THE THEORY AND PRACTICE OF ASSESSMENT IN COUNSELING

Richard S. Balkin
Texas A&M University, Corpus Christi

Gerald A. Juhnke
University of Texas at San Antonio

Boston   Columbus   Indianapolis   New York   San Francisco   Upper Saddle River
Amsterdam   Cape Town   Dubai   London   Madrid   Milan   Munich   Paris   Montreal   Toronto
Delhi   Mexico City   São Paulo   Sydney   Hong Kong   Seoul   Singapore   Taipei   Tokyo

Vice President and Editorial Director: Jeffery W. Johnston
Senior Acquisitions Editor: Meredith Fossel
Editorial Assistant: Krista Slavicek
Vice President, Director of Marketing: Margaret Waples
Senior Marketing Manager: Christopher Barry
Senior Managing Editor: Pamela D. Bennett
Production Project Manager: Carrie Mollette
Production Manager: Laura Messerly
Creative Director: Jayne Conte
Cover Designer: Suzanne Duda
Cover Art: Fotolia
Full Service Project Management: Jogender Taneja/Aptara®, Inc.
Composition: Aptara®, Inc.
Printer/Binder: Courier/Westford
Cover Printer: Courier/Westford
Text Font: ITC Garamond Light

Credits and acknowledgments for material borrowed from other sources and reproduced, with permission, in this textbook appear on the appropriate page within the text.

Every effort has been made to provide accurate and current Internet information in this book. However, the Internet and information posted on it are constantly changing, so it is inevitable that some of the Internet addresses listed in this textbook will change.

Library of Congress Cataloging-in-Publication Data

Balkin, Richard S.
  The theory and practice of assessment in counseling/Richard S. Balkin, Gerald A. Juhnke.
    pages cm
  ISBN-13: 978-0-13-701751-5
  ISBN-10: 0-13-701751-0
  1. Psychological tests. 2. Behavioral assessment. 3. Counseling psychology.
I. Juhnke, Gerald A. II. Title.
  BF176.B35 2014
  158.3028'7—dc23

                                                                         2012044287

10 9 8 7 6 5 4 3 2 1

ISBN 10:   0-13-701751-0
ISBN 13: 978-0-13-701751-5

To my parents: Howard and Susanne Balkin

Dad, I think you would have gotten a kick out of this.
Mom, I know you are proud.

—*RSB*

PREFACE

This book was initially conceived as a textbook that would emphasize the practice of assessment in counseling. When I teach assessment, as well as other courses that emphasize research methods and statistics, I often find students overwhelmed with the mathematical concepts and quite anxious about the course work. Assessment, like most core areas of counseling, has a theoretical basis and a pertinent, practical component. However, this practical component often gets lost in the application of the skills and use of instruments that heavily rely on psychometric properties.

Statistics are an influential component to assessment in counseling. If you are like many students and get mired in the mathematical concepts, I encourage you to take a step back and relax. Yes, there will be some math discussed and applied in this textbook, but we hope you will find that the explanation of the computations are provided to emphasize the process, as opposed to focus on only the product. In my experience, most counseling students who express some intimidation with the statistical concepts do so as a result of past experience. My hope is that you will see these concepts expressed in a new or different light with focus on application, rather than the mere computation.

My co-author and I worked hard to focus on the application of the theoretical and measurement concepts of assessment in counseling. We attempted to use a conversational style of writing and introduce two case studies that we follow throughout the text. This is different from other textbooks that also present similar principles but do not demonstrate the application of said principles. Through this format, you will, we hope, see examples of assessment principles that may be applied to a variety of settings. Our goal is for this textbook to serve as a guide for administering, scoring, interpreting, and communicating assessment results.

ORGANIZATION OF THIS BOOK

We organized this book to provide a logical flow for the material we introduce. Chapters 1 through 5 represent foundational elements for assessment in counseling. In these chapters, you will learn about the background, history, and relevance of assessment and the properties of assessment instruments. Chapters 6 through 8 include practical issues related to selecting, administering, scoring, and interpreting assessment instruments. Chapters 9 through 15 include information on specific types of instruments, particularly for areas of specialization, fundamentals in interpreting and communicating results, and accountability issues. Each chapter ends with information related to applying the material presented in the chapter. In most cases, we use the case studies from Chapter 2 to demonstrate how the material may be utilized in a counseling setting.

CHAPTER 1 We introduce assessment as a continuous process in counseling. Counselors have some choices with respect to the populations they serve and the modalities they employ, but assessment is an integral component to all populations and used within all models. Key terms are defined. We also cover the history of assessment, emphasizing past mistakes and connections to current practice. Ethical and legal issues are highlighted.

CHAPTER 2 We introduce two case studies that will be used throughout the text. We highlight the basic elements of an intake interview, which are addressed in detail in Chapter 7. We also provide information related to writing and maintaining progress notes and highlight common note-taking methods.

CHAPTER 3 This chapter is likely the most statistically focused chapter in the text. We cover basic concepts of measurement and address procedures in computing and conceptualizing scores on assessment instruments. Students will be able to differentiate between norm-referenced and criterion-referenced tests and compute and interpret measures of central tendency, variability, and correlation and convert the scores into meaningful information in order to make comparisons and formulate a conceptualization of the client.

CHAPTER 4 We highlight reliability in this chapter. One important consideration is to understand reliability as a characteristic of test scores and not the test or scales. We focus on the various methods of evaluating reliability of scores, particularly as they relate to the normative sample. Applications of reliability estimates to the case study are provided.

CHAPTER 5 We provide the most up-to-date definitions of test validation with comparisons to previous iterations of test validity and how the concept evolved. The five types of validity evidence are emphasized and tied to the development of instruments. Students will learn how to evaluate validity in order to be informed consumers of instruments.

CHAPTER 6 This chapter provides an opportunity to revisit the concepts in Chapters 1 through 5 and apply these concepts to selecting appropriate instruments. We emphasize the qualifications necessary to use specific instruments. We also highlight how counselors can obtain information on tests through the use of tests reviews from various databases. We address information included in test reviews and keys to interpreting and using test reviews in order to be an informed consumer of assessments instruments.

CHAPTER 7 The clinical interview, initially addressed in Chapter 2, is presented in detail with emphasis on the psychosocial intake, using the CLISD-PA model, and the mental status exam. We emphasize different types of intake data and specifically address substance abuse intake. We also provide information on using basic counseling skills as an integral part of the intake interview. We apply the concepts of the clinical interview to the case studies.

CHAPTER 8 This chapter on multicultural issues in assessment is a foundational chapter exploring such issues as test bias versus test fairness, assessment with special populations, and the limitations to generalizability from typical normative samples. We explore issues related to testing accommodations and how such accommodations may affect the interpretation of scores. Finally, we address how counselors can improve their cross-cultural competence as assessment professionals and explore multicultural implications in the case study.

CHAPTER 9 We introduce theories of intelligence and provide information related to instruments that were designed to measure intelligence, as well as the extent to which the instruments correspond to theories of intelligence. We also highlight research on emotional intelligence and some of the criticisms of emotional intelligence. Finally, we discuss three common intelligence measures and address applications to a case study.

CHAPTER 10 We discuss similarities and differences of achievement and aptitude tests and place these constructs into the context of ability testing. We also discuss the development of achievement tests, how scores are reported, and the relationship of achievement and aptitude to general cognitive ability. Applications to a case study are addressed.

CHAPTER 11 The nature of multiaxial diagnosis and an overview of common mental health disorders is presented in this chapter. We introduce one of the most important personality measures, the Minnesota Multiphasic Personality Inventory—2 (MMPI-2) and the MMPI-2—Restructured Form (MMPI-2-RF), and provide a narrative related to the case studies, emphasizing how these tests can be used to facilitate diagnosis and treatment.

CHAPTER 12 In this chapter, we focus on how career assessment may provide valuable information to guide career counseling and overall wellness of clients served in multiple settings such as schools, agencies, organizations, and practices. Theories and elements of career assessment are presented, as well as an overview of common measures used in career assessment. We focus specifically on the O*NET system and applying career assessment to the case studies.

CHAPTER 13 This chapter is devoted to specialty areas of assessment, including assessment in marriage, couples, and family counseling; substance abuse counseling; and suicide assessment interventions. We provide information on scales related to these areas and apply them to our case studies. In addition, we provide a model for assessing suicide and an overview of instruments that may be used.

CHAPTER 14 Now that we presented various types of assessment commonly used in counseling, we provide an overview of how to write an assessment report. We highlight both the structure and contents of the assessment report and provide clear examples, using the case studies, as to how reports may be written for clients, referral agents, and stakeholders.

CHAPTER 15 We conclude this text with an overview of accountability and program evaluation in counseling and the role of assessment in these areas. We discuss standardized and nonstandardized measures of accountability and apply issues of accountability to our case studies. Furthermore, we provide an overview of a program evaluation model and how assessment ties into program evaluation.

APPENDICES Additional resources were included in the appendices. These resources include a table (Appendix A) that will be very helpful in interpreting scores from standardized tests by providing percentiles for standard scores, explained in Chapter 2. Various standards and statements from professional counseling organizations were included in latter appendices, which were referenced throughout the text.

ACKNOWLEDGMENTS

Rick, first and foremost, thanks his wife, Melissa, and his children, Abigail, Gabriela, and Isabel, for their support during this writing endeavor. Melissa, you lived this book with me and willed me through it. Abigail, thank you for your own contribution to this product. I also want to thank my Department Chair, Robert Smith, for your support, friendship, and mentorship. I want to extend a big thank you to my friend and colleague, Jerry Juhnke, for completing this journey with me and making such a wonderful contribution to the book. Carl Sheperis, my friend and colleague, thank you for the inspiration and stimulus for this project. Finally, I wish to thank my Acquisitions Editor, Meredith Fossel, for your enthusiasm, optimism, and patience.

Jerry thanks Deborah, Bryce, Brenna, Gerald, and Babe Juhnke for their love and support during this writing endeavor. As well, Jerry thanks his very good friend and professional colleague, Rick, for allowing him the privilege of co-authoring this text with him.

The authors also wish to express their appreciation for those individuals who reviewed the manuscript throughout its development: Kandis Croom, Arkansas Tech University; Donna M. Gibson, University of South Carolina; Susan Guzzo, Argosy University; Clarrice Rapisarda, UNC Charlotte; Gail Rizzo, Cincinnati Christian University; Chester R. Robinson, Texas A&M University of Commerce; Leo R. Sandy, Plymouth State University; and Chiachih Wang, University of Missouri–Kansas.

BRIEF CONTENTS

CONTENTS

CHAPTER 1

The Role of Assessment in Counseling

OBJECTIVES

After reading this chapter, you will be able to:

1. Understand the importance and role of assessment in counseling.

2. Identify psychological constructs and associated operational definitions.

3. Distinguish between standardized and nonstandardized assessments.

4. Identify relevant historical issues of assessment and the implications for assessment today.

5. Recognize the role and importance of professional organizations with respect to the practice of assessment.

6. Identify competencies related to assessment practices.

7. Identify ethical and legal codes affecting assessment.

WHAT IS ASSESSMENT?

The practice of assessment entails the collection of information in order to identify, analyze, evaluate, and address the problems, issues, and circumstances of clients in the counseling relationship. Assessment is used as a basis for identifying problems, planning interventions, evaluating and/or diagnosing clients, and informing clients and stakeholders. Many novice counselors may make the mistake of identifying assessment as a means to an end, such as providing a label or diagnosis to a client. In this text, assessment will be viewed as a process essential to all elements of counseling. Whether practicing in a school, private practice, agency, or other health care setting, assessment plays an integral role. Assessment moves beyond the administration of measures. Assessment involves identifying statements, actions, and procedures to help individuals, groups, couples, and families make progress in the counseling environment. Although counselors have the opportunity to limit their scope of practice with respect to modalities, theories, and types of clients, a counselor cannot function without an understanding of the processes and procedures of assessment in counseling.

practicality of treatment. both, and.

1

Some academics may discern between assessment and testing (Cohen & Swerdlik, 2002; Gladding, 2009). The focus of assessment is on gathering information; *testing* refers to the measurement of psychological constructs through instruments or specified procedures. In this sense, a *construct* refers to a phenomenon that exists but cannot be directly observed. For example, variables such as height and weight can be directly observed. Measurement systems for height and weight are available to minimize errors and guarantee accuracy of results. However, not all variables can be directly observed. Emotional states such as depression or happiness, or cognitive traits such as intelligence, or even psychological states such as stress, cannot be directly observed or measured. How often has a friend told you "I feel fine" rather than acknowledged something was wrong? Constructs may not be identified so easily. In addition, a construct may vary, depending on the *operational definition*—how the construct is measured. For example, Michael Jordan was labeled a *brilliant* basketball player. Does this imply that Michael Jordan was creative, had a high level of intelligence, or had superior analytic skills? Quite simply, an operational definition would need to be applied in order to measure the construct of brilliance, and this definition may vary depending on the instruments used or the experts' theoretical underpinnings of the measure.

The process of assessing, and sometimes testing, is necessary to understand a client. However, differentiating between assessment and testing may be viewed as an academic exercise. Often, these terms may be interchangeable, as the process of testing (i.e., administering, scoring, and interpreting an instrument) cannot be separated from the assessment process. Testing, therefore, is part of assessment. A distinction is made between standardized and nonstandardized assessment. *Standardized* assessment refers to a formal process in which a specific set of rules and guidelines related to administration, scoring, and interpretation are followed consistently to ensure accurate results over a period of time and across populations. Standardized assessments include instruments developed under a rigorous process and produce results that may be generalizable to a population or meaningful to an individual in the context of a population. Instruments such as achievement tests, aptitude tests, and personality tests fit this description. Nonstandardized assessment refers to a process of gathering information without adherence to a strict set of rules or guidelines. *Nonstandardized* assessments may include clinical interviews. Even when such interviews follow a formula or pattern, deviations in administrations occur because of the personal nature of the interactions and of addressing the client's personal needs. Such assessments may not adhere to a rigid administration, scoring, and interpretation process.

HISTORY OF ASSESSMENT

The Council for Accreditation of Counseling and Related Educational Programs (CACREP, 2009) directed accredited counseling programs to address "historical perspectives concerning the nature and meaning of assessment" (p. 12). Such discussions may appear to lack relevance and come across as tedious and uninteresting when in fact the history of assessment and testing practices may shed light on how assessment practices evolved and why specific procedures, which may appear foreign or confusing, are used today (Gregory, 2007). More important, a review of assessment history may shed light on the past misuse of assessment instruments in order to ensure valid practice in the future.

Issues of testing and measurement are by no means new to the social sciences. As early as 2200 B.C.E., public officials in China were issued an examination every third year by the Chinese emperor (Cohen & Swerdlik, 2002; Gregory, 2007). Although these examinations were nothing like the type of standardized measures given today—such exams throughout the Middle Ages emphasized archery, equestrian abilities (Cohen & Swerdlik, 2002), poetry composition, handwriting, and elements of military, agriculture, and civil law—the exams were used for employment considerations (Gregory, 2007).

The foundation for modern testing began in the 19th Century among biologists, particularly Charles Darwin (1809–1882) and Sir Francis Galton (1822–1911). Darwin's work had two important contributions to assessment. First, Darwin linked human development to animals, thereby influencing the use of animals to study human behavior. Second, Darwin identified the notion of individual differences when noting the relationship of children to parents, which led to increased studies in heredity (Cohen & Swerdlik, 2002).

Because Francis Galton was a cousin of Darwin (Cohen & Swerdlik, 2002), the fact that he commenced studies in heredity and individual differences was not likely a coincidence. Interestingly, one area that Galton is known for turned out to be somewhat irrelevant to assessment by modern standards. Galton investigated the relationship between physical characteristics and mental capacities. For example, Galton would examine such physical characteristics as height, weight, arm span, head length, and finger length and make comparisons to such mental/behavioral characteristics as auditory and visual acuity, grip strength, and reaction time. Galton set up a laboratory at the 1884 International Exposition and charged individuals a minimal fee to take these tests (Anastasi & Urbina, 1997). One of Galton's primary interests was noting the individual differences in regard to perceptions of the senses. Galton noted that individuals with severe mental retardation were indifferent to sensory perceptions, such as hot, cold, or pain, which led to the investigation of how physical characteristics may be related to discerning sensory information (Anastasi & Urbina, 1997). Although biased sampling and the type of data may be criticized, three important contributions should be noted:

1. Galton believed anything could be measured. This belief is important to modern assessment practices, as counselors attempt to measure processes that are not directly observable, such as interests and emotional states.
2. Although Galton was not able to connect physical traits to mental capacities, the insignificant relationship is nevertheless important. Sometimes, knowing where not to look for answers is as important as knowing where to find answers.
3. Galton devised a standardized method for gathering information and recording results (Gregory, 2007), which influenced modern practices of assessment.

Although the notion that physical characteristics relating to mental capacities may seem more closely aligned with the late 17th-Century Salem witch trials, in which daily events were connected to unlikely phenomena—in this case, supernatural occurrences— the astute counselor may notice that society still searches for answers with overly simplistic explanations, such as attributing the achievement gap to differences in ethnicity. Many school districts across the country break down academic achievement levels across ethnicity. How different is that from identifying intellectual capacities based on arm length?

A contemporary of Galton was Wilhelm Wundt (1832–1920), who studied mental processes over 20 years prior to Galton's work at the 1884 International Exposition. In 1879, Wundt established the first psychological laboratory in Leipzig, Germany. Unlike Galton, who was interested in individual differences, Wundt was interested in similarities among humans, particularly with variables such as response time, perception, and attention

(Cohen & Swerdlik, 2002). Wundt used a calibrated pendulum to measure what he thought would be "swiftness of thought" (Gregory, 2007, p. 6). As the pendulum would swing back and forth, a bell would be struck and participants would be asked to identify the position of the pendulum when the bell was struck. Wundt ultimately concluded that the speed of thought varied among individuals. Wundt did not account for threats to experimental validity, such as variations in attention span or differences in the environment, so findings would be summarily dismissed using modern standards of assessment and research practices; however, studies by Wundt and Galton provided a foundation and interest in assessment practices (Gregory, 2007). These were initial attempts to measure mental processes.

James McKeen Cattell (1860–1944) studied the works of Galton and Wundt and was highly influenced by Galton's study of individual differences. Cattell coined the term mental test, and the focus of Cattell's work was to examine differences in reaction time for various mental tests, such as reaction time after hearing a sound, judgment of 10 seconds of time, and short-term memory. Similar to Galton, Cattell also studied physical characteristics. One portion of a mental test included the strength of a hand squeeze and the degree of pressure needed to cause pain by pressing a rubber tip against the forehead (Cohen & Swerdlik, 2002; Gregory, 2007). Once again, although some of these practices may appear preposterous today, keep in mind that many tests (e.g., American College Testing [ACT], Wechsler Intelligence Scale for Children—Fourth Edition [WISC-IV], Test of Variables of Attention) that help counselors examine aptitude, achievement, intellectual functioning, and mental process are timed or have timed elements.

Not until 1901 did a student of Cattell, Clark Wissler, identify that the processes measured by Galton and Cattell had no correlation to academic achievement. Unfortunately, response times, not what criteria qualified as a mental test (e.g., grip strength), were summarily dismissed for about 70 years until researchers on intelligence readdressed the value of response time. Shortly thereafter, Alfred Binet (1857–1911) created what would become known as the first *intelligence test* in 1905 (Gregory, 2007).

Binet was influenced by the works of J. E. D. Esquirol (1772–1840) and Edouard Seguin (1812–1880), who spearheaded a modern approach for identifying and working with individuals with mental retardation. Gregory (2007) noted that Binet's intelligence tests were developed "to identify mentally retarded children who would not likely profit from ordinary schooling" (p. 12). Binet's tests would be adopted internationally and would influence later works by David Wechsler, who would initially introduce intelligence tests specifically geared for adults (Cohen & Swerdlik, 2002).

Unfortunately, the popularity of intelligence testing led to blatant misuse. Gregory (2007) described the misuse of intelligence testing by Henry Goddard (1866–1957), who translated Binet's scale from French to English in 1908. Goddard believed that individuals with low intellectual functioning should be segregated from society and that restrictions should be placed on such individuals in order to control procreation. Goddard was commissioned by Ellis Island to administer the Binet-Simon Intelligence Test to immigrants as they were arriving. Tests were administered by translators in various languages, such as Yiddish, Russian, and Italian, and compared to the French norms established by Binet. The result, of course, was that over 80% of the immigrants tested were identified with low intellectual functioning.

Ultimately, the popularity of intelligence testing led to the construction and use of instruments to measure personality and aptitude. Freud and Jung developed theories of

eugenics?

personality in the late 19th and early 20th Centuries. Cohen and Swedlik (2002) identified World War I (1914–1918) as the precursor to group testing. The military needed to identify individuals who may not be intellectually or emotionally fit for duty. The first self-report personality assessment, the Woodworth Personal Data Sheet, was not used until 1919–1920 by the U.S. Army (Butcher, 2010). The instrument consisted of 116 self-report items related to "physical problems, social behavior, and mental health symptoms" such as 'Have you ever seen a vision?" "Do you have a great fear of fire?" "Do you feel tired most of the time?" "Is it easy to get you angry?" (Butcher, 2010, p. 5). The Personal Data Sheet was adapted for children in 1924. The Personal Data Sheet served as a precursor for the Minnesota Multiphasic Personality Inventory (MMPI). The MMPI revolutionized personality testing. Butcher indicated that large sets of items were developed and selected based on how homogeneous groups of psychiatric patients answered the items. Items that discriminated between diagnostic categories were retained. Items on the MMPI and MMPI-2 may seem to lack evidence based on test content. In other words, items may appear ambiguous, because the items may not have been developed to measure a particular symptom. For example, "I like mechanics magazines" may discriminate individuals with elevations on Scale 4, psychodeviance. Consider the implications—the MMPI and associated instruments (i.e., MMPI-2, MMPI-2—Restructured Form [MMPI-2-RF], and MMPI-A [for adolescents]) are among the most widely used instruments with over 19,000 articles and books published in relation to these instruments (Butcher, 2010); yet, the items were not created with a particular construct in mind to measure. Clearly, the lack of obvious connection between items and potential mental distress or disorders is a legitimate criticism.

The development of the MMPI and subsequent adaptations and revisions (i.e., MMPI-2 and MMPI-A) spawned additional diagnostic and personality measures, such as the Millon Clinical Multiaxial Inventory (MCMI), which measures personality issues. Whereas the MMPI focused on Axis I disorders, the MCMI focused on Axis II disorders. In the 1950s, interest in general personality, as opposed to assessing clinical problems, spawned the emergence of the 16 Personality Factor Questionnaire (16-PF) and the California Psychological Inventory. These instruments served as predecessors to the NEO Personality Inventory (NEO-PI) in the 1980s. The NEO-PI assesses individuals on a five-factor model of personality, including openness, agreeableness, neuroticism, extraversion, and conscientiousness, also known as the "'Big Five' personality dimensions" (Butcher, 2010, p. 9).

In the 1960s to the present, measures were developed to focus on specific psychological constructs, such as depression, with the Beck Depression Inventory. Today, counselors may find instruments that measure a variety of constructs such as diagnostic categories, anxiety and trauma, suicide, wellness, and substance abuse. Many instruments today are used less for diagnosis and more for identifying problem areas or strength-based areas. Many of these instruments continue to rely on self-report, which may be problematic in terms of producing a valid response from a client who may not be well. Therefore, the use of assessment instruments that focus on observations from parents, teachers, clinicians, and/or significant others was a natural progression. Such instruments as the Behavior Assessment System for Children and the Child Behavior Checklist were developed in the 1990s and include report forms for the client and observers (e.g., parent, teacher).

Refinement related to assessment and testing is ongoing, as are the issues. The standards for test construction are evolving continually. As a result, instruments constructed, normed, and validated in the 1980s may be out-of-date by today's standards. How instruments are used and individuals are compared is an ongoing debate. Issues related to educational placement, incarceration, job placement and promotion, and differential diagnoses permeate the counseling profession. Counselors need to be aware of the multicultural and social justice issues that emerge from testing and comparing populations.

THE DEVELOPMENT OF COUNSELORS AS ASSESSMENT PROFESSIONALS

As mentioned before, assessment is an integral part of counseling practice, and therefore training in assessment is essential. CACREP (2009) identified assessment as one of the "eight common core curricular areas" (p. 8) required for all students in accredited counseling programs. Although counselors receive training and practice in assessment, the right for counselors to practice assessment is not a given, as such rights are dictated by state licensing boards. However, in general, counselors may use a variety of instruments, with projective assessments being the least available. Many state licensing boards have rules that prevent professionals outside of psychology from using projective tests, such as the Rorschach Technique (Pearson Assessments).

The Association for Assessment and Research in Counseling (AARC)

The AARC (formerly known as the Association for Assessment in Counseling [AAC] and the Association for Assessment in Counseling and Education [AACE]) is a division of the American Counseling Association (ACA), whose mission is "to promote and recognize excellence in assessment, research, and evaluation in counseling." (AARC, 2012). AARC and ACA produced statements with respect to counselors' use of standardized instruments. In addition to being a division of ACA, AARC represents counselors in a variety of work groups representing counselors' interests in assessment, measurement, evaluation, and diagnosis. In addition, ACA appointed individuals from AARC/ACA to represent counselors on the Joint Committee on Testing Practices (JCTP). The JCTP was established in 1985, along with such groups as the American Educational Research Association, the National Council on Measurement in Education, and the American Psychological Association, to address testing practices in education and clinical settings. The JCTP disbanded in 2007, but it published several documents related to test use. In terms of practicing assessment, counselors should be aware of guidelines in the *Responsibilities of Users of Standardized Tests (RUST,* Appendix H; Wall et al., 2003*), Standards for Qualifications of Test Users* (Erford, Basham, Cashwell, Juhnke, & Wall, 2003), and the *ACA Code of Ethics* (ACA, 2005), as well as the qualification requirements for each test publisher.

RESPONSIBILITIES OF USERS OF STANDARDIZED TESTS (RUST)   The RUST statement (see Appendix H) was developed for the purposes of educating counselors and educators on ethical use of standardized tests. AACE addressed guidelines across seven areas: (a) Qualifications of Test Users, (b) Technical Knowledge, (c) Test Selection, (d) Test Administration, (e) Test Scoring, (f) Interpreting Test Results, and (g) Communicating Test Results (Wall et al., 2003). Wall et al. (2003) indicated that the responsibility of ensuring appropriate test use lies within the counselor or educator administering the test. An understanding of measurement to select, score, and interpret results, as well as of protocols for administering and scoring tests, is pertinent. Efforts should be made to communicate test results to clients and stakeholders in a manner that is understandable and useful while also addressing any limitations to selected tests.

STANDARDS FOR QUALIFICATIONS OF TEST USERS   The RUST statement was a precursor to the *Standards for Qualifications of Test Users,* a document that was adopted by the ACA (Erford et al., 2003) related to the training and skills necessary for counselors to use psychological tests. As noted previously, this document was developed, in part, to address concerns of legislative bodies that received pressure from outside organizations related to counselors' right to use psychological measures. Among the issues addressed in the document was that assessment is not a stand-alone practice. Assessment should be integrated along with counseling theory and never used with populations or issues outside the counselor's scope of practice. Similar to the RUST statement, counselors should have knowledge and skill in areas related to measurement, test development, administration, scoring, and communicating results. ACA also addressed counselors' responsibility to promote fairness in assessment practices by understanding the role of diversity and the legal and ethical implications of assessment.

The *ACA Code of Ethics* (2005)

Section E of the *ACA Code of Ethics* (2005) covers evaluation, assessment, and interpretation. ACA addressed ethics in both formal and informal assessments. The primary goal is to promote client welfare. This section of the *ACA Code of Ethics* (COE) is extensive and covers 13 areas. Some of the information in the COE is similar to the RUST statement and *Standards for Qualifications of Test Users,* particularly with respect to counselor competence, instrument selection, administration, scoring, interpretation, and attention to diversity. However, in addition to outlining the responsibilities of counselors, the COE also covers the rights of clients, including informed consent and release and security of assessment data. Clients have a right to know the nature of the assessment and how the assessment results may be used prior to administration. Clients also have the right to receive the results and identify qualified professionals, if any, with whom the results may be shared. Confidentiality may not be compromised, and this is an issue that needs to be addressed before administering an assessment, especially if the client is referred by an organization, agency, court, or other professional. For example, the U.S. Department of Transportation (DOT) has policies and procedures related to who may administer substance abuse assessments for transportation employees and how the results should be communicated. Courts may order an individual for psychological testing and expect a report related to the results. Counselors, therefore, need to be proactive in addressing issues of informed consent and confidentiality, especially with regard to who will have access to the results and the implications of said results.

When administering assessments, counselors need to be aware of administration conditions, as tests should be administered under similar conditions in which the norms were established. However, accommodations may be necessary, especially if assessing individuals with any disability or impairment.

As mentioned before, diagnosis is an aspect of assessment and perhaps represents an area that differs considerably from ethical codes in other mental health professions. As the counseling profession follows a developmental model, as opposed to a medical model focused on diagnosis and treatment, counselors need to be aware of the conditions and issues in providing a diagnosis. These issues include using multiple methods and data sources when providing a diagnosis and awareness of the impact that such a label may bring. The cultural context of the client should be considered with respect to providing a diagnosis. Perhaps an additional area in which counseling is unique is that ACA (2005) indicated that "counselors may refrain from making and/or reporting a diagnosis if they believe it would cause harm to the client or others" (p. 12). Thus, when a diagnosis is not in the best interest of the client, the counselor may refrain from providing a diagnosis.

A growing area in the field of counseling is forensic evaluation. As in other types of assessment, ACA addressed competency and consent, but one area of difference is the stipulation that counselors do not evaluate their clients for forensic purposes and avoid relationships with individuals related to forensic evaluation, including the individual being evaluated and personal relationships associated with the individual.

The *ACA Code of Ethics* is used by licensure boards across the country. Assessment is an integral part of counseling and emphasized in the COE. Counselors need to implement the ethical codes into their practice and be particularly attentive to the manner in which assessments should be introduced, consent and assent procedures, rules regarding disclosures, issues of diversity, and the impact of diagnosis.

Fair Access to Tests

In the past, state psychology boards attempted to limit the use of psychological assessments to licensed psychologists (Naugle, 2009).

> While some professional groups are seeking to control and restrict the use of psychological tests, the American Counseling Association believes firmly that one's right to use tests in counseling practice is directly related to competence. This competence is achieved through education, training, and experience in the field of testing. Thus, professional counselors with a master's degree or higher and appropriate coursework in appraisal/assessment, supervision, and experience are qualified to use objective tests. With additional training and experience, professional counselors are also able to administer projective tests, individual intelligence tests, and clinical diagnostic tests. (Erford et al., 2003, p. 1)

The right to use psychological tests is not a simple issue, as the debate includes licensing boards, professional organizations, and test publishers. Licensing boards address scope-of-practice issues. Turf battles ensue when licensing boards of one profession attempt to limit the scope of practice of another profession through legal wrangling. However, counselor licensure laws in most states clearly identify the right of counselors to use assessments, although the type of assessments may be limited, and such limitation vary from state to state. Professional organizations provide guidelines for training, practice, and ethics in assessment. Test publishers are responsible for "monitoring the competencies of those who purchase and utilize assessment instruments" (Naugle, 2009, p. 32). Note that these organizations have missions that may be aligned or have competing interests. As noted earlier, an effort to protect a professional turf may have an effect on individuals who purchase and use assessment instruments, which does not benefit test publishers. Although guidelines are necessary to protect the public from poor practice, the public does not benefit when professions duly qualified are limited in assessment practice.

The Fair Access Coalition on Testing (FACT), along with the ACA and the National Board of Certified Counselors who both serve on FACT, advocate for counselors and other qualified professionals for fair test use. FACT plays an important role in collaborating with other professionals who use standardized instruments and works to protect the rights of counselors and other associated professionals (e.g., school psychologists, speech–language pathologists).

In 1997, Indiana passed counselor licensure. This law was followed by legislation allowing the Indiana State Psychology Board to create a restricted test list. In 1998, the Indiana State Psychology Board submitted a list of 318 tests as restricted for sole use by psychologists. FACT, along with ACA, AACE, and the National Board for Certified Counselors (NBCC), provided letters and testimony to the Indiana state legislature and governor. In 2007, the Indiana state legislature repealed the law allowing the Indiana State Psychology Board to create a restricted test list. Other states (e.g., Maryland) have attempted to restrict use of assessment instruments (FACT). In addition, some states (e.g., Arkansas, Texas) included restrictions on using projective techniques in the counselor licensure laws (Naugle, 2009). Counselors should be aware of their rights as test users and stay abreast of legal challenges that attempt to limit said rights. The importance of joining and maintaining memberships to state and national counseling associations (e.g., ACA) cannot be overemphasized, as such organizations play a leading role in advocating for the rights of counselors.

Test Publisher Qualifications of Test Users

The Association of Test Publishers is also represented on FACT. As noted earlier, test publishers also monitor test use, by providing an application process or qualification process to administer assessment instruments. Some test companies use a tiered system. In the first tier, often referred to as *A level*, individuals with minimal training, a bachelor's degree, or certification may administer tests. In the second tier, often referred to as *B level*, individuals with a master's degree and/or membership in a professional organization (e.g., ACA) and/ or professional licensure may administer tests. In the third tier, often referred to as *C level*, individuals with a doctoral degree and/or specialized training may administer tests.

Although this system appears to be the most common among test publishers, it is not the only system employed by test publishers. Pearson Assessments, for example, includes an additional fourth tier, *Level Q*, in which test users need to include a specific background related to the instrument (Naugle, 2009). Application procedures for other test companies may include information related to licensure, highest educational degree, specialized training, continuing education, certifications, and membership in professional associations.

LEGAL ISSUES

In addition to organizations that represent counselors' interests in assessment and ethical codes that address rights and responsibilities of counselors and clients, familiarity of legal and legislative issues that affect assessment practice in counseling are important. Laws that affect assessment practices may not necessarily be created with assessment in mind, but the practice of assessment may be affected in a variety of environments (Whiston, 2009), including health care, education, business, and public service.

Health Care Legislation

The Health Insurance Portability and Accountability Act (HIPAA; 1996) is a complex law of regulations concerning the privacy of health care records. Counselors working in agencies and private practice need to be familiar with HIPAA guidelines. In essence, HIPAA provided clients with increased control and access to health care information (Erard, 2004). Clients have a right to their assessment results and reports and may decide who receives this information. HIPAA affects the manner in which counselors, agencies, and organizations operate, such as providing a privacy notice to all clients regarding their records and obtaining permission to release information to third-party payors for reimbursement. Counselors should also be aware of exceptions to HIPAA policies, such as laws related to being a mandated reporter in cases such as physical/sexual abuse of a minor. Counselors working in a private practice or agency setting should seek training regarding adherence to HIPAA guidelines and implementation.

Civil Rights Legislation

Civil rights legislation dates back to 1866 with the emancipation of slaves. Since that time, seven additional civil rights acts were passed. The 1964 and 1972 civil rights acts mandated discrimination-free workplaces. These laws affected employment-based testing, which led to disputes related to fair testing practices in the workplace, resulting in the Civil Rights Act of 1991 (Whiston, 2009). The Civil Rights Act of 1991 places the responsibility of appropriate test practices on the employer. In other words, employers must be able to demonstrate that employment testing relates to the duties of the job that are to be performed by employees. In addition, the use of separate norms based on race, ethnicity, sex, or religion was prohibited (Whiston, 2009).

In 2009, a lawsuit was filed against the city of New Haven, Connecticut, on behalf of firefighters who cited discrimination related to promotion. In *Ricci v. DeStafano*, an exam for the rank of lieutenant and captain was administered to 118 firefighters, in which the top scorers would be appointed to the vacant positions. None of the top scorers were African American, and only two Latino/a candidates were eligible for promotion. White candidates were eligible for all of the vacancies. The city of New Haven opted to disregard the test results on the notion that to use the results would be discriminatory. The lawsuit was filed by those who passed the test and were denied promotion. The U.S. Supreme Court ruled that the city acted wrongly in not accepting the results, as the test was created by a third party, I/O Solutions, and represented a reliable and valid result. In fact, testimony demonstrated the test items were related to the duties required for the jobs in question.

The Americans with Disabilities Act of 1990 required employers to provide reasonable accommodations related to employees with disabilities (Koch, 2000), and naturally this extends to testing. Note that this policy is in line with the *ACA Code of Ethics* (2005). Although ACA indicated that assessments should be administered under the same conditions in which the instrument was standardized, ACA acknowledged that accommodations may be necessary, such as with individuals with disabilities, but the accommodations need to be addressed in the interpretations and the overall validity of the test. Koch's use of the term "reasonable accommodations" (p. 103) is in line with the wording from the Americans with Disabilities Act. Whiston (2009) identified that counselors should be cautious with respect to implementation, as the term *reasonable* is somewhat ambiguous and subject to interpretation.

Educational Legislation

Congress passed the Individuals with Disabilities Act (IDEA) in 1997 and reauthorized the act in 2004. IDEA was a reauthorization and extension of PL-94-142, the Education for All

Handicapped Children Act in 1975. Telzrow and McNamara (2001) identified three new areas of IDEA that impacted assessment: "(a) increased parental involvement in educational decision-making; (b) greater emphasis on accountability and student results; and (c) the development of new assessment technologies" (p. 105). As IDEA mandated individualized education plans for children diagnosed with a disability, parental involvement was a core area, in which the parent/guardian has decision-making authority. Schools cannot evaluate a child for a disability without parental consent. Once parental consent is provided, the school has 60 days to conduct an evaluation on the student. School counselors may not be responsible for the educational evaluation, but they typically serve as a member of the committee developing the individualized educational plan in collaboration with the parent(s)/guardian(s). Parental consent for testing was not a new issue, as this right was also addressed in the Family Educational Rights and Privacy Act of 1974 (FERPA). FERPA also limited the release of educational records to parents/guardians and students over the age of 18. One issue that may be affected is counseling records, which are not generally part of the students' educational file, but may be included. School counselors should be aware of district policy regarding counseling notes about students (Whiston, 2009).

Similar to IDEA, the No Child Left Behind legislation (2002) established accountability measures in educational settings. A major outcome of NCLB was the mandate for the implementation of high-stakes testing (Duffy, Giordano, Farrell, Paneque, & Crump, 2008). Schools became accountable through the implementation of minimal proficiency standards established by the state but approved by the U.S. Department of Education. The implementation of high-stakes testing resulted in increases in student testing, such as using preparatory testing procedures to increase performance on the state-mandated test. Additional criticisms include an overreliance on test scores to address educational shortcomings and the presence of increased anxiety over test performance among children. During the writing of this text, President Barack Obama requested Congress to overhaul NCLB, citing a high rate of school failure based on measures enacted by NCLB. Counselors need to stay aware of ongoing educational legislation, as such legislation affects clients and the advocacy efforts of counselors on behalf of their clients.

AN OVERVIEW OF ASSESSMENT IN MENTAL HEALTH SETTINGS, SCHOOLS, REHABILITATION COUNSELING, AND HIGHER EDUCATION SETTINGS

Assessment is used across all counseling settings in a variety of ways. Assessment is integral to the clinical interview. Assessment includes diagnosis and treatment planning. As counselors meet with their clients, they make decisions on what problems to address and what interventions to attempt. Hence, assessment permeates every aspect of the counseling process.

Assessment is also used for advocacy and placement. Through careful assessment, clients can be provided with needed services that otherwise may have been unattainable. When clients are active participants in the assessment process, they have the opportunity to learn something about themselves, including personal strengths, challenges, interests, and activities that promote growth and wellness.

Counselors, therefore, are both consumers and producers of assessment data. Counselors need to be aware of the various types of assessment tools in order to select the best instruments for their clients. Counselors need to be well rounded in their delivery of services; application of both standardized and nonstandardized assessment strategies is integral to being a competent counselor. In addition to being aware and able to implement a variety of assessment tools, counselors need to be adept in administering, scoring, and interpreting assessment instruments. Counselors are not only accountable to their clients but also to the general public and stakeholders who demand accountability and effective practice.

References

American Counseling Association. (2005). *ACA code of ethics.* Alexandria, VA: Author.

Anastasi, A., & Urbina, S. (1997). *Psychological testing* (7th ed.). Upper Saddle River, NJ: Prentice Hall.

Association for Assessment and Research in Counseling (2012). AARC statements of purpose. Retrieved from http://www.theaaceonline.com/about.htm

Butcher, J. N. (2010). Personality assessment from the nineteenth to the early twenty-first century: Past achievements and contemporary challenges. *Annual Review of Clinical Psychology*, 6, 1–20. doi:10.1146/annurev.clinpsy.121208.131420

Council for Accreditation of Counseling and Related Educational Programs. (2009). 2009 *CACREP standards.* Alexandria, VA: Author.

Cohen, R. J., & Swerdlik, M. E. (2002). *Psychological testing and assessment* (5th ed.). Boston, MA: McGraw-Hill.

Duffy, M., Giordano, V. A., Farrell, J. B., Paneque, O. M., & Crump, G. B. (2008). No Child Left Behind: Values and research issues in high-stakes assessments. *Counseling and Values*, 53, 53–66.

Erard, R. E. (2004). Release of test data under the 2002 ethics code and the HIPAA privacy rule: A raw deal or just a half-baked idea? *Journal of Personality Assessment,* 82, 23–30. doi:10.1207/s15327752jpa8201_4

Erford, B. E., Basham, A., Cashwell, C. S., Juhnke, G., & Wall, J. (2003, March 22–24). *Standards for qualifications of test users.* [Approved by the American Counseling Association Governing Council]. Alexandria, VA: American Counseling Association.

Gregory, R. J. (2007). *Psychological testing: History, principles, and applications* (5th ed.). Boston, MA: Allyn & Bacon.

Gladding, S. T. (2009). *Counseling: A comprehensive profession* (6th ed.). Upper Saddle River, NJ: Pearson Education.

Koch, L. C. (2000). Assessment and planning in the Americans with Disabilities Act era: Strategies for consumer self-advocacy and employer collaboration. *Journal of Vocational Rehabilitation*, 14, 103–108.

Naugle, K. A. (2009). Counseling and testing: What counselors need to know about state laws on assessment and testing. *Measurement and Evaluation in Counseling and Development,* 42, 31–45. doi: 10.1177/0748175609333561

Ricci v. DeStefano. (2012). In *Encyclopædia Britannica.* Retrieved from http://www.britannica.com/EBchecked/topic/1540641/Ricci-v-DeStefano

Telzrow, C. F., & McNamara, K. (2001). New directions in assessment for students with disabilities. *Work: Journal of Prevention, Assessment & Rehabilitation,* 17, 105–116.

Wall, J., Augustin, J., Eberly, C., Erford, B., Lundberg, D., & Vansickle, T. (2003). *Responsibilities of Users of Standardized Tests (RUST)* (3rd ed.). Alexandria, VA: Association for Assessment in Counseling and Education.

Whiston, S. C. (2009). *Principles and applications of assessment in counseling* (3rd ed.). Belmont, CA: Brooks/Cole.

CHAPTER 2

Case Studies and Progress Notes

OBJECTIVES

After reading this chapter, you will be able to:

1. Describe the case studies of Ms. Eva Marie Garza and Mr. Robert Jones.

2. Recognize the basic elements contained within a typical clinical assessment intake interview—including but not limited to (a) general demographics, (b) client presentation and statements, (c) identified treatment goals, (d) marriages and significant other relationships, (e) family of origin and family history, (f) previous counseling and psychiatric hospitalization history, (g) educational experiences, (h) work–career history, (i) legal history, (j) medical history, and (k) diagnosis.

3. Indicate the purpose of progress notes and the major components included within typical progress notes.

4. State the similarities and differences among SOAP, DART, and diagnostic-based progress notes.

OVERVIEW

The intent of this chapter is fourfold. First, the chapter provides two case studies. These case studies are used throughout the upcoming chapters. They will help readers understand how specific psychological assessment instruments can be used with persons presenting with concerns similar to the case study examples and how similar presenting persons will likely score on psychological assessment instruments. Second, the chapter will help readers gain a general understanding of typical assessment intake interviews. Third, the authors will describe the purpose and major components included within counseling progress notes. Finally, the chapter will provide an overview of three common progress note taking methods.

CASE STUDIES

During our joint 30-plus years of clinical experience and teaching psychological assessment to doctoral and master's students as well as frontline counseling professionals, we have learned many important and helpful teaching strategies. One strategy frequently cited as helpful by those we have trained is using one or two case study examples across the many different psychological assessment instruments. In other words, students and professionals alike find it helpful when we provide just one or two thorough case studies and then discuss how to use different psychological instruments with the same one or two clients. Based on teaching evaluations and feedback, our adult learners report limiting case studies reduces confusion and the intermingling of client scenarios.

Thus, this chapter provides two fictional case studies. The case studies are continuously used throughout the book. The portrayed clients, although fictional, are based on an aggregate of clients previously treated or supervised by the authors. Names, circumstances, and potentially identifying characteristics have been changed to protect true client identities. However, the case studies are representative of clients frequently referred to and treated by counselors.

Anxiety and mood disorders (e.g., depression) are the most common mental health disorders diagnosed among American adults with more than 6.8 million Americans diagnosed with generalized anxiety disorder in 2005 (Kessler, Chiu, Demler, & Walter, 2005). Anxiety and mood disorders constitute the largest single portion of our clinical supervisees' caseloads. Many of the clients we have counseled fulfilled the complete diagnostic criteria necessary for such disorders. Thus, given the frequency of anxiety and mood disorders—especially from the robust increase in clients reporting "anxiety" as their chief presenting complaint since the onset of the reported double-dip recession—our first clinical vignette reflects a client presenting with generalized anxiety disorder.

Clients who experience severe anxiety suffer an especially debilitating mental illness that significantly interferes with daily living and greatly compromises life satisfaction. They are wracked with excessive, irrational, and uncontrollable worry; the vast majority of our supervisees' clients and the clients with whom we have counseled have experienced clinically significant anxiety throughout much of their lives. Ms. Eva Marie Garza is such a person.

Although most clients succinctly provide sufficient information to complete a clinical assessment intake interview in approximately 90 minutes, this was not the case with Eva Marie. Despite her above-average intelligence, she was remarkably nervous and distraught during the first 45 minutes of her original meeting. At that time, her markedly elevated anxiety inhibited her ability to adequately focus and concentrate on counselor-asked questions or to respond in a succinct manner. Thus, until approximately halfway through the first session, her speech was noticeably tangential and pressured. Her responses to relatively simple, straightforward questions such as "Tell me how you arrived at my office today?" were loquacious, loosely associated to the asked question, and often difficult to follow or comprehend. Therefore, the clinical intake assessment interview required two sessions. During the latter half of the first session and following the first 10 minutes of her second session, Eva Marie's anxiety greatly diminished and it became evident via her more focused and detailed question responses that she was feeling far more comfortable and less nervous. Below is Eva Marie's case study. You will want to become thoroughly familiar with Eva Marie because we will refer to her throughout the remainder of the book.

Case Study: Ms. Eva Marie Garza

The following psychosocial report is a summary of observations, client statements, and responses made by Ms. Eva Marie Garza during two clinical assessment intake interviews. The first interview occurred June 7, 2011, between 9:30 A.M. and 11 A.M. The second occurred June 14, 2011, between 11 A.M. and noon. Eva Marie was remarkably anxious during the first clinical assessment intake interview. Because of the severity of her anxiety, Eva Marie was unable to complete the standard initial clinical intake assessment in its entirety on June 7. The clinical intake was completed during our second interview, one week later on June 14. Both interviews were conducted by Gerald Juhnke, Ed.D., LPC, at his office located at 345 Colorado Street, San Antonio, Texas. No attempt was made to verify the veracity of Ms. Garza's statements or self-report. Exact quotations were used whenever possible to most accurately reflect Ms. Garza's responses.

Ms. Eva Marie Garza is a 40-year-old, married, Mexican-American female. She was oriented to person, place, and time. Based on the complexity of language she used and the sophistication of the questions she asked within sessions, she appeared as having above-average intelligence. Eva Marie's overall mood was anxious. Eva Marie's speech was noticeably pressured and fast. During the first 45 minutes of her initial June 7 intake, her responses to counselor-asked questions were often tangential and only loosely associated with asked questions. During that time, she was especially loquacious, and she demonstrated slight to mild psychomotor agitation. On first entering the initial intake session, Eva Marie sat in the counseling office chair. She slowly rocked back and forth as she responded to verbal questions. Approximately halfway through the first session, she seemed to relax and discontinued her rocking. When she was more relaxed, her question responses became more focused, less tangential, and more succinct. However, she continued to demonstrate slight psychomotor agitation at times by tapping her feet, slightly bouncing her legs up and down, and tapping her fingers on the chair armrest.

Eva Marie was appropriately dressed wearing a clean, dark blue dress with matching dark blue, "pump" shoes. Her dark red nail polish was unchipped and appeared recently applied. She wore no jewelry. Eva Marie's personal hygiene was appropriate and unremarkable. Eva Marie is 5 feet, one inch tall, and weighs 109 pounds. She looked healthy and was neither visibly overweight nor gaunt. Eva Marie works as an "assistant to the librarian" at Our Lady of Mercy Elementary School. When asked the reason for entering counseling, Eva Marie abruptly began to weep and reported "extreme anxiety" and "complete dissatisfaction" with her life. As her weeping slowed, Eva Marie stated, "I don't know what to do." Moments later she stated, "I'm so anxious and miserable. I've been this way all my life and want to change."

IDENTIFIED TREATMENT GOALS   When asked to identify the two most pressing concerns she would like to address in counseling, Eva Marie immediately responded, "I want to live without being anxious." Asked to clarify her response, Eva Marie reported significant levels of "anxiety and worry that have permeated my life forever." She reported her experienced anxiety is not limited to one behavior, a specific circumstance or place, or a single aspect of her life: "Worry and anxiety haunt me from the moment I awake until I finally fall asleep…. I can't even sleep the whole night because I'm so worried about everything." When asked about specific circumstances, events, persons, or places that promote, cause, or increase her anxiety, Eva Marie stated, "Everything." When queried about her statement "Everything," she responded, "I'm overwrought by worry and it isn't limited to one specific thing." She continued by reporting that her mind "races" and claims to "worry about anything and everything I think about." Eva Marie reported "great fatigue" and "an inability to relax." She later stated, "I'm so nervous my head, neck, and shoulders constantly ache." She indicated that she often experienced "stress headaches" and complained of "stomach upsets" that often were correlated to "more stressful times." Eva Marie indicated difficulty performing daily tasks and a lack of concentration throughout the day from her "overwhelming" worry and anxiety: "My mother says I should 'stop worrying and enjoy life.' I can't. My mind races with worry. I constantly worry about what's going to go wrong next in my life." Eva Marie continued, "What I'd really like to do is simply go on a cruise and get away from Momma and my husband for about a year. However, they both need me, and as an only child, I have to take care of my mother. It would be a sin not to. It's like I'm taking care of two youngsters who need constant attention and care. Ugh!"

Asked about the second most pressing thing she would like to address via counseling, Eva Maria shook her head and said, "I'm too worried to think about a second thing [to address in counseling]." When asked to scale her degree of anxiety between "0" or no anxiety and "10" or overwhelming anxiety, Eva Marie reported "11." She then stated, "Anxiety has ruined my life. I can't function because it [anxiety] is so bad."

MARRIAGES AND SIGNIFICANT OTHER RELATIONSHIPS   Eva Marie is married to 55-year-old Ernest. The couple has been married for 21 years. This is Eva Marie's first marriage and Ernest's second. The couple has no children, "Ernest never wanted kids. His dad was an alcoholic. Kids were never his thing." Eva Marie continued by reporting she thought once she married Ernest her anxiety would diminish and her lonesomeness would "disappear." Immediately after making this statement, Eva Marie again began to cry and her rocking quickened. When asked what three words she would use to describe Ernest, Eva Marie quickly said "absent" and "emotionless." Eva Marie struggled to identify a third word to describe Ernest. After considerable thought, Eva Marie asked, "May I stop at two [two words to describe Ernest]?" When asked about Eva Marie's marital satisfaction level, she responded, "Can one be married and happy?" Later, Eva Marie reported "little marital satisfaction" and stated her marriage was one of "convenience." She quickly added that she was "jilted" by her "high school boyfriend...we [high school boyfriend and Eva Marie] had planned to marry during college." One week after being jilted, Ernest introduced himself to Eva Marie. This occurred at a parish social event where Eva Marie was working as food buffet server. The couple wed within two weeks. Eva Marie reported that the quick marriage ended her fears of being "forever lonesome and alone." She then stated, "I never realized one could be hopelessly lonesome and married. I can't wait for my mother to die so I can divorce Ernest without being told I'm a bad Catholic."

When asked about her dating history prior to Ernest, Eva Marie said, "My mother is Catholic. Dating before high school was absolutely forbidden." She reported her "only high school boyfriend" was Karl. He invited Eva Marie to the high school homecoming dance and later the prom her senior year. According to Eva Marie, she was "ecstatic. I had a huge crush on Karl." Eva Marie reported the high school homecoming occurred following a fall semester football game, "I was so anxious about going and had no idea what to wear." She described in great detail the events leading to the homecoming dance and the dance itself. When asked about anxiety when dating Karl, Eva Marie indicated, "Karl was almost as anxious as me." She indicated Karl's humor and frankness regarding his anxiety kept her from focusing on her own anxiety. According to Eva Marie, the couple exclusively dated each other throughout their senior year and into the following year. Eva Marie reported "the plan was" that she would complete her accounting associate's degree through Piedmont Community College. Given that Karl was attending Georgia Tech University, Eva Marie believed the couple would marry during Karl's junior year and live in married student housing: "I'd get a bookkeeping job downtown, and he'd complete his chemistry degree. It never happened." Eva Marie reported that Karl failed multiple classes and dropped out of college, "He interacted less and less with me until he just disappeared...not even a telephone call." Eva Marie said she was "devastated" and survived by focusing on her multiple jobs. One week later, she met Ernest.

Eva Marie reported that the most important person in her life was her 56-year-old mother: "Momma is the center of my life." When asked to describe her mother in three words, Eva Maria stated, "nurturing, kind, and supportive, but ever since she has gotten elderly, she is often crotchety—I'd say, 'bitchy' but good Catholics aren't suppose to swear."

FAMILY OF ORIGIN AND FAMILY HISTORY   Eva Marie is an only child. She resides with her husband and mother at her mother's home located at 94213 South West Clark Road, San Antonio, Texas. Eva Marie's mother and father moved Eva Marie from Mission, Texas, in the Rio Grande River Valley to Atlanta, Georgia, when Eva Marie was 7 years old. Eva Marie reported, "It was horrible. We were the only Mexican-American family there [Atlanta]" and "...everybody made derogatory racial slurs about us." Eva Marie indicated that her mother and she wished to immediately return to "The Valley," but her father reported he could earn more money in Atlanta than in Texas. Eva Marie stated, "I cried myself to sleep, almost every night when we moved to Atlanta." According to Eva Marie, she felt "ostracized" by others at her school, because she was Mexican American: "No one befriended me." Despite ridicule and hardships, the family stayed in Atlanta while her father worked odd construction jobs. When Eva Marie was 11, her father was killed in a construction accident: "It was horrible. Momma tried to move us back to Mission [Texas], but we had no money or family to help."

Once Eva Marie and Ernest married, they moved in with Eva Marie's mother: "Ernest and I didn't have enough money for our own place." Two years ago, Eva Marie's grandmother passed away. Her grandmother left Eva Marie's mother her estate, including the home where Eva Marie, her mother, and Ernest now reside in San Antonio: "Mother wanted to move back to Texas. So, with the help of our assistant parish priest and youth group, we packed up and here we are." Eva Marie reported that had it not been for her mother, she would have stayed in Atlanta, divorced Ernest, and never let her mother know that she had divorced Ernest.

Eva Marie described her mother as "strong willed and crotchety at times, but very loving. And, she never means everything that she says—she is just getting elderly." When queried, Eva Marie smiled and stated, "Momma was the best momma in the whole world. But, as she has gotten a whole lot older, she has gotten a whole lot more cantankerous." When asked what three words she would use to describe her father, Eva Marie said, "Loving, genuine, the perfect father." Eva Marie described her father as "the most caring and kind man I ever met." Eva Marie reported her parents had a "perfect" marriage: "They constantly held hands and shared in each other's lives." When asked which parent Eva Marie is most similar to, she stated, "I'm a blend of both. I look exactly like my mother, but I have my father's sense of kindness towards others."

Eva Marie stated her first memory of her mother was singing a "church hymn": "She sang church hymns all the time." Her first memory of her father was of "him teaching me how to pray at our kitchen table. I must have been about three." She denies any corporal punishment or abuse within her family of origin experience. Eva Marie reported herself as "very religious" and indicated, "I grew up in a proud Catholic family with a proud Catholic tradition." When asked what this meant, Eva Marie reported that she had learned to "follow God's rules" and "God's way" from her parents and her involvement in the Catholic Church.

PREVIOUS COUNSELING AND PSYCHIATRIC HOSPITALIZATIONS   Eva Marie denies any previous counseling or psychiatric hospitalizations. She claims that she first noticed she was "nervous" when her father started praying that God would help her "relax" and "feel more comfortable" at elementary school. Eva Marie reported that in kindergarten and elementary school she often would awake early in the morning and "race" to her mother and father's bedroom: "I'd get them up at 5 A.M. and demand my father immediately take me to school. I was worried I'd be late and fail the grade." According to Eva Marie, she would cry until father walked her to school. Reportedly, the two would sit on the school steps and wait until the janitors arrived at 6 A.M.

EDUCATIONAL EXPERIENCES   Eva Marie reported being an "A student." She stated, "I was always so nervous I would flunk classes that I studied very hard." She was inducted into the National Junior Honor Society in sixth grade and continued Honor Society until she graduated high school. According to Eva Marie, "I had four or five close friends [during her middle and high school years], and we stayed close friends from middle through high school." She proudly continued discussing how she and her friends would get together weekly until she moved her mother back to Texas 2 years ago. Eva Marie graduated from Downtown Central Catholic High School in Atlanta, Georgia, and completed her associate's degree in accounting from Piedmont Community College. When asked if she had considered entering a 4-year college upon graduating from Piedmont Community College, Eva Marie stated, "Never. I wanted to get a real job and earn money."

WORK-CAREER HISTORY   Eva Marie reported, "I worked at home, cooking, canning, and cleaning, until high school." During her high school years, Eva Marie's mother required that Eva Marie work at their local Catholic parish, St. Patrick's Cathedral. Eva Marie reported that she was "good with numbers," so mother secured Eva Marie a job on the "Tithing Committee." Eva Marie smiled and her rate of speech significantly quickened as she described how she "worked my way up to bookkeeping [at the parish]." Eva Marie reported she "loved" bookkeeping, "It [bookkeeping at the parish] gave me a sense of purpose, and I was less nervous." She continued her work at the parish until she graduated from community college and began work as a bookkeeper at a local drug store. The drug store was owned by a fellow parish member: "Mr. Alexander knew I had just graduated from Piedmont and needed a job. He needed someone to get his books in order." Eva Marie took great pride in her perceptions that Mr. Alexander greatly valued her work. According to Eva Marie, Mr. Alexander put Eva Marie in charge of the pharmacy's local advertising campaign where she enjoyed making daily decisions about what items to advertise and what special sales would appear in the local newspaper advertisements: "It was great because I enjoyed telling others what to do and how to accomplish our advertising goals." She worked there "14 years" until her mother decided to move back to Texas: "I didn't want to move back to Texas, but I can't abandon my mother." Eva Marie went on to describe how a "good Catholic" would never abandon a parent who had been as dedicated to her child as Eva Marie's mother had: "God would strike me dead if I left her. And, she needs me." Eva Marie continued, "It probably sounds bad, but I will feel so much freer when she passes." When asked to explain, Eva Marie described how her mother is aging and "crotchety," how overwhelming it is to take care of her given mother's declining self-care and "crabbiness," and how no matter what decisions Eva Marie makes, her mother finds fault with Eva Marie's decisions: "It is like I can never fully please her."

When Eva Marie moved to San Antonio she had a difficult time finding work: "I didn't know anyone, and I couldn't find a bookkeeping job." Ten months ago, Eva Marie "took" a position as "assistant to the chief librarian" at Our Lady of Mercy elementary school: "I hate the job, but I get to work at the parish school, and it gets me out of the house and away from Ernest and my mother." She reports the thing she likes most about working as the assistant to the librarian is "making decisions for the chief librarian." When asked to clarifying her response, Eva Marie indicated she had the ability to synthesize data and make rapid decisions regarding what books to purchase, how many books to purchase, and what to do to make the library more "user-friendly."

Eva Marie smiled when she discussed her work abilities and skills. When the counselor commented on Eva Marie's smile as she described her purchasing skills, Eva Marie responded, "I like to make sound business decisions, and I like it when people pay attention to me. Momma never lets me make decisions at home, and Ernest...I have to make every decision for him. It's like I'm married to an eight-year-old." She continued by reporting that although she "hates" her job, she likes being at work rather than at home because she could "take responsibility for myself" and "make things happen."

LEGAL HISTORY   Eva Marie denies any previous arrests or pending legal actions.

MEDICAL HISTORY   Eva Marie has high blood pressure; temporomandibular joint disorder (TMJ) reportedly resulting from her "constant grinding and clinching of my teeth and jaw"; "chest pain, headaches, and nausea caused by my constant worrying"; and "sleep problems." She is under medical treatment for each of these disorders and takes the following medications as prescribed by either her general physician, Dr. Sylvia Torres, or her dentist, Dr. Robert Hartman:

Lisinopril 20 mg per day prescribed by Dr. Torres (blood pressure)

Xanax 5 mg per day (*Note:* This medication is jointly prescribed and monitored by both Drs. Torres [to reduce anxiety leading to chest pain and sleep disturbance] and Hartman [muscle relaxant for TMJ]). These doctors are working in unison with the prescription and thus the total amount of Xanax she is taking per day is 5 mg, not 10 mg.

Eva Marie denies previous surgeries, head or spinal injuries, drug use, or medical conditions.

Diagnostic Statistical Manual (DSM) Diagnosis

Axis I:	300.02	Generalized Anxiety Disorder
	V61.10	Partner Relational Problem
	V62.89	Phase of Life Problem

Axis II: V71.09   No Diagnosis on Axis II

Axis III: High blood pressure and TMJ; currently under the care of physician and oral surgeon for both

Axis IV: Marital dissatisfaction; husband and client living with mother; job dissatisfaction

Axis V: Current Global Assessment of Functioning (GAF) score: 62

Highest GAF score previous 12 months: 65

This case study reflects the types of detailed information gathered during a typical counseling intake or psychosocial assessment. Upcoming Chapters 7 and 13 will describe in far greater detail both the face-to-face interview process and how to author psychological reports. Therefore, we will not go into great detail here. However, for the purposes of this chapter, it is important to note that the counselor has documented Eva Marie's age, ethnicity, appearance, behaviors within session, mental status, and home address. Even the client's reported treatment goals are identified. Furthermore, the typical assessment process investigates the many complex domains of Eva Marie's life and reflects the synergy between these domains. Specifically, the counselor gathers information regarding marriages and significant other relationships, including Eva Marie's family of origin and family, as well as her perceptions of mother and father. In addition, Eva Marie's previous counseling and psychiatric hospitalization, education, work/career, legal, and medical histories are probed.

The intake assessment reveals Eva Marie's immediate anxiety symptoms are acute, problematic, unpleasant, and debilitating. It becomes strikingly evident that at least some of Eva Marie's poorer past decisions were made in an attempt to escape her anxiety. Unfortunately, these decisions have resulted in additional life problems and stressors. For example, in an attempt to lessen her anxiety and eliminate her lonesomeness, she married Ernest within days of being "jilted" by the man she wanted to marry. Unfortunately, her decision to quickly marry Ernest did not bring about her desired outcomes and now even magnifies Eva Marie's anxiety.

It is important to note that Eva Marie's overwhelming and expansive anxiety is her chief presenting concern. She likes making everyday decisions for herself without the need for excessive amounts of advice or reassurance from others. She also enjoys making work-related decisions—especially for her boss. Concomitantly, Eva Marie does not have an unrealistic fear of being left alone when her mother dies. Instead, Eva Marie wishes she could escape her mother and husband to enjoy personal "alone time." In addition, Eva Marie likes initiating and completing work-specific projects without unrealistic needs for reassurance by others.

Like many clients, Eva Marie becomes more comfortable as she spends time with the counselor and the intake process becomes more familiar. This lessens her extreme anxiety and allows Eva Marie to use her precise language. The counselor recognizes Eva Marie's precise language and understands the correlation between such language and intelligence. Hence, the counselor can make a statement about her intelligence.

Our second case study highlights a male client fulfilling the DSM (4th edition, text revision; *DSM-IV-TR*) diagnostic criteria for antisocial personality disorder. Like Eva Marie, the second described client is fictional and based on an aggregate of clients counseled or supervised by the authors. Given the significant number of court-mandated clients counseled by our students and clinical supervisees, we believe this case is highly representative of clients served by professional counselors. In addition, it provides a case example that demonstrates the rigid and inflexible behaviors associated with a characterlogical, Axis II disorder. Like the T-shirts we have seen at the beach with a cartoon of a ferocious-looking, sharp-toothed shark that reads, "I don't get ulcers, I give 'em," persons with certain Axis II personality disorders, such as antisocial personality disorder and narcissistic personality disorder, often do not find their behaviors or symptoms necessarily noxious or debilitating. Instead, those around them suffer by the characterlogically disordered clients' behaviors. Most often, clients fulfilling antisocial personality disorder criteria are mandated into treatment by the courts, professional licensure or certification boards (e.g., nursing, counseling), or employers. Many times, personality-disordered clients deny an understanding of the reasons for their mandated counseling or claim the supposed behaviors that caused the mandated counseling were erroneous, mistaken, or "only one time, atypical" events simply blown out of proportion by others. However, as one listens to the client's self-reported history, it often becomes strikingly evident that the same behaviors that resulted in the current mandated counseling have a long history. These experiences are consistent with the next case study.

Case Study: Mr. Robert Jones

The following psychosocial report is a summary of observations, client statements, and responses made by Mr. Robert Jones during a clinical intake interview. This September 29, 2011, interview was conducted between 1 P.M. and 2:51 P.M. at the counseling office of Gerald Juhnke, Ed.D., LPC, located at 345 Colorado Street, San Antonio, Texas. No attempt was made to verify the veracity of Mr. Jones's statements or self-report. Exact quotations are used whenever possible to reflect Mr. Jones's exact responses.

Robert Jones is a 37-year- old, twice-divorced Caucasian male. He was oriented to person, place, and time. He seemed to have somewhat above-average intelligence given the preciseness of his speech, the sophistication of his chosen words, and his engaging manner of interacting. Robert was appropriately dressed. He wore clean clothing, including khaki-colored trousers, an overly noticeable starched and pressed, white, button-down shirt, and Sperry Topsider-type shoes. His personal hygiene was appropriate and unremarkable. Robert is 6 feet tall and weighs 210 pounds. His appearance was trim and muscular without noted obesity. He works as a "heavy-duty equipment and tractor salesman" for a large, national road equipment company. When asked the reason for his visit, Robert stated, "My attorney told me to begin counseling." When pressed, Robert indicated he was arrested on January 3 of this year for "grand larceny and possession of stolen property in excess of $100,000." Robert indicated the arrest was "a big misunderstanding." Robert stated the situation was "blown out of proportion by my former employer." He indicated his former supervisor "was a jealous old fool." Robert claimed the larceny and possession of stolen property charges stemmed from a "jealous boss" and Robert's "earning more on commission sales" than his former supervisor did. Robert claimed his former supervisor fabricated a story that made it appear Robert was stealing company equipment. Instead, Robert reported he was "warehousing" commercial road construction equipment—"graders, backhoes, excavators, and the like"—on his property until he could get the equipment back to the company. Robert's scheduled trial date is October 30 in Oxford County Superior Court A.

IDENTIFIED TREATMENT GOALS   Robert initially denied any clearly identifiable or desired therapeutic treatment goals. Instead, he reported his primary purpose for attending counseling was to comply with his attorney's recommendations. However, after further discussion, Robert reported having "minor issues" related to three other recent arrests within the last 6 months. Two of these reported arrests were specific to driving under the influence. These arrests occurred on June 1 and July 4 of this year. It should be noted that June 1 was part of the long Memorial Day weekend; July 4 was also part of a long weekend. The third arrest was specific to domestic violence and "other charges" associated with an August 14, 2011, arrest.

Robert stated, "Others constantly get me into fights." When asked specifically who the "others" were, Robert reported, "Mostly my live-in girlfriend, Catherine." The primary behavior reported by Robert as leading to his domestic violence arrest was his alcohol consumption. "She pressed my buttons, so I started downing six packs of brew until I couldn't hear her anymore." When asked what three words he would use to describe himself after he begins consuming alcohol, he reports "argumentative," "angry," and "aggressive."

MARRIAGES AND SIGNIFICANT OTHER RELATIONSHIPS   Robert and his reported "live-in girlfriend" of 5 months (April 2011), Ms. Catherine O'Donnell, reside at North Hunting Hill Apartments, 1115 NW Cherry Street, San Antonio, Texas. Robert and Catherine met at Knotty's Bar. She was a cocktail server at the bar. According to Robert, he made numerous flirtatious passes at Catherine the evening they initially met. Instead of completing her scheduled work shift, she left Knotty's and immediately moved in with Robert at the above residence. When asked "What three words would you use to describe Catherine?" Robert responded, "Very sexy, blonde, and tall...did I mention very sexy?" Robert reported he has "no interest" in marrying Catherine: "I've been married twice before. It [marriage] destroys relationships."

Robert stated his relationship with Catherine was "on its final legs." When asked to further clarify and explain this response, Robert said he does not anticipate the couple will stay together "much longer." According to Robert, he is "tired" of paying the bills without "equal financial support from Catherine." Robert reported Catherine is an "addict" who uses approximately $300 per week in cocaine and alcohol. Robert states that he "doesn't trust" Catherine. He stated his level of trust "greatly disintegrated" after Catherine called the police in August and charged Robert with domestic violence. Those charges, as well as other charges that same evening, including drunk and disorderly conduct and aggravated assault to a police officer, resulted in Robert's incarceration in the county jail for a period of 31 days.

Robert reported his previous live-in partner was "Andi." Robert met Andi at an Alcoholics Anonymous (AA) meeting in March of 2010. Robert moved into Andi's trailer within days of meeting. Robert resided with Andi and her two children until "Halloween 2010." When asked why the relationship ended, Robert reported, "The sex got old, and I couldn't stand living with all those whining kids." Robert denied any domestic violence allegations by Andi and stated, "Although I sometimes got rough with Andi, she never would have filed charges." Robert, however, reported occasions when he physically struck Andi or pulled Andi's hair. According to Robert, these behaviors were precipitated by his alcohol consumption: "I only hit her when I was drunk and I didn't know what I was doing."

Robert reported "four or five" live-in relationships prior to meeting Andi. He stated those relationships were "meaningless" and occurred so he could have free lodging, sex, and alcohol. Robert claimed each relationship "lasted less than a couple weeks." When asked whether Robert remained in contact with these live-in partners, he responded, "Why would I do that?"

Robert married his high school sweetheart, Emma Mae Cronkite, in 1992. The couple had three sons, Cody (18 years old [born 1993]), Kyle (16 years old [born 1995]), and Carter (13 years old [born 1998]). Robert denied any violent behaviors towards Emma. "Never. She accepted me for who I was." When queried about the reason for the marriage's dissolution, Robert reported Emma Mae's father (who also was Robert's employer at the time) "started rumors" insinuating Robert's infidelity: "It [the alleged infidelity] never happened. I drank a lot, but I never ran around on Emma Mae." Emma Mae and the boys currently reside with Emma Mae's father and mother in Ohio. In lieu of alimony, Robert agreed to award Emma Mae full custody of the boys in 1999 as part of their divorce settlement.

Robert married Lisa McKinney in 2000. Robert stated, "It was my shotgun-rebound marriage." When asked to clarify the stated "shotgun-rebound" term, Robert indicated Lisa's father "forced" him into the marriage, "because Lisa was pregnant." Further, Robert reported he was "rebounding" from his divorce with Emma Mae. Robert and Lisa lived together from February until May 2000. The couple wed in June of 2000 when Lisa revealed she was pregnant. The couple separated in 2001 because of Robert's drinking and domestic violence. Lisa divorced Robert in 2003. "She petitioned the court and has had my paychecks garnished ever since." Robert stated, "Just eight more years of paying for that kid, and I'll have my full paycheck again."

FAMILY OF ORIGIN AND FAMILY HISTORY   Robert is the oldest of four siblings (Robert [37], Donny [36], Eddy [34], and Trish [30]). Robert's biological parents were Robert "Senior" and Martha Jones. Robert described "Senior" as a "self-centered, son-of-a-bitch" and "no good, alcoholic." Martha was described as a "saint with a drinking problem." When queried, Robert stated his first memories of his father were of being "pounded by his fists for waking him [his father] up." Robert reported he looked "more like" Senior than Martha— "I've got his big nose, crooked smile, and small ears"—and had more of Senior's personality traits—"I can be stubborn and ornery like him." Robert indicated his parents had a "loveless" marriage, and his father was verbally and physically abusive to his mother and the children. His father was reported as physically absent throughout Robert's youth: "he wasn't home often." Robert at first expressed anger towards his father because of this absence, but quickly responded, "Actually, it [his father's absence] was probably best." When queried about this statement, Robert indicated his father often was under the influence of alcohol when home and would "act violently" towards Martha, Robert's siblings, and Robert. Therefore, Senior's absence "probably kept us from getting killed." When asked about his fondest memory of his father, Robert smiled and stated, "His [Senior's] absence." Robert's father died in a "drunk-driving accident" in 2009. Robert denied experiencing any grief or loss feelings resulting from his father's death and responded, "Nope. He never was really part of my life." Robert continued by describing how he and his mother celebrated Senior's death by drinking shots of tequila after Senior's funeral.

Robert stated his earliest memories of his mother revolved around her crying—"she cried all the time." He indicated that his mother "rarely fed us...she was too busy crying or sleeping." Robert reported his mother frequently fell and often was unable to stand because of her intoxication, "We [Robert and his siblings] would laugh at her, because she was too drunk to get up." Robert enthusiastically described occasions when he would tease his intoxicated mother in hopes of having her chase him. He reported that when his mother was intoxicated and chased him, she would often run into walls or trip. Robert stated this was a "sport" with him. When pressed to explain, Robert smiled and said, "Sport—like playing cards or hunting. I did it because it was fun."

Robert indicated embarrassment during his middle and high school years "because" of his mother's alcohol consumption: "Everybody knew she [his mother] was a drunk." According to Robert, his mother has "ill-health" and resides with Robert's sister, Trish, in a trailer outside Lubbock, Texas. Robert reported he last visited his mother approximately 2 years ago. According to Robert, he called his mother on her birthday last year. However, "She was too drunk to have a conversation."

When queried regarding his siblings, Robert stated, "We were never close." Robert indicated that he and Donny had a "strained relationship." Robert stated the two were in "constant competition" with each other during middle and high school. Robert reported Donny joined the Army after high school and is believed to reside in Georgia near Fort Benning. According to Robert, the two have not talked "in years." Eddy, Robert's 34-year-old brother, is a computer technician and works for a local community college informational technology department. Robert reported, "He [Eddy] got the brains of the family." Robert indicated he stopped by Eddy's apartment on New Year's Eve last year, and they talk "a couple times a year" by telephone. Robert claimed Trish was "the real mother of the family." Robert reported his sister "constantly calls," but he actively screens her calls via his voicemail. He further indicated, "Trish has always taken care of mother." Robert reported he feels "sorry" for Trish for assuming the caretaker role for "everyone in this frigged up family." According to Robert, Trish is a "nondrinker" who "tries to save men from their drugs. It's too bad she can't save herself."

PREVIOUS COUNSELING AND PSYCHIATRIC HOSPITALIZATIONS Robert first began counseling with Oxford County Community Mental Health (OCCMH) when he was 8 years old. Counseling was court mandated. Robert stabbed a classmate with a sharpened pencil and stole the classmate's basketball shoes. Robert "couldn't remember" how long he counseled with OCCMH but reported, "It was only a couple sessions." During middle school, Robert participated in group counseling experiences for children of substance-abusing parents. Robert stated, "It was a total waste of time." Robert also participated in "substance abuse counseling" with Dr. Garrie Watts. Robert entered counseling with Dr. Watts immediately following Robert's divorces in 1999 and 2003. Robert signed a confidential release of information requesting Dr. Watts's clinical reports and a summary regarding those counseling sessions be forwarded to this counselor. In both instances, Robert discontinued treatment within "three to five sessions for money reasons." According to Robert, Dr. Watts "put a collection agency on me, but it didn't work." Robert reported he "inconsistently" attended AA meetings from 1996 to the present: "I attend for a couple of months. Then I stop once I'm doing better…but it is a great place to pick up ladies." Robert denied any other psychotherapy experiences or inpatient psychiatric hospitalizations.

EDUCATIONAL EXPERIENCES Robert reported he was "mostly a B or C student" during his elementary, middle, and high school years. He indicated difficulties with authority figures, especially male teachers who challenged him to do better in classes. When queried, Robert reported the thing he liked best about high school was "playing football." Robert discontinued playing football because of his alcohol consumption, difficulties following team policies and rules, and arguments with coaches and players. Robert graduated from John Greely Williams High School in Clemmons, Texas, with a "college prep type high school diploma." He initially wanted to attend The University of Texas in Austin, but never enrolled. Instead, he attended a local community college and discontinued after a year of studies: "I started making more money as a used car salesman than I would with my degree anyway."

WORK–CAREER HISTORY Robert began working in fifth grade. He worked as a bus boy at a local restaurant: "I worked 4 to 8 [P.M.] every night." He indicated this work was "a necessity," because there "rarely" was food in his home. By seventh grade, he sold magazines and books door to door after school and bused tables at night. In high school, Robert was befriended by an "AA guy" named "Karl." Karl was a neighbor who brought food to Robert's mother and unsuccessfully encouraged Robert's dad to attend AA. Karl repaired tractor engines and farm equipment while Robert watched: "He [Karl] could do everything and anything with engines." Karl talked his employer into hiring Robert as a "go-for boy." According to Robert, this meant he would "fetch" whatever tools or parts Karl needed from the repair truck or garage. Over time, Karl taught Robert how to repair "anything related to motors." By the time Robert entered 11th grade, he was earning $700 per week at the farm equipment company (Terry's Tractors and Farm Equipment) doing the same engine repair work as Karl. According to Robert, this angered the other older engine mechanics and "Karl eventually became jealous of me, too." Robert reported the anger and jealousy of his coworkers resulted in Robert being "framed and fired" for stealing shop parts and tools.

After termination from the farm equipment company, Robert worked as an auto mechanic at his girlfriend's father's family-owned and -operated car dealership "Cronkite Cars." He worked there his high school senior year. Robert's speech rate noticeably increased, and he grinned as he described selling his first car at the dealership. According to Robert, a customer initially brought a car into the dealership for repairs. Robert informed the customer that the necessary repairs would cost more than purchasing a new car, "So, I walked him [the customer] onto the sales floor and acted like a salesman." Robert sold the customer a new car "at sticker price." Robert stated he "triple whammed the guy." When asked what this statement meant, Robert reported that he sold the customer a car at the "full sticker price" noted on the car window, sold the customer a "bogus full warranty package" that added over $2,700 to the basic sticker price, and received the customer's old car for free—"basically, it [the old car] only needed new spark plugs, wires, and a rotor cap." The dealership owner was so pleased that he immediately moved Robert from the repair shop to the sales floor. Robert reported being the "third highest grossing salesperson" during his senior year in high school. When he enrolled in community college, he was the highest producing salesperson at the dealership and the fourth highest producing salesperson in the district. Robert worked at Cronkite Cars from 1991 to 1998. He was terminated by the dealership owner, who was also his father-in-law, amid accusations of drinking on the job and having sex with customers and the dealership's receptionist.

From 1999 to 2006, Robert had a checkered history of working as a used car salesperson at multiple dealerships. In March of 2006, Robert became a "tractor and heavy equipment leasing agent" at Worldwide Tractor and Road Equipment. In 2010, he was terminated from that position amid accusations of theft. Criminal charges of "grand larceny and possession of stolen property in excess of $100,000" were levied against Robert in 2011 by Worldwide Tractor and Road Equipment related to incidents that led to his 2010 termination. In 2011, Robert began working at American Transnational Road Equipment as a "heavy-duty equipment and tractor salesman." Robert reported, "I get a buzz from sales." When asked if he ever considered other career options, Robert stated, "Never. This [equipment sales] is my 'calling.' I love it."

LEGAL HISTORY   Robert reported a checkered legal history. He reported stealing "candy, chips, and cigarettes" from neighborhood convenience and drugstores before age 8. He stated that during the times he got caught for stealing, the store owners or police would feel sorry for him once they realized his mother was an alcoholic and his father was abusive: "I could have won an Academy Award for the shows I used to put on for the cops." At age 8, he stabbed a classmate with a pencil. He later stole the same classmate's "Air Jordan" basketball shoes. Robert noted that when Oxford County Juvenile Court investigated these charges against him and completed a family evaluation, his mother's alcoholism, father's absence, and the neglect of the children became apparent. Thus, Oxford County Child Protective Services placed his siblings in foster care homes and his mother was court mandated to complete a 21-day, inpatient, substance abuse program. Robert was expelled from school for the stabbing and served 47 days in juvenile detention. He reported, "[After being at the detention center] I vowed never to get caught again."

Robert reported that the "only times" he has been "caught for breaking the law" since his juvenile detention incarceration were his (a) January 3, 2011, grand larceny and possession of stolen property in excess of $100,000 arrest; (b) June 1 and July 2011, driving under the influence (DUI) arrests; and (c) August 14, 2011, domestic violence arrest that included additional charges of drunk and disorderly conduct and aggravated assault to a police officer. This combination of charges during his August 14, 2011, arrest resulted in his incarceration in the Oxford County Justice Center for a 60-day period.

When queried about other arrests or incarcerations, Robert smiled and stated, "You can check my record. Those are the only charges against me." When queried why the arrests all occurred in 2011, Robert claimed, "It was a bad year."

Robert's scheduled trial date for his January 3, 2011, arrest is October 30 in Oxford County Superior Court A, the Honorable Judge Steven Wisneski is presiding.

MEDICAL HISTORY   Robert denied any significant past or present medical issues. He reported his mother mentioned nothing remarkable regarding Robert's birth—"not that a drunk could remember anything anyway." He denied any head traumas or surgeries. Robert reported that his last medical evaluation occurred on March 9, 2011, as part of a pre-hire screening physical required by his current employer. He had "no high cholesterol problems or anything."

DSM Diagnosis

Axis I:	303.90	Alcohol Dependence
Axis II:	301.83	Antisocial Personality Disorder
Axis III:	None	
Axis IV:	Pending court trial; relationship dissatisfaction	
Axis V:	Current GAF score: 48	
	Highest GAF score previous 12 months: 50	

Robert's intake assessment demonstrates a number of reoccurring themes and behaviors that warrant discussion. First, Robert repeatedly has broken the law, harmed others, or ignored the rights and feelings of others; he appears to take great pleasure in describing how he conned or took advantage them. These behaviors began before age 8 and have continued unto today. Multiple examples of Robert's characterlogical disorder are evident. As a youth, Robert constantly teased his intoxicated mother in an effort to get her to chase him and trip or run into things while in pursuit of Robert. He called this a "sport" and lacked empathy towards his mother. In addition, Robert reported stealing candy, chips, and cigarettes from neighborhood stores as a youngster; at age 8, Robert stabbed a peer with a pencil and stole the peer's shoes. Robert later stated he could have been the recipient of an Academy Award for the way he conned police and storekeepers to escape punishment. Furthermore, it seems Robert tends to enter relationships with others to obtain what he wants with little attention or support for the other persons. Once he has attained his desires, he ends the relationship with little concern for the others. These behaviors demonstrate an ingrained and pervasive pattern of thinking and behaving that supports the Axis II antisocial personality disorder diagnosis.

One of the common behaviors we encounter with persons fulfilling antisocial personality disorder criteria is alcohol and substance abuse or dependence. In Robert's case, alcohol dependence seems to be commonly associated with his reckless disregard for others' safety. Whether driving under the influence or assaulting a police officer, Robert's alcohol dependence seems connected with his impulsivity and acting-out behaviors. However, his alcohol dependence is a symptom of his personality disorder, not necessarily the entire cause of his many antisocial behaviors. Even if Robert were not drinking, his blatant disregard for others and their safety, his impulsivity and deceitfulness, and his lack of remorse exist.

These two case studies reflect interesting persons who will complete psychological assessment instruments in upcoming chapters. Their symptomatology and ways of behaving and thinking will become more apparent as we review their test results Of course, clinical assessment intakes are not the only time we document what clients say and do. In the following, we will provide a general overview of progress notes and describe three common methods of recording such information.

PROGRESS NOTES

Progress notes are critically important. They establish a written summary of each counseling session, promote treatment efficacy and continuity, and potentially insulate counselors from wrongful liability. Counselors merely need to review previous session progress notes to remind them of pressing topics, themes, and assignments that require attention within the upcoming treatment session. Progress notes further provide documentation of what was said and done within the counseling session. Therefore, from a legal and reimbursement standpoint, progress notes are vitally important. They prove what services were rendered, what services should be reimbursed, and the ethical manner in which services were provided.

Despite the potential importance and benefits of well-written progress notes, there exists wide variation among agencies regarding progress note taking requirements and policies. Minimally, progress notes should describe (a) any significant changes in client symptoms or diagnoses, (b) changes in presenting concern severity, (c) the counseling modality used (e.g., individual, family, group), (d) the counseling theory or model used (e.g., motivational interviewing, cognitive-behavioral theory), (e) a summarization of interventions used to address each client-presenting concern, and (f) any prescribed assignments or important communications within the session. Should clients present with suicidal, homicidal, or violent ideation or verbalize or suggest harmful intent, progress notes must clearly report what the clients said or did to denote such ideation or intent, the interventions created to sufficiently neutralize the potential threat and ensure safety, consultations with professional peers and superiors to ensure adequate safety, and generated follow-up plans. Finally, given the importance of summarizing and documenting client sessions and to ensure the most accurate recall and reporting, we ask supervisees to complete progress notes immediately following each session. Therefore, we strongly encourage our charges to use 50 minutes of each treatment hour for counseling and the remaining 10 minutes to author corresponding session progress notes. In addition, we require progress note completion by the end of the agency's treatment day. In other words, counselors complete all progress notes within their typical 8-hour work schedule, when memories and recall can adequately provide exact details regarding the session. It has been our experience when counselors fail to complete multiple progress notes prior to the end of the agency's treatment day that the later authored progress notes are void of important details. Concomitantly, the counselors often have a difficult time adequately describing session benefits and concerns.

Standardized Progress Note Formats

SOAP PROGRESS NOTES   Early in our education, we were trained to use SOAP Notes. SOAP is a mnemonic that uses the first letters of four words: Subjective, Objective, Assessment, and Plan (J. Owen, personal communication, September 9, 1985; Shaw, 1997). Each letter and word corresponds to a specific component of the counselor-authored progress note. Thus, SOAP Notes start with a Subjective component, proceed through Objective and Assessment components, and end with a Plan component. Typically, at the top of the first and following pages of the SOAP Notes the client's name, the date and time of the session, and the counselor's name are prominently displayed. Counselors sign and date the Notes after written content is added to the SOAP Plan component. The signature is placed immediately under the last line of the Plan component. This indicates that the progress notes for that session are complete and whole. Furthermore, the signature placement helps ensure that others cannot add or delete written content. On the right-hand side next to the counselor's signature are the counselor's highest academic degree (e.g., M.A., M.S., Ph.D.) and professional license and certification initials such as LPC (Licensed Professional Counselor), LMHC (Licensed Mental Health Counselor), or NCC (National Certified Counselor).

The SOAP Notes Subjective component includes client-provided information. Thus, the information is completely subjective. The information contained within the Subjective component involves the client's perceptions of the chief presenting concerns or reasons for treatment. Here, the client describes symptoms including onset, duration, severity of the concern, and factors perceived by the client as influencing the concern. The SOAP Notes Objective component is intended to contain impartial and unbiased data from external information sources. Height and weight measurements, findings from physical examinations, or blood pressure measurements are the types of information contained in medical SOAP Notes. However, within the realm of counseling, truly objective information is at best difficult to attain. Here, counselors may include direct client observations such as descriptions of clothing worn; predominate presenting affect; person hygiene; speech volume, rate, and tone; and eye contact. Yet, we believe this information is typically far more subjective than implied by the SOAP term "Objective." In general, the Objective component contained within most SOAP Notes we have read are typically scant of clinically useful or significant information. Thus, the clinical utility of the Objective component for mental health treatment providers is questionable. The third SOAP component is Assessment. Assessment typically includes a corresponding DSM diagnosis, counselor perceptions regarding client intelligence, cognitive functioning, emotional state, and behavioral symptoms, counselor-observed discrepancies between what the client states and does, and the identification of persons reported by the client as significant. Plan is the final SOAP Notes component. Here, counselors indicate future treatment plans and recommendations, as well as client agreed-upon assignments and treatment goals.

DART PROGRESS NOTES   DART Notes and SOAP Notes are similar. Like SOAP Notes, DART Notes use a four-letter mnemonic. Each letter represents a corresponding progress note component. These components include *Data*, *Action*, *Response*, and *Teaching* (Baird, 2008). However, unlike the previously described SOAP components, DART Notes combine both subjective and objective information within a single progress note component. This component, Data, is the first letter of the DART Notes mnemonic. Data contains both the subjective client-reported symptoms and presenting concerns as well as the counselor's direct observations of the client. Action is the second DART component. Action describes the counseling interventions used within the treatment session. Thus, if the counselor used the familiar Solution Focused Miracle Question (Juhnke & Hagedorn, 2006) as the means for identifying client goals, this action is described. Client responses to these described actions are noted in the third DART Notes component, Response. Both favorable and unfavorable client responses to counselor-engendered intervention techniques are recorded. Thus, if the intervention was reported helpful by the client or perceived clinically useful by the counselor, the counselor would document the positive outcome. Teaching is the final DART component. Professional counselors often use psychoeducation and teaching within treatment sessions (Granello & Juhnke, 2009; Juhnke, 2002; Juhnke, Granello, & Granello, 2010; Kelly & Juhnke, 2005). For example, if the counselor provided psychoeducation about the addictive properties of cocaine to a substance-abusing client or taught a client how to identify triggering events that occur prior to arguing with a spouse, these would be documented within the DART Notes Teaching component.

DIAGNOSTIC-BASED PROGRESS NOTES   Over the years, we have found Diagnostic-Based Progress Notes provide the most comprehensive session documentation, greatest client treatment satisfaction, and increased insurance reimbursement probability. In addition, because Diagnostic-Based Progress Notes require each client-identified concern from the clinical intake assessment to be thoroughly assessed and ranked according to client-perceived importance, severity, and frequency, as well as counselor-noted clinical significance, clients and counselors collaborate to create treatment goals and objectives believed most helpful in reducing or eliminating diagnostic-related symptoms. Stated differently, it is impossible for clients to be dissatisfied with treatment, because they identify and rank order their concerns. Clients and counselors then jointly cocreate treatment goals and objectives they believe will best alleviate the diagnoses corresponding to these concerns. These cocreated treatment goals and objectives are the core of Diagnostic-Based Progress Notes.

Diagnostic-Based Notes are far more structured than either SOAP or DART Notes and use both the standardized DSM diagnosis and the first four DSM Axes noted within the clinical assessment intake. Hence, treatment goals and objectives specific to the client's chief presenting complaint (Axis I), personality disorder or mental retardation (Axis II), client's general medical conditions (Axis III), and psychosocial and environmental problems or concerns (Axis IV; American Psychiatric Association, 2000, p. 27) are ranked ordered under the corresponding axis. At the conclusion of each counseling session, each corresponding component's goal is reported as "Addressed," "Partially Addressed," or "Not Addressed" and a description documenting how the goal or objective was addressed is entered.

The best way to demonstrate Diagnostic-Based Progress Notes is via example. Jeff is a 25-year-old depressed male. He presents at your counseling practice requesting treatment. During the clinical assessment intake, you learn Jeff and his wife of 4 years separated. According to Jeff, his wife had an extramarital affair with her work supervisor and moved into her supervisor's apartment 6 months ago. Jeff reports "complete devastation" and "overwhelming depression" ever since. He is unable to sleep or concentrate, and finds no pleasure in his former hobbies of fly fishing and mountain biking. After a thorough clinical assessment intake, you determined the following four axis DSM diagnoses:

Axis I:	296.22	Major Depressive Disorder, Single Episode
	V61.10	Partner Relational Problem
Axis II:	V71.09	No Diagnosis on Axis II
Axis III:	None	
Axis IV:	Separation from wife	

Using this clinical vignette, the counselor would help Jeff identify useful treatment goals and objectives for each Axis where concerns are identified. In Jeff's case, concerns are identified under Axis I (the chief presenting complaint) and Axis IV (psychosocial and environmental problems or concerns). Thus, the counselor might say something like, "Jeff, from the list of all the concerns you want to address in counseling, which one item do you wish to address first?" Jeff might reply, "I really want to get over my depression." Given the enormity of this goal, the counselor will help Jeff identify stepping-stones or objectives that will help him move towards accomplishing this significant goal. Let's read how the counselor will do this and help Jeff create his first Axis-based goal and objectives that will be used in his progress notes.

COUNSELOR: "Getting over your depression is an excellent goal, Jeff. However, it is a big treatment goal. My clients often find it helpful to identify small stepping-stones or objectives that will help them begin moving toward their larger treatment goals. What stepping-stones could you use to start moving you closer to your goal of getting over your depression?"

JEFF: "I don't know."

COUNSELOR: "Well, some of my clients consult with a psychiatrist to determine if antidepressant medications might be helpful. Might this be something you would like to do?"

JEFF: "That makes sense."

COUNSELOR: "So, let's help you identify a psychiatrist and see if antidepressant medi-ations may be helpful."

JEFF: "Okay."

COUNSELOR: "What other baby steps will help you move towards your goal of get-ting over your depression?"

JEFF: "I'm really lonesome. Emily was my life. Once she left, I was all by myself. All I do is work or stay home. When I am at home I can't stop thinking about Emily."

COUNSELOR: "So, am I hearing you saying another way to begin to get over your depression would be to get out, socialize, and make new friends?"

JEFF: "Yes. I'm tired of being lonely and ruminating on Emily's leaving me."

COUNSELOR: "What are some things you could do to get out of the house and start socializing with other people?"

JEFF: "Well, my company has a volleyball league. Some coworkers have been asking me to play."

COUNSELOR: "Would that be of interest to you, Jeff?"

JEFF: "I think it would. I'd like to try."

COUNSELOR: "How about if we use the behaviors you have just identified for our first treatment goal and objectives? Would those work for you?"

JEFF: "Certainly."

COUNSELOR: "May I make one minor suggestion?"

JEFF: "What's that?"

COUNSELOR: "Well, I have learned over the years that it is easier to achieve goals that add behaviors and ways of thinking rather than attempt to eliminate behaviors and thinking. Instead of saying our goal is to 'help Jeff get over his depression,' would you mind if we slightly modify our goal? Maybe we could say Jeff's number one goal is to 'increase the fre-quency of nondepressed times'? In other words, our goal will be to increase times when you are happy."

JEFF: "That will work."

COUNSELOR: "So, our major goal will be to 'increase the frequency of nondepressed times.' Our stepping-stones or objectives that you have identified as potentially helpful in moving you closer to accomplishing that goal are to consult with a psychiatrist to determine if antidepressant medications may be helpful and to identify and engage in social events and inter-personal interactions such as signing up for your company's volleyball team. How does that sound?"

JEFF: "I think those are good places to start."

The Diagnostic-Based Progress Notes use these client-identified goals and objectives. Next to each written goal or objective, the counselor indicates "Addressed," "Partially Addressed," or "Not Addressed." Under each goal and objective is a succinct description of what occurred within the session related to the goal or objective. In this way, the progress notes exactly report what goals and objectives were addressed in session and how the goals and objectives were addressed. Thus, Jeff's Diagnostic-Based Progress Notes are written like this:

Axis I, Goal I: Increase the frequency of nondepressed times. (Addressed.)

During today's session, Jeff identified his first treatment goal. That treatment goal is to increase the frequency of his nondepressed times. According to Jeff, he wishes to "get over" his depression. Jeff identified two stepping-stones or objectives that he reports will help move him towards his first treatment goal. These objectives are indicated below.

Axis I Objective Number I: Consult with a psychiatrist to determine if antidepressant medications may be helpful. (Addressed.)

During today's treatment session, Jeff contacted Blue Cross of Texas to identify a psychiatrist within 5 miles of Jeff's home zip code. Three such providers were identified by Blue Cross. One of the providers, Dr. David Lundberg, was contacted by Jeff and an appointment was scheduled for Tuesday of next week. Jeff signed releases of confidential information, allowing Dr. Juhnke and Dr. Lundberg to discuss, consult, and apprise each other of treatment progress, plans, and any potential relevant treatment issues that might arise. The release of confidential information also allows Dr. Juhnke to provide Dr. Lundberg a copy of Jeff's psychosocial and clinical intake report.

Axis I Objective II: Identify and engage in social events and increased interpersonal interactions. (Addressed.)

During today's treatment session, Jeff reported that after work he usually returned home and ruminated for hours about Emily. Jeff further indicated that he believed it would be helpful to engage in social events that would foster increased interpersonal interactions and get his mind off Emily. One such opportunity revolved around Jeff's company's volleyball league. Jeff reported he was asked by coworkers to join the league. After discussing this opportunity during today's counseling session, Jeff believed it would be in his best interests to join the company volleyball league and engage in social activities with his coworkers. Jeff reported he would enroll in the league tomorrow when he returns to work.

An important Diagnostic-Based Progress Note feature is that client-presenting concerns generate diagnoses and diagnoses encourage relevant and thoughtful treatment. Thus, all Axis I, Axis II, Axis III, and Axis IV diagnoses require corresponding treatment goals and objectives. Therefore, unlike SOAP or DART progress notes where detailed goals and objectives are not required and progress notes may not document what specifically occurred within each treatment session to address client-identified goals or corresponding diagnoses, Diagnostic-Based Progress Notes ensure counselors document how all diagnoses were addressed via corresponding Axis I, II, III, and IV goals and objectives. Such documentation ensures treatment continuity and reduces the probability of overlooking important client-identified concerns. In addition, the documentation of each goal and objective enhances the probability of full insurance reimbursement.

Jeff's diagnoses include two Axis I concerns. Axis I represents the client's reported concerns that are the main counseling foci (Juhnke, 2002). Depression is the most pressing issue reported by Jeff. Therefore, depression is ranked first and placed above Jeff's second greatest concern, the separation from his wife. Jeff's marital separation qualifies for the diagnosis V61.01 Partner Relational Problem. Interestingly, Jeff's second concern is related to Jeff's pertinent psychosocial concerns and environmental concerns. Psychosocial and environmental concerns are typically addressed under Axis IV. However, in this case, because Jeff has identified his separation from his wife as a major concern that he wishes to address within counseling, the concern is listed under Axis I—concerns that are the main counseling foci. When asked about his separation, Jeff and his counselor cocreated the following second Axis I goal and objectives:

Axis I, Goal 2: Jeff will investigate whether or not he wishes to pursue his marriage with Emily or divorce. (Addressed.)

Jeff reported great confusion over whether or not he wished to invest the time and energy to "win Emily back" or "simply file for divorce." He reported mild to moderate marital dissatisfaction during the "last 2 years" of his marriage. In addition, he discussed his "disbelief" that Emily would reject him for her supervisor: "She always told me what a jerk he [the supervisor] was." During today's treatment session, Jeff reported he needed "time to figure out what I want to do [related to his marriage]."

Goal 2, Objective I: Jeff will identify and contact an attorney whose office is within 5 miles of Jeff's home zip code. (Partially Addressed.) Although this objective was established in today's treatment session, Jeff reported he was "far too depressed to look for an attorney today" or schedule a meeting with an attorney.

Goal 2, Objective II: Jeff will read, *A Man's Survival Guide to Divorce*, watch the corresponding prechapter DVDs, and complete the corresponding discussion questions at the ends of each video vignette and book chapter. (Partially addressed.) During today's session, Jeff received the book *A Man's Survival Guide to Divorce* and observed the book's corresponding prechapter DVD for Chapter 1. Following the vignette, Jeff and I discussed the prechapter DVD and the discussion questions. Jeff noted that unlike the prechapter DVD vignette of Angry Allen, Jeff has no intention to harm or harass Emily. Jeff agreed if he experienced feelings or thoughts of harming himself or others that he would contact the Oxford County Crisis Services telephone number at 1-800-555-5555. That number was given to Jeff on a business card and he signed for receipt of same. Jeff reported he would read Chapter 1 of the book in its entirety and be prepared to discuss it during next week's scheduled counseling session.

As you can readily see from this vignette, Diagnostic-Based Progress Notes are highly structured and use client-identified goals and objectives. We have found the Diagnostic-Based Progress Note method superior to others. Once our students and supervisees become familiar with this method, they often prefer it to other progress note methods. When goals or objectives are fulfilled, counselors write "Goal Achieved" next to the goal or "Objective Achieved" next to the objective. Counselors and clients then create a new goal or object to take the place of the achieved one. Thus, once Jeff consults with the psychiatrist, the counselor would write the words "Objective Achieved" after the objective and tell how the objective was achieved. This is demonstrated below.

Goal I, Objective Number I: Consult with a psychiatrist to determine if antidepressant medications may be helpful. (Achieved.)

Jeff consulted with psychiatrist Dr. David Lundberg, 2222 Sontera Place, San Antonio, Texas on July 24, 2011. Dr. Lundberg believed Jeff would respond well to the antidepressant

Prozac, and gave Jeff a prescription for 20 mg of Prozac a day for 30 days. Jeff's follow-up appointment with Dr. Lundberg regarding potential experienced benefits is August 23, 2011, at 2 P.M. Given that this objective has been achieved, Jeff and this counselor have identified a new objective to replace this achieved objective. The new objective is that "Jeff will participate in monthly medical monitoring of Jeff's antidepressants with Dr. David Lundberg."

Jeff's goals and objectives are relatively simple and used for instructional purposes only. In most cases a minimum of three treatment goals with each goal having at least two objectives are used. In addition, all client-identified treatment goals should be noted at the onset of treatment. However, these goals should be ranked ordered by the client and counselor according to the most pressing and clinically significant concerns. Thus, issues specific to self-harm or potential harm to others (e.g., suicidal ideation, suicide intent, domestic violence, homicide intent) or psychotic features are priority concerns and addressed first.

DISCUSSION

Chapter 2 has provided two thorough case studies that will be used throughout the upcoming chapters. Ms. Eva Marie Garza presents with three identifiable Axis I disorders. Generalized anxiety is the most predominant. Thus, generalized anxiety disorder is listed first. Mr. Robert Jones presents with alcohol dependence as his chief presenting Axis I disorder and antisocial personality disorder as his Axis II disorder. These case studies have demonstrated to readers the basic elements contained within typical clinical assessment intake interviews. This chapter has further indicated the general purpose and use of progress notes. Finally, the chapter has provided an overview of three different progress note taking methods and described potential benefits of using Diagnostic-Based Progress Notes.

References

American Psychiatric Association. (2000). *Diagnostic and statistical manual of mental disorders.* (4th ed., text rev.). Washington, DC: Author.

Baird, B. N. (2008). *The internship, practicum, and field placement handbook: A guide for the helping professions* (5th ed.). Upper Saddle River, NJ: Pearson.

Granello, P. F., & Juhnke, G. A. (2009). *Case studies in suicide: Experiences of mental health professionals.* Upper Saddle River, NJ: Merrill-Pearson.

Juhnke, G. A. (2002). *Substance abuse assessment: A handbook for mental health professionals.* New York, NY: Brunner-Routledge.

Juhnke, G. A., Granello, D. H., & Granello, P. F. (2010). *Suicide, self-injury, and violence in the schools: Assessment, prevention, and intervention strategies.* Hoboken, NJ: John Wiley & Sons.

Juhnke, G. A., & Hagedorn, .W. B. (2006). *Counseling addicted families: An integrated assessment and treatment model.* New York, NY: Brunner-Routledge.

Kelly, V., & Juhnke, G. A. (2005). *Critical incidents in addictions counseling.* Alexandria, VA: ACA Press.

Kessler, R. C., Chiu, W. T., Demler, O., & Walters, E. E. (2005). Prevalence, severity, and comorbidity of twelve-month DSM-IV disorders in the National Comorbidity Survey Replication (NCS-R). *Archives of General Psychiatry, 62*(6), 617–627.

Shaw, M. (1997). *Charting made incredibly easy.* Springhouse, PA: Springhouse.

CHAPTER 3

The Fundamentals of Assessment Results

OBJECTIVES

After reading this chapter, you will be able to:

1. Distinguish between norm-referenced tests and criterion-referenced tests.
2. Define the various types of scales of measurement.
3. Understand the basic elements of a frequency distribution.
4. Compute and interpret measures of central tendency and variability.
5. Understand the role of the normal curve and its purpose in norming assessments and interpreting scores.
6. Identify, define, and interpret various types of standard scores.
7. Compute and interpret correlation coefficients.

THE MEANINGS OF TEST SCORES

Scores on assessment results only have meaning based on the context in which the assessment was administered. A score, by itself, is essentially meaningless. However, when the score is placed in proper context, related to the purpose of the assessment, the nature of the administration, the interpretation of the score(s), and the manner in which the results are used, a score can be quite meaningful. For example, a score on an achievement test is meaningful only when compared to an established criterion, past performance, or other individuals who completed the instrument. Each of these scenarios presents a way to understand and use test scores.

Criterion-Referenced Tests

Criterion-referenced tests refer to scores on instruments that are compared to a preestablished standard (Cohen & Swerdlik, 2002). The standard for comparison could be defined in many different ways, such as a knowledge base or cut-score. Most exams given in a classroom are criterion-referenced exams—the teacher is testing a student's knowledge of information. The percent correct or score is an estimate of the amount of knowledge a student answered correctly. The score is a comparison to the total amount of information being evaluated by the exam. Often a *cut-score*, a score indicating a minimum for passing a standard, is used to indicate sufficient mastery of material. For example, an individual taking an exam to obtain a driver's license may be required to pass the exam with 70% correct to be eligible for a license. Cut-scores are not exclusive to criterion-referenced tests, and may be used in norm-referenced tests as well. Criterion-referenced tests may be used to examine mastery of a knowledge base, determine the amount of knowledge understood about a particular phenomenon, or make comparisons of how much knowledge was gained within an individual or group, such as by using a pretest or baseline measure and comparing to a posttest.

Because criterion-referenced tests may be used more informally, such as by classroom teachers to assess gained knowledge of a subject area, test construction may not be adequate. These types of assessments may not be created with regard to current testing standards, so issues compromising fairness and accuracy of the test may be evident. Proper training in devising assessments is essential to ethical practice of assessment.

Norm-Referenced Tests

Norm-referenced instruments use scores that compare an individual or group to a *norm group*—a group representing an estimate of the population of interest for a given phenomenon. Scores on norm-referenced tests are expressed in ways that compare the individual or group to the norm group. For example, percentile scores, such as those expressed on a standardized test, make comparisons based on how an individual's performance compares to others with similar characteristics. A student scoring in the 97th percentile has performed at or above 97% of the norm group. This could be interpreted as the individual scoring in the top 3% of a given phenomenon for individuals with similar characteristics.

Because norm-referenced tests rely on comparisons based on a norm group, also known as a *normative sample*, construction of norm-referenced tests should follow the most current guidelines in the 1999 *Standards for Educational and Psychological Testing* discussed in Chapters 3 and 4. There are many ways to express, understand, and interpret scores and comparisons made to a norm group. The following sections will address the manner in which scores are expressed, known as *scales*, and various methods of understanding and interpreting test scores.

SCALES OF MEASUREMENT

In some cases, phenomena of interest can be directly observed. A counselor can observe a student in class and count the number of disruptive behaviors the student exhibits. A judge can score a gymnastics routine. Scores generated from such events are a result of some objective criteria based on direct observation. However, not all phenomena of interest can be measured through direct observation. *Constructs* are phenomena that exist but cannot be directly observed. Psychosocial variables such as depression may be observed but not objectively scored without the use of an *instrument*, a set of objective criteria designed to measure a construct. Other common constructs that are measured include intelligence, achievement, aptitude, and a wide range of psychological variables (e.g. depression, aggression, stress, wellness). Constructs can also refer to characteristics such as gender identity or multicultural competence. When an instrument is used in a study to measure a construct, the measurement may be a variable in the study. Thus, variables can be based on objective criteria or a measured construct. To understand and communicate assessment results, counselors need to understand the types of scales that may define a variable.

A *nominal* scale refers to a variable that is classified. Examples include sex, ethnicity, religion, and so forth. Each nominal scale includes a set of categories or labels, and no label is quantitatively higher or lower than another label. Comparisons can be based only on the count for each label. For example, the Beck Depression Inventory—II (BDI-II) was normed on 500 outpatients and 120 college students. The label of *outpatients* and *college students* refer to nominal variables—categories that describe the individuals in the sample.

An *ordinal* scale denotes an order or ranking. No comparisons beyond the order or ranking can be made. Such rankings are often used in schools to denote valedictorians and salutatorians. The labels by themselves denote a one–two position in graduation but do not include an amount of the difference between the two categories. Only the rank is considered and not the extent to how each rank was measured. Another example may be in voting, where it may not matter by how much a vote wins but simply which decision was made by the most participants. In assessment, having participants rank preferences in a survey or instrument is an example of ordinal data.

An *interval* scale denotes equality between levels with no true zero. A *true zero* refers to an absence of a particular variable. Celsius temperature would be an example of an interval scale. When measuring temperature, 0°Celsius (C) does not refer to an absence of temperature but merely freezing temperature. One hundred degrees Celsius refers to boiling water. Each degree above, below, or between is based on an equal measure. The distance between 10°Celsius and 32°Celsius is the same as the distance between 20°Celsius and 42°Celsius. Thus, interval data can be subjected to mathematical operations. In counseling research, however, true interval scales are rarely used. Often, researchers assume choices on a scale are of equal distance, when in fact they are not. For example, the directions in the BDI-II instruct the participant to "pick out the one statement in each group that best describes the way you have been feeling. . ." (Beck, Steer, & Brown, 1996, p. 8). Each statement will reference a number that can be added or subtracted to form a total score. However, the degree to which an individual believes a certain statement, such as feeling sad, is true may differ between and among individuals. So, whereas one person believes he or she experiences sadness frequently, another individual may interpret the same degree of sadness as occurring more often. Another example is often seen in Likert and Likert-type scales (pronounced 'lick-urt') in which participants are asked to identify the level of agreement for a particular item similar to the following choices: (1) *strongly disagree*, (2) *disagree*, (3) *neither agree nor disagree*, (4) *agree*, and (5) *strongly agree*. The assumption is that for each data point, the distance is equal. The distance between a 2 and a 4 is the same as the distance between a 3 and a 5. However, the extent that would lead a person to choose, for example, *strongly agree* versus *agree* differs between and among individuals. So, although these items are treated as if they occur on an interval scale and used with mathematical operations, in actuality they do not. When researchers treat such scales as interval data, the scale may be termed as *quasi-interval*.

A *ratio* scale denotes equality between levels with a true zero. In this case, the absence of a measured phenomenon is possible. This could be, for example, the number of items answered correctly on a test, where zero refers to no items answered correctly, amount of income, or age. In counseling research, items related to the number of suicidal ideations a client has experienced in a given week can be a ratio variable. Because mathematical operations can be conducted on interval or ratio variables, they are often termed *continuous variables*, given the wide range of possible answers. When variables have a finite number of categories (i.e., nominal variables), they are often referred to as *discrete variables*.

UNDERSTANDING ASSESSMENT SCORES: FREQUENCY DISTRIBUTIONS AND PERCENTILES

There are many different methods of presenting information garnered from assessments. Frequency distributions provide a variety of important information about the nature of a set of scores. By using frequency distributions, counselors can evaluate how each individual scored and make comparisons to the whole group.

For the purposes of explaining the measurement concepts in this chapter, we will use a data set consisting of 108 at-risk adolescents who were administered the MMPI-A. For this group of adolescents, we will use only one scale of the MMPI-A, Scale 2 (D), which measures depression. Caution, however, should be noted when drawing any conclusions from a single scale, especially on the MMPI-A, as interpretations are based on entire profiles and not just a single scale (Whiston, 2009). From the 108 participants, scores ranged from 36 to 93. We have arranged the scores in descending order in Table 3.1 and have provided the following information:

Frequency refers to the number of adolescents who have the exact same score on the Depression Scale of the MMPI-A.

Percent refers to the percentage of adolescents who have the same score; it is the frequency divided by the total sample (108).

Cumulative frequency refers to the number of adolescents who are at or below the corresponding score. To obtain the cumulative frequency for a corresponding score, simply add each frequency to the cumulative frequency below the corresponding score. The first frequency and first cumulative frequency will be equal. The highest cumulative frequency will equal the total sample.

Cumulative percent refers to the percentage of adolescents who are at or below the corresponding score. To obtain the cumulative percent for a corresponding score, simply add each percent to the cumulative percent below the corresponding score. The first percentage score and first cumulative percent will be equal. The highest cumulative percent will equal 100%.

Frequency distributions can also be demonstrated visually through a histogram. A histogram is a bar graph with the scores on the X-axis and the frequencies on the Y-axis. Histograms also show the shape of a distribution, which you can see in Figure 3.1. Frequency distributions with larger sample sizes often approximate a bell-shaped distribution, which will be discussed later in this chapter.

Frequency distributions may also be displayed through intervals, especially when counselors are more interested in a range of scores. There are numerous ways to create a frequency distribution using intervals. One method (Table 3.2) is demonstrated. Notice the distribution maintains the same shape, regardless of the use of intervals (Figure 3.2).

TABLE 3.1	Frequency Distribution for Scale D on the MMPI-A (n = 108)			
Score	Frequency	Cumulative Frequency	Percent	Cumulative Percent
93	1	108	1.00%	100.00%
92	1	107	1.00%	99.00%
91	4	106	3.50%	98.00%
90	1	102	1.00%	94.50%
89	1	101	1.00%	93.50%
87	1	100	1.00%	92.50%
85	2	99	2.00%	91.50%
83	3	97	2.50%	89.50%
81	3	94	2.50%	87.00%
79	3	91	2.50%	84.50%
77	1	88	1.00%	82.00%
75	3	87	2.50%	81.00%
73	6	84	5.50%	78.50%
71	6	78	5.50%	73.00%
69	2	72	2.00%	67.50%
67	5	70	5.00%	65.50%
65	11	65	10.00%	60.50%
63	3	54	3.00%	50.50%
62	2	51	2.00%	47.50%
61	5	49	5.00%	45.50%
60	2	44	2.00%	40.50%
59	2	42	2.00%	38.50%
58	1	40	1.00%	36.50%
57	3	39	2.50%	35.50%
56	1	36	1.00%	33.00%
55	4	35	3.50%	32.00%
53	3	31	2.50%	28.50%
52	4	28	4.00%	26.00%
51	3	24	2.50%	22.00%
50	7	21	6.00%	19.50%
48	6	14	5.50%	13.50%
46	2	8	2.00%	8.00%
45	2	6	2.00%	6.00%
41	1	4	1.00%	4.00%
40	1	3	1.00%	3.00%
38	1	2	1.00%	2.00%
36	1	1	1.00%	1.00%

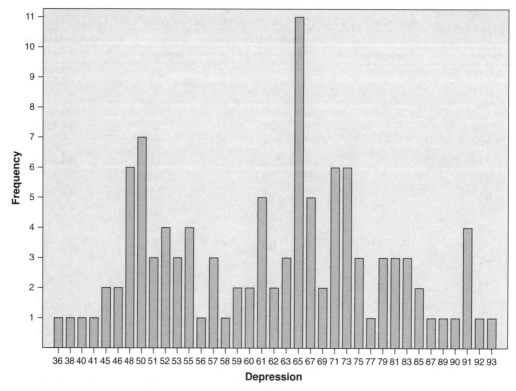

FIGURE 3.1 Histogram of Frequency Distribution for Scale D on the MMPI-A (*n* = 108)

TABLE 3.2	Interval Distribution for Scale D on the MMPI-A (*n* = 108)			
Interval	Frequency	Cumulative Frequency	Percent	Cumulative Percent
91–95	6	108	5.50%	100.00%
86–90	3	102	2.50%	94.50%
81–85	8	99	7.50%	92.00%
76–80	4	91	4.00%	84.50%
71–75	15	87	14.00%	80.50%
66–70	7	72	6.50%	66.50%
61–65	21	65	19.50%	60.00%
56–60	9	44	8.50%	40.50%
51–55	14	35	13.00%	32.00%
46–50	15	21	14.00%	19.00%
41–45	3	6	2.50%	5.00%
36–40	3	3	2.50%	2.50%

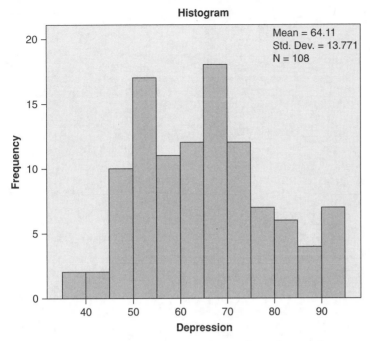

FIGURE 3.2 Histogram of Interval Distribution for Scale D on the MMPI-A (*n* = 108)

Frequency distributions provide a visual organization of the data and a method of making comparisons. An individual who achieves a particular score can easily be compared to the entire group. For example, approximately half of the participants scored 63 or below, as evidenced by the cumulative percentage of 50.5% for participants who scored 63 on Table 3.1. On the MMPI-A, scores are generally considered elevated on a clinical scale above 65. In Table 3.1, about 40% of the adolescents from this particular sample of 108 may be identified as elevated on the depression scale based on the cumulative percentage at 65—60.5% scored at or below 65. By default, the rest of the sample (39.5%) is above this range.

Frequency distributions and histograms also provide a visual representation of data. By examining frequencies, common scores among a group are easily identified, and these commonalities can been seen as spikes. Table 3.1 shows scores of 65 had the highest frequency (*f* = 11) with 10% of the group scoring 65.

This spike in the scores can be seen in Figure 3.1 near the center of the distribution. When counselors are more interested in a range of scores, frequency distributions and histograms that use intervals (Table 3.2 and Figure 3.2) may be more useful.

MEASURES OF CENTRAL TENDENCY

Although frequency distributions may demonstrate how an individual fits into a group of scores, measures of central tendency indicate how a group performs on a given instrument or task. A school counselor may want to know how a group of students score on a particular assessment, such as the ACT. A mental health counselor or director may wish

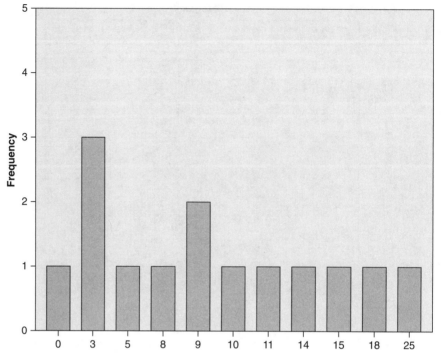

FIGURE 3.3 Histogram of BDI-II Scores (*n* = 14)

to ascertain the degree to which clients treated at a particular setting manifest various levels depression using the BDI-II. To understand a particular set of scores, three types of scores will be explained: (a) the mean, (b) the median, and (c) the mode. Each measure of central tendency is used as indication of how a group scored on a measure. No information related to the distribution of scores is provided with the mean, median, or mode. In other words, when looking at a measure of central tendency, you will not know the extent to which individuals scored above or below the mean. You will only know a general idea of how the group scored and with the raw data you may get an indication of the shape of the distribution as demonstrated in Figures 3.3 and 3.4 (as well as Figures 3.1 and 3.2 for MMPI-A scores). Put more succinctly, measures of central tendency describe a group. To explain each component of central tendency, we will be using a data set of 14 scores, which range from 0 to 25, on the BDI-II (Table 3.3).

The Mean

Stated simply, the *mean* is an average score for a group. The mean is the most common measure of central tendency and is an integral component to research, measurement, and evaluation in the counseling profession. Most studies and statistics rely on this measure.

TABLE 3.3	BDI-II Scores (*n* = 14)												
25	18	15	14	11	10	9	9	8	5	3	3	3	0

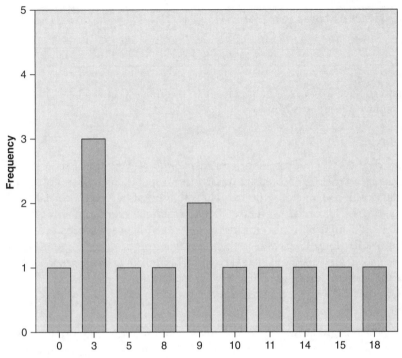

FIGURE 3.4 Histogram of BDI-II Scores Without Outliers (*n* = 14)

COMPUTING THE MEAN   The mean ($\bar{x}$) is the sum (Σ) of all raw scores (*x*) divided by the total number of scores (*n*):

$$\bar{x} = \frac{\Sigma x}{n}$$

Consider the 14 scores on the BDI-II as shown in Table 3.3. The sum of all of the scores is 133. Thus,

$$\bar{x} = \frac{\Sigma x}{n} = \frac{133}{14} = 9.5$$

Now, take a look at the scores again, but this time in a histogram as seen in Figure 3.3. Is the mean an accurate depiction of how the group scored?

Based on the histogram, it is hard to tell. The mean score of 9.5 is not exactly in the center of the distribution, nor does 9.5 reflect the most common score, which is 3. Another confusing facet is that the mean represents only an average of the group. It is not necessarily the reflection of any obtained score. On the BDI-II, it is impossible to score a 9.5. Despite the mean being one of the most useful scores in statistics, when the sample size is small, as is the case here, the mean may not be an accurate reflection of a group. The mean may be highly influenced by extreme scores. Extreme scores are often termed *outliers*, as they represent an individual whose score is not consistent with the rest of the group. Although extreme caution should be used when analyzing data with outliers or removing outliers, notice what happens to the distribution when the score of 25 is

TABLE 3.4	BDI-II Scores ($n = 14$)

25	18	15	14	11	10	9	9	8	5	3	3	3	0
						Middle Scores				Mode			

removed and replaced with 9, a value closer to the mean (Figure 3.4). The mean of 8.36 is more centralized in the distribution!

The Median

The *median* denotes the middle score in a *distribution*—a group of scores. Whereas the mean represents an average score, the median represents which score occupies the center or middle position. Therefore, the median is that point in which one half of the scores are below and one-half of the score are above. When an even number of scores exist in a distribution, the median is the midpoint between the two scores. To calculate the median, the distribution of scores is placed in ascending or descending order. The score in the middle position represents the median. From Table 3.3 and Table 3.4, there are 14 scores but each of the middle scores is 9. Therefore, the median is 9.

The Mode

The mode represents the score that occurs most often in a distribution. It is also possible for more than one mode to exist. Among the 14 scores in Table 3.3 and Table 3.4, a score of "3" was obtained by three participants. Therefore, the mode is 3.

What Is the Best Measure of Central Tendency?

The measure of central tendency that would be the most accurate for a distribution depends on many factors: (a) the number of scores in the distribution, known as *sample size*, (b) the presence of outliers, and (c) the shape of the distribution. As shown in Figure 3.5, when

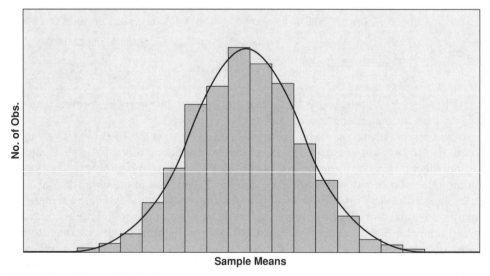

FIGURE 3.5 Normal Distribution

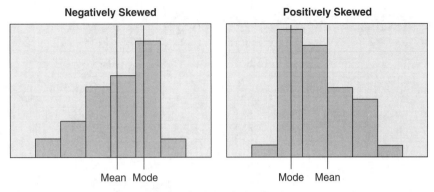

FIGURE 3.6   Negatively and Positively Skewed Distributions

the mean, median, and mode are equal, the distribution of scores is said to be normal and the distribution will resemble a bell-shaped curve.

Notice the distribution in Figure 3.2. The large number of scores minimizes the influence of outliers. The mean, median, and mode are relatively equivalent at 64.11, 64, and 65, respectively. The shape of the distribution is similar to the bell-shaped curve. These qualities are not shared by the scores in Figure 3.3, in which the distribution is small and more easily influenced by outliers, and the mean and median of 9.5 and 9, respectively, are quite different from the mode of 3. In addition, the shape of the distribution is not normal. Rather, the distribution in Figure 3.3 is *positively skewed*, in which the mode is less than the mean. In a *negatively skewed distribution*, the mode would be greater than the mean. Figure 3.6 presents a side-by-side comparison of skewed distributions. So, when a distribution is normal, the mean, median, and mode are all accurate estimates, with the mean being the more preferable term because of its usefulness in statistics. However, when distributions are small, often the median or the mode represent the better measure of a distribution. In summary, the mean is an indicator of the average score; the median is the position of the center score; the mode is the most common score.

MEASURES OF VARIABILITY

As mentioned earlier, measures of central tendency allow counselors to evaluate the performance of an individual when compared to a group. Throughout this text, we will use the case studies in Chapter 2 to discuss the application of various assessments. For example, using the case study of Eva Marie (Chapter 2) and reviewing her score on the Kaufman Brief Intelligence Test-2 (KBIT-2) in Chapter 9, Eva Marie obtained an IQ Composite score of 119, which classifies her in the above average range of intellectual functioning and ranks her at the 90th percentile when compared with others in the same age group. Thus, we can compare Eva Marie's score of 119 to the mean or average intelligence score of 100 and identify Eva Marie with above average intellectual functioning. Measures of central tendency can also be used to represent the performance of a group. For example, Figure 3.2 shows the interval distribution for 108 adolescents admitted in to an inpatient psychiatric hospital on the Depression Scale for the MMPI-A. This group has a mean of 64.11. On the MMPI-A, a score of 50 is considered average. Therefore, this group of adolescents

TABLE 3.5	BDI-II Scores ($n = 14$)	
x	$(x - \bar{x})$	$(x - \bar{x})^2$
25	15.5	240.25
18	8.5	72.25
15	5.5	30.25
14	4.5	20.25
11	1.5	2.25
10	0.5	0.25
9	−0.5	0.25
9	−0.5	0.25
8	−1.5	2.25
5	−4.5	20.25
3	−6.5	42.25
3	−6.5	42.25
3	−6.5	42.25
0	−9.5	90.25
$\bar{x} = 9.5$	$\Sigma(x - \bar{x}) = 0$	$\Sigma(x - \bar{x})^2 = 605.5$

appears to have a higher level of depression from what we would expect of the general adolescent population. However, when a single score is used to represent the performance of a group or population, more information is needed. An understanding of whether or not the mean is a good indicator of the group performance is necessary.

Referring back to Table 3.1, notice that 108 individuals scored between 36 and 93 on Scale D of the MMPI-A. Does the mean score of 64.11 truly represent the level of depression among the group? The answer of course is both yes and no. Although the mean of 64.11 indicates an average score and the distribution appears to resemble the bell-shaped curve (Figure 3.1), when looking at the distribution of scores (Table 3.1), no one scored a 64. As a matter of fact, individuals scoring between 63 and 65 represent only 13% ($n = 14$) of the distribution. Also notice the BDI-II data in Table 3.5. The mean ($\bar{x} = 9.5$) and median ($Md = 9$) are close, but neither score represents the most common score of the distribution—the mode ($Mo = 3$). So, when means are used to signify the performance of a group, additional information is needed to identify if the mean is truly representative of group performance. This is the rationale for measures of variability—to provide information on how much error is included in the mean or the degree of consistency (i.e. how closely participants scored to the mean) for the group. Three measures of variability are described to address amount of error in a distribution when using the mean to describe the performance of a group.

The Range

The range is simply a value indicating the span of score and may be expressed as the highest value minus the lowest value plus one:

$$(\text{highest value} - \text{lowest value}) + 1$$

In Table 3.3 of the BDI-II scores, the highest value is 25 and the lowest value is 0, so the range is as follows:

$$(25 - 0) + 1 = 26$$

The purpose of the range is to provide an indication the span of values. The reason for adding 1 to the formula is make sure we are inclusive of the most extreme values in the distribution. However, the range does not offer any indication of the relationship of scores to the mean.

The Standard Deviation and Variance

The *standard deviation* is one of the more useful terms in statistics. Although the mean indicates the average score for a distribution, the standard deviation indicates *the average distance from the mean*. As discussed earlier, whenever a single score is used to represent an entire group, error will be present, because not everyone scores at the mean. Just how close the scores are to the mean is indicated by the standard deviation.

The *variance* is also a measure of dispersion and is directly related to the standard deviation. The variance is the *squared average distance from the mean*. The variance has many important properties relevant to counseling research, and in order to compute the standard deviation, the variance is computed first. Computation of the variance and standard deviation will be discussed following a discussion of population versus sample statistics.

ESTIMATING THE POPULATION   At times, a measure of a population is easy to determine. College entrance exams, such as the SAT and ACT, serve as an example of estimating the population. Most universities require the SAT or ACT be taken before entering college. As a result, ETS, the company that created the SAT, and ACT, Inc., collect scores for every person who takes these tests. Thus, they have a population. Each individual who takes the SAT or ACT has the scores documented by the respective company. So, it is easy for ETS or ACT to make estimates on the population. We might even say that they can make an unbiased estimation, as each individual score from the respective test can be accounted for with minimal error. This of course does not include error that could occur from non-uniform testing conditions and other extraneous factors.

More often, however, counselors attempt to make generalizations about a population based upon a sample. So, how do researchers make sure that the results garnered from a sample can be generalized to a population? Researchers demonstrate generalizability in two ways: (a) by describing the sample with respect to characteristics (e.g. age, ethnicity, sex) so that evidence to the appropriate population can be demonstrated and (b) by using mathematical procedures that take into account the size of the sample in order to generalize to a population. However, if mathematical adjustments are being made, how do we know that they are accurate? To discuss the nature of the mathematical formulae and proofs is beyond the scope of this book (thank goodness); we can just be glad that statisticians such as Pearson, Gosset, and Fisher created such formulae and provided the evidence so that we can apply this knowledge to the field! We will now present the formulae for computing the variance and standard deviation for both a population and a sample.

THE FORMULA FOR THE VARIANCE   Recall that the variance, the squared average distance from the mean, has many important properties relevant to counseling research, and to compute the standard deviation, the variance is computed first. The formula for the variance is represented as the sum of the squared deviation scores divided by the sample size. Let's break down this formula.

The *sum* will be represented by Σ, and therefore refers to the process of adding a set of values.

A *deviation score* is a raw score minus the mean. We will represent the deviation score as $(x - \bar{x})$, where x is a raw score such as the scores you see in Table 3.3 and $\bar{x}$ is the mean, 9.5.

Sample size will vary, based on whether we are using the formula for a population or a sample. For a population, the sample size will be noted as n and be the total number of participants, 14. Therefore, we say $n = 14$. For a sample, the sample size will be noted as $n - 1$ and be the total number of participants minus 1, 13. Therefore, we say $n - 1 = 13$.

Using statistical notation for the above information, the formula for the variance when using a population is as follows:

$$s^2 = \frac{\Sigma(x - \bar{x})^2}{n}$$

and for a sample is as follows:

$$s^2 = \frac{\Sigma(x - \bar{x})^2}{n - 1}$$

COMPUTING THE VARIANCE   Using the data from Table 3.3, we will compute the variance using the population formula and the sample formula. Regardless of whether computing for a population or a sample, the numerator, $\Sigma(x - \bar{x})^2$, is computed in the same way. First, compute a deviation from each raw score by subtracting the mean from each raw score as shown in the second column of Table 3.5.

Notice that the deviation score can be positive or negative. Also notice that when we sum the deviation scores, we always end up with 0. This is an important point. If our eventual goal is to compute the standard deviation, the average distance from the mean, an average cannot be computed when 0 is divided by any value. So, to eventually compute the standard deviation, we need to get rid of the 0 by eliminating the negative numbers. We can do this by squaring each deviation score as shown in the third column of Table 3.5. By squaring each deviation score and summing the scores, we obtain the *sum of the squared deviations* (605.5). The next step is to compute the variance of a population and sample and obtain an average of sorts using the sum of the squared deviations. To compute the variance, simply divide by the number of cases (n) for a population or the sample size minus 1 ($n - 1$) for a sample.

Population

$$s^2 = \frac{\Sigma(x - \bar{x})^2}{n} = \frac{605.5}{14} = 43.25$$

Sample

$$s^2 = \frac{\Sigma(x - \bar{x})^2}{n - 1} = \frac{605.5}{14 - 1} = 46.58$$

COMPUTING THE STANDARD DEVIATION   Keep in mind an average is simply a sum of scores divided by the number of scores. In the case of the variance, the deviation scores are squared, which is why the variance is the squared average of distance from the mean. To find the standard deviation—the average distance from the mean—simply take the square root of the variance.

Population

$$s = \sqrt{\frac{\Sigma(x - \bar{x})^2}{n}} = \sqrt{\frac{605.5}{14}} = \sqrt{43.25} = 6.58$$

Sample

$$s = \sqrt{\frac{\Sigma(x - \bar{x})^2}{n - 1}} = \sqrt{\frac{605.5}{14 - 1}} = \sqrt{46.58} = 6.82$$

So, for the sample of 14 participants who completed the BDI-II, the average score was 9.5, but the average amount of variation from the mean was 6.82. With a range of 26, a standard deviation of 6.82 may seem like a large amount of variation from the mean. One reason this occurs is the small sample size. If the mean is an indication of how a group scored, the standard deviation expresses the degree to which that mean is representative of the group. In other words, are the scores in the group consistent with the mean? With an average difference of 6.82 from the mean, the mean may not be that consistent. Now, look at the data from Table 3.1 using the D Scale of the MMPI-A. Notice that we have a range of 58, yet the mean is 64.11 and the standard deviation is 13.77. When attempting to get an idea of the consistency of a group, consider the mean, standard deviation, and the range of scores. We will now discuss how the standard deviation may affect the interpretation of a group.

THE NORMAL CURVE

The normal curve is a theoretical concept for understanding the nature of scores based upon probability theory. Best and Kahn (2003) indicated that the normal curve does not actually exist, but measures of populations tend to demonstrate this distribution. The normal curve (Figure 3.7) is symmetrical with 50% of the scores above and below the

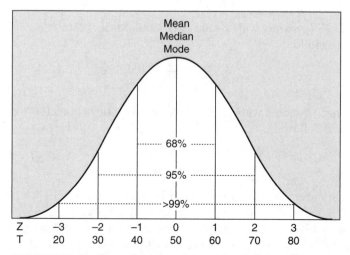

FIGURE 3.7   The Normal Curve and Corresponding Area Estimates

mean. The mean, median, and mode all have the same value, and the scores cluster around the center.

Although data are not usually perfectly described by the normal distribution, an independent measure taken repeatedly will eventually resemble a normal distribution. Figure 3.1 appears to demonstrate this concept, as enough data ($n = 108$) were collected to demonstrate a more normalized distribution. On the other hand, Figure 3.3, with a small sample size of 14, is less like a normal distribution. Why? The sample size is insufficient to be an accurate estimate of the population.

Confidence Intervals

One characteristic of the normal curve is that counselors can look at assessment scores and determine where an individual falls with respect to a normally distributed population. In a normally distributed population, as illustrated in Figure 3.7, 50% of the distribution lies before and after the mean. Between -1 and $+1$ standard deviation units is 68% of the distribution. Between -2 and $+2$ standard deviation units is 95% of the distribution. Between -3 and $+3$ standard deviation units is 99% of the distribution. This is known as the *68-95-99 rule*. For the MMPI-A, the scales are standardized to have a mean of 50 and a standard deviation of 10. So, 68% of the distribution would fall between -1 and $+1$ standard deviation units—between 40 and 60; 95% of the distribution would fall between -2 and $+2$ standard deviation units—between 30 and 70; 99% of the distribution would fall between -3 and $+3$ standard deviation units—between 20 and 80.

We can establish *confidence intervals*, estimates of where we expect scores to fall based on the mean and standard deviation. A confidence interval (CI) expresses the range of scores that is likely to be obtained using the following formula:

$$CI = M \pm SD$$

To express a range of scores with within one standard deviation (68% confidence), we would compute as follows:

$$CI = 50 \pm 1(10)$$
$$[40, 60] = 50 \pm 10$$

To express a range of scores with within two standard deviations (95% confidence), we would compute as follows:

$$CI = 50 \pm 2(10)$$
$$[30, 70] = 50 \pm 20$$

To express a range of scores with within three standard deviations (99% confidence), we would compute as follows:

$$CI = 50 \pm 3(10)$$
$$[20, 80] = 50 \pm 30$$

The normal curve provides information in interpreting scores for an individual or group. To do this, we will use the z table in Appendix A and the 68-95-99 rule.

Assume we wish to compare the group mean of the 108 adolescents on the D Scale of the MMPI-A to the normed population. Recall that the sample had a group mean of 64.11. This score would be 1.4 standard deviations above the mean. We can use a z table in Appendix A to estimate the percentile of the group. The z table provides the amount of area (or the percentage of the distribution) that lies to the left of a score expressed in standard deviation units, known as a z score. In other words, the z table provides the corresponding percentile (the percentage of participants who scored at or below a given score) for a given z score. Using the above example, with a mean of 50 and a standard deviation of 10, the group mean of the sample of adolescents ($M = 64.11$) is approximately 1.4 standard deviation units above the mean or a z score of 1.4 (we will discuss how a z score is computed later in the chapter, but for right now we will only focus on understanding Appendix A).

1. Using Appendix A, follow the left column down until you see 1.4. The row on top expresses the z score to the nearest hundredth. So, you will actually use 1.4 on the left column and .00 on the top row to find the corresponding percentile for 1.40.
2. The corresponding value under 1.40 is .9192, which can be converted to a percentile, 91.92% or about the 92nd percentile.
3. In this case, a sample mean of 64.11 is approximately in the 92nd percentile (.9192) of a normed population.

Another way to estimate is to use the 68-95-99 rule (see Figure 3.8).

We know that 50% of the distribution is before or after the mean and that 68% of the distribution is between -1 and $+1$ standard deviation units. Therefore, the distance between the mean and $+1$ standard deviation units is 34% (one-half of 68%) plus 50% (the other half of the distribution). Therefore, the score of 64.11 must be above the 84th percentile. Between -2 and $+2$ standard deviation units is 47.5% of the distribution before and after the mean. We can add 47.5% to 50% and find that a score of 64.11 must be below the 98th percentile. Thus the value is about halfway between the 84th and the 98th percentile (1.4 standard deviation units—around the 92nd percentile).

In summary, the normal curve can be used to determine where scores fall with respect to probability and percentiles by examining (a) the percentage of total space included between the mean and a given standard deviation, (b) the percentage of cases or n values that fall between a given mean and standard deviation, (c) the probability that an event will occur between the mean and a given standard deviation, (d) the percentile rank of scores in a normal distribution, and (e) the extent to which a distribution of scores is normalized. "The normal curve has a smooth, altogether handsome countenance—a thing of beauty" (Glass & Hopkins, 1996, p. 83).

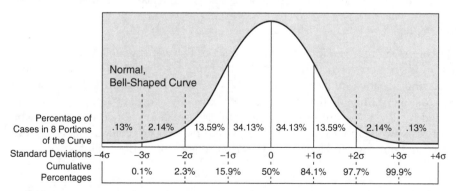

FIGURE 3.8 Estimates of Area Underneath the Normal Curve

STANDARD SCORES

Expressing scores in standard deviation units, as opposed to raw scores, is quite useful. When scores are expressed in standard deviation units, we refer to them as _standard scores_. With such information, we can compare scores across different instruments that measure the same construct and provide an interpretation of raw scores. For example, an individual who scores a 21 on the ACT is approximately in the 50th percentile. Because the SAT also measures aptitude, a comparable score would be about 1550, also in the 50th percentile. Knowing the mean and standard deviation of each exam allows us to make comparisons when the same construct is measured. Similarly, we can take a single score and make a comparison to the normed distribution.

z Scores

Given that raw scores may not have much meaning, z scores can be used to make comparisons of an individual or group score to a distribution by simply converting the raw score to a score expressed in standard deviation units. A basic formula is used to convert a raw score to a z score:

$$z = \frac{x - \bar{x}}{\sigma},$$

where x is raw score;

$\bar{x}$ is the mean;

σ is the standard deviation.

From the data presented in Table 3.3, an individual college student scored a 25 on the BDI-II. For the college population, the BDI-II has a mean of 12.56 and a standard deviation of 9.93 (Beck et al., 1996). We can convert the individual score of 25 to a standard score in order to determine the percentile of the individual compared to the normative sample of college students. _using a z score table_

$$z = \frac{x - \bar{x}}{\sigma} = \frac{25 - 12.56}{9.93} = 1.25$$

Thus, an individual scoring a 25 on the BDI-II is about 1.25 standard deviations above the mean—the 89th percentile (by using Appendix A)! We could determine that this individual is in the top 11% when compared to other college students with respect to depression.

T Scores

The T score is another version of a standard score that is (a) widely used for interpreting scores on instruments, (b) converted directly from z scores, and (c) avoids the use of decimals and negative numbers. T scores have a mean of 50 and a standard deviation of 10. So, for every unit of increase or decrease in a z score, a T score is increased or decreased by 10. A T score of 60 is one standard deviation above the mean, while a T score of 30 is two standard deviations below the mean. The relationship of z scores and T scores can be shown in Figure 3.7. The T score is computed as follows:

$$T = 50 + 10Z$$

and rounded to the nearest whole number.

Using the example above, the college student who scored 25 on the BDI-II and obtained a z score of 1.25 could be converted to a T score:

$$T = 50 + 10z$$
$$T = 50 + 10(1.25) = 62.5$$

We would round this to a T score of 63, knowing that 60 is one standard deviation above the mean and 70 is two standard deviations above the mean. A T score of 63 is close to the z score of 1.25.

Other Types of Standard Scores

Although T scores and z scores tend to be commonly used, many instrument developers use their own methods of standard scores, such as the SAT, which uses a mean of 500 and a standard deviation of 100, or intelligence tests with a mean of 100 and a standard deviation of 15 (e.g., KBIT-2). For example, in the case study of Chapter 2 and information in Chapter 9, Eva Marie has an IQ Composite score of 119 on the KBIT-2. A z score can easily be computed from the standard score of the KBIT-2:

$$z = \frac{x - \bar{x}}{\sigma} = \frac{119 - 100}{15} = 1.27$$

Both the IQ Composite score of 119 and the z score of 1.27 indicate that Eva Marie is above the mean with respect to intelligence—the 90th percentile (the top 10%) using Appendix A.

We could do the same with a score on the SAT. A student who scores 420 on the verbal section of the SAT is below the mean of 500, and therefore would have a z score in the negative range:

$$z = \frac{x - \bar{x}}{\sigma} = \frac{420 - 500}{100} = -.80$$

Using Appendix A, such a score would place the student in the 21st percentile $(.50 - .2881 = .2119)$.

UNDERSTANDING CORRELATION COEFFICIENTS

One of the more useful statistics in social science research is the correlation coefficient. In counseling research, it is helpful to know the relationship between variables, such as the relationship between aptitude and achievement, self-esteem and behavioral disruptions, and so forth. Correlations are also used to compare scores on instruments. For example, a strong relationship would be expected between SAT and ACT, because both measure aptitude. A correlation coefficient is the expression of a linear relationship between two (and only two) paired variables or data sets (Cohen & Swerdlik, 2002). A correlation coefficient is most commonly expressed as r and may range from -1.00 to $+1.00$. Correlation coefficients are interpreted by examining two facets: (a) direction and (b) magnitude. Direction refers to the sign of the correlation, either positive $(+)$ or negative $(-)$. In a positive correlation, as the values in one variable increases, so do the variables in the other variable. For example, there is a positive correlation between the number of years using drugs and the severity of drug abuse. In other words, the longer someone has used

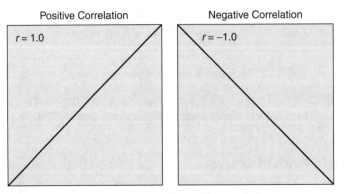

FIGURE 3.9 Perfect Positive and Negative Correlations

drugs, the more severe the addiction is likely to be. In a negative correlation, as the values in one variable increases, the values in the other variable decreases. Such an example may be evident with exercise and depression. The more one engages in physical exercise, the fewer depressive symptoms may be evident. An illustration of positive and negative correlations is in Figure 3.9.

So, while the sign of the correlation reflects direction, the number reflects magnitude. In Figure 3.9, both correlations are *perfect correlations*. A perfect correlation has a value of +1.00 or −1.00. The magnitudes are the same. In a perfect positive correlation, for every unit of *increase* in one variable, there is an equal unit of *increase* in the other variable. In a perfect negative correlation, for every unit of *increase* in one variable, there is an equal unit of *decrease* in the other variable. In counseling research, you will not find a perfect correlation. More likely, you will see correlations that reflect various relationships. Best and Kahn (2006) recommended the following guidelines in interpreting correlation coefficients (see Table 3.6):

Note that the categories in Table 3.6 are regardless of direction, as there is no difference between a −.30 and a positive .30 in terms of magnitude. Both signify relationships as *low*.

There are two common types of correlation coefficients, although others exist as well. The most common type is the *Pearson product moment correlation coefficient*, often referred to as a *Pearson r* or just *r*, which indicates the relationship between two variables or data sets that contain scores at the interval or ratio level of measurement. A second common type of correlation coefficient is an adaptation of the Pearson *r*, known as the *Spearman rho correlation coefficient*, which computes a correlation coefficient from ordinal data.

TABLE 3.6	Interpretation of Correlation Coefficients
.00 to .20	Negligible
.20 to .40	Low
.40 to .60	Moderate
.60 to .80	Substantial
.80 to 1.00	High to very high

Calculating a Pearson r

The most common formula for computing the Pearson r relies on concepts already learned for computing the variance and standard deviation.

$$r = \frac{\Sigma xy}{\sqrt{(\Sigma x^2)(\Sigma y^2)}}$$

where

$\Sigma x^2 = \Sigma(X - \bar{X})^2$, the squared sum of the deviation scores for variable x

$\Sigma y^2 = \Sigma(Y - \bar{Y})^2$, the squared sum of the deviation scores for variable y

$\Sigma xy = \Sigma(X - \bar{X})(Y - \bar{Y})$, the sum of the *covariance* scores—each deviation score for x is multiplied by the corresponding deviation score for y and then summed.

Table 3.7 is a heuristic example of data for x and y in which the computation of a Pearson r will be illustrated. Keep in mind that variables x and y could stand for any pair of variables

TABLE 3.7	Computation of a Pearson r					
Pretest (x)	Posttest (y)	x	y	x^2	y^2	Xy
15	1	5.50	$\overline{6.57}$	30.25	43.16	−36.14
10	6	0.50	1.57	0.25	2.46	−0.79
11	12	1.50	4.43	2.25	19.62	6.65
9	11	$\overline{0.50}$	3.43	0.25	11.76	−1.72
3	2	$\overline{6.50}$	$\overline{5.57}$	42.25	31.02	36.21
0	0	$\overline{9.50}$	$\overline{7.57}$	90.25	57.30	71.92
3	4	$\overline{6.50}$	$\overline{3.57}$	42.25	12.74	23.21
14	12	4.50	4.43	20.25	19.62	19.94
18	15	8.50	7.43	72.25	55.20	63.16
5	5	$\overline{4.50}$	$\overline{2.57}$	20.25	6.60	11.57
25	21	15.50	13.43	240.25	180.36	208.17
8	9	$\overline{1.50}$	1.43	2.25	2.04	−2.15
9	2	$\overline{0.50}$	$\overline{5.57}$	0.25	31.02	2.79
3	6	$\overline{6.50}$	$\overline{1.57}$	42.25	2.46	10.21
Mean 9.50	7.57					
Sum				605.50	475.43	413.00

being measured. In this case, we will use data collected on a study for exercise and depression by Balkin, Tietjen-Smith, Shen, and Caldwell (2007). Fourteen college females participated in a control group. The participants were administered the BDI-II on two occasions at 6 weeks apart. Because this group did not have any intervention, the expectation would be that there would be minimal change in the scores from one administration to the next. Thus, a high correlation between the two administrations was anticipated.

$$r = \frac{\Sigma xy}{\sqrt{(\Sigma x^2)(\Sigma y^2)}}$$

$$r = \frac{413}{\sqrt{(605.50)(475.43)}} = .77$$

Using Table 3.6, a correlation coefficient of .77 is indeed substantial because of the similarities in the scoring patterns.

WHAT TYPES OF SCORES ARE REPORTED?

Throughout the various chapters in this text, you will see assessment results reported, often using standard scores. For example, in Chapter 11 scores on the MMPI-2 are reported for the case studies addressed in Chapter 2. The MMPI-2 uses T scores and the trained counselor can easily determine where clinically significant aspects of personality are evident. For example, Robert will show elevations in PD (psychopathic deviate), contributing to the antisocial personality that was evident in his case study. In Chapter 9, standard scores are used to represent intelligence test scores. These scores are essential in drawing comparisons to the general population.

Not all tests use standard scores; although as shown in this chapter, a standard score may be obtained if the mean and standard deviation of the norm group is used. Such information is consistently reported in test manuals for this reason. An example that we addressed earlier is the BDI-II, which simply uses a raw score to identify whether a client is mild, moderate, or severe in depressive symptoms. Moreover, by using the manual for the BDI-II, counselors can draw comparisons to clinical and nonclinical subgroups. In other words, when the counselor administers the BDI-II, standard scores may be derived by comparing the client to a clinical population, such as other clients seeking outpatient counseling, or a nonclinical population, such as undergraduate college students. A client with moderate depression, for example, may be slightly higher than the mean for the clinical population, over 1 standard deviation above the mean when compared to the nonclinical norm group. Overall, having knowledge of standard scores and their relationship to percentiles is important to identifying the degree to which a person may be viewed with issues or concerns pertinent to counseling.

References

American Educational Research Association, American Psychological Association, & National Council of Measurement in Education. (1999). *Standards for educational and psychological testing*. Washington, DC: American Educational Research Association.

Balkin, R. S., Tietjen-Smith, T., Caldwell, C., & Shen, Y. (2007). The relationship of exercise and depression among young adult women. *Adultspan Journal*, 30–35.

Beck, A. T., Steer, R. A., & Brown, G. K. (1996). *BDI-II manual*. San Antonio, TX: The Psychological Corporation.

Best, J. W., & Kahn, J. V. (2006). *Research in education* (10th ed.). Boston: Allyn & Bacon.

Cohen, R. J., & Swerdlik, M. E. (2002). *Psychological testing and assessment* (5th ed.). Boston: McGraw-Hill.

Glass, G. V., & Hopkins, K. D. (1996). *Statistical methods in education and psychology* (3rd ed.). Boston: Allyn & Bacon.

Whiston, S. C. (2009). *Principles and applications of assessment in counseling* (3rd ed.). Belmont, CA: Brooks/Cole.

CHAPTER 4

Current Standards of Reliability

OBJECTIVES

1. Identify different types of reliability.
2. Define key terms related to reliability.
3. Understand the role of reliability in determining the usefulness of assessment results.
4. Interpret reliability estimates and apply them to case conceptualization.

DEFINING RELIABILITY

Inherent in the practice of assessment is the repeated administration of an instrument, either to a single individual across time or across multiple individuals. An example of the former is a counselor who may wish to use the Beck Depression Inventory (BDI-II) to evaluate whether clients have experienced a reduction in depressive symptoms after a time. As an example of assessing multiple individuals, the expectation is that individuals with similar characteristics, such as adults diagnosed with depression and participating in group counseling, will demonstrate similar scoring patterns. Thus, *reliability* is the consistency of a measure (American Educational Research Association, American Psychological Association, & National Council of Measurement in Education [AERA, APA, & NCME], 1999; Cohen & Swerdlik, 2002). In these examples, *consistency* refers to stability over time and across populations.

When dealing with objective measures, such as an individual's weight, an individual can step on a scale, read the weight, step back on, and more than likely read the same weight. There is very little variance on the weight. Individuals of similar build will likely have similar weights, so the scale is a reliable measure of weight. However, the same cannot be said for measuring *constructs*. Not every phenomenon of interest can be directly observed. *Constructs* are theoretically guided phenomena that cannot be directly observed or measured. Intelligence, various mood states (e.g., depression, happiness, stress, antisocial personality) all serve as constructs in the counseling profession. For example, an athlete may be labeled as brilliant for an ability to think quickly and react in creative ways, but such behavior may not translate into high scores on an intelligence test. Yet, such behavior is an act of creativity that could be recognized as a measure of intelligence. Therefore, constructs are limited by an *operational definition*, a method of explaining and limiting how a construct will be measured. Referring to the previous example of using the BDI-II, clients completing the instruments are evaluated for depression partially based on how each symptom is defined on the BDI-II. Other instruments, such as the Minnesota Multiphasic Personality Inventory—II (MMPI-II) or the Suicide Probability Scale, also evaluate depression, but they do so differently. Although correlations may exist between or among the instruments, each instrument employs a separate operational definition based on having different items evaluating depression.

Reliability is a term extended from classical test theory (CTT), derived from Spearman (1904), as well as other more contemporary contributors (e.g., Guttman, Likert, Lord, Thurstone). The premise of CTT was based on two postulates: (a) the measurement of attributes of an individual that contribute to a consistent response set and (b) the measurement of attributes unrelated to the construct being measured but affect the test scores (Gregory, 2007). So, although the first postulate relates to attributes of the construct, the second postulate is a reflection of extraneous factors that contribute to measurement error (see Postulates of Classical Test Theory table).

Postulates of Classical Test Theory

1. The measurement of attributes of an individual contributes to a consistent response set.
2. The measurement of attributes consists of unrelated elements to the construct being measured and affects the test scores.

Although CTT is the more popular theory related to assessment and measurement, other theories are present, particularly *item response theory* (IRT), also known as latent-trait theory. IRT addresses the extent to which an item measures a particular trait (Cohen & Swerdlik, 2002). The rest of this chapter will address aspects of reliability with respect to CTT.

True Score

Note that the postulates of CTT indicate that an individual's responses are measures of an attribute but that unanticipated events or factors also contribute to the measurement. Therefore, measurement is fraught with error. Any score obtained from the measurement of a construct includes three elements: (a) the observed score, (b) the true score, and (c) error. If O represents and observed score, T represents a true score, and E represents error, then the following equation expresses the relationship of the observed score to the true score and error:

$$O = T + E$$

The equation is theoretical in nature. The true score is never actually known (Gregory, 2007). For example, an aspiring college student takes the SAT and scores 510 on the quantitative section. The student decides to retake the SAT in an effort to get a higher score and obtains a 530. Which score is the true measure of the aspiring student's aptitude? According to CTT, the true score is within a range of scores in which 510 and 530 are included.

With respect to the above equation, error can be positive or negative. Assume that the true score in the aforementioned example is 520 (again, we will never know the true score in actuality). In one administration, the error term is positive, denoting the aspiring student's aptitude to be higher than what was initially measured; whereas the error term is negative in the second administration, indicating an overestimation of aptitude.

Error

To understand the relationship of an observed score to a true score, it may be helpful to rearrange the equation:

$$T = O - E$$

Notice that in this equation the smaller the error term, the more accurate the observed score is to the true score. If it were possible for no error to be present in a measure (i.e., $E = \emptyset$), then the true score and the observed score would be equal. *Measurement error* is the difference between the observed score and the true score (AERA et al., 1999).

$$E = O - T$$

Measurement error occurs because of *random error*, chance, unplanned phenomena, or events that affect the measure of a construct. Stanley (1971) provided a comprehensive overview of measurement error, but the following issues were regarded as the most pertinent and likely in assessment: (a) construction of the instrument, (b) administration of the instrument, (c) scoring of the instrument, and (d) interpretation of the instrument (Cohen & Swedlik, 2002; Gregory, 2007).

CONSTRUCTION OF THE INSTRUMENT   The construct being measured by the instrument is based on a finite number of items consistent with the operational definition of the construct. With any construct of interest, there are an infinite number of possibilities for items, and the construct will ultimately be defined by a finite number of items chosen by the author(s) of the instrument. For example, the BDI-II uses items that reflect one of two aspects of depression: affect and somatic. Eight items were chosen to reflect the affect (or mood) of the client and 13 items were selected to reflect somatic issues (or physical complaints). Could more of these items have been created? Naturally, there are certainly many possibilities in adding to or revising the questions asked. Generally, authors of instruments seek to identify items that will provide information to measuring the construct based on the operational definition. Items that tend to elicit the same information as another item or fail to provide new information about the construct may be eliminated. Certainly, the failure to eliminate such items using statistical procedures and expert review will lead to measurement error.

Because the operational definition of a construct may lend subjectivity to the measure of the construct, instruments that measure the same construct may produce varying results. For example, an adolescent who is administered the Reynolds Adolescent Depression Scale (RADS) may score differently than if the BDI-II had been administered. That each instrument has a different item pool for measuring the same construct may produce different results. Furthermore, the instruments may employ variations in the operational definition of depression.

When items are developed, a respondent answers each item from a subjective interpretation of the item. Any ambiguity in the interpretation or system of scoring contributes to random error. For example, the RADS uses a response pattern of four choices across 30 items to assess depressive symptoms using the following response format: 1 = *almost never*, 2 = *hardly ever*, 3 = *sometimes*, 4 = *most of the time*. Notice the subjective nature of the response format. The decision, for instance, to choose a 3 = *sometimes* versus a 4 = *most of the time* is not universal. What one person views as a "3" for a specific symptom may be viewed as a "2" or a "4" by another person. Although reliability coefficients attempt to estimate the consistency of the responses, random error affects the accuracy of these estimates.

Scaling items are similar to multiple-choice items, except that these types of items are usually used to discern a degree to which a behavior, thought, or action exists. In this case, there is no correct response but rather a response that may describe how a client thinks, feels, or behaves. One of the more common types of scales used in assessment is a Likert-type scale. In a Likert-type scale, items range from 1 to 5, in which lower scores indicate disagreement or negativity toward a construct and higher scores are indicative of agreement or affirmation toward a construct. A classic example is items in which a respondent indicates 1 = *strongly disagree*, 2 = *disagree*, 3 = *neither agree nor disagree*, 4 = *agree*, and 5 = *strongly agree*. Likert-type items may be scored reliably but differences between the negative components (*strongly disagree* and *disagree*) or positive components (*strongly agree* and *agree*) may be difficult to differentiate. In addition, justifying that the measures are truly interval, that the degree of difference between two scores is universal for each respondent, is a limitation. For example, Rye (1998) developed the Forgiveness Scale as part of a study involving college women who had previously been wronged in a relationship. A sample item included "I spend time thinking about ways to get back at the person who wronged me" in which the respondent indicated 1 for *strongly disagree* to 5 for *strongly agree*. Can researchers assume that respondents who indicate 4, *agree*, are the same? The extent to which an individual indicates *agree* may not be universal. A respondent who answers *agree* may experience the same degree of a construct as another respondent who answers *strongly agree*. Think of it this way—imagine going to a comedy club and the comedian tells a joke. Some in the audience laugh; others do not. Yet, each audience member was subjected to the same event. Some members may say the joke was funny; others may say the joke was very funny. The extent to which one finds a joke funny or very funny may not be the same across each individual. This is a limitation with Likert-type items, because such items are treated as interval data but are really more ordinal in nature.

Other types of common scales include Guttman scaling and Thurstone scaling (Trochim, 2006). Guttman scaling includes developing dichotomous items (*yes* or *no* responses) that build on one another to develop a cumulative measure. For example, a researcher could develop a series of items to measure religious tolerance that would be placed in a logical order:

1. I appreciate perspective from individuals of different faiths.
2. I would have no problem if my son/daughter dated an individual from a different faith.
3. I would have no problem if my son/daughter married an individual from a different faith.

Notice that each item can be answered with *yes* or *no*. In addition, an argument could be made that the items increase in intensity. The number of items in which the respondent answers *yes* could be the scale score. Usually a scale will consist of a larger series of items than the three used in this example.

The Thurstone scale is similar to the Guttman scale in that the items are dichotomous (*yes* or *no* responses; *agree* or *disagree* responses), but the development of the scale is much more complex and involves evaluating a large series of items and weighting the items to draw conclusions from respondents. Unlike the Guttman scale, the items are not necessarily presented in an ascending fashion and the scoring of the items is more involved.

ADMINISTRATION OF THE INSTRUMENT   Variability in the administration of instruments is common and can have a haphazard effect on the results. Even though instrument developers may pay careful attention to standardizing the instrument through the gathering and analyzing of scores across a chosen population, random errors related to the testing environment, the individual(s) completing the instrument, or the individual(s) administering the instrument may occur. Although items on an instrument can be evaluated for consistency, evaluation of the scores based on other factors simply does not occur on a consistent basis and rarely considered when an instrument is scored and interpreted.

Errors within the testing environment include the variability with each testing environment. Areas may be spacious or cramped; temperatures may fluctuate; participants could be exposed to uncomfortably high or low temperatures. Rooms may be noisy or there could be disruptive activities outside of the testing area, such as construction work. Characteristics of the room in which the instrument is administered may have qualities that distract examinees, such as posters or carvings on walls or desks. Lighting in the room may be poor. Some desks have poor writing surfaces, or perhaps issues exist with technology when computer-based instruments are administered. Older students in particular may be less adept at computer-based administrations. These attributes, as well as others, could have an effect on the participants' abilities to concentrate and be comfortable in the testing environment.

Counselors are responsible for identifying nonstandard environmental conditions or favorable testing conditions when interpreting assessment results (American Counseling Association [ACA], 2005). When nonstandard testing conditions occur, such conditions should be disclosed and reflected in the interpretation of the scores. Indeed, counselors should be cautious in the interpretation and subsequent use of test scores obtained from nonstandard testing conditions, as such scores compromise reliability of the instrument.

Individuals responsible for administering group-based assessments, such as school counselors who coordinate testing for schools, may encourage students to get adequate rest and food before the examination. However, the fact that each individual has unique characteristics related to the administration of the instrument cannot be overlooked. Students may come to the examination with varying levels of motivation, energy, and health. Some students may be overly tired or hungry; others may be ill. Issues related to test anxiety might play a role in test performance. Inadequate attention to testing protocol, such as poor time management on timed exams or mistakes made in the reading or interpretation of the items, may result in random error. Participants may mistakenly blacken the wrong oval corresponding to the item number (e.g., mistakenly marking the oval for Item 6 when answering Item 5) and thereby making the following items incongruent with the intended responses. Items may be mistakenly skipped or omitted. Such random errors can have disastrous consequences for scoring, interpreting, and even placing participants in appropriate programs or services.

Individuals administering instruments also contribute to random errors. Any accidental departure from the standardized procedures may contribute to random error. Verbal and nonverbal communications may have an impact as to how participants may respond to a protocol. For example, an abrupt verbal response or nod could indicate to a participant that an answer is incorrect (Gregory, 2007). In particular, any type of exam that has an oral administration, such as various intelligence tests, is highly susceptible to random errors on the part of the administrator. Cadence, rhythm, and accent in the examiner's speech may affect performance on an instrument and lend to variability from other examinees that have a different administrator for an instrument.

High-stakes testing has had a serious impact on some individuals who administer assessment instruments. Hacker (2007) documented evidence of cheating from 700 schools in Texas on the Texas Assessment of Knowledge and Skills, an achievement test used to comply with No Child Left Behind policies. In addition to teachers leaking questions out to other teachers in order to facilitate test preparation for the students, Hacker (2007) stated the following:

> In most cases, the cheating involved individual pairs or small groups of students . . . [b]ut in a few cases . . . an overwhelming number of students' answers were incredibly similar. So aside from the statistical equivalent of lightning striking the same place 10 times, those students were either all copying one source, or an adult was doctoring answer sheets. (p. 20)

The ramifications of such errors are serious. Consumers of research use test scores to make policy decisions in education. Parents use test scores to make decisions on where to send their children to school. Test scores are often used as evidence for appropriate student placement in programs for various schools, such as gifted and talented programs. Often counselors play a pivotal role in the procedures of administering various assessments, and training for administering instruments in a standardized format cannot be overlooked.

SCORING OF THE INSTRUMENT   Computer-based scoring may reduce random errors by increasing consistency to the scoring process. However, counselors typically use many instruments that are hand scored or scored by scantrons. Problems may persist, especially when score sheets contain erasure marks or lightly blackened answers that may be misread by scantrons. Although instruments that rely on open-ended items, such as intelligence tests, often include substantial training to standardize scoring methods, subjectivity in scoring items may still occur, thereby compromising instrument reliability.

However, another type of scoring issue that is often overlooked when evaluating the psychometric properties of the instrument is the response format on an instrument. Forced-choice items, such as on the MMPI-II, may have less subjectivity in terms of participants understanding the item and choosing a response, yet the limited responses available may not accurately reflect the construct of interest for the participant. In contrast, Likert scale items (i.e., 5-point scales ranging from *strongly disagree* to *strongly agree*), as mentioned earlier, are often used as interval scale items, which can be summed and incorporated into mean scores. However, the response format is quite subjective, as some participants may choose *agree* while others choose *strongly agree* with no verifiable measure of whether the intensity of the construct is truly different from participant to participant. Another example would be scales that measure chronic pain. Some individuals may have a higher pain tolerance and provide lower scores, yet still be in as much or more pain as someone who is endorsing higher levels of pain. Technically these items could be considered ordinal, but researchers who use these instruments treat such items as interval scales to facilitate the use of parametric statistics, many of which are included in the test manuals to support reliability and validity of the instrument. So, although the practice of quasi-interval scales is common among instrument developers, the potential for random error and subsequent effect on instrument reliability is evident.

INTERPRETATION OF THE INSTRUMENT Many instruments provide the opportunity for counselors to use computer-generated reports once scores are tabulated. The ACA (2005) categorized the use of computer-generated reports as an extension of "professional-to-professional consultation" (p. 13). Therefore, when pre-generated reports are used to communicate test results to the client, the onus of responsibility for the accuracy of the report lies with the counselor or service provider who assumes ultimate responsibility for the communication of results. In the case of using assessments for diagnostic purposes, counselors administering and creating reports are accountable for the accuracy and errors of the assessment report. However, in the case of participants contracting with testing companies to provide an assessment, such as an aptitude test, the test company assumes responsibility for the accuracy of the results.

Another source of measurement error is *systematic error*, when the instrument measures something other than the construct. In an attempt to measure commitment to safety for adolescents admitted to a crisis unit, Balkin (2004) created items that also loaded on an individual's ability to process coping skills. The end result was the reliability of a scale designed to measure commitment to safety was compromised. The development of scales that consistently assess one and only one construct is improbable and compounded by the fact that systematic errors may go unnoticed. Cronin and Goodman (2008) documented the legislative approval of using the Scholastic Aptitude Test (SAT), a college-entrance examination used to predict first-year success in college, as the exit exam for high school students. In other words, an instrument designed to assess *aptitude* was implemented to assess academic *achievement*. Despite efforts from Maine counselors, the American Counseling Association, and the Association of Assessment in Counseling and Education, a major systematic error was placed into educational policy. The good intentions of legislators to boost college admissions has resulted in students being evaluated on material that may not be covered in a high school academic curriculum and therefore serving as an unreliable indicator of academic achievement.

ESTIMATING RELIABILITY

Because of the presence of error, estimating the reliability of an instrument (i.e., the consistency in which a construct is measured) can be problematic. Moreover, different methods are used and more than one reliability estimate may be reported. Three terms are common in estimating reliability: (a) reliability coefficient, (b) standard error of measurement, and (c) reliability index.

Reliability Coefficient

To estimate reliability, a *reliability coefficient* is computed to quantify the relationship of observed scores on an instrument: r_{xx} is the correlation between two observed scores.

Reliability coefficients range from 0 to 1. A perfect correlation between observed scores is 1.0, meaning that a set of examinees will obtain the same score each time the test is administered. Consequently, a reliability coefficient of 1.0 is not likely to occur for instruments commonly used to measure psychological constructs. Scores may be similar for individuals who retake an instrument, but slight variations are expected. Ultimately, perfect reliability is difficult to obtain, even when more objective measures are used. For example, measures of blood pressure, resting heart rate, or even weight rarely show the exact values when done repeatedly in a given time frame. The reliability coefficient is the most commonly reported estimate of reliability. There are different methods of reporting the reliability coefficient, which are discussed later in the chapter.

STANDARD ERROR OF MEASUREMENT   Recall that the standard deviation typically refers to the average amount of error from the mean for a given sample or population. A mean, therefore, represents the average score for a particular group and the standard deviation indicates how much each individual will differ from the group mean, on average. When administering an instrument, the standard deviation provides an indication of how a particular individual's score is similar or different from a given group, but the standard deviation is not an indication of the instrument being a consistent measure of a construct for the individual.

SD = avg amt error in group.

For example, the BDI-II for adults in outpatient settings has a mean of 22.45, a standard deviation of 12.75, and a reliability coefficient of .92 (Beck, Steer, & Brown, 1996). Beck et al. (1996) suggested guidelines of total scores for diagnosing major depression (see Table 4.1):

A client who scores a 20 on the BDI-II would be classified in the moderate range for major depression according to Beck et al.'s guidelines. But how likely would the client be to get the same score on a second administration of the BDI-II if no other intervention or change in life circumstances has taken place? To answer this question, counselors use the *standard error of measurement*, which indicates the average amount of error for an individual if the instrument were to be administered repeatedly. So, although the standard deviation indicates variability within a group, the standard error of measurement (*SEM*) indicates variability of a score for an individual.

SEM: avg amt error in individual (w/ repeated trials)

The *SEM* can be computed with the following formula:

$$\sigma_e = \sigma \sqrt{1 - r_{xx}}$$

where σ_e is the standard error of measurement, σ is the population standard deviation, and r_{xx} is the reliability coefficient. So, although an instrument has error, participants may not obtain the same score when administered an instrument repeatedly under similar conditions, and although the true score of an individual is never really known, the *SEM* can be computed to indicate the range in which the true score lies.

TABLE 4.1	Total Score Guidelines for Diagnosing Major Depression
Total Scores	**Range**
0–13	Minimal
14–19	Mild
20–28	Moderate
29–63	Severe

Referring back to the previous example of the BDI-II, if the test has a standard deviation of 12.75 for individuals receiving counseling services in an outpatient setting and a reliability index of .92, then SEM for the BDI-II can be computed as follows:

$$\sigma_e = 12.75\sqrt{1 - .92} = 3.61$$

Notice the attributes of the *SEM*. If the standard deviation remains constant and the reliability coefficient increases (moves closer to 1, demonstrating higher consistency), the *SEM* becomes smaller; likewise, instruments that are less reliable have more error indicated by a larger *SEM*. For example, the reliability of the BDI-II for a college sample was .93:

$$\sigma_e = 12.75\sqrt{1 - .93} = 3.37$$

When the reliability coefficient remains constant and the standard deviation decreases, the *SEM* once again becomes smaller and would increase if the standard deviation were to increase. When the BDI-II was administered to participants who had a previous diagnosis of a mood disorder, the mean score was 26.57 and the standard deviation was 12.15.

$$\sigma_e = 12.15\sqrt{1 - .92} = 3.44$$

On any given assessment period, the *SEM* provides information about the true score within a specific range of confidence, known as a *confidence interval*. Now, we can identify the range in which the true score lies using the information we learned in Chapter 3 Within 1 standard deviation, we can be 68% confident that the true score will lie $\pm 1\sigma_e$ of the observed score; within 2 standard deviations, we can be 95% confident that the true score will lie $\pm 2\sigma_e$ of the observed score; within 3 standard deviations, we can be 99% confident that the true score will lie $\pm 3\sigma_e$ of the observed score. The range for the true score can be expressed in the following way:

For 68% confidence, $T = O \pm 1\sigma_e$

For 95% confidence, $T = O \pm 2\sigma_e$

For 99% confidence, $T = O \pm 3\sigma_e$

In our example for the client who scored 20 on the BDI-II:

We can be 68% confident that the client's true score is between 20 ± 3.61 or between 16.39 and 23.61, inclusive.

We can be 95% confident that the client's true score is between 20 $\pm(2)3.61$ or between 12.78 and 27.22, inclusive.

We can be 99% confident that the client's true score is between 20 $\pm(3)3.61$ or between 9.17 and 30.83, inclusive.

Referring back to the suggested interpretative guidelines of the BDI-II, the *SEM* has some implications for the client, as the client may fall in between the mild to moderate range of depression, again reinforcing the importance of caution in the interpretation of assessment results.

Indeed, *SEM* can play a pivotal role when assessments are used. All too often educational settings overrely on scores to address placement and service issues. A student who tests in the range of borderline intellectual functioning may be refused services on the basis of the score when in fact the *SEM* indicates that the student may have tested in the mildly mentally retarded range of intellectual functioning.

RELIABILITY INDEX The *reliability index* is the relationship between the true score and the observed score and is a less common term than the reliability coefficient to provide estimates of reliability. The reliability index, r_{TX}, quantifies correlation of the true score (*T*) to the observed score (*O*), as opposed to the reliability coefficient, which identifies the relationship between two forms or administrations of an instrument. The reliability index is related directly to the reliability coefficient and is computed as follows:

$$r_{TX} = \sqrt{r_{xx}}$$

As the reliability coefficient increases or decreases, the reliability index increases or decreases respectively. A perfect reliability coefficient, 1.0, would indicate no error in consistency between administrations; therefore, a perfect reliability index, 1.0, would also be present as there would be no error in predicting the true score from the observed score.

TYPES OF RELIABILITY MEASUREMENT

Several methods are used to calculate reliability coefficients (r_{xx}). As r_{xx} approaches 1.0, the instrument is deemed more consistent. This section will address four different forms of computing reliability coefficients: (a) test–retest, (b) parallel/alternate forms, (c) internal consistency, and (d) interscorer reliability. When reliability estimates are reported for an instrument, common practice includes the use of more than one method to demonstrate reliability of the instrument.

Consistency Over Time: Test–Retest Reliability

Test–retest reliability refers to the correlation of two administrations of the same instrument. Often referred to as stability over time, reliability is evaluated by examining the relationship of the same instrument, measuring the same construct at two different time periods. A Pearson product moment correlation coefficient can be computed between the two scores to determine the relationship. This is an appropriate measure to use when the construct being measured remains stable (i.e., does not change) over time.

Psychosocial constructs, however, may change over time—even if no intervention has occurred. Balkin, Tietjen-Smith, Caldwell, and Shen (2007) studied the effect of exercise on depression for young adult women and noted a nonsignificant decrease in scores on the BDI-II for the control group (nonexercise group) when the BDI-II was administered for baseline and then 6 weeks later. Although depression may decrease over time when there is no intervention, that no statistically significant decrease was evident may be linked to the high test–retest reliability of the BDI-II. Beck et al. (1996) reported a test–retest reliability for the BDI-II at $r = .93$ when the BDI-II was administered twice at an interval of 1 week apart. Test–retest reliability is related to the amount of time between the two administrations (Trochim, 2000). Shorter time periods between administrations may yield higher reliability coefficients. A limitation in the test–retest methodology is the assumption that no meaningful changes have occurred that would alter the measurement of the construct being investigated. In addition, the presence of a *testing effect*, previous exposure to the instrument by the examinee, may alter the manner in which the examinee responds. For example, after an initial administration of the BDI-II, an examinee decides to look up symptoms of depression. In an effort to appear less depressed, the examinee could answer the items differently, because previous exposure to the items from the first administration took place.

Estimates of Equivalency: Parallel or Alternate Forms

When more than one form of the same instrument exists, the equivalency of the forms can be assessed by correlating scores on the two forms of the instrument. Although the terms *parallel* or *alternate* are used interchangeably, there is a technical difference. Parallel forms maintain the same means and variances across the various forms; alternate forms are constructed with the intention of being parallel but may not have the same descriptive information (Cohen & Swerdlick, 2002).

A Pearson product moment correlation coefficient can be computed between the two scores on each of the forms to determine the relationship. In this case, highly consistent forms will have different items that cover the same content. Instruments that measure a specific knowledge base or aptitude (e.g., SAT, ACT, Graduate Record Examination [GRE], National Counselor Examination [NCE]) should not differ across *item difficulty*, the percentage of participants answering an item correctly, or *item discrimination*, the extent to which an item distinguishes those who vary on a given construct. To compute item discrimination, the top scoring 27% of participants and the lowest scoring 27% of the participants are used in the following calculation: percent from upper group answering item correctly minus percent from lower group answering item correctly.

The challenge in using parallel forms to evaluate the reliability of an instrument is the development of items that measure the same aspects of a construct for different forms of the instrument. A much larger item pool is necessary to develop equivalent forms. For example, a counselor who is required to take the NCE for a second time would likely encounter items that were different from the first administration but cover the same content areas. Developing items that fit the criteria for an alternate form would be much easier than developing items for a parallel form, as providing evidence for similar item difficulty and discrimination would be necessary.

Internal Consistency

Both test–retest and equivalent forms can be time-consuming methods to estimate reliability, as either the instrument must be administered twice or another form of the instrument must be created. However, another way to estimate reliability may be to examine the *internal consistency* of the instrument—analyzing the relationships of the items on the instrument. There are several methods to evaluating the internal consistency of an instrument: (a) split-half, (b) coefficient alpha, and (c) Kuder-Richardson formulas.

SPLIT-HALF Assuming that all of the items measure the same construct, the instrument can be split into equivalent halves. A Pearson product-moment correlation coefficient can be computed between the two halves on each of the forms to determine the relationship or reliability coefficient. Splitting the instrument into two equivalent halves can be complicated. For example, the BDI-II may not be a good instrument to use this method of reliability estimation. The BDI-II has 21 items, and each item measures a distinct characteristic of depression. So, identifying two equivalent halves of the instrument may not be possible. However, to use this method on the NCE may be easier, as there could be several items that measure knowledge in ethics, the helping relationship, group theory, and so forth, and these items could be equally divided between two halves of the exam.

TABLE 4.2 Reliability Estimates Using Split-Half and Spearman-Brown Formulas	
Split-Half Reliability Coefficient	**Spearman-Brown Reliability Coefficient**
0.70	0.82
0.80	0.89
0.90	0.95

An additional problem occurs in reliability estimation when the split-half method is used. Reliability estimates fluctuate depending on the length of the exam. An increase in items leads to an increase in reliability estimates (Gage & Damrin, 1950), and shorter tests are less reliable. When an instrument is split in half, the reliability coefficient will be underestimated. The *Spearman-Brown formula* adjusts for the underestimation of the split-half method and can be computed as follows:

$$r_{sb} = \frac{2r_{hh}}{1 + r_{hh}}$$

where r_{sb} is the reliability coefficient using the Spearman-Brown formula and r_{hh} is the reliability coefficient using the split-half method. Recall that the split-half method will compare two half-tests, while the Spearman-Brown adjusts for this error by providing a reliability estimate for the whole test. Using the above formula, the following adjustments found in Table 4.2 can be noted. Because of the underestimation of the split-half method, Cohen and Swerdlick (2002) recommended that the Spearman-Brown formula always be used when estimating reliability using the split-half method.

COEFFICIENT ALPHA   As mentioned previously, test developers may have difficulty justifying how an instrument can be divided into two equivalent halves. In addition, there can be many ways to divide an instrument in half. Cronbach (1951) devised a mathematical formula, *coefficient alpha* or *Cronbach's alpha*, to take into account all possible split-half methods to evaluate the internal consistency of an instrument. The formula for coefficient alpha is as follows:

$$r_\alpha = \left(\frac{n}{n-1}\right)\left(1 - \frac{\Sigma\sigma_i^2}{\sigma^2}\right)$$

where r_α is coefficient alpha (this term is often referred to as α when discussing reliability estimates in published research), n is the number of items on the instrument, $\Sigma\sigma_i^2$ is the sum of the variance for each item, and σ^2 is the total variance of the instrument. Although this statistic is quite labor-intensive when computed by hand, the use of computer programs has made coefficient alpha the most widely reported and preferred method for estimating reliability.

KUDER-RICHARDSON   The coefficient alpha formula is actually an extension of an earlier formula developed to evaluate internal consistency for dichotomous items. Whereas coefficient alpha can be used to estimate reliability for items that have a range of responses (i.e., Likert scale items—*strongly agree* to *strongly disagree*), the Kuder-Richardson formula (KR-20) is used to evaluate internal consistency when items can be scored a 1 or 0 (e.g., *right* or *wrong; relapse* or *no relapse*). The KR-20 formula is as follows:

$$r_{KR20} = \left(\frac{n}{n-1} \right)\left(1 - \frac{\Sigma pq}{\sigma^2} \right)$$

where r_{KR20} is the Kuder-Richardson reliability coefficient, n is the number of items, p is the proportion of participants who answer the item correctly or positively, q is the proportion of participants who answer the item incorrectly or negatively, and σ^2 is the total variance of the instrument. Although the KR-20 can be used only for dichotomous items, coefficient alpha will produce the same results as KR-20 for dichotomous items and can be extended to nondichotomous items as well.

Interscorer Reliability

Some measures are dependent on scoring from standardized procedures. Measures of intelligence, performance, or other subjective indicators may vary as a result of the scorers, as opposed to actual variance in the construct. For example, each year at the Olympics, a controversy ensues over scores by various judges. Sports such as figure skating, gymnastics, and boxing often experience questionable scoring procedures. These types of issues may also exist in many types of tests in which the presence or absence, pass or failure of an attribute is dependent upon a scorer's perspective. *Interscorer reliability*, often referred to as *interrater reliability*, refers to the relationship between or among scores issued by raters. Consistency among scorers is dependent on the use and training of objective criteria to rate a construct. When low correlations exist among raters, some type of training is needed to get the raters using similar criteria.

The Pearson product-moment correlation coefficient may be computed to assess the consistency between two judges. When more than two judges are being evaluated, a more sophisticated statistic, called the *intraclass correlation coefficient*, can be computed using computer programs. The intraclass correlation coefficient provides the average rating for a single judge. To account for more than one judge in the average, adjustments can be made using a Spearman-Brown correction:

$$\frac{j(icc)}{1 + (j-1)icc}$$

where j is the number of judges and icc is the intraclass correlation coefficient. An approximation of the icc may be determined from the average of the Pearson product-moment correlation coefficients from all raters.

INTERPRETATION OF RELIABILITY

When deciding whether or not to use a particular psychosocial instrument, the interpretation of reliability data is pertinent. Counselors should be aware of reliability estimation methods, the conditions in which reliability estimates were derived, and the description of the participants from whom the data were collected. "General statements to the effect that a test is 'reliable' or that it is 'sufficiently reliable to permit interpretations of individual scores' are rarely, if ever, acceptable" (AERA et al., 1999, p. 31).

Each method for determining reliability contains sources of error related to time, content, scoring error, and sampling variance. Test–retest is limited by time, as longer periods of time between administrations may decrease reliability estimates. Reliability estimates related to using equivalent forms may be limited by content, as alternate content may be inadvertently used because of the need to generate larger item pools. Although coefficient alpha appears to address limitation in test content that occurs with split-half methods, items that are less likely to measure the homogeneous nature of a construct will lower reliability. Identifying items that measure more heterogeneous attributes of a construct may need to be eliminated. Reliability estimates, with respect to interscorer reliability, are affected by inherent biases, as well as subjective scoring procedures. Objective criteria and training may increase reliability estimates but not eliminate the error variance.

An important consideration outside of computing reliability estimates is the nature of the group in which the reliability estimates are obtained. As a rule of thumb, a heterogeneous group will provide higher reliability estimates, regardless of the method used. Imagine if a group being administered the BDI-II all scored in the severe range. There would be no way to correlate this group's depression with other characteristics, because there was no difference evident from the scores in depression—everybody scored similarly. Having a diverse sample provides evidence that attributes can be consistently measured, as they vary from person to person.

In another example, consider the construct of introversion–extroversion. There would be little relationship to any other construct, such as propensity for substance abuse or self-esteem, if each participant scored high on extroversion. Correlations would be low because of the lack of variability in the sample. With respect to interscorer reliability, if everyone obtained the highest score possible on a construct such as creativity, there would be no way to rank the participants with respect to creativity. The issue of variance in the sample underlies the importance for counselors to be familiar with whom the instrument was normed.

The nature of the instrument is another important consideration. Many instruments, especially instruments geared toward measuring aptitude and ability, rely on speed and/or power measures. *Speed measures* contain simple items that the examinee will likely get correct but the time limit is restricted, preventing the examinee from completing all of the items. *Power measures* provide adequate time to complete the instrument, but include items of difficulty, which may prevent one from obtaining a perfect score. Many instruments (ACT, SAT, GRE, Wechsler Intelligence Scale for Children—Fourth Edition [WISC-IV]) employ a combination of these measures. Because of the nature of speeded tests, traditional split-half methods, such as comparing odd and even items, may produce very high reliability estimates. A better method would be to use a test–retest method on two separately timed tests or correlate to half-tests with a Spearman-Brown formula (Gregory, 2007).

Given the limitations of reliability estimates, what constitutes adequate reliability? Hopkins, Stanley, and Hopkins (1990) indicated that standardized tests, such as those used for placement and college admission, should have reliability coefficients of .90 or higher. Yet, many psychosocial instruments are used with reliability estimates near .70. Certain constructs, such as psychosis, have been difficult to measure and reliability estimates may be lower.

Reliability estimates should not be used alone to assess the consistency of the scores. Standard error of measurement should also be considered. Although reliability estimates account for consistency of the instrument, standard error of measurement provides an indication of accuracy. Recall that the standard error of measurement incorporates two terms: a reliability coefficient and measurement error. Therefore, an instrument may be reliable, but could also be inaccurate.

WHAT ARE THE IMPLICATIONS FOR RELIABILITY?

Because of the many different aspects of reliability, determining whether an instrument is reliable is not a simple matter and requires a multifaceted approach. Instruments may have strong reliability evidence in one area yet be lacking in another area. Such an issue is apparent in the Child Behavior Checklist (CBCL). Although the CBCL is a popular instrument, the reliability of the instrument may be questioned in some regards. Test–retest after 1 week and internal consistency scores for composite scales average .80; but internal consistency scores for the subscales may be as low as .50. The attributes of the raters may also be a factor with interrater reliability averaging .66 on the parent forms (Doll, 2004). Similar to the CBCL, the MMPI-2 maintains strong test–retest reliability, averaging .83, but internal consistency reliability for the clinical subscales has a broader range, .34 to .87 with a median range of .63 (Matz, Altepeter, & Perlman, 1992).

Educational and cognitive tests may have higher reliability estimates because of the nature of measuring academic performance or intelligence, as opposed to psychopathology, which may be considered more diverse and complex in nature to measure. Reliability estimates for the Wechsler Adult Intelligence Scale—III (WAIS-III) are quite good. Test–retest coefficients range from .80 to the low .90s. Interscorer agreement is in the low to middle .90s (Hess, 2004). The Wechsler Intelligence Scales have a standard error of measurement of ±5 points, so this needs to be considered when applying labels and determining services for individuals. For example, if a school district employs a cut-score of 70 IQ to provide services, and a student scores 72, the *SEM* indicates that the student could fall in the range of mild mental retardation to borderline intellectual functioning.

Again, the popularity of an instrument is not a guarantee of reliable assessment results. Each of the assessments used in this sample profile are more widely known and can easily be referenced in the *Mental Measurement Yearbook* or peer-reviewed literature. Counselors should be aware of the error related to measurement and assessment. Standardized assessments are only a tool and should never stand alone in determining treatment or diagnosis.

References

American Counseling Association. (2005). *ACA code of ethics*. Alexandria, VA: American Counseling Association.

American Educational Research Association, American Psychological Association, & National Council of Measurement in Education. (1999). *Standards for educational and psychological testing*. Washington, DC: American Educational Research Association.

Balkin, R. S. (2004). Application of a model for adolescent acute care psychiatric programs. *Dissertation Abstracts International, 64*, 2391.

Balkin, R. S., Tietjen-Smith, T, Caldwell, C., & Shen, Y. (2007). The relationship of exercise and depression among young adult women. *Adultspan Journal*, pp. 30–35.

Beck, A. T., Steer, R. A., & Brown, G. K. (1996). *BDI-II manual*. San Antonio, TX: The Psychological Corporation.

Cohen, R. J., & Swerdlik, M. E. (2002). *Psychological testing and assessment* (5th ed.). Boston, MA: McGraw-Hill.

Cronbach, L. J. (1951). Coefficient alpha and the internal structure of tests. *Psychometrika, 16,* 297–334.

Cronin, J. M., & Goodman, R. H. (2008). Is New England ready for P-20? A report card on efforts to expand the K-12 notion from preschool to grade 20. *The New England Journal of Higher Education, 22,* 15–17.

Doll, B. (2004). Test review of the Child Behavior Checklist. From J. C. Impara & B. S. Plake (Eds.), *The thirteenth mental measurements yearbook* [Electronic version]. Retrieved July 16, 2009, from the Buros Institute's *Test Reviews Online* Web site: http://www.unl.edu/buros

Gage, N. L., & Damrin, D. E. (1950). Reliability, homogeneity and number of choices. *Journal of Educational Psychology,* pp. 385–404.

Gregory, R. J. (2007). *Psychological testing: History, principles, and applications* (5th ed.). Boston, MA: Allyn & Bacon.

Hacker, H. (2007). Against the odds. *IRE Journal, 30,* 19–20.

Hess, A. (2004). Test review of the Wechsler Adult Intelligence Scale—Third Edition. From J. C. Impara & B. S. Plake (Eds.), *The thirteenth mental measurements yearbook* [Electronic version]. Retrieved July 16, 2009, from the Buros Institute's *Test Reviews Online* Web site: http://www.unl.edu/buros

Hopkins, K. D. (1998). *Educational and psychological measurement and evaluation* (8th ed.). Boston, MA: Allyn & Bacon.

Matz, P. A., Altepeter, T. S., & Perlman, B. (1992). MMPI-2: Reliability with college students. *Journal of Clinical Psychology, 48,* 330–334.

Spearman, C. (1904). "General Intelligence," objectively determined and measured. *American Journal of Psychology, 15,* 201–293.

Stanley, J. C. (1971). Reliability. In R. L. Thorndike (Ed.), *Educational measurement* (2nd ed.). Washington, DC: American Council on Education.

Trochim, W. (2000). *The Research Methods Knowledge Base* (2nd ed.). Cincinnati, OH: Atomic Dog Publishing.

CHAPTER 5

Current Standards
for Validity

OBJECTIVES

1. Understand the historical context of validity.
2. Understand the current standards for validity.
3. Differentiate the current standards of validity with the triadic model of validity.
4. Understand the methods for demonstrating evidence of validity.
5. Identify whether test developers sufficiently address validity issues in their assessments.

DEFINING VALIDITY: A BRIEF HISTORY

In assessment, *validity* refers to the development, administration, scoring, interpretation, and utilization of an instrument. An instrument is valid if the instrument is an actual measure of a given construct. "Validity refers to the degree to which evidence and theory support the interpretations of test scores entailed by proposed uses of tests...[and is] the most fundamental consideration in developing and evaluating tests" (American Educational Research Association, American Psychological Association, & National Council of Measurement in Education [AERA, APA, & NCME], 1999, p. 9).

Validity is an evolving process. The manner in which validity was defined in the early 20th century is quite different from the current definition and criteria. Initially, validity was viewed as a fixed, stable attribute of a measure. Guilford (1946) indicated "a test is valid for anything with which it correlates" (p. 429). Thus, validity was evaluated via a correlation coefficient, which became known as a *validity coefficient.* The effect was to rely on statistics to determine evidence of validity. Issues of item content were not even considered (Reynolds & Kamphaus, 2003). Research continued to develop in this area with the definition of validity being extended to *criterion evidence* (Gulliksen, 1950), which is a relationship to a construct or phenomenon, and convergent and *discriminant* evidence (Campbell & Fiske, 1959), the extent to which items on an instrument for different scales are strongly intercorrelated (i.e., convergent evidence) or show weaker relationships (i.e., discriminant evidence). For example, an individual who endorses the item "I feel sad all of the time" on the Beck Depression Inventory-II (BDI-II) may also endorse other similar items related to depression (convergent evidence), which all could relate to depressive disorder (criterion evidence). On another note, some instruments contain more than one scale. For example, the Substance Abuse Subtle Scale Inventory—3 (SASSI-3) has scales that focus on more objective criteria related to chemical dependency, such as the amount of alcohol or drugs consumed, but it also has other scales that measure more subtle symptoms, such as feelings of guilt after using. An item measuring guilt may not correlate with objective items, but could correlate with items related to feelings that occur as a result of drug or alcohol use. Both convergent and discriminant evidence would show that feelings of guilt correlate with subtle symptoms of chemical dependency (i.e., convergent evidence) and correlate less with objective symptoms of chemical dependency (i.e., discriminant evidence).

Cronbach and Meehl (1955) identified four types of validity in their seminal article, "Construct Validity in Psychological Tests": (a) predictive validity, (b) concurrent validity, (c) content validity, and (d) construct validity. The concept of criterion validity was separated into two aspects: (a) *predictive validity*, which is attained when an instrument is administered and scores are correlated to some criterion that is obtained later, and (b) *concurrent validity*, which is attained when an instrument is administered while simultaneously obtaining another score on a criterion. For example, when the Strong Interest Inventory is used to guide a client to a career path, predictive evidence is demonstrated; that the Strong Interest Inventory may correlate with the interest inventory on O*NET demonstrates concurrent evidence. *Content validity* referred to the acceptance that the items of an instrument measure the intended construct. The process of evaluating content validity was quite ambiguous. According to Cronbach and Meehl (1955), "Content validity is ordinarily to be established deductively, by defining a universe of items and sampling systematically within this universe to establish the test" (p. 282). Cronbach and Meehl further elaborated that content validity was demonstrated through "*acceptance* of the...content" (p. 282). Thus, content evidence may be demonstrated through a review of previous published research on a phenomenon of interest, expert review, or documentation of preestablished acceptance or standards. Cronbach and Meehl suggested *construct validation* be investigated when a phenomenon of interest lacked an operational definition. "Construct validity must be investigated whenever no criterion or universe of content is accepted as entirely adequate to define the quality to be measured" (p. 282). Construct validity could be established through the investigation of (a) group differences, (b) correlational procedures such as factor analysis, (c) evaluations of internal structure, such as reliability and the consistency of responses from a homogeneous sample, (d) evaluations because of changes in conditions, such as the insertion or removal of a test condition, and (e) observations of an individual performance or process of completing an instrument.

In 1966, APA AERA, and NCME published the *Standards for Educational and Psychological Tests and Manuals*. Although this was not the first time these organizations published standards for testing and measurement, it was the first joint publication for the three groups. The main change from Cronbach and Meehl's (1955) conceptualization of validity was use of the term *criterion-related validity*, which addressed specific types of predictive and concurrent evidence related to the measure (Hubley & Zumbo, 2001). The 1966 *Standards* yielded the trinity view (Goodwin & Leech, 2003; Hubley & Zumbo, 2001) of validity. Although the 1966 *Standards* related three distinct types of validity, the

1985 *Standards* identified test validity as a single concept and that content, criterion, and construct validity were merely different types of evidence for validity (AERA et al., 1985; Goodwin & Leech, 2003). Thus, a trend evolved to describe validity as a single conceptual element of evaluating instruments, in which different types of evidence may be examined to determine the extent to which an instrument meets standards of validity.

A PRESENT VIEW OF VALIDITY

In the 1999 *Standards for Educational and Psychological Testing* (AERA et al.), validity was described as the incorporation of evidence and theory required to support the proposed interpretation and use of test scores. Validity, therefore, not only included the gathering of data to support the interpretation of scores but also in how scores were used. For example, the use of an aptitude test to assess academic achievement (as explained in Chapter 4) and to be used as an exit exam for high school students may be contrary to the explicit definition of validity. "The process of validation involves accumulating evidence to provide a sound scientific basis for the proposed score interpretations....When test scores are used or interpreted in more than one way, each intended interpretation must be validated" (AERA et al., 1999, p. 9).

When evaluating an instrument for use with a client, counselors should focus on the statements related to validity. Essentially, counselors should ask, "Is this the appropriate instrument for this client? Will the interpretation of test scores be used in a manner to which the instrument was designed and interpreted in a manner that is appropriate to the client?" Previously, reliability—the accuracy and consistency of a measure—was defined and described. Reliability and validity are essential to responsible test use. However, sole evaluation of reliability would be a mistake. An instrument may be reliable without being valid. For example, Lawson (2007) asserted that counselor wellness affects the quality of services clients receive. Although items that measure wellness may be consistent and accurate, would the presence of such items on a licensure exam compromise the validity of the licensure exam? In this case, the validity of the licensure exam may be compromised, as the exam was designed to measure a different construct, and such items would adversely effect the interpretation of the instrument. The responsibility to evaluate validity is on both the counselor and the test developer. The developer is responsible to furnish the evidence related to test interpretation and use; the counselor is responsible for evaluating such evidence and using the instrument, scores, and interpretation in an ethical manner (American Counseling Association [ACA], 2005; AERA et al., 1999). The 1999 *Standards for Educational and Psychological Testing* emphasized five types of evidences for test validity.

EVIDENCE BASED ON TEST CONTENT

The contents of an instrument (i.e., test items) should represent the intended domain or construct being measured. "Test content refers to themes, wording, and format of the items, tasks, or questions on a test, as well as the guidelines for procedures regarding administration and scoring" (AERA et al., 1999, p. 11). Evidence based on test content replaced the term *content validity*, but also expanded the definition. Rather than merely focusing on what the instrument contains, evidence based on test content also incorporated procedures related to test use and interpretation. Counselors should be able to identify the extent to which scores and interpretations of an instrument are generated from the items administered and the tasks or processes placed upon the examinee. For example, administering a Wechsler Intelligence Scale for Children—Fourth Edition (WISC-IV) to a child with deafness may not be valid, as the processes required by the examinee involve verbal explanations of questions asked. If the examinee has difficulty responding to the questions and queries as a result of hearing impairment and not of intellectual impairment, then the measure ceases to be valid because of the inappropriate tasks and processes being placed upon the examinee. Many complications can arise that make a test invalid, such as administering a self-report inventory to an individual diagnosed with dyslexia. Counselors who use assessment instruments must consider carefully the ramifications of scoring and interpreting instruments, given the abilities of each individual client.

A term that is often confused with evidence based on test content is *face validity*, which refers to a superficial evaluation of the instrument according to how the instrument looks. In other words, an instrument would be deemed as valid if it appears valid to the individuals who decide to use it (Anastaci & Urbina, 1997). Face validity is not evidence based, and therefore is not considered as sufficient evidence of validity.

How Is Evidence Based on Test Content Evaluated?

Analysis and evaluation of evidence based on test content occurs both logically and empirically (AERA et al., 1999). Test developers should document how items were derived. Relevant reviews of literature and developed theories should be cited. Often, expert opinion is cited and test developers may revise, add, or delete items according to suggestions from reviewers. In creating the *Latino/a Values Scale,* Kim, Soliz, Orellana, and Alamilla (2009) documented an extensive review of the literature, which was used to create "Latino/a value dimensions" (p. 75). These dimensions were critiqued by a research team, reduced to fewer dimensions, and then placed in a survey to a professional association to solicit feedback.

An empirical method for demonstrating evidence based on test content is the index of item-objective congruence, developed by Rovinelli and Hambleton (1977). In this method, a test developer identifies an objective to be measured by each item and expert raters evaluate each item and provide the following ratings: 1 for an item that *clearly measures the objective,* −1 for an item that *clearly does not measure the objective,* and 0 for items in which the *measurement of the objective is unclear* (Turner & Carlson, 2003). Raters may have different ratings for each of the items, depending on their own subjective evaluations. An index for item-objective congruence may be computed to assess the degree to which the raters identified that an item measured a particular objective using the following formula:

$$I_{ik} = \frac{N}{2n - 2}(\mu_k - \mu)$$

where I_{ik} is the index of item-objective congruence for item I on objective k, $N =$ the number of objectives, $\mu_k =$ judges' mean rating of item I on objective k, and $\mu =$ the judges' mean rating of item I on all objectives (Crocker & Algina, 1986, p. 221).

A generally accepted value for an index score is .75 (Turner & Carlson, 2003). Although the specific computations of the index of item-objective congruence are outside the scope of this text, readers who have an interest in using the index of item-objective congruence may find more information about the measure in the cited materials. The important element of this discussion is that empirical methods of evaluating evidence based on test content may be used in test development.

EVIDENCE BASED ON RESPONSE PROCESSES

Test developers should gather evidence demonstrating that the actual responses of participants on test items is a valid operation for evaluating the construct being investigated (AERA et al., 1999). When an item appears on an instrument, the assumption is that individuals will interpret the item the same way. But this is not always true. For example, Whiston (2009, p. 141) identified a common question related to substance abuse assessment, "Has drinking or taking drugs ever caused you any problems?" Such questions can be ambiguous, because individuals who use drugs or alcohol are often in denial about the problematic nature of their use/abuse. Thus, an individual who drinks only on weekends may answer "yes" while another individual who smokes marijuana every day may answer "no." The same item may be answered unexpectedly different by each examinee. Often, outside factors that are irrelevant to the measured construct can influence test responses and performance. For example, students from low socioeconomic backgrounds may test lower because they own fewer books in the home or did not have a good meal before the exam.

How Is Evidence Based on Response Processes Evaluated?

By examining the individual responses of examinees and even questioning examinees about their responses or how the responses were derived, test developers may gain insight to the extent to which a desired construct is being measured. There are various types of responses that can be monitored, such as the speed of the response, tasks engaged in developing a response, or physiological responses to an item. When individual differences are noted in terms of a response to an item, the test developer may wish to consider alternative formats to an item.

One aspect that is generally acknowledged in standardized testing is the issue of bias. Bias occurs when the interpretation of an instrument is different across various groups. Test developers need to be cautious when subgroups perform differently on an instrument. Investigations into ways items may be interpreted or meaning conveyed is essential so that the instrument remains relevant across a diverse population.

EVIDENCE BASED ON INTERNAL STRUCTURE

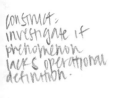

Previously labeled as *construct validity*, evidence based on internal structure refers to the interrelationships of the items and the relationships of the items to variables, constructs, or components/factors being measured. For example, when subscales are developed for an instrument, the expectation is that items on one subscale have higher correlations to each other, as they are measuring the same construct, and have lower correlations to items measuring a separate subscale, as the construct may be quite different.

The extent to which items on the same subscale have higher intercorrelations is known as *convergent evidence*; the extent to which items on one subscale have lower correlations to items on a separate subscale is known as *discriminant evidence*. Trochim

TABLE 5.1	Convergent and Discriminant Evidence in the GASS (Balkin & Roland, 2007)					
	Problem Identification			Commitment to Follow-up		
	PI_1	PI_2	PI_3	CF_1	CF_2	CF_3
PI_1	1.00					
PI_2	**0.85**	1.00				
PI_3	**0.80**	**0.86**	1.00			
CF_1	0.40	0.41	0.37	1.00		
CF_2	0.41	0.42	0.35	**0.81**	1.00	
CF_3	0.43	0.43	0.39	**0.68**	**0.80**	1.00

(2000) identified methods for examining item correlations to establish convergent and discriminant evidence. For example, in development of the *Goal Attainment Scale of Stabilization* (GASS; Balkin & Roland, 2007), subscales were developed to measure the extent to which adolescent clients in psychiatric hospitalization attained therapeutic goals designed around problem solving and coping strategies and commitment to a follow-up plan upon discharge from the hospital. In this study, convergent evidence was demonstrated in the problem identification and commitment to follow-up subscales. You can see that sample items were strongly related to items identified as measuring problem identification and less related to items measuring commitment to follow-up (see Table 5.1). A similar model appears in commitment to follow-up.

Note that items in bold demonstrate strong intercorrelations. These items demonstrate convergent evidence in that items on the same subscale are more highly correlated to each other. Also note that the values that are not bolded are weaker correlations. These items demonstrate discriminant evidence, as items on one subscale do not correlate with items on another subscale. Each subscale measures something unique in client therapeutic goal attainment.

How Is Evidence Based on Internal Structure Evaluated?

When developing instruments, items should fit the appropriate construct of interest both theoretically (i.e., evidence based on test content) and statistically. Examining intercorrelations of items, as mentioned earlier, is one method. However, often more sophisticated methods are used to determine whether items actually measure a construct in question. Common methods include principal component analysis (PCA), exploratory factor analysis (EFA), and confirmatory factor analysis (CFA). The goal of PCA and EFA is to identify items that measure a latent trait and eliminate items that do not contribute to a measure. A *latent trait* refers to a variable or construct that is not directly observed or measured. For example, in the development of the BDI-II (Beck, Steer, & Brown, 1996), 21 items were used to measure depression. These 21 items may or may not represent the entire pool of items in which data were collected. Items that had low correlations, for instance, may have been removed. Beck et al. conducted an EFA and two latent traits emerged. Items indicating levels of sadness, agitation, loss of interest, and indecisiveness, for example, loaded on a latent trait, which was identified by the authors as Cognitive-Affective dimension. These items were indicative of cognitive or affective symptoms of depression. A second factor emerged consisting of items such as tiredness, loss of energy, and changes in appetite. These items were somatic in nature and therefore labeled as Somatic dimension. Thus, two latent traits emerged from the EFA.

An important note is that both PCA and EFA are exploratory procedures. Although a theory was in place to create items that measure depression, based on *Diagnostic Statistical Manual* (4th ed.; DSM-IV) criteria, the latent traits were identified through exploratory procedures. The test developers created the items and then studied the factor loadings, which were used to label the latent traits. In exploratory procedures, a theory is developed through both item content and statistical analyses. Many test developers do not run additional analyses beyond the exploratory procedures. However, CFA represents a method to statistically test a theory once the factors have been identified. CFA procedures may be more respected, because statistics are used to test a preestablished theory, as opposed to using statistics in theory development. A strong instrument is one in which both exploratory and confirmatory procedures on separate samples are used in test development.

EVIDENCE BASED ON RELATIONS TO OTHER VARIABLES

When developing an instrument, analyses to external variables related to the measure is pertinent to establishing evidence of test validity. Relationship to external variables may be ascertained by examining concurrent evidence and predictive evidence; similar to evaluating evidence of internal structure, convergent and discriminant evidence may also be examined with respect to external variables.

Concurrent evidence refers to an analysis of a relationship between two measures at the same time. For example, Balkin and Roland (2007) administered two instruments, the GASS to measure therapeutic goal attainment for adolescents at the time of discharge from psychiatric hospitalization, and the Clinician Problem Scale—Revised (CPS-R) to measure psychiatric symptoms at the time of discharge. Concurrent evidence was demonstrated on the GASS as a significant relationship was found between the GASS and CPS-R scores, indicating that increases in therapeutic goal attainment (GASS scores) were related to decreased psychiatric symptoms (CPS-R scores).

Predictive evidence is demonstrated when an instrument is related to a specific future outcome. For example, universities often use the ACT or SAT as an admission criterion, because universities believe that college entrance scores may be predictive of success in college. Predictive evidence, however, can be challenging to evaluate. In developing the Suicide Probability Scale (SPS), Cull and Gill (1982) attempted to demonstrate the extent to which scores on the SPS differentiated between clinical and nonclinical populations. In a clinical population, 70.8% of potential attemptors were misclassified as nonsuicidal and 76.9% of nonattemptors were misclassified as suicidal. In a nonclinical population, 41.5% of nonattemptors were misclassified as suicidal (Golding, 2004).

Similar to evidence based on internal structure, an evaluation of convergent and discriminant evidence to external variables may provide important evidence for validity. For the purposes of evaluating relationships to other variables, stronger correlations between similar measures would be apparent in convergent evidence and weaker correlations would be apparent in discriminant evidence. For example, Beck et al. (1996) demonstrated convergent evidence by correlating scores on the BDI-II with the Hamilton Psychiatric Rating Scale for Depression (HRSD). Because both instruments measure the same construct, depression, the correlation, as expected, between the two instruments was high ($r = .71$). Discriminant evidence was less evident, as the BDI-II was correlated with the Beck Anxiety Inventory (BAI). The relationship between the BDI-II and the BAI was .60. Beck et al. identified that this finding was not unexpected, as "depression and anxiety have been found to be correlated in clinical evaluations" (p. 27).

How Is Evidence Based on Relations to Other Variables Evaluated?

Correlational designs, as noted earlier, tend to be common in identifying evidence of relationships to other variables. Typically, correlations of measures and regression analyses may be used to demonstrate concurrent, predictive, convergent, and discriminant characteristics between measures. Occasionally, tests of significance between administrations of two or more measures may be analyzed to demonstrate evidence of validity. Beck et al. (1996), in their revision of the Beck Depression Inventory—IA to the BDI-II conducted t tests to evaluate whether scores were significantly different between the two instruments. Beck et al. identified that more items were endorsed on the BDI-II than on the BDI-IA by a sample of outpatient clients. Despite this difference, which may be used to justify the revision, correlation between the two instruments was strong (.84).

EVIDENCE BASED ON CONSEQUENCES OF TESTING

In a break from the trinity model, the 1999 *Standards* emphasized the need to identify the benefits, as well as consequences, of using a measure. The benefits of using an instrument should be both stated and implied. When a test is administered, users should be able to glean information and insights that are useful and beneficial to the client and/or to society. At times, measures may be used in which the intended construct of interest is either lacking evidence of validity or the instruments measure a construct that is unrelated. A clear example of testing consequences can be examined through the advent of high-stakes testing. When No Child Left Behind was passed in 2002, accountability through the examination and demonstrated improvement of student performance was legislated, with the withholding of federal funds as a consequence for poor test scores (Thorn & Mulvenon, 2002). Hence, students are now placed under enormous pressure to achieve higher test scores. In many states, the extent to which the test measures academic progress, as well as the students' ability to work under a pressure situation, has come under scrutiny. Although no change in the present system is likely to occur, the debate about the benefits and the consequences of the test and the practice of high-stakes testing is central to obtaining evidence based on consequences of testing. AERA et al. (1999) cautioned that differentiating between social policy issues versus test validity issues may be difficult. The intent of obtaining evidence of consequences of testing is not to influence social policy but to make sure that interpretations of instruments provide the intended information. As the emphasis on consequences for testing is relatively new, Goodwin and Leech (2003) indicated that few guidelines have been established. Although the intended focus on the benefits and consequences of a test is important, test developers have not identified methods for demonstrating this aspect of validity.

WHAT ARE THE IMPLICATIONS FOR TEST VALIDITY?

Despite the fact that the *Standards for Educational and Psychological Testing* were last revised in 1999, neither developers nor reviewers have adhered strongly to the most recent standards. The Minnesota Multiphasic Personality Inventory—II (MMPI-II), in fact, was revised in 1989, and evidence of validity still follows the 1985 *Standards*, with emphasis on comparing norms and scales between the MMPI-II and the MMPI. Even instruments that were revised after the 1999 *Standards* tend to adhere to much older standards of validity. With respect to the WISC-IV, "rather than presenting traditional concurrent and predictive validity evidence, the technical manual refers to Campbell and Fiske's (1959) terminology of convergent and discriminant...validity" (Maller, 2005). Modern test reviews in *Mental Measurements Yearbook* still incorporate the terms from the 1985 *Standards*.

Although the instruments in the case studies are all well established and common to the field, validity studies using the most recent standards are lacking. Counselors should be careful consumers when engaging in standardized assessment practices. Attention to reviews of instruments is essential in identifying the appropriateness of using various assessment tools. When evaluating whether the use of an instrument would be valid for a client or group of clients, counselors should consider the following issues:

1. To what extent was the instrument developed under a theoretical framework? This is essential to evidence of test content. What theory or theories were used to develop the instrument? In addition, identification of some type of review by experts is important to providing evidence that the instrument was theoretically derived.

2. To what extent do the processes involved in responding to items provide a meaningful measure of the construct in question? For example, if the instrument is a self-report inventory, is this appropriate for the client and the construct being measured? Counselors should consider the nature and type of questions that clients are exposed to and identify if the scores obtained are likely to reflect a valid measure for the client. Certainly, being aware of reliability evidence, as discussed in Chapter 4, is essential here.

3. What strategies were used to demonstrate evidence of internal structure? Most tests are validated using sophisticated statistical analyses, such as exploratory and confirmatory factor analysis. Although many master's-level counselors will not have course work covering the details of these analyses, being aware of attempts to establish factor structure is important. Look to see that the subscales in the measure are identified as part of the factor structure. The overall structure of the instrument should account for a large proportion of the variance in the model but there are no good rules of thumb on this, with some instruments as low as 40% (or possibly lower) and others much higher.

4. What measures were used to correlate to the instrument in question? Counselors should look for evidence that the instrument being evaluated was correlated with other instruments that measure a similar construct. If the instrument correlates moderately to another existing measure, that serves as evidence that the scores obtained from administration of the instrument may be valid for a particular use.

5. What are the consequences for using a test for a specific client? Counselors should be aware of the issues related to test use and abuse. The scores obtained on a particular assessment measure can help direct or guide treatment, or may inadvertently label a client, which may not serve his/her best interest. Counselors should ensure that the scores obtained from a measure would be used appropriately.

References

American Counseling Association. (2005). *ACA code of ethics*. Alexandria, VA: American Counseling Association.

American Educational Research Association, American Psychological Association, & National Council of Measurement in Education. (1985). *Standards for educational and psychological testing*. Washington, DC: American Psychological Association.

American Educational Research Association, American Psychological Association, & National Council of Measurement in Education. (1999). *Standards for educational and psychological testing*. Washington, DC: American Educational Research Association.

American Psychological Association, American Educational Research Association, & National Council of Measurement in Education. (1966). *Standards for educational and psychological tests and manuals*. Washington, DC: American Psychological Association.

Anastaci, A., & Urbina, S. (1997). *Psychological testing* (7th ed.). Upper Saddle River, NJ: Prentice Hall.

Balkin, R. S., & Roland, C. B. (2007). Reconceptualizing stabilization for counseling adolescents in brief psychiatric hospitalization: A new model. *Journal of Counseling & Development, 85,* 64–72.

Beck, A. T., Steer, R. A., & Grown, G. K. (1996). *BDI-II manual*. San Antonio, TX: The Psychological Corporation.

Campbell, D. T., & Fiske, D. W. (1959). Convergent and discriminant validation by the multitrait-multimethod matrix. *Psychological Bulletin, 56*(2), 81–105. doi:10.1037/h0046016

Crocker, L., & Algina, J. (1986). *Introduction to classical modern test theory*. Orlando, FL: Harcourt Brace Jovanovich.

Cronbach, L. J., & Meehl, P. E. (1955). Construct validity in psychological tests. *Psychological Bulletin, 52,* 281–302.

Cull, J. G., & Gill, W. S. (1982). *Suicide Probability Scale (SPS) manual*. Los Angeles, CA: Western Psychological Services.

Golding, S. L. (1985). [Review of the Supervisory Practices Inventory]. In J. V. Mitchell, Jr. (Ed.), *The ninth mental measurements yearbook*. Lincoln, NE: Buros Institute of Mental Measurements.

Goodwin, L. D., & Leech, N. L. (2003). The meaning of validity in the new *Standards for Educational and Psychological Testing*: Implications for measurement courses. *Measurement and Evaluation in Counseling and Development, 36,* 181–191.

Guilford, J. P. (1946). New standards for test evaluation. *Educational and Psychological Measurement, 6,* 427–438.

Gulliksen, H. (1950). *Theory of mental tests*. New York: Wiley.

Hubley, A. M., & Zumbo, B. D. (2001). A dialectic on validity: Where we have been and where we are going. *The Journal of General Psychology, 123,* 207–215.

Kim, B., Soliz, A., Orellana, B., & Alamilla, S. (2009). Latino/a Values Scale: Development, reliability, and validity. *Measurement and Evaluation in Counseling and Development, 42,* 71–91.

Lawson, G. (2007). Counselor wellness and impairment: A national survey. *Journal of Humanistic Counseling, Education & Development, 46,* 20–34. Retrieved from Academic Search Complete database.

Maller, S. J. (2005). [Review of the Wechsler Intelligence Scale for Children—Fourth Edition]. In R. A. Spies, & B. S. Plake (Eds.). (2005). *The sixteenth mental measurements yearbook*. Lincoln, NE: Buros Institute of Mental Measurements.

Rainelle, R. J., & Hamilton, R. K. (1977). On the use of content specialists in the assessment of criterion-references test item validity. *Dutch Journal of Educational Research, 2,* 49–60.

Reynolds, C. R., & Kamphaus, R. W. (2003). *Handbook of psychological and educational assessment of children: Intelligence, aptitude, and achievement* (2nd ed.). New York, NY: Guilford Press.

Thorn, A., & Mulvenon, S. (2002). High-stakes testing: An examination of elementary counselors' views and their academic preparation to meet this challenge. *Measurement & Evaluation in Counseling & Development, 35,* 195–206.

Trochim, W. (2000). *The research methods knowledge base* (2nd ed.). Cincinnati, OH: Atomic Dog Publishing.

Turner, R. C., & Carlson, L. (2003). Indexes of item-objective congruence for multidimensional items, *International Journal of Testing, 3,* 163–171.

Whiston, S. C. (2009). Principles and applications of assessment in counseling (3rd ed.). Belmont, CA: Brooks/Cole, Cengage Learning.

CHAPTER 6

How to Choose an Assessment Instrument

OBJECTIVES

1. Identify ethical and legal considerations in selecting an assessment instrument.
2. Interpret the technical quality of an instrument.
3. Understand the format and information in an instrument review.
4. Determine the appropriateness of an instrument.
5. Understand the factors that compromise the quality of an instrument.
6. Understand the limitations and strengths of a selected assessment instrument.
7. Identify factors that may affect performance.

DEFINING THE PURPOSE OF THE ASSESSMENT INSTRUMENT

Counselors' decisions to use an assessment instrument should be based on the construct or phenomenon to be measured, the benefit to the client, the expertise/training of the counselor, the potential to yield appropriate decisions for the client, and the cultural sensitivity of the instrument (American Counseling Association [ACA], 2005; American Educational Research Association, American Psychological Association, & National Council of Measurement in Education [AERA, APA, & NCME], 1999). When selecting an instrument, counselors should have in mind a specific purpose for which the instrument will be used. George (1997) identified three such purposes: (a) describe a client or client population, including characteristics of the client or client population, (b) identify specific needs of a client or client population, and (c) evaluate interventions and/or programs that serve clients or client populations. Ultimately, counselors need to determine the degree to which the information will be useful and contribute to timely interventions for the client or client population (Sederer, Dickey, & Eisen, 1997).

In terms of usefulness, consider the following:

1. How will the client benefit from the assessment?
2. How will the counselor use assessment results to provide best practice for the client?

In administering the assessment, both the client and counselor will expend time, energy, and money to obtain some result. Often counselors attempt to identify problems, measure baseline behaviors, or diagnose in order to develop effective treatment plans and improve client conceptualization by the counselor. Clients might benefit by gaining insight into problem areas or identifying a particular diagnosis that help explains the problem areas, such as a parent learning that a son or daughter has Asperger's syndrome.

As mentioned in previous chapters, counselors should consider the psychometric qualities of an instrument. "Counselors carefully consider the validity, reliability, psychometric imitations, and appropriateness of instruments when selecting assessments" (ACA, 2005, p. 12). The reliability of an instrument can range from 0 to 1, with coefficients of .70 or above considered adequate for sufficient reliability evidence of scores on an instrument. Statements about validity should also be evaluated, with indications that the instrument was evaluated with respect to content, internal structure, relationships to other variables, response processes, and consequences of testing. Rarely are all aspects of validity mentioned in manuals and reviews, and many instruments are evaluated based on the 1985 standards. Counselors should be cautious when using instruments that selectively disclose validation procedures. Also remember that instruments are not deemed reliable and/or valid. Rather, authors demonstrate evidence for reliability and validity and make a judgment or interpretation based on the estimates and evidence presented.

Beyond reliability and validity, a suitable instrument is sensitive to change (Lambert & Hawkins, 2004; Sederer et al., 1997). For example, the Youth Outcome Questionnaire—SR 2.0 (Wells, Burlingame, & Rose, 1999) is a self-report inventory designed to measure treatment progress over time for adolescents (ages 12 to 18) receiving mental health services. As such, when clients make progress in counseling, a well-designed instrument should be able to detect such change, even if the change is somewhat limited. A well-designed instrument will also demonstrate variability between different client groups. For example, the Beck Depression Inventory—II (BDI-II; Beck, Steer, & Brown, 1996) differentiates between minimal, mild, moderate, and severe ranges of depression. So, sensitivity to change may refer to change over time or change in the extent to which clients may be classified or diagnosed. Instruments that lack sensitivity to change may be limited by broad ranges of categories or ineffective in demonstrating accountability.

The appropriateness of an assessment instrument also is determined by the qualifications/training of the counselor using the assessment instrument.

> Counselors utilize only those testing and assessment services for which they have been trained and are competent. . . . Counselors responsible for decisions involving individuals or policies that are based on assessment results have a thorough understanding of educational, psychological, and career measurement, including validation criteria, assessment research, and guidelines for assessment development and use. (ACA, 2005, p. 12)

However, the ethics and legality of the use of assessment instruments by counselors is also determined by test publishers and state counselor licensure laws. There are no uniform guidelines, and differences exist depending on where the instrument is published and the state in which the counselor practices.

Generally, publishing companies for assessment instruments ask for proof of training to verify qualification to use an assessment instrument. Publishing companies often print this information in their catalogues and Web sites. Counselors should consider their qualifications before purchasing or using an assessment instrument. As a general rule, publishing companies list three types of qualifications:

Level A: This level includes instruments in which there is no specific training necessary to purchase the instrument.

Level B: Some test companies may require test users to have a 4-year degree and specific related training to use an assessment. Other companies may require a master's degree and/or specific training with an instrument. In addition, membership to a professional organization or certification/licensure may be required. Appropriate training usually includes course work in assessment ethics, administration, scoring, and interpreting of assessment instruments. Generally, counseling students graduating with a Council for Accreditation of Counseling and Related Educational Programs (CACREP) accredited master's degree in counseling qualify as Level B.

Level C: To accommodate for master's-level psychologists who may not be licensed in some states, Level C often refers to folks with Level B training plus licensure or certification and a doctoral degree with formal training in assessment procedures. Some companies will accept specialized training in lieu of a doctorate. In addition, a doctoral degree does not guarantee Level C qualifications. Many instruments require specialized training that is not necessarily provided in a doctoral degree (e.g., intelligence tests such as the Wechsler Intelligence Scales and diagnostic instruments such as the Minnesota Multiphasic Personality Inventory—II [MMPI-II]).

Once a counselor decides to use an assessment instrument, the counselor becomes responsible for the delivery of assessment services, including a report and an explanation to the client related to the findings and the decisions made based on the assessment results and the recommendations. "Counselors are responsible for the appropriate application, scoring, interpretation, and use of assessment instruments relevant to the needs of the client, whether they score and interpret such assessments themselves or use technology or other services" (ACA, 2005, p. 12).

Counselors who practice in assessment may receive referrals from other counselors or mental health practitioners (e.g., physicians, social workers) for assessment services. Most often counselors will develop a report related to a clinical interview, selected assessments administered with a rationale for each instrument, and a report of the findings, including standard scores, interpretations, and recommendations. That a client is referred only for assessment services does not relieve the counselor of the responsibility to discuss assessment results and implications with the referred client.

When selecting an assessment instrument, counselors should be aware of issues of bias. Most assessment instruments normed on a sample may lack representation from diverse groups. Assessments deemed reliable and valid may only be so for a particular group in which the assessment was normed and not across all populations (Sedlacek,

2004). In general, the idea that a measure can be developed and be fair for all groups is misguided (Sedlacek, 1994). Counselors should be wary of using assessment instruments with culturally diverse clients if no norming data is available for the group (ACA, 2005). Indeed, culture can be a factor that affects the problems clients manifest and how they cope. Thus, when using assessment to diagnose, label, or develop a treatment plan for a client, counselors should be aware of the cultural implications related to the assessment process. For example, the *Diagnostic Statistical Manual* (4th ed., text rev.; DSM-IV-TR; American Psychiatric Association, 2000) outlines symptoms of depression to include irritability and inattentiveness, which are typical for adolescent males. Thus, counselors may miss this detail and misdiagnose a client as oppositional-defiant disorder, as opposed to a depressive disorder. A culturally sensitive counselor will take the client's culture into account when engaging in the assessment process.

Counselors also need to be aware of how instruments are scored and interpreted. Many instruments may be scored by hand. However, hand scoring can be cumbersome for some complex instruments, and computer-based scoring is available. However, counselors sometimes opt out of using computer-based scoring because of cost. At other times, however, computer-based scoring is the only scoring available. One benefit of computer-based scoring is that counselors have the ability to obtain interpretive reports. Although interpretive reports can be helpful in conceptualizing the results, counselors should use such results with extreme caution. Obviously, computerized results rely solely on the scores of the instrument. The assessment instrument, however, is merely one tool. Without the benefits of a clinical interview, other assessment tools/ strategies, or previous counseling history, a computerized assessment report is lacking. Regardless if administration and interpretation services are used, the counselor assumes full responsibility for the administration, scoring, and interpretation of the assessment instrument (ACA, 2005). For this reason, counselors should scrutinize computer-based interpretative results very carefully and use only the results that fit the particular aspects of the client.

REVIEWING ASSESSMENT INSTRUMENTS

Because of the ethical and legal implications for using assessment instruments, careful consideration of the properties of an instrument is important. Hence, counselors not only have to be aware of ethical and legal considerations of assessment, but also the importance of the psychometric characteristics identified in an instrument. Using instruments that are weak in terms of psychometric quality can lead to serious consequences. Consider Golding's (1985) critique of the Suicide Probability Scale (SPS) in which 70.8% of potential attemptors were misclassified as nonsuicidal and 76.9% of nonattemptors were misclassified as suicidal. In a nonclinical population, 41.5% of nonattemptors were misclassified as suicidal. Extant research related to the SPS continues to be limited and the instrument tends to be highly regarded (Eltz et al., 2007). As an assessment instrument designed to provide insight as to whether a client may be a danger to self or others, decisions based on this instrument could be disastrous. Not only should counselors be able to properly review an assessment instrument in order to be an informed consumer, but counselors should also be reminded of the limitations of assessment instruments in general and never base decisions solely on the results of a single instrument. In the effort to inform counselors on reviewing assessment instruments, two databases are covered: the

Mental Measurements Yearbook (MMY) and test critiques from the Association for Assessment and Research in Counseling (AARC), formerly the Association for Assessment in Counseling and Education (AACE).

Details of a Mental Measurements Review

The Buros Institute of Mental Measurements (BIMM) publishes the MMY. Currently, there are 18 volumes of the MMY. Not all instruments are evaluated in each volume. Rather, each volume contains selected measures for an evaluation. For a comprehensive list of all known published assessment instruments, counselors should use *Tests in Print*, which is also published by BIMM. *Tests in Print* contains bibliographic information on a published measure and the volume of MMY that a review may be found. Not all instruments listed in *Test in Print* have a review in MMY. To determine if an assessment instrument was reviewed in MMY, a free Web site is available at http://buros.unl.edu/buros/jsp/search.jsp. Although this Web site will provide information related to the status of a review, users will need to either locate the review using a library database, use a hard copy of MMY, or purchase the review from BIMM.

MMY reviews are usually conducted by two independent reviewers with terminal degrees (i.e., Ph.D., Psy.D., Ed.D.) and have no conflict of interest in the test review. Each review goes through an editorial process before it is accepted, and reviews may be rejected. BIMM identified the purpose of test reviews: (a) to inform test users, (b) to encourage the development of instruments with strong psychometric properties and discourage the use of instruments with poor quality, and (c) to encourage test publishers to fully disclose the strengths, limitations, and possible misuses of assessment instruments (Buros Institute of Mental Measurements, 2010).

A test review from MMY consists of a 1000- to 1500- word document covering five areas: (a) description, (b) development, (c) technical, (d) commentary, and (e) summary. The beginning of each test review includes basic information of the test including test name, test publisher, type of scores yielded from administration, a brief statement of purpose, the intended population, the test acronym, type of administration (i.e., group or individual), instrument pricing, time to administer the instrument, and authorship. The Buros Institute of Mental Measurements (2010) covers the guidelines for test reviews.

Under the test description, the purpose and intended population are covered in a brief narrative. In addition, reviews will include information on test administration, scoring, and intended use of the scores. Usually a more in-depth review of the purpose and use of the scores are provided. Reviews also provide information on the procedures to administer and score the instrument. Many reviews also expand on the intended population and indicate where bias may occur and any inappropriate uses of the instrument. For example, Sandoval's (2007) review of the Draw-A-Person Intellectual Ability Test for Children, Adolescents, and Adults noted that the instrument might be inappropriate for individuals with visual or motor impairments. Such limitations are important to consider when deciding to use an assessment instrument. Other important considerations include reading level of the instrument, assuming the instrument is self-report, and the client's mastery of the language in which the instrument is administered.

A section on test development includes information on underlying theories or operational definitions of the construct measured that led to the origination or evolution of the instrument. Counselors should pay particular attention to both the theoretical underpinnings and the manner in which the construct is operationally defined. For example, the

Myers-Briggs Personality Type Indicator (MBTI) is a popular personality instrument used in educational, clinical, career, and industrial settings. The instrument evolved from the personality theory of Carl Jung (Fleenor, 2001). Counselors not familiar with Jung's theory of psychological types may see minimal benefit to using this instrument. Recall that an operational definition is essential to measuring any construct. Be aware of the how the construct is being defined for the purposes of the instrument. Such information is important to discern how the findings may be used. For example, professional athletes may be described as brilliant by the way they compete, but would this type of ability translate to scores on an achievement test? Operational definitions provide a clear purpose for what is being measured, but also limit the use of the instrument to a specifically defined objective.

The technical section of an MMY review includes information on the process of standardization and the psychometric properties of the instrument. Specifically, information on the norm group is mentioned. Counselors should have an understanding of the age, gender, and cultural characteristics of the sample from which the instrument was normed. An instrument may be limited as a cross-cultural tool if variances in ethnicity, gender, disability status, and so forth were not considered. Often, strengths and limitations of the sample, specifically related to gender and ethnic differences, are identified or noted.

Psychometric considerations in the technical section include statements about the evidence of reliability and validity of the scores in the normative sample and the instrument. Counselors should keep in mind how the instrument is administered and scored when assessing reliability. For example, if the instrument is a behavioral rating scale completed by the counselor, parent, teacher, and so forth, a statement about interrater reliability of the scores in the normative sample is appropriate. Self-report inventories often include test–retest reliability on the scores of the normative sample. Tests with multiple forms, such as aptitude and achievement tests used in educational settings, should include an assessment of parallel forms to demonstrate that each version of an instrument is similar in terms of consistency. Most instruments also have a measure of internal consistency, noted by Cronbach's alpha (often referred to as coefficient alpha). Expect that each measure of reliability to be separate and distinct from other reliability measures, but a good instrument will have strong reliability coefficients from scores on the normative sample. Often, reviewers will provide comments on reliability estimates. For example, reliability estimates for measuring psychotic symptoms in clients tend to be low across most existing instruments. Thus, coefficients in the range of .50 are fairly typical.

With respect to reporting validity, reviewers in the MMY generally focus on the evidence that is presented in testing manuals to determine the degree to which an instrument measures what it is purported to measure. If, for example, an instrument is designed to diagnose or classify individuals or groups, then evidence related to this outcome must be presented. Generally, authors do not provide evidence of all aspects of validity as noted in the *Standards for Educational and Psychological Testing* (AERA et al., 1999). Rather, focus is on displaying evidence that indicates the measure provides meaningful information as outlined in the purpose of the instrument and the operational definition of the construct.

Based on the evidence presented in the above sections, reviewers provide a summary of strengths and weaknesses of the instrument in the commentary section. Information related to the theoretical underpinnings of the instrument and the extent to which the theory is tested is presented. The reviewer may also include a statement related to the consequences (either positive or negative) of using this instrument.

A brief summary section completes an MMY review. This section includes conclusions and recommendations of the test reviewer. Explicit statements from the reviewer related to recommendations or problem areas of the instrument are common to MMY reviews. At times, reviewers may include alternative assessments that they recommend in lieu of the instrument reviewed. Although counselors should pay particular attention to the summary section, the review should be considered holistically. Attention to how the summary is or is not congruent with the evidence presented in the review should be evaluated. Taken as a whole, the MMY review is an important resource for counselors considering using an assessment instrument, as the reviews in MMY tend to be professional and free of bias.

AARC Critiques

Test reviews from the Association for Assessment and Research in Counseling (AARC), formerly AACE, are available to the public from the AACE Web site: http://www.theaaceonline.com/. Although many of the tests reviewed on the AARC Web site are also reviewed by BIMM, the reviews in the MMY are from tests that are available only through test publishers. AARC test reviews may fall into the category of academic assessments and not be available through national test publishers. For example, at the time the Five Factor Wellness Inventory was reviewed by AACE in 2006, MMY had not reviewed the instrument. A review in MMY appeared in the 17th edition (2007). Thus, in addition to more established instruments, AARC may review instruments that are more avant-garde.

An AARC test review will be comprised of five main areas: (a) general information, (b) purpose and nature of instrument, (c) practical evaluation, (d) technical considerations, and (e) evaluation. Much of the information in these areas is similar to the information in an MMY review. General information includes similar information in the beginning of an MMY review, including (a) title; (b) author; (c) publisher (if available); (d) date of publication (if available); (e) forms specific to various administration or populations (e.g., child, adolescent, or adult versions); (f) practical features; (g) general type—related to how the instrument is administered (e.g., self-report, rating scale); (h) cost of the instrument, forms, manuals, and so forth; (h) time required to administer; and (i) purpose of the instrument. Keep in mind the importance of the general information. A brief review of the general information provides counselors with purpose, cost, and contact information of the publisher should the counselor wish to find more information or purchase the instrument. From the general information, counselors can determine if the instrument is appropriate, cost-effective, and usable in their practice.

The section on purpose and nature of the instrument provides a more in-depth review of how the instrument is used. Beyond the stated purpose of the instrument in the previous section, this section provides information on test, item, and score descriptions. The types of items, a description of tasks to complete the instrument, and the nature of the scores are elucidated upon. Reviews often include information on the type and number of subscales, the types of scores, and how the scores are interpreted. Unlike the MMY, which is geared toward general assessment practitioners, this section will also include specific information of the instrument relevant to counseling. Counselors may garner an understanding of how the instrument may be useful in clinical, academic, and vocational settings.

The practical evaluation covers information relevant to administering and scoring the instrument, including usefulness of the manual, adequacy of directions, qualifications of the examiner, and scoring provisions. The technical manual of an instrument often includes information about the psychometric qualities of the instrument and, without advanced course work in psychometrics, may be difficult to understand. So, the practical evaluation may be helpful for practitioners in highlighting useful aspects of the manual that relate to administration, scoring, and interpretation. Often, the adequacy of the instructions is highlighted in this section, providing counselors with insight into the ease of administration. A statement regarding the qualifications of the examiner is provided, so counselors are aware of the degree to which their training prepares them to administer, score, and interpret the instrument. Scoring provisions are also covered, providing an overview of how the instrument is scored. For example, some instruments cannot be hand scored because the scoring is not made available. Thus, extra cost may be incurred to score the instrument or use computer-based administration and/or scoring services. Although many instruments can be hand scored, such scoring can be timely and complex. Counselors often purchase computer-based scoring methods to save time and assist with interpretation.

The technical considerations in an AARC review are similar to the content of what is seen in an MMY review: (a) normative sample, (b) reliability, and (c) validity. Again, statements about the norming process, including descriptive information about the population, are provided. The evidence pertaining to reliability and validity is presented, so counselors can ascertain the degree to which the instrument measures what is implied in a consistent and accurate manner.

The evaluation section of an AARC review includes (a) comments of reviewers and (b) a general evaluation. In the event that the instrument is recently developed, no published reviews may be available. Otherwise, sources are cited, such as reviews from MMY. The general evaluation includes comments from the reviewer based on the data and information presented. A critique is provided and an opinion may be rendered about the instrument. AARC reviews provide statements about the efficacy and application of the instrument to assessment practice.

UNDERSTANDING THE TECHNICAL QUALITY OF AN INSTRUMENT

As mentioned before, technical manuals may be complex to counselors who do not have advanced training in psychometrics. In this section, information related to understanding the technical quality of an instrument is provided. As noted by the discussion of MMY and AARC reviews, evidence related to representativeness of the normative sample, reliability, and validity are essential in evaluating the technical quality of an instrument.

Evaluating the Normative Sample

Before deciding to use an assessment instrument, counselors should consider the population used to develop the instrument. In other words, does the client or clients being administered this assessment fit into the normative group of the sample? For example, Beck et al. (1996) stated that the BDI-II is appropriate for measuring the severity of depression for adolescents and adults 13 years old and above. Whether the BDI-II is truly a valid measure for this large age range is dependent on sampling groups used in developing the instrument. Beck et al. indicated in the BDI-II Manual that two outpatient samples were used. The first sample was a sample of 500 outpatients from four different outpatient clinics. Clients who were administered the BDI-II ranged from 13 to 86 years old with a mean age of 37.20 (*SD* = 15.91). Ninety-one percent of the sample was identified as White with the remaining 9% being African American, Asian American, and Latino/a. The second sample consisted of 120 college students from Canada with a mean age of 19.58 (*SD* = 1.84).

Based on this sample description, counselors may have difficulty discerning whether the BDI-II is appropriate for their practice. Clearly, the majority of participants were adults over the age of 18. So, without knowing how many adolescents received the BDI-II, evidence for the appropriateness of the BDI-II with clients as young as 13 years old is limited. In addition, data related to minority responses on the BDI-II are also limited. Counselors may wish to examine research articles in which the BDI-II was used with minority participants to evaluate the appropriateness of the instrument across non-White clients. Endorsement of depressive symptoms may differ across various ethnic groups. However, Carmody (2005) administered the BDI-II to 502 college students, 41% of which were ethnic minority students. Carmody concluded that the BDI-II is appropriate as a measure of depression for students of diverse ethnicity. Numerous psychometric instruments are normed using a college student population. Limitations related to the over-reliance of this demographic should be noted to avoid overgeneralizing results for a client that are based on a normed sample that has little in common with the client. In addition to the technical manuals, tests reviews usually include this information, so counselors can easily ascertain whether the instrument is appropriate for a specific client or client population. Although test manuals may not be all-inclusive with respect to the development of the test and the normative sample, research using well-established instruments is quite common. Counselors should actively seek out articles about an instrument when a gap in the development is apparent in order to determine if the gap was addressed.

Evaluating Reliability Evidence of an Instrument

When evaluating reliability, consider the type of reliability reported and the magnitude of the coefficients. Reliability coefficients range from 0 to 1, with coefficients from .70 and above considered as adequate evidence for measuring accuracy and consistency of an instrument. Reliability coefficients should be interpreted. Keep in mind the types of reliability you expect to see in a study. The most common reliability coefficient reported is internal consistency, often reported as Cronbach's alpha or coefficient alpha. This reliability coefficient is easily computed with statistical software and is used to demonstrate that the scale meets a standard of measuring a construct consistently using multiple items. Larger sample sizes are needed to demonstrate internal consistency.

If an instrument has different forms, such as in many aptitude and achievement tests (e.g., SAT, ACT, GRE, NCE), then evidence indicating consistency over different administrations of the instrument is important. Strong reliability coefficients, in this case a positive correlation between the alternate forms (e.g., $r = .80$), are expected.

Recall that authors of instruments may also provide evidence of stability over time through test–retest. Essentially, a strong correlation (i.e., .70 or above) is expected when an assessment is administered and then administered again a short time later. For example, Beck et al. (1996) reported the BDI-II has a test–retest reliability coefficient of .93, indicating a very strong relationship between an administration of the BDI-II and a second administration 1 week later. When evaluating test–retest reliability, consider how much time lapsed between administrations. Also, understand that not all instruments may be evaluated for test–retest reliability, particularly instruments that are time sensitive.

Interrater reliability can be an important consideration for instruments that use a rating scale. Essentially, test developers want to establish a high correlation among practitioners who use the instrument. Thus, if two counselors are using a behavior rating scale to evaluate a child, an instrument with high interrater reliability will show similarity between the scores of the counselors. As with other measures of reliability, this could be ascertained through examining correlation coefficients. In this case, however, rating scales completed by multiple examiners would be correlated.

In summary, interpreting reliability is an important consideration. When reliability coefficients fall below .70, that does not mean the instrument should not be used. Rather, counselors should keep in mind what scales are prone to low reliability estimates and be careful to evaluate the client in these areas. Essentially, counselors need to ask, "Are these the scores I expect for this client?" If the answer is "no," then the counselor needs to consider whether the score is reliable, the administration is valid, or the assessment instrument is providing new information about the client not previously considered. Keep in mind not all constructs can be measured with a high level of accuracy and consistency. Psychosis is one construct that has low reliability across many different measures.

Evaluating Validity Evidence of an Instrument

As mentioned previously, rarely will all five evidences of validity (evidence of test content, response process, internal structure, relations to other variables, and consequences of testing) be discussed in a technical manual. In addition, the statistical methods used are usually quite sophisticated, which may make counselors without advanced knowledge of psychometrics and statistics feel inadequate about interpreting such information. One point to keep in mind is that nearly all of these procedures are correlational in nature. Specifically, authors of instruments tend to demonstrate five criteria:

1. There is a theoretical framework that guided the development of this instrument (evidence of test content). When reviewing the technical manual or instrument reviews, the theory driving the development of the items should be clearly explained. The author(s) identify how the tasks involved in the assessment instrument measure the intended construct.
2. The authors attempt to demonstrate that the instrument measures the theoretical structure by examining the intercorrelations of items. When an instrument has separate subscales, such as the MMPI-II or the Behavior Assessment System for Children (BASC), then some demonstration of how the items correlate on the subscale is in order. This is usually done through factor analysis, in which the extent of how each item loads on each subscale is reported. Generally, factor loadings of .40 for each item on a subscale are considered adequate. Sometimes we will see an item load on more than one subscale of the instrument, and then the author needs to justify the rationale for placing a particular item with a selected subscale. When this type of evidence is not reported, an instrument is likely suspect in terms of validity. Such analyses require large sample sizes, usually 5 to 10 participants per item.
3. The authors evaluate the relationship between the instrument and another instrument(s) that measures the same or similar construct. Once again, this is demonstrated through the use of correlations, in which each participant is administered

two assessment instruments and the results between the instruments are correlated. Higher correlations demonstrate stronger convergent evidence, or that both instruments are measuring the same intended construct.

4. The authors evaluated the relationship between the instrument and another instrument(s) that measures a different construct. In other words, evidence is provided that the instrument is measuring a similar, yet separate construct. For example, in the development of the BDI-II, Beck et al. (1996) demonstrated discriminant evidence with the Beck Anxiety Inventory (BAI). As both depression and anxiety are related, a moderate correlation between scores on the BDI-II and the BAI might be expected. In this case, the BDI-II was moderately correlated to the BAI ($r = .60$). Thus, the BDI-II is measuring a similar yet separate and distinct construct, as the BAI.

5. Evidence related to the consequences of testing may be difficult to demonstrate. Extant literature is limited in terms of how to demonstrate such evidence (Goodwin & Leech, 2003). However, some acknowledgement of the strengths and limitations of the assessment tool is appropriate.

Although the *Standards for Educational and Psychological Testing* (1999) are explicit in terms of the types of evidence for validity, many authors who developed instruments prior to 1999 and revised after 1999 do not comply with these standards. Counselors should evaluate the type of validity evidence provided to ascertain the appropriateness of a selected assessment tool.

UNDERSTANDING FACTORS THAT MAY AFFECT PERFORMANCE

Even if an instrument is deemed to have strong evidence of reliability and validity, external factors may influence the performance of a client on a particular measure. Assessment may be bound by time and context. In other words, an underlying assumption in the assessment process is that the performance measured at a particular moment in time is representative of how the individual would perform generally. However, this is not always the case. An otherwise high-achieving student who takes the SAT when sick with a 102° fever, may have an uncharacteristically poor performance on a rather high-stakes exam. The same problems could occur when administering other types of psychosocial instruments, such as measuring anxiety when a client has a particularly good or trying day.

Testing conditions can also be a factor. Clients often receive several instruments at one time, resulting in test fatigue. Instruments administered at the beginning of the sequence may be more accurate in measuring the desired construct than instruments at the end of the sequence. The opposite may also be true. The client could be less defensive at the end of the process than at the beginning. In addition, consider the environment in which the test is administered. Is the environment suitable for an extended period of time to complete an assessment procedure?

The client's ability to complete the tasks is an important factor to consider. Does the client possess the reading ability to understand the instructions and items? If the instrument is timed, does accommodation need to be provided? Are there any interpersonal factors (e.g., disability, medical condition) that interfere with the administration or completion of the assessment? Again, ongoing research on specific assessment instruments is often available, and counselors may need to consult the literature to identify the conditions of accommodation and alternate interpretations.

FACTORS IN CRITERION-REFERENCED TESTS: THE ITEM ANALYSIS

So far, the examples and issues identified in selecting and administering assessments revolve around norm-referenced tests. However, counselors should be aware of issues related to criterion-referenced tests. Recall that criterion-referenced tests are based on a score against preestablished criteria. Therefore, most exams in academic settings fall into this category. When a student earns 85% on an exam, the score is interpreted as the student correctly answered 85% of the material. School counselors, especially, can serve as important resources for faculty, as criterion-referenced tests are used extensively to determine grades.

When criterion-referenced tests are used, attention to item development is essential. We advocate that users of criterion-referenced tests conduct an *item analysis*. Two prominent issues related to an item analysis include item difficulty and item discrimination.

Item Difficulty

Item difficulty is simply the proportion of students who correctly answered the item. For each item on an exam, the proportion of students who got the item correct is calculated. Therefore, item difficulty ranges from 0.0 to 1.00, with 0.0 referring to an item that no one got correct and 1.00 referring to an item that all participants answered correctly. The formula for item difficulty can be expressed as follows:

$$P = \frac{\#\,of\,correct\,responses}{total\,\#\,of\,responses}$$

where P is the proportion of correct responses, the numerator is the number of respondents who correctly answered the item, and the denominator is the total number of respondents. Easy items are closer to 1.00; more difficult items are closer to 0.0.

Item Discrimination

Item discrimination is useful in determining the extent to which an item differentiates different levels of mastery. For example, a teacher would expect that a student who has proficiency over material will be able to answer more items correctly than a student who lacks proficiency. Not only will some items be more difficult, but students who have more knowledge of the material should be able to answer more difficult items, and students with less mastery of material may have more difficulty answering items correctly. Simply because few students answer an item correctly does not necessarily mean the item is bad, especially if the item was answered correctly by the top students. In other words, an item can discriminate between those students who have a solid understanding of material versus those who do not.

To evaluate item discrimination, participants should be divided into three groups: the upper 27% of scores, the middle 46% of scores, and the lower 27% of scores. For the purposes of calculating item discrimination, only the upper and lower groups are used. Item discrimination indices only use 54% of the participants. Similar to item difficulty, item discrimination indices need to be calculated for each item:

D = (% of the upper group who correctly answered the item)
　　− (% of the lower group who correctly answered the item)

So, if 80% of the upper group answered an item correctly and 20% of the lower group answered the same item correctly, the discrimination index would be .80 − .60 = .40.

Item discrimination indices may range from −1.00 to +1.00. When an item perfectly discriminates (+1.00), that means everyone in the upper group answered the item correctly and everyone in the lower group answered the item incorrectly. Thus, even if the difficulty index was low, the item may still be valid, as the item helps differentiate those with more advanced knowledge with respect to this item. However, when item discrimination is low (e.g., .20), the item discriminates poorly. The closer the index is to 0.0, the less the item discriminates, and equal numbers of participants in the upper and lower groups are answering the item incorrectly. This might indicate an item in which the material was not taught well or covered adequately. Items in this category may not be good items, and removal should be considered. When an item discrimination index is negative, more people who are in the lower group (i.e., participants with lower scores) answered the item correctly than those in the upper group did. This often occurs with poorly worded items or a result of guessing on the answer. Items with negative discrimination indices should be removed.

For criterion-referenced tests, item analyses are essential in determining the appropriateness of the questions. A limitation to item discrimination indices is that 46% of the participants are not included in the analysis. Counselors should carefully evaluate items on the basis of difficulty and discrimination, as neither measure should stand alone. School counselors may also be a valuable resource in teaching faculty to use item analysis in order to improve test administration.

REVIEW OF ASSESSMENTS IN THIS TEXT

Many of the instruments referenced this text may be reviewed in MMY, and some of them can be found on the AARC Web site. In general, the instruments are widely established as assessment tools for measuring constructs of interest in counseling.

In our case examples throughout the text, we provide an overview of assessments that may be used with clients, such as assessments related to intelligence and ability, career, personality, substance abuse, and so forth. Keep in mind that instruments designed to measure constructs across numerous age groups throughout the lifespan may not always be appropriate. Considering the developmental gap that is covered between early adolescence to older adulthood, instruments that claim to be geared toward such a vast age range likely fall short in terms of normative sampling procedures unless careful, representative sampling methods were used, which is often the case with intelligence tests. Careful thought should go into what assessments are appropriate for a given population.

References

American Counseling Association. (2005). *ACA code of ethics.* Alexandria, VA: Author.

American Educational Research Association, American Psychological Association, & National Council of Measurement in Education (1999). *Standards for educational and psychological testing.* Washington, DC: American Educational Research Association.

American Psychiatric Association. (2000). *Diagnostic and statistical manual of mental disorders* (4th ed., text rev.). Washington, DC: Author.

Beck, A. T., Steer, R. A., & Brown, G. K. (1996). *BDI-II manual*. San Antonio, TX: The Psychological Corporation.

Buros Institute of Mental Measurements. (2010, June 6). *Becoming a reviewer for the mental measurements yearbook*. Retrieved June 6, 2010, from http://www.unl.edu/buros/bimm/pdf/07Reviewer Brochure.pdf

Buros Institute of Mental Measurements. (2010, June 6). *Organization of test reviews for the mental measurements yearbook series*. Retrieved June 6, 2010, from http://www.unl.edu/buros/bimm/html/revieworg.html

Carmody, D. (2005). Psychometric characteristics of the Beck Depression Inventory-II with college students of diverse ethnicity. *International Journal of Psychiatry in Clinical Practice*, 9, 22–28. doi:10.1080/13651500510014800

Eltz, M., Evans, A., Celio, M., Dyl, J., Hunt, J., Armstrong, L., et al. (2007). Suicide Probability Scale and its utility with adolescent psychiatric patients. *Child Psychiatry & Human Development*, 38, 17–29. doi:10.1007/s10578-006-0040-7

Fleenor, J. W. (2001). [Review of the Myers-Briggs Type Indicator, Form M]. In B. S. Plake & J. C. Impara (Eds.), *The fourteenth mental measurements yearbook* (pp. 1033–1038). Lincoln, NE: Buros Institute of Mental Measurements.

Geisinger, K. F., Spies, R. A., Carlson, J. F. & Plake, B. S. (2007). *The seventeenth mental measurements yearbook*. Lincoln, NE: Buros Institute of Mental Measurements.

George, L. K. (1997). Choosing among established assessment tools: Scientific demands and practical constraints. *Generations*, 21, 32–36.

Golding, S. L. (1985). [Review of the Suicide Probability Scale]. In J. V. Mitchell, Jr. (Ed.), *The ninth mental measurements yearbook*. Lincoln, NE: Buros Institute of Mental Measurements.

Goodwin, L. D., & Leech, N. L. (2003). The meaning of validity in the new *Standards for Educational and Psychological Testing: Implications for measurement courses. Measurement and Evaluation in Counseling and Development*, 36, 181–191.

Lambert, M. J., & Hawkins, E. J. (2004). Measuring outcome in professional practice: Considerations in selecting and using brief outcome instruments. *Professional Psychology: Research and Practice*, 35, 492–499.

Sandoval, J. (2007). [Review of the Draw-A-Person Intellectual Ability Test for Children, Adolescents, and Adults]. In K. F. Geisinger, R. A. Spies, J. F. Carlson, & B. S. Plake (Eds.), *The seventeenth mental measurements yearbook* (pp. 498–502). Lincoln, NE: Buros Institute of Mental Measurements.

Sederer, L. I., Dickey, B., & Eisen, S. V. (1997). Assessing outcomes in clinical practice. *Psychiatric Quarterly*, 68, 311–325.

Sedlacek, W. E. (1994). Issues in advancing diversity through assessment. *Journal of Counseling & Development*, 72, 549–553.

Sedlacek, W. E. (2004). *Beyond the big test: Noncognitive assessment in higher education*. San Francisco, CA: Jossey-Bass.

Wells, M. G., Burlingame, G. M., & Rose, P. M. (2003). *Administration and scoring manual for the Y-OQ-SR 2.0 (self-report version of the Youth Outcome Questionnaire)*. Salt Lake City, UT: American Professional Credentialing Services LLC.

CHAPTER 7

Conducting an Initial Interview

OBJECTIVES

After reading this chapter, you will be able to:

1. Identify the purpose and scope of the clinical interview.
2. Address the advantages of using structured interview approaches versus unstructured interviews.
3. Identify the elements of the CLISD-PA Model (Juhnke, 2002).
4. Identify essential elements of the clinical interview.
5. Examine specific areas of interest related to substance abuse.
6. Apply the concepts of the clinical interview to the case study and various clinical settings.

PURPOSES OF THE INITIAL INTERVIEW

Previous chapters emphasized the standardized nature of assessment. In other words, the development and use of standardized assessment instruments quite often are regimented, with specific procedures in place to make sure that the assessment process is not compromised and accurate and meaningful information is conveyed. However, to describe the counseling process as regimented and standardized is inaccurate. Juhnke (2008) suggested assessment also implies a stochastic process, that is, understanding and preparing for random processes that occur throughout assessment in counseling. For example, the focus of this chapter is the clinical interview—a process of gathering relevant information about the client in order to conceptualize the client accurately, identify a treatment plan and/or therapeutic goals, and plan for appropriate interventions. However, the type of information disclosed by the client may change the direction of the clinical interview. In the midst of gathering such information, what happens if the client, say a 14-year-old female, identifies a past history of sexual abuse? Suddenly, the current process may be put on hold, as the present disclosure must be dealt with, including gathering different information, assessing client safety, and making a mandated report.

The clinical interview most likely presents the first time the counselor will be meeting with the client. Counseling skills are ingrained in the assessment process. Although accurate intake information is essential, so is the establishment of rapport and initiation of the counseling process. Counselors often enter into an initial session with a plan to obtain specific information related to the client's presenting problem and relevant history. The type of information sought by the counselor in the initial interview often follows a general procedure, but counselors should be aware of the stochastic nature of the assessment process (Juhnke, 2008), as issues may arise that move the counselor and client in a different direction than initially anticipated. Clients may even get frustrated if the counselor's preoccupation of a specific issue is not reflective of the client's goals or desire toward further processing. Counselors should keep an open mind to the type of information presented in the counseling process. Owen (2008) found that counselors are more likely to ask questions that confirm their initial impressions about a client as opposed to questions that might contradict or disaffirm such impressions. Thus, counselors should be proactive in asking questions that challenge their initial assumptions about a client in order to identify potential issues and rule out any differential diagnostic implications. For example, if a counselor believes an adolescent male has attention deficit disorder because of the presence of low frustration tolerance, impulsivity, and inattentiveness, the counselor should also make sure there are not additional indicators of unstable mood that could indicate a mood disorder.

SCOPE OF THE INITIAL INTERVIEW

The initial interview can broadly be categorized into two distinct areas: the psychosocial history and the mental status exam. The purpose of the psychosocial history is to identify relevant present issues and past history. Vacc and Juhnke (1997) advocated for using a structured interview format to encourage accuracy, consistency, and meaningfulness of the information gathered. Unstructured interviews may be the least trustworthy method of gathering information because of erratic questions and various methods of gathering information, which may cause response variance—a client answering a question differently based on the various ways the question may be asked. For example, a client may respond differently when asked, "How often do you drink?" versus, "How many drinks do you have in a given week?" In the first case, the client might respond, "I drink 1 to 2 times per week." In the latter case the client might respond, "Depending on what I am drinking, I usually drink until I feel drunk." Clearly the responses are different despite the similarities between the questions. As mentioned earlier, counselors tend to ask questions that confirm their initial impressions about a client (Owens, 2008), and this can lead to inappropriate decisions made on behalf of the client by the counselor. Counselors need to balance the stochastic nature of assessment (Juhnke, 2008) with the need to gather standard and pertinent information. According to the *Standards for Assessment in Mental Health Counseling* (2009):

> Mental health counselors use structured and semi-structured clinical interviews, and qualitative assessment procedures (e.g., role playing, life line assessments, direct and indirect observation). Mental health counselors are able to:
>
> 1. Define the differences and similarities between structured and semi-structured clinical interviews.

2. Describe the advantages and disadvantages of structured and semi-structured clinical interviews in practice.
3. Use both structured and semi-structured clinical interviews as a means to develop goal setting and treatment intervention plans.
4. Understand the advantages and disadvantages of qualitative assessment procedures.
5. Apply the concepts of continuous assessment and wraparound services. (Association for Assessment in Counseling and Education & American Mental Health Counselors Association, 2009, p. 1)

The clinical interview is the primary element that will lead both the counselor and the client to establishing the client problem areas, determining the need for additional assessments, and developing and implementing a treatment plan/counseling strategy. Juhnke (2002) developed a four-tiered system, referred to as the Clinical Interview, Standardized Specialty, Drug Detection, Personality Assessment (CLISD-PA) Model. The first two tiers of the CLISD-PA begin with a clinical interview of the client and significant other. Once the clinical interviews are concluded, additional questions or concerns may be evident. For example, perhaps after interviewing an adolescent and a parent, the counselor notes some inconsistencies between what the client self-disclosed and what the parent reported. Although a parent may report that the adolescent client is noncompliant and unruly, the adolescent client could report that the parent is rigid and unreasonable. At this point in time, additional data may be necessary.

Tier III of the CLISD-PA includes the administration of standardized specialty instruments and drug detection devices, which might be helpful in providing additional information about the client and how to weight the disclosures from the interviews. Standardized specialty instruments might include instruments that provide some additional information on a specified attribute, such as the Beck Depression Inventory-II (BDI-II), the Substance Abuse Subtle Scale Inventory—3 (SASSI-3), and the Reynolds Adolescent Adjustment Screening Inventory (RASSI). If during the clinical interview, the counselor identified no past history of depression and substance use but that the adolescent client recently experienced a drop in grades, appeared easily angered or frustrated, and lost interest in previously enjoyed activities, the counselor may opt to administer a BDI-II and the SASSI-A—the adolescent version of the SASSI-3. Such instruments may be helpful in assessing the nature of the behavioral change in the client. If the client revealed on the SASSI-A that he/she is using substances, then additional drug detection tests may be warranted, especially if the client is not forthcoming.

Tier IV includes the administration of personality assessments, such as the Minnesota Multiphasic Personality Inventory-II (MMPI-II), and the Millon Multiaxial Clinical Inventory—III. Such instruments may be helpful in identifying Axis I and Axis II disorders, respectively. Often these instruments include child and/or adolescent versions. These instruments also provide insight into personality and character traits. Such instruments can be time-consuming and expensive. Many of these instruments require specialized training or advanced course work/degrees (i.e., Ph.D.). However, when counselors require more information about a client because of the client's divergent behavior or cognitive processes, or when the clinical interview and subsequent measures have not yielded a helpful or conclusive conceptualization of the client, personality assessments can be a valuable tool.

Essential Elements of a Psychosocial History

As evidenced from the CLISD-PA Model (Juhnke, 2002), the initial session is a comprehensive process. Initial sessions, in fact, may be longer than a typical 50-minute counseling session, so counselors should plan accordingly. As mentioned previously, the clinical interview sets the stage for identifying presenting problems, obtaining relevant history, and determining if further assessment procedures are warranted. With this in mind, we turn our attention to gathering a psychosocial history. These elements include the following: (a) presenting problem, (b) relevant history, (c) mental status, (d) medical history, (e) family history/issues, (f) social support, (g) educational/occupational/economic issues, and (h) cultural/spiritual concerns.

PRESENTING PROBLEM   Consider how the initiation of the counseling relationship begins. Clients may complete a standard intake form, complete with insurance information and statements about the Health Insurance Portability and Accountability Act of 1996 (HIPAA) and confidentiality. A counselor may begin with a brief introduction and a restatement about confidentiality and safety for the client. At this point, the client may be asked any number of questions to begin the process, such as "What brings you here today?" The possibilities of opening the session to begin a dialogue with the client are endless, and so the counselor must choose his or her words carefully and consider what questions will assist the client in presenting the nature of why they are seeking services, as well as fit the counselor's theoretical orientation. The nature of the presenting problem will likely guide treatment planning, therapeutic goals, and outcomes of counseling, in addition to providing justification for a diagnosis should one be necessary. Counselors should consider various methods that present the opportunity to identify and differentiate the presenting problem the client presents. Presenting problems often are identified on Axis I or II for the *Diagnostic Statistical Manual* (4th ed., text rev.; DSM-IV-TR) multiaxial system (American Psychiatric Association, 2000).

RELEVANT HISTORY   Although the role of past events may be weighted differently depending on the counselor's theoretical orientation, an understanding of how past events relate to present distress is pertinent, as well obtaining an accurate history of past counseling experiences. Discussion of past experiences in counseling may shed light on issues important to the client and past approaches to counseling that led to more or less meaningful experiences in the counseling process. In addition, counselors should be aware of informed consent processes in order to obtain documents from the client's counseling history.

MENTAL STATUS EXAM   The mental status examination (MSE) is a component of the initial interview that provides information related to client functioning. The MSE can be instrumental in identifying baseline status of the client, diagnosing, treatment planning, and justifying intervention to stakeholders and third-party payors. The MSE is a combination of objective and subjective data, based on the counselor's observations and information provided by the client (Polanski & Hinkle, 2000). Six elements are considered when assessing mental status: (a) appearance, attitude, and activity; (b) mood and affect; (c) speech and language; (d) thought process, thought content, and perception; (e) cognition; and (f) insight and judgment. These elements will be addressed more specifically later in the chapter.

MEDICAL HISTORY Medical history may be relevant when dealing with a multitude of disorders such as depression, addiction, and disordered eating. From a diagnostic perspective, counselors need to be careful when medical issues are disclosed. Medical issues may preclude the diagnosis of many psychiatric disorders, and therefore need to be considered in the assessment process. Not only should medical issues be addressed as part of the psychosocial history, but medical issues are also identified on Axis III of a multiaxial diagnosis (American Psychiatric Association, 2000).

FAMILY HISTORY/ISSUES Depending on the counselor's view of family interventions and systems theory (i.e., couples, marriage, and family counseling) and the client's presentation, family issues may be the primary presenting problem when a client initiates counseling. Family issues may pertain to significant events, such as divorce or death, as well as ongoing conflicts and sources of dysfunction (e.g., addiction, infidelity). Counselors practicing couples, marriage, and family counseling should be able to "conduct structured clinical interviews, obtain an accurate biopsychosocial history and assess intergenerational dynamics and contextual factors related to clients' family of origin (e.g., genograms)" (Association for Assessment in Counseling and Education & International Association for Marriage and Family Counselors, 2010, p. 2). Family issues may also be noted in Axis IV of a multiaxial diagnosis (American Psychiatric Association, 2000).

SOCIAL SUPPORT Social support includes an assessment of the client's support system, most often outside of the home environment. Support systems may not be healthy and may be a contributing factor to the presenting problem. For example, an adolescent who engages in antisocial behavior (e.g., drug use, truancy, criminal activity) may associate with other adolescents who engage in similar behavior. Often, changes in social support are important to making overall changes to the presenting problem. Issues of social support may also be noted in Axis IV of a multiaxial diagnosis (American Psychiatric Association, 2000).

EDUCATIONAL/OCCUPATIONAL/ECONOMIC ISSUES Educational, occupational, and economic issues predominate child, adolescent, and adult lifestyles. Therefore, problems in these areas often motivate individuals to seek counseling services. Adjustment problems, failure, and stress in occupational and academic settings may be presenting problems or additional issues that require intervention or processing with the client. Educational delays, past diagnoses, and testing should be noted. Educational/occupational issues may also be noted in Axis IV of a multiaxial diagnosis (American Psychiatric Association, 2000). Economic issues may be challenging, especially when society exhibits bias toward the underprivileged and homeless. In addition, clients with limited economic resources may have difficulty obtaining necessary services, such as mental health care, medication, and medical care.

CULTURAL/SPIRITUAL CONCERNS In the *ACA Code of Ethics*, the American Counseling Association (ACA; 2005) included a guideline under Section E. Evaluation, Assessment, and Interpretation that "counselors recognize that culture affects the manner in which clients' problems are defined" (p. 11). Counselors have an ethical obligation to be competent with multicultural issues related to assessment and in the clinical interview. Understanding the implications of "age, color, culture, disability, ethnic, group, gender, race, language preference, religion, spirituality, sexual orientation, and socioeconomic status"

(ACA, 2005, p. 13) in the assessment process may affect the counselor's conceptualization of the client. As a result, counselors should employ questions that gauge clients' attitudes toward their perceptions of culture and any implications to presenting issues.

SUMMARY   The summary includes a general statement of the overall assessment process, highlighting any issues of concern and providing a general focus of future counseling sessions. Often counseling goals and preliminary plans will be identified in the summary section.

Determining Mental Status

The MSE was adapted from psychiatry as a way to assess a client's overall level of functioning. In this respect, the MSE is, at the very least, a semistructured component of a clinical interview. The domains represented in the MSE are well documented (Polanski & Hinkle, 2000; Trzepacz & Baker, 1993; Whiston, 2009), and although the domains may be standardized, the manner in which the counselor gathers the information is more subjective and may vary because of varying degrees of rapport established with the client. The mental status exam may be an integral part of the clinical interview and/or diagnostic process for clients. Establishing rapport is important to gathering information from the client, and the MSE is not an exception (Polanski & Hinkle, 2000). Third-party payors, in particular, may be interested in data collected from the MSE. Polanski and Hinkle suggested that counselors be sure to document each of the noted areas of the MSE, provide quotes from the client to support findings related to appropriate elements of the MSE (e.g., mood, language, thought content), and identify any issues in the MSE that support diagnosis.

APPEARANCE, ATTITUDE, AND ACTIVITY   Dress, cleanliness, and overall grooming may be considered in appearance, as well as more objective traits such as health and disability status. Appearance may also be tied to development, as how clients present themselves may provide insight into their personality (e.g., disheveled, unorganized, seductive, uncaring). Appearance may relate to the manner in which a client is aware of his/her own feelings, thoughts, concept of self, and overall mood. Thus, appearance can relate to a client's diagnosis. However, counselors would be wise not to confuse appearance with other sociocultural factors such as socioeconomic status and religious identity. Notes the counselor makes related to appearance may generally be identified as objective. The counselor may identify a subjective intent of a client appearance, but then support it with objective criteria. For example:

> The client is a 35-year old White male. The client appeared disheveled. Hair was uncombed. The client did not appear clean. The client's shirt was tucked and untucked erratically, and the client sat with poor posture, legs straight out, and poor eye contact.

The attitude of a client may be assessed through observations and disclosures related to his/her motivation and understanding of counseling and the clinical interview. For adults, in particular, many of these clients approach counseling voluntarily. However, in many circumstances, adults may be court ordered, such as in court-mandated counseling (e.g., domestic violence, driving under the influence [DUI]), and therefore adults may approach counseling less willingly. Children and adolescents may show resistance as well, and either be unwilling participants or in denial of the need for services. The assessment of attitude, therefore, may be an indication of client motivation and amiability toward counseling. Counselors should remember to focus on both verbal and nonverbal behaviors when assessing attitude. For instance, a client's disclosure of a desire for counseling can be somewhat superficial when incongruent nonverbal behaviors accompany the disclosure. "Yes, I really want some help" may come across as insincere with the type of body language displayed in the above scenario.

Activity is an indication of the client's ability to control physical movements. Activity may refer to behaviors that are purposeful (e.g., stomping feet to demonstrate anger, yelling, laughing, crying), subconscious (e.g., biting fingernails), unconscious (e.g., shaking, fidgeting), and/or involuntary (e.g. motor tics, stuttering). As with appearance and attitude, activity may have diagnostic implications (e.g., obsessive-compulsive disorder, attention deficit disorder [ADD], depression). Activity may also be relevant to features more medically related, such as traumatic brain injury, Alzheimer's, and Parkinson's. Counselors should keep in mind the broad array of activity levels, which may be overactive (e.g., mania), delayed (e.g., Alzheimer's), or nonexistent (e.g., catatonia).

MOOD AND AFFECT   Mood and affect are related terms but refer to distinct processes. Mood refers to an internal state with six categories: (a) euthymic (normal), (b) dysphoric (dissatisfied feeling), (c) euphoric (elated or over satisfied feeling), (d) angry, (e) anxious, and (f) apathetic (Polanski & Hinkle, 2000; Trzepacz & Baker, 1993). Affect refers to an external state, in which feelings are overtly expressed. Whereas mood is assessed generally through client disclosure, affect may be observed through both verbal and nonverbal behaviors. For example, body language and overt behaviors such as laughing or crying provide an indication of affect. Generally, affect can be assessed across two dimensions: range and intensity (Polanski & Hinkle, 2000). During an interview, counselors should note if affect changes and the breadth of affect demonstrated during the session. A client may move from crying to laughing within the same session. Intensity may be evaluated by noting the degree to which a particular emotional state is demonstrated and the client's ability to function within that emotional state.

SPEECH AND LANGUAGE   Language refers to the understanding and communication of verbal and nonverbal expressions. Speech refers to the pattern or rhythm of the expressed ideas (Polanski & Hinkle, 2000). Therefore, during an MSE the counselor pays particular attention to the content and manner of expression. Polanski and Hinkle noted three areas of common deficits in speech and language:

(a) Derailment, also known as loose associations, refers to the expression of unrelated ideas to the counselor, although the disconnected ideas may appear to make sense from the perspective of the client. Two common types of derailment include flight of ideas and tangential speech. In flight of ideas, the client uses a word or phrase to identify another idea that is weakly associated. For example, "I went on a date. It was Tuesday. Tuesday night is taco night. I love tacos." For tangential speech, the client may make responses to the counselor that appear unrelated to the inquiry:

COUNSELOR: "What is your relationship like with your parents?"

CLIENT: "I like chocolate milk."

(b) Poverty of speech refers to the absence or delay of speech. Clients exhibiting poverty of speech may be more constrained. For example, clients with depression may be less likely to engage in spontaneous discourse, not because of resistance but rather because of an inability to converse resulting from delayed cognitive and/or motor processes. In addition to delayed speech, clients may also experience increased latency, an increase in response time during discourse (Polanski & Hinkle, 2000).

(c) Pressured speech refers to an increased rate of verbalizations, often noted during a manic episode. Clients with pressured speech both speak and respond more rapidly, creating discourse that may seem tangential or even incoherent. However, pressured speech is specific to the rate of speech and the decreased response time during discourse, often referred to as decreased latency (Polanski & Hinkle, 2000).

THOUGHT PROCESS, THOUGHT CONTENT, AND PERCEPTION Hallucinations and delusions may result in perceptual distortions. Hallucinations refer the presence of phenomena that are not actually being experienced. Hallucinations may be categorized as an aspect of sensory perception: auditory, visual, tactile, olfactory, and gustatory (Polanski & Hinkle, 2000). For mental health issues, auditory and visual hallucinations are more common (American Psychiatric Association, 2000). Delusions, like hallucinations, also affect perception, but are characterized as only beliefs about a situation. Beliefs tend to be unrealistic and also unaltered when confronted. A client is identified as ego-dystonic when an awareness of the distorted perceptions is present; a lack of awareness of the distorted perceptions is ego-syntonic (Trzepacz & Baker, 1993).

COGNITION Assessing cognition requires the counselor to be aware of the client's clarity in thought and orientation. On a subjective level, the counselor should be able to determine if clients are thinking clearly and making sense about their situation. A more objective manner to determine cognition is to assess orientation. Orientation refers to the client's awareness of person, place, time, and situation.

Counselors should be careful about assessing orientation, as clients who are completely oriented, documented as *oriented x 4*, may find such questions as either ridiculous because they are completely lucid, or frustrating because of their awareness of being unable to answer questions that they should know. For example, asking a client "What is your name? Where are you? What is the date?" may feel more like an interrogation as opposed to a therapeutic interview meant to build rapport. Rather, see if the client is able to introduce him/herself through social cues. To see if the client is aware of his/her situation, try asking, "What brings you here today?" Keep in mind that lucid individuals frequently have to check their calendar to know the exact date, but knowing the month, day, and who the president is may be appropriate lines of questioning to assess orientation.

INSIGHT AND JUDGMENT Clients often have difficulty identifying how their total behavior (i.e., feelings, cognitions, actions [Glasser, 1998]) leads to their current situation, which is a lack of insight. How insight or a lack thereof leads to decisions (healthy or unhealthy) is the basis for judgment. Counselors often refer to clients having good or poor insight into their situation or problem. Often, clients may identify beliefs related to their situation or have expectations related to their behavior that are unrealistic. For example, an adolescent client may feel that it is okay to get high because he is not hurting anyone. This is known as poor reality testing, when a client identifies unrealistic expectations related to behaviors. Poor reality testing may be a result of internalizing or externalizing problems. For example, adolescents who blame their disruptive behavior in school on a teacher may be externalizing their behavior—the problems being experienced are the result of someone or something else. Clients may also accept responsibility or blame for a problem, known as internalizing, such as a child who identifies guilty feelings over a parent's drinking.

Factors Affecting Mental Status

Throughout the discussion of mental status, focus was placed on alterations of mental status issues because of Axis I diagnoses. In other words, associated problems with mental status may occur as a result of such psychiatric diagnoses as mood, psychotic, and anxiety disorders or disorders normally diagnosed in childhood and adolescence. Counselors should be thorough and cautious in assuming the reason for deviations in mental status. Mental status may be compromised from substance use/abuse, mismanaged medication, or organic issues (e.g., traumatic brain injury, stroke, infections [delirium]). When evaluating a client whose mental status appears compromised, the counselor may wish to obtain consent from the client to have a family member or other significant person present to confirm history, problems, and so forth.

Clients whose mental status appears compromised may indeed be a danger to self or others. Even if the client is not identifying suicidal thoughts, the client may not be able to engage in independent living activities (e.g., cooking, cleaning, grooming). Counselors need to carefully address the disposition of the client when mental status is compromised. Does the client require 24-hour supervision? Is the client able to function adequately and responsibly? Who is available should the client's situation further deteriorate? In cases such as this, a referral to a crisis residence, a brief in-patient hospitalization for the purposes of observation, assessment, and stabilization, is necessary.

TYPES OF INTAKE DATA

The clinical interview, as well as other intake information, may assume a standardized or nonstandardized format. In a nonstandardized format, counselors may gather information and focus on issues that arise at the moment. The advantage of the nonstandardized format is that the client drives the focus of the initial session more so than a prearranged questionnaire. However, the potential of missing information or failure to obtain important history or presenting issues may be problematic with a nonstandardized format. Advantages of using a standardized format include consistency of information obtained, ability to manage information across various settings, and liability protection. Vacc and Juhnke (1997) noted that nonstandardized interviews are the least trustworthy assessment procedure because of the variability in the type and quality of the information gathered. Structured interviews provide more consistency in gathering information. Counselors are less likely to leave, omit, or skip important aspects of the client's presenting issues. Keep in mind that many third-party payors require an initial diagnosis and supporting documentation after the initial session for the client to be eligible to receive services. Many insurance companies use the right to refuse payment for services if the insurance company views the services as unnecessary. Standardized interviews help ensure that counselors collect adequate information to warrant care.

As counselors are required to use evidence-based techniques in their practice (ACA, 2005), standardized assessments allow for counselor to track information obtained from their clients. Consistent information allows counselors to evaluate who they treat, the types and severity of issues encountered, and the strategies that appear effective. Standardized assessments may be more useful in identifying baseline data to track client progress. For community-based mental health centers and hospitals, data may be more easily recorded and reported to stakeholders, such as state departments of health or accrediting agencies.

When counselors collect information consistently, and the information gathered is what is supported in best practice literature, counselors protect themselves. Counselors need to be able to explain and defend why they practice in a particular manner. When the nature of the practice is ethical, thorough, and consistent, the counselor is less likely to be held liable for problems that may occur as a result of the type of services rendered.

So far, we identified and explained the psychosocial history and MSE as primary components to the clinical interview. However, other types of data are essential in order to place information garnered from the clinical interview into proper context. Basic demographic data should be noted, including sex, age, ethnicity, and level of education. Such information provides context into present problems and development. In regard to children, for example, counselors should pay particular attention to level of education and age, as discrepancies may need to be investigated with respect to any educational delays, learning disabilities, past evaluations, and so forth.

Direct questions related to the client's living situation and past history are essential. Counselors should document with whom the client lives, past family issues (e.g., separation, divorce, remarriage), and any history of abuse, whether physical, emotional, or sexual abuse. In the case of abuse, counselors must document if a report was filed and the outcome of the report/investigation. Further follow-up from the counselor may be warranted. Essentially, counselors should assess the safety of the client's living situation.

Not only is the past psychosocial/medical history of the client important, but so is the past psychosocial/medical history of family members. Issues of suicide, abuse, addiction, and psychiatric diagnoses are important indicators of potential problems with clients. Genetic predispositions for addiction, mood, and anxiety disorders are well documented (American Psychiatric Association, 2000). In addition, such information may provide insight into the home environment. Processing coping strategies to help an adolescent avoid drugs and alcohol may be more complicated if drug and alcohol use/abuse is in the home environment.

Particular attention to problems and symptoms should be noted. The American Psychiatric Association emphasized impairment as criteria to diagnoses. The frequency, duration, and severity of symptoms should be noted, as well as the effect that such symptoms have on the client's life. In the case of substance abuse, much more information is necessary.

Substance Use/Abuse Intake

The Substance Abuse Mental Health Services Administration (2009) reported 20.1 million individuals aged 12 years old and above used illicit drugs in the past month, representing 8% of the population. Substance use and abuse represents one of the most common diagnoses encountered by counselors. As a result, knowledge of interviewing strategies related to substance abuse and dependence is essential.

One particular area of difficulty for counselors conducting an interview in which substance abuse is apparent is the level of the client's denial. Individuals who abuse drugs/alcohol demonstrate recurrent use and often refuse to acknowledge the harmful effects or problems resulting from the substance abuse. Counselors may need to ask and

Current use:

Substance abuse history:

Type	Drug Name	Age Started	Duration of Use	Frequency of Use	Amount Used	Route	Last Used
Cannabis							
Cocaine							
Other stimulants							
Hallucinogenics/ narcotics							
Depressants							
Inhalants							
Alcohol							

Age of first drink:

Age of first drug use:

What problems do you have related to your drinking/using?

How have you attempted to reduce your use or quit using drugs/alcohol?

FIGURE 7.1 Substance Abuse Assessment

re-ask questions in different ways in order to obtain informative or truthful responses. In particular, counselors need to avoid close-ended questions such as "Have you ever tried to quit?" and opt for more open-ended questions such as "Tell me about a time when you tried to cut down on your use."

Counselors may wish to evaluate substance abuse by noting the types of substances abused. Counselors should evaluate each type of drug, including alcohol, nicotine, opiates, amphetamines, inhalants, marijuana, hallucinogens, and prescription drugs. In noting each substance used, counselors may document the frequency of use, duration, and route (e.g. injected, smoked, snorted, swallowed). How the substances are obtained is also important. With respect to substance dependence, the time spent to acquire, use, and recover from the effects of the substance is a noted criteria for dependency (American Psychiatric Association, 2000). Counselors should note patterns of use, and include a history of when the substance use began. Consequences and legal problems should be documented, keeping in mind that many clients will deny that the substance abuse plays a role in such problems. Often, clients may externalize (i.e. blame others or events) rather than accept responsibility or admit to the role substance abuse is playing in the present circumstances. Rationalization and denial of substance abuse problems are viewed as part of the nature of addiction. Figure 7.1 serves as an example of a standardized form for substance abuse assessment that may be incorporated into the clinical interview.

APPLYING COUNSELING SKILLS TO THE INTERVIEW PROCESS

Throughout the counseling process, implementation of the core conditions (i.e. unconditional positive regard, empathic understanding, congruence [Rogers, 1957]) is essential, and the clinical interview is no exception. Although, not every counselor may ascribe to

Roger's theoretical framework, other counseling theories uphold similar frameworks. Glasser (1965) identified *involvement* as essential to the therapeutic relationship. Other theoreticians from complimentary theories (e.g., Adlerian, existentialism, cognitive-behavioral) include a collaborative relationship. Counselor–client rapport is a necessary therapeutic condition for gathering information from the client. The mere fact that a client will sit down with a complete stranger and begin to disclose highly personal information is worthy of respect for the courage and risk that accompanies this scenario.

In the traditional counseling setting, attending skills are essential to rapport building. However, the initial interview requires documentation to support the need for services, develop a treatment plan, address disposition, and establish case notes. As a result, counselors need to be able to document information, which may interfere with the traditional attending skills.

Counselors may wish to consider the assessment environment. How can the counselor communicate helpfulness, build rapport, establish comfort and confidentiality, and document the necessary details of the clinical interview? Helpful attending techniques may include sitting across from the client and writing on a note pad or clipboard, as opposed to having a desk separating the counselor and client. The counselor should use nonverbal, attending skills essential to building rapport, and focus on using open-ended questions. More time may be needed for a clinical interview than for a regular session. The counselor should make sure that the boundaries of confidentiality and the counselor–client consent and agreement are stated up front. An initial opening may include a brief introduction of the counselor, the nature of the counseling relationship, and statement about confidentiality such as the following:

> I want you to know that what you say in here will stay in here. However, confidentiality may be compromised in three conditions: if you tell me you are going to hurt yourself; if you tell me you may hurt someone else; or if you disclose physical or sexual abuse or tell me you have abused a minor.

Because of the nature of the clinical interview, especially when standardized methods and models are employed, the client–counselor interaction may appear atheoretical. Keep in mind that the goal of the clinical interview is to establish rapport, gather information, assess need for services and desired interventions, and perhaps commit to future counseling sessions.

TYPES OF INFORMATION DERIVED FROM OUR CASE STUDIES

Each of the case studies presented in Chapter 2 contains information derived from the clinical interview. Just as the clients vary in the case studies, so does the information gathered during the clinical interview. A description of some of the similarities and differences with respect to the clinical interview follows.

Both the cases of Eva Marie Garza and Robert Jones begin with a physical description of the client, relevant demographic information, and a description of mental status. In the authors' experience, knowledge and use of the MSE is very important, but is often overlooked, particularly by novice counselors. For this reason, we point out specifically where mental status was addressed in the case studies of Eva Marie Garza and Robert Jones. For Eva Marie, five of the six elements of the mental status examination— (a) appearance, attitude, and activity, (b) mood and affect, (c) speech and language,

(d) thought process, thought content, and perception, and (e) cognition—were addressed with (f) insight and judgment addressed later:

> She was oriented to person, place, and time. Based on the complexity of language she used and the sophistication of the questions she asked within the session, she appeared as having above-average intelligence. Eva Marie's overall mood was anxious. Eva Marie's speech was noticeably pressured and fast. During the first 45 minutes of her initial June 7 intake, her responses to counselor-asked questions were often tangential and only loosely associated with asked questions. During that time, she was especially loquacious, and she demonstrated slight to mild psychomotor agitation. On first entering the initial intake session, Eva Marie sat in the counseling office chair. She slowly rocked back and forth as she responded to verbal questions. (Chapter 2)

Similar observations were made about Robert Jones:

> He was oriented to person, place, and time. He seemed to have somewhat above-average intelligence given the preciseness of his speech, the sophistication of his chosen words, and his engaging manner of interacting. Robert was appropriately dressed. He wore clean clothing, including khaki-colored trousers, an overly noticeable starched and pressed, white, button-down shirt, and Sperry Topsider-type shoes. His personal hygiene was appropriate and unremarkable. Robert is 6 feet tall and weighs 210 pounds. His appearance was trim and muscular without noted obesity. (Chapter 2)

In terms of insight and judgment, we can turn to some of the quotes by the clients. For example, Eva Marie appears to have good insight into her issues. She admits to having "'extreme anxiety'" and 'complete dissatisfaction' with her life" with compromised judgment, as indicated by her statement "I don't know what to do."

In contrast to Eva Marie, Robert shows very poor insight and judgment. Robert accepts no responsibility, admitting, "My attorney told me to begin counseling." In addition, Robert externalizes his problems, blaming his employer for his legal problems.

In terms of addressing the presenting problem in the case studies presented, it seems that as each section of the case study is presented, additional problems may be noted. For example, Robert admits to alcohol abuse and poor anger control, but later we also see that Robert has had tumultuous relationships (he is twice divorced) and has previous charges of domestic violence, aggravated assault on police, and drunk and disorderly conduct. Other issues may be apparent stemming from Robert's family of origin, such as his father's physical abuse and mother's neglect. Clearly, Robert also has a troublesome work history, along with legal issues.

So, when identifying presenting problems with Robert, where do we start? A more psychodynamically oriented counselor may wish to address Robert's lack of attachment to his parents. A counselor specializing in a systems approach may wish to address Robert's relationship issues. From a mental health perspective, Robert is unlikely to make any changes if he cannot abstain from alcohol. Many of his legal issues, and probably work performance issues as well as his poor anger control, can be tied to his drinking. For this reason, addressing issues of sobriety may be first and foremost. Even with the presence of mental health problems and diagnoses, a client who is not clean and sober will be unable to develop insight, judgment, and positive growth.

For Eva Marie, the presenting problem—anxiety—addressed under "Identified Treatment Goals" is complicated by other extenuating issues addressed in subsequent areas of her case study. Eva Marie is in an unhappy marriage to a husband she describes as "absent" and "emotionless." Eva Marie is very unhappy in her current job and is also burdened with caring for her mother, whom she is quite dependent upon.

From the clinical interview with Eva Marie, a counselor may feel challenged with helping Eva Marie find some alleviation for her anxiety given all of the issues that trigger stress in her life. Once again, depending on the theoretical and professional orientation of the counselor, Eva Marie's anxiety may be addressed in a multitude of ways. From a systems perspective, Eva Marie's role in the family, perspectives on marriage, and problematic relationships could receive primary consideration. Eva Marie has a long history of a dependent relationship with her mother, and her religious and cultural foundations have also played a significant role in the decisions she makes. From a mental health perspective, a long history of anxiety appears evident, and she is currently on medication to address her anxiety.

Notice that each of the case studies concludes with a five-axis diagnosis, consistent with DSM-IV-TR guidelines. The concept of providing a diagnosis after a clinical interview is controversial. On one hand, third-party payors expect, and even require, a diagnosis. On the other hand, the *ACA Code of Ethics* (2005) has indicated that counselors have the right not to provide a diagnosis, particularly if the provision of a diagnosis is not in the client's best interest. Moreover, how appropriate is it to provide a diagnosis after an initial clinical interview? Keep in mind that a diagnosis can be changed. As more information is learned about the client, the need to amend treatment goals or re-evaluate the direction of counseling is important. At the early stage of a clinical interview, counselors may view diagnosis as provisional and note that it may evolve—they may even identify the need to rule out specific diagnoses. At other times, however, sufficient evidence may be presented during the clinical interview to formulate a more conclusive picture of the presenting issues, such as with Robert's alcohol dependence or Eva Marie's anxiety.

The subsequent sections that appear in a clinical interview, beyond the presenting problem, have a role in informing the counselor either about the presenting problem or addressing relevant concerns about the presenting problem, thereby lending credence to the various models of the clinical interview presented in this chapter. Thorough attention to the various components of the clinical interview provided a more comprehensive picture for each of the case studies presented. The subsequent sections provide more depth to understanding the presenting problem(s), as well as provide background information and present information on contributing factors or additional issues that may arise and be addressed through counseling.

Summary

The clinical interview is an integral component of the assessment process and pertinent to establishing treatment goals, treatment plans, and therapeutic rapport. Clinical interviews should be comprehensive. Beginning counselors should use models and standardized formats to collect relevant information and identify problem areas. Structured clinical interviews provide a framework for documentation that enable the counselor to provide ethical, evidence-based, comprehensive care. In addition, stakeholders (e.g., agencies, third-party payors) utilize information and data to ascertain that best practices are being utilized for clients.

A comprehensive clinical interview is atheoretical and therefore can be implemented from a variety of therapeutic approaches in a myriad of settings. From the case studies presented in Chapter 2, counselors, regardless of professional orientation and setting, can use the information from the clinical interview. Juhnke (2002) outlined a structured clinical interview format (CLISD-PA) that provides a comprehensive, atheoretical approach to the clinical interview.

References

American Counseling Association. (2005). *ACA code of ethics*. Alexandria, VA: Author.

American Psychiatric Association. (2000). *Diagnostic and statistical manual of mental disorders* (4th ed., text rev.). Washington, DC: Author.

Association for Assessment in Counseling and Education & American Mental Health Counselors Association. (2009). *Standards for assessment in mental health counseling*. Alexandria, VA: Author.

Association for Assessment in Counseling and Education & International Association for Marriage and Family Counselors. (2010). *Marriage, couple and family counseling assessment competencies*. Alexandria, VA: Author.

Glasser, W. (1965). *Reality therapy: A new approach to psychiatry*. New York: Harper & Row.

Health Insurance Portability and Accountability Act of 1996, 42 U.S.C. § 1320d-9 (2010).

Juhnke, G. A. (2002). *Substance abuse assessment: A handbook for mental health professionals*. New York, NY: Brunner-Routledge.

Juhnke, G. A. (2008, March). *Utilizing stochastic processing and continuous assessment methods to produce evidenced based informed outcomes*. Keynote Speaker Association for Assessment in Counseling and Education, Honolulu, HI.

Owen, J. (2008). The nature of confirmatory strategies in the initial assessment process. *Journal of Mental Health Counseling, 30*, 362–374.

Polanski, P. J., & Hinkle, J. S. (2000). The mental status examination: Its use by professional counselors. *Journal of Counseling & Development, 78*, 357–364.

Rogers, C. (1957). The necessary and sufficient conditions of therapeutic personality change. *Journal of Consulting Psychology, 21*, 95–103.

Substance Abuse and Mental Health Services Administration. (2009). *Results from the 2008 National Survey on Drug Use and Health: National Findings* (Office of Applied Studies, NSDUH Series H-36, HHS Publication No. SMA 09-4434). Rockville, MD: Author.

Trzepacz, P. T., & Baker, R. W. (1993). *The psychiatric mental status examination*. New York, NY: Oxford University Press.

Vacc, N. A., & Juhnke, G. A. (1997). The use of structured clinical interviews for assessment in counseling. *Journal of Counseling & Development, 75*, 470–480.

Whiston, S. C. (2009). *Principles and applications of assessment in counseling* (3rd ed.). Belmont, CA: Thomson Brooks/Cole.

CHAPTER 8

Multicultural and Special Population Assessment Issues in Counseling

OBJECTIVES

After reading this chapter, you will be able to:

1. Identify issues of multicultural competence for assessment in counseling.
2. Identify standards and statements related to multicultural issues in assessment.
3. Address skills necessary to practice assessment in a multicultural world.
4. Identify issues of bias and perception of assessment from a multicultural perspective.

BIAS IN ASSESSMENT

Perhaps no issue in assessment is as controversial as the presence and effect of assessment bias. The existence of bias in assessment is well documented, but the reason for assessment bias is far more complex. In other words, counselors may recognize that bias exists in the assessment process but still be at a loss of what can be done about it. At times, assessment instruments may be biased, but the reason for the bias is not known.

Bias occurs when groups or subgroups experience differences in scores or score interpretations on an instrument. *Item bias* is the result of different response patterns occurring from individuals of different group membership; when such differences can be attributed to both the scores and other variables, *predictive bias* is evident (American Educational Research Association, American Psychological Association, & National Council of Measurement in Education [AERA, APA, NCME], 1999). For example, females tend to endorse depressive symptoms more often than males (American Psychiatric Association [APA], 2000). Beck, Steer, and Brown (1996) noted statistically significant mean differences between males and females on the Beck Depression Inventory—II (BDI-II). Yet, cut-scores indicating mild, moderate, and severe depression are the same for both males and females, which could lead to false-positive results for females or false-negative results for males. Thus, although the BDI-II is a highly efficient and often utilized instrument, some gender bias may be evident.

The *Standards for Educational and Psychological Testing* (AERA et al., 1999) may be the gold standard publication to which assessment and psychological tests aspire to meet, but other theories of test bias were evident in past research. Item bias and predictive bias may be seen as general categories to which other types of bias may fit. Walsh and Betz (2001) outlined several types of test biases, including cultural, content, internal structure, selection, slope, intercept, and sex bias.

Internal structure relates to the reliability and validity information of an assessment instrument. Clearly, if scores, items or subscales lack accurate or consistent response sets or fail to measure the intended construct, biased results may be a logical consequence. Slope and intercept bias are related to predictive bias. In a slope bias, an outcome for one group is predicted differently over the same outcome for another group. Using the above example of the BDI-II, should women be diagnosed with depression more often than men because of the tendency to identify depressive symptoms more often for women? The difference could be from social influences, rather than the development of a psychiatric disorder. Intercept bias occurs when a test overestimates or underestimates a particular group. For example, the number of ethnic minorities diagnosed with disruptive behavior disorders compared to nonminorities diagnosed with mood disorders may be an example. Although statistical biases may be data driven, they are the result of social and contextual issues related to assessment. Statistics may be useful in examining bias, but the statistics are not the problem. The problem lies in the interpretation and utilization of the information, as well as the item development of the instrument.

Content bias is a type of item bias, which occurs when the wording of an item is interpreted differently among different groups. This could result in scoring patterns that are different for one group over another. Chernin, Holden, and Chandler (1997) highlighted sex bias as an example, in which items on instruments may be biased if negative connotations or lack of references to minority groups are evident.

To be clear, test bias is an important component to test fairness. However, simply because an instrument is biased does not mean the instrument is unfair. The idea that all groups have comparable scores across an instrument defies the explicit rationale for conducting assessments. For example, in assessing wellness, should participants in a clinical setting identify different levels of wellness from participants in a nonclinical setting? In education, should students who have fewer resources have lower levels of achievement? Often, the answer to these rhetorical questions is a resounding "Yes!" Bias is expected, but instruments should be carefully evaluated when bias is found. The scores on an achievement test may vary from group to group because of unequal opportunities to learn, such as in comparing a college preparatory school with a school in a rural area of the United States.

The problem, therefore, is not test bias, but test fairness. To address test fairness, AERA et al. (1999) identified the following conditions: (a) test scores must be used and interpreted the same across all participants; (b) opportunity to prepare and/or complete the instruments must be the same for all participants, such as standardized instructions, tasks, and preparation; (c) all participants complete the instrument in similar conditions. These attributes are essential to any standardized testing process. For example, schools go through great lengths to ensure the same process is provided for all students, including the reading of directions, the amount of time provided, and the similarity in test-taking environment. Many instrument developers take time to describe the process of administering the instrument in the test manual. Scoring procedures are provided to ensure similar interpretations for all individuals being evaluated. Counselors should take time to read the manuals carefully, as scoring procedures may be different across gender, age, and grade. Intelligence, achievement, and aptitude tests often provide different norms, administration, and scoring procedures for different age and grade levels.

The Achievement Gap: An Heuristic Example of Test Bias Versus Test Fairness

Tests will be biased, but to address test fairness, variables that are not being measured should not be different. Perhaps where bias and fairness become most troublesome is with disparities in scores across ethnic groups. In educational settings, comparisons across ethnic groups are commonplace at the local, state, and federal levels, with an abundance of research on the achievement gap. Addressing the achievement gap is complicated. Although the comparison of ethnic groups predominates research on the achievement gap, ethnicity does not account for the disparities in achievement. Ethnic disparities in standardized testing occur, but the reason for the disparities is unclear. To suggest that race is the mitigating factor behind scoring differences is blatantly racist. Common variables explored include socioeconomic status, parents' level of education, resiliency, culture, and so forth. The issue is multifaceted. For example socioeconomic status can account for some differences, as the opportunity to access materials and support in the home environment may play a role in academic achievement; however, socioeconomic status cannot account for differences solely, as Asian groups typically out-perform Caucasian students, despite having lower socioeconomic status (Fangzhou & Patterson, 2010).

Attempts to explain the achievement gap fall short because the variables involved are more numerous and complex to measure. Too often researchers engage in demonstrating evidence of *construct-irrelevant variance*, which refers to differences in test scores based on factors unrelated to the construct being measured (AERA et al., 1999). When researchers look for gender and racial differences in constructs such as academic achievement, they are postulating that achievement differences are from gender and/or racial differences, rather than recognizing that such factors are irrelevant to academic achievement. Racial groupings are not part of the definition of academic achievement, so why emphasize such differences when racial groupings are irrelevant to the criteria to measure academic achievement (Helms, 2006)?

Rather than focusing on irrelevant factors, Helms (2006) suggested researchers should focus on *construct underrepresentation*—when the items fail to measure the important aspects of an intended phenomenon of interest (AERA et al., 1999). In other words, maybe unintended group differences exist because of poorly constructed items, or the items do not measure the construct comprehensively.

Researchers who follow the guidelines for constructing and administering instruments should review the literature thoroughly to develop items and use a formal process of addressing whether the items address sufficient evidence of test content. Although items may be dropped because of psychometric instability (e.g., poor reliability), items are less likely to be dropped because of construct irrelevancy, as such items would not have been placed into the item pool initially. Wohlgemuth (1997) indicated that dropping items often results in decreases in accuracy, consistency, and usefulness. Care must be taken in modifying instruments.

As a result of a growing pluralistic society, instruments are commonly translated into multiple languages and re-normed according to cultural groups. Although such changes may be appropriate for instruments that measure emotional or behavioral constructs, which may be more sensitive to variations in cultural norms, instruments that assess academic achievement may be less sensitive to cultural issues. If culture does indeed play a role in predicting academic achievement, how can culture be measured and the effect of culture be accounted for in a competent, nonbiased way? Counselors must be aware that any changes to an assessment may compromise reliability and validity. In addition, the cost of norming an instrument according to specific demographic groups (e.g., sex, ethnicity, age, sexual orientation) would be an unrealistic burden on test developers because of data collection, costs, and varying interpretations (Wohlgemuth, 1997).

However, the role of culture can be acknowledged and the unique qualities of an individual's culture can be recognized. Sedlacek (2004) encouraged higher education institutions to use noncognitive variables, such as community involvement, preference for long-term goals, leadership experience, and realistic self-appraisal, as predictors of success in higher education, as opposed to merely focusing on high-stakes testing results. An emphasis on noncognitive variables may decrease the weight of high-stakes testing in predicting performance and level the playing field for ethnic minority students who may not perform as well on high-stakes tests because of a variety of factors.

ASSESSMENT WITH SPECIAL POPULATIONS

An instrument becomes standardized as a result of a rigorous norming process (e.g., establishing meaningful statistics from the norm group, reliability, validity). A *special population*, therefore, is a group that was not included in the norming of an instrument. There are reasons why groups may be excluded from the norming process:

1. The process involved in addressing a relevant portion of special populations is daunting, time-consuming, and improbable when taking into account sample size and the breadth of issues related to potential specialized populations (e.g., gifted, low socioeconomic status, various disabilities). For example, to obtain a sufficient amount of data to norm an instrument using more elementary methods of standardization (e.g., exploratory factor analysis), a ratio of 10 to 20 participants per item is necessary. More advanced procedures (e.g., confirmatory factor analysis) in standardization may require a separate sample of similar size as well. Thus, a 32-item instrument may require an initial norm group of 320 participants to simply get started.
2. Instruments often are developed with a particular population in mind. For example, the Reynolds Adolescent Adjustment Screening Inventory was designed to address potential problem areas faced by adolescents. Providing norming information for individuals older or younger than the adolescent age range would go against the intended design of the instrument. Thus, populations may be purposefully ignored.

The potential for an instrument to be useful among a broad range of populations is known as *generalizability*. Recall from Chapter 3 that researchers demonstrate generalizability in two ways: (a) by describing the sample with respect to characteristics (e.g., age, ethnicity, sex) so that evidence to the appropriate population can be demonstrated and (b) by using mathematical procedures that take into account the size of the sample in order to generalize to a population. Hence, when instruments are used with individuals similar to the norm group, the results may be assumed generalizable. However, when an instrument is used with individuals who may be different from the norm group, as indicated by demographic data, events, or circumstances, then the validity of the results may be called into question.

Comparing Special Populations to Normative Samples

Counselors should be cautious about using instruments in which an individual or group outside of the normative sample completes an instrument. Standardized instruments frequently lack representatives related to sociocultural demographic factors (e.g., ethnic minorities, English as second language, low socioeconomic status) and various physical, mental, and behavioral deficits (e.g., cerebral palsy, autism, attention deficit hyperactivity disorder). However, as explained earlier, to expect test developers to include all potential members of various subgroups to norm an instrument is unreasonable. Thus, individuals outside of norm groups are administered tests. Although counselors should be cautious in interpreting results, counselors should also be aware of when results may be pertinent and generalizable to an individual or group. To evaluate when an instrument may be appropriate for an individual or group from a special population, counselors should be aware of the norming process and current research related to the instrument.

Counselors should familiarize themselves with the norming process of the instrument as addressed in the test manual or relevant articles. By noting the demographic/descriptive factors of the norm group, counselors may be able to ascertain whether the instrument is an appropriate assessment tool. For example, Balkin, Miller, Ricard, Garcia, and Lancaster (2011) used the Reynolds Adolescent Adjustment Screening Inventory (RAASI) to examine influencing characteristics on recidivism for a predominately adolescent, Latino, court-referred group. However, the RAASI included a normative sample from 1827 adolescents who were primarily Caucasian (72.1%), with only 6.4% of the group identified as Hispanic. In addition, most of the norm group lived with both parents (61.8%; Reynolds, 2001). This norm group may be quite different from the group used in the Balkin et al. (2011) study, in which the majority of participants who were administered the RAASI were Latino coming from single-parent homes. So, was the use of the RASSI valid in the Balkin et al. study? There may be factors, such as number of parents in the home, that may have an effect on the socialization of adolescents, and therefore the use of the RAASI with at-risk youth may have some limitations. On the other hand, counselors should be wary of construct-irrelevant variance, in which the application of variables, such as ethnicity, is inconsistent with the operational definition of the construct (i.e., adolescent adjustment) being measured.

When using an instrument for an individual or group outside of the normative sample, counselors should review current literature to identify recent research on the instrument, particularly as the research relates to special populations. Researchers often shed light on additional generalizability issues once an instrument is published. Journals such as *Measurement and Evaluation in Counseling and Development* include articles in which established instruments are revalidated using a special population. For example, Canel-Çınarbaş, Cui, and Lauridsen (2011) examined validity of the BDI-II across a Turkish sample and compared the finding to a U.S. sample. In this case, Canel-Çınarbaş et al. (2011) was able to show how the BDI-II could be used with a special population.

Not all validated instruments come from established measures. Rye, Loiacono, Folck, Olszewski, and Madia (2001) developed the Forgiveness Scale "as part of a study involving college women who had been wronged in a romantic relationship" (Rye et al., 2001, p. 264). However, the author reworded items to address any type of wrongdoing by an individual and correlated the measure to a more established instrument, the Enright Forgiveness Inventory. Thus, the instrument was revalidated with a more generalizable population and may prove useful in future research and practice related to forgiveness issues in counseling.

As shown in this example, not all instruments are published by test companies. For example, the Multicultural Awareness Knowledge and Skills Survey was used to assess multicultural competence in numerous studies (e.g., Cartwright, Daniels, & Zhang, 2008; Constantine, 2001; Brabeck et al., 2000), but this instrument is not published by a testing company. When assessment instruments are published in journals, as opposed to test companies, validation across many different special populations may be easier because of access to the instrument and the inexpensive nature of conducting the research.

Counselors using assessment instruments with individuals from special populations need to assess carefully the nature of the special population, the consequences of testing and interpretation, and the relevant literature associated with the instrument. The process of validating an instrument across special populations may be just as intensive as the initial validation. When evaluating a research article or review of an instrument for use with a special population, counselors should look carefully at the methods employed in obtaining a representative sample for the special population, the reliability estimates for the special population as compared to the normative sample, and the validation procedures used, which often improve on the initial validation procedures for a given instrument.

Adapting Assessment Instruments and Procedures

Accommodations refer to processes and procedures for individuals who may be disadvantaged from a disability or condition and require a change in the processes and/or procedures of an administered assessment. Accommodations can include a multitude of measures such as additional time, verbal administration, assistance completing the instrument, and alternate response strategies. Federal guidelines, such as Individuals with Disabilities Education Act (IDEA) in education and the American Disabilities Act of 1990 (ADA) for employers (see Chapter 1), require efforts to create a fair environment for individuals with disabilities. Counselors should be careful about implementing accommodations and interpreting the results. Some issues to address when considering an accommodation include legal implications, the validity of the accommodation(s), and available resources.

Counselors who work in schools, agencies, and businesses often rely on the organization for establishing protocols related to test accommodations. For example, universities often address compliance with ADA through specific services for students with disabilities, while businesses may employ professionals in human resources. In addition, school districts often include administrative personnel who oversee accommodations in testing. Such personnel will identify specific accommodations that are required for students, employees, and so forth. Such a procedure prevents personnel from implementing different protocols and procedures. Therefore, the decision to offer an accommodation and the type of accommodation offered may be streamlined and less subjective. For example, a student with a diagnosis of attention deficit disorder (ADD) may require additional time on a test, and this accommodation may be established through an individualized education plan.

Compliance with policies and procedures for individuals with disabilities is important, and counselors should be aware that the decision to offer an accommodation should be considered carefully. Consider the implications if an organization offers an accommodation for an undocumented condition. For example, an applicant for graduate school is administered a timed essay. However, the student has a cold that day and the administrator allows the individual more time to complete the essay. Would such an accommodation be fair? Other students who may not have felt healthy but did not ask for an accommodation may be at an unfair disadvantage. In addition, to what extent should an accommodation be offered? Should the student require documentation of illness? Is the illness severe enough to warrant an accommodation? The consequences may be that the process of assessing the aforementioned applicant and making comparisons to other applicants is invalid.

When an accommodation is offered, counselors should be aware of the validity of the accommodation and consider under what conditions an accommodation may be acceptable. For example, a high school student diagnosed with ADD wishes to obtain an accommodation for the ACT. In this scenario, such an accommodation may be important for allowing the student the opportunity to demonstrate college preparedness. Contrast this with a scenario in which a parent requests an accommodation for a child diagnosed with mild mental retardation who will be administered an intelligence test. In this case, such an accommodation is invalid, as the test is designed to evaluate the construct (i.e., intelligence) that is a basis for the diagnosis. As a general rule, counselors should be aware of policies, procedures, and existing literature (test manuals, research studies) related to accommodations for a test. The following issues presented serve as examples of issues related to accommodations in tests.

SPEED VERSUS POWER TESTS   Recall from Chapter 4 that speed tests refer to items or tests that are time limited; power tests include items that may increase in difficulty and therefore may not be completed or may be incorrectly answered. Although accommodations on a power test may be infrequent, accommodations for a speed test through the allowance of increased time occur quite frequently. One factor to keep in mind is that many tests may be speed tests as an unintended consequence. Such a circumstance occurs often in educational settings. A student is administered an exam during a class and has the class period to complete the exam. Incompletion of the exam is not necessarily a result of a lack of knowledge; rather, an incomplete exam may be the result of running out of time to finish. Thus, time can be added to the exam if the properties of the exam are left intact. In this case, if the purpose of the exam is to test an understanding of information, then time is not an issue.

LANGUAGE BARRIERS   The increase in a multicultural, diverse society results in a proliferation of individuals with English as a second language (ESL). This is an area in which failure to offer an accommodation can have deleterious effects. Consider the consequences of Henry Goddard's (1866–1957) actions of administering the Binet scale to assess intelligence of immigrants as they were arriving to Ellis Island. Not only were the individuals in poor physical condition to take a test, but the translation of the test may have been inconsistent and was certainly not normed. Thus, even when a translation of an instrument is offered, if the translation is not normed, then the use of the test is not valid. Counselors may wish to consider alternative tests that may be administered nonverbally. For example, the Test of Nonverbal Intelligence, 4th edition (TONI-4), tests intelligence and aptitude but does not require the use of language.

PHYSICAL IMPAIRMENTS   Counselors should be aware when physical impairments, such as visual, auditory, and motor disorders, interfere with the validity of an assessment. For example, Block Design is a subtest on the Wechsler Intelligence Scale for Children (WISC-IV). This subtest requires the examinee to manipulate blocks in order to create a visual representation of a designated shape, and the process is timed. Clients diagnosed with motor impairments could have difficulty manipulating the blocks, which could affect their ability to complete the task in a specified time frame. Not only is time allotment a concern, but also individuals may become frustrated in attempting the task. Thus, the subtest may not be a valid measure of intelligence. When physical impairments are evident and affect the test or testing process, counselors should consider alternative measures or alternative scoring methods if the tasks cannot be completed. If an alternative scoring method is used, test manuals and existing literature should support the decision.

COGNITIVE DISORDERS   Cognitive disorders can affect the speed in which tasks are processed. Thus, a delayed reaction could alter the interpretation of a test, particularly when speed is an issue and incorporated into the score of a test, which is typical on aptitude, achievement, and intelligence tests. In addition, counselors should address the client's understanding of the tasks presented. In many tests, instructions are standardized, particularly in the areas of aptitude, intelligence, and achievement. If the instructions are not understood, an accurate measure in these areas may be compromised. The decision to alter instructions can affect how a client responds, and careful consideration of the wording, so as not to lead the client to respond in a certain way, is pertinent.

EMOTIONAL DISORDERS   An array of emotional disorders, such as depression, ADD, and anxiety, may affect the processing of tasks because of reactions to the stress of the test-taking environment or delayed processing. Time accommodations are common with emotional disorders. However, counselors should be aware if the test manual or existing literature offers a rationale and empirical evidence for accommodations on a specific test. Again, consideration of the purpose of testing is essential. Time accommodations are appropriate when the purpose of the test is to investigate a construct that is not predicated on the speed of the response. Although achievement tests often do not require a timed component, evaluating the speed of a response in intelligence and aptitude testing is common practice.

DEVELOPING MULTICULTURAL COMPETENCE AS AN ASSESSMENT PROFESSIONAL

In light of the multicultural issues that emanate from assessment practices, counselors should be aware of the information garnered from the assessment process and view it as a single tool, used in conjunction with other tools, to make appropriate recommendations to clients. "Culturally skilled counselors have knowledge of the potential bias in assessment instruments and use procedures and interpret findings keeping in mind the cultural and linguistic characteristics of the clients" (Arredondo et al., 1996, p. 3). Counselors should keep in mind that the counseling profession maintains an inclusive definition of multiculturalism: "the diversity of racial, ethnic, and cultural heritage; socioeconomic status; age; gender; sexual orientation; and religious and spiritual beliefs, as well as physical, emotional, and mental abilities" (Council for Accreditation for Counseling and Related Educational Programs [CACREP], 2009, p. 61). The application for multicultural competency in assessment covers a wide range of populations and special groups. Counselors need to consider carefully how the assessment process, from the type of assessment through the administration, scoring, and interpretation of the results, may be attributed to cultural issues of the client. In terms of skills, Arredondo et al. (1996) indicated that counselors "not only understand the technical aspects of the instruments but are also aware of the cultural limitations. This allows them to use test instruments for the welfare of culturally different clients" (p. 3).

Sedlacek and Kim (1995) identified common misuses of assessments from a multicultural perspective. Counselors should be aware of labeling for diverse groups. Labels have changed for various groups over the past 50 to 60 years, but the change in labels has done little to affect bias and prejudice for disenfranchised groups and populations. Although this issue can apply to various domains across the counseling profession, specific assessment issues include the creation, norming, and interpretation of assessments. Assessment instruments should be created for use among diverse populations, but many of the theories employed for the constructs that counselors measure (e.g., intelligence, achievement, depression) come from a Eurocentric worldview (Helms, 1992; Sedlacek & Kim, 1995). In addition, even if instruments are developed for use among various groups, the norm groups of many instruments often lack reflection of a diverse sample. Development of assessments overwhelmingly is dependent upon college student populations of primary European American descent. As a result, assessment instruments may lack generalizability to minority groups. Counselors should then consider how an assessment instrument and the scores produced from it are a valid measure when used with a culturally diverse client. Sedlacek and Kim (1995) warned that individuals who develop instruments might lack training in multicultural issues. As a result, counselors should be cautious when using assessment instruments in which such considerations are not outlined in the manual.

Awareness of Perceptions of Counseling and Assessment Among Various Cultures

Generally, the practice of counseling in the United States assumes a Western-valued process, which may be inherently biased toward persons of color. Historically, ethnic minorities are less likely to use and be satisfied with counseling services. Extant research is quite limited with respect to the role of assessment and multicultural issues. In addition, past research focused more on counselor training related to multicultural competence and less on client perceptions. Ethnic minorities are less likely to seek out counseling services. "Historically, ethnic minorities have been under-represented with respect to accessing services in the mental health system" because of disparities in the judicial system, access to private health care insurance, and increased risk of psychological and behavioral disorders (Balkin, 2006, p. 50). Jones and Markos (1997) found that the clients' attitude toward counseling is related to the clients' perception of effectiveness of counseling services. Constantine (2002) added to this research by elucidating on the relationship between the clients' attitude toward counseling and satisfaction with counseling services. Furthermore, Constantine found that satisfaction with counseling services was related to the clients' perception of multicultural competence by the counselor. In other words, client satisfaction increased when the client perception of multicultural competence increased; client satisfaction decreased when the client perception of multicultural competence decreased. Li and Kim (2004) examined the relationship of Asian values across counselor effectiveness, counselor empathy, working alliance, session depth, and cross-cultural counseling competence. The extent to which clients adhered to Asian values was not a factor in relationship to the above measures. However, Asian clients did show a preference for directive counseling methods.

One emerging area of research that may indicate negative perceptions of counseling and assessment from minority clients is in the area of racial microaggressions in the counseling relationship. "*Racial microaggressions* refers to subtle and commonplace exchanges that somehow convey insulting or demeaning messages to people of color" (Constantine, 2007, p. 2). Racial microaggressions in the counseling relationship may occur because of the counselors' denial of cultural differences, minimization of racial cultural issues, patronization, engagement in stereotypical behaviors, and so forth (Constantine, 2007). Constantine (2007) specifically examined racial microaggressions in the counseling relationship with African American clients who received counseling from White counselors. When African American clients perceived racial microaggressions, both the therapeutic alliance and satisfaction with counseling services were negatively impacted.

The need to adhere to multiculturally competent practices in the assessment process cannot be overstated, as the assessment process may indeed be the introductory step to beginning counseling for many clients. Arredondo et al. (1996) addressed assessment competencies for multicultural counseling in terms of "knowledge of potential bias," interpretation with respect to client characteristics, and "training and expertise in the use of traditional assessment and testing instruments" (p. 3). In the assessment process, culturally competent counselors take into consideration cultural values and issues of the client, avoid stereotyping the client, and continue to broaden awareness and understanding of diversity (Skiba, Knesting, & Bush, 2002). Counselors need to be aware of labels as a characteristic of the assessment process. Labels may be helpful or harmful depending on the context. The practice of labeling may contribute to over-representation of ethnic minorities. For example, in the school setting a disproportionate number of ethnic minorities may be labeled with a disability in order to receive special education services. Counselors, and school counselors in particular, may need to advocate for assessment strategies that identify the need for intervention and remediation, rather than eligibility for placement (Skiba et al., 2002).

The determination of ethnic differences across constructs, despite being irrelevant to the measurement of the construct, is not a practice that is likely to cease in the near future. Counselors need to be able to address ethnic differences on tests by being knowledgeable about noncognitive variables. As mentioned previously, disparities in access to academic resources and/or motivation toward counseling, treatment goals, achievement, and so forth may be evaluated independent of ethnicity and may account for variation on measured constructs.

Counselors should be aware of the norm groups for an assessment instrument. Application to a particular ethnic group or culture may be inappropriate if minorities were underrepresented in the norm group. There is a need to examine norm differences when assessment tools are used. For example, using an assessment instrument like the Reynolds Adolescent Adjustment Screening Inventory on Latino/a youth may require re-norming if this population was not part of the original standardization of the instrument.

Although studies on assessment training in the counseling literature may be limited, one factor that appears to increase multicultural competence for counselor trainees is clinical supervision with more non-White clients (Vereen, Hill, & McNeal, 2008). Thus, practice with non-White clients may be essential to developing multicultural counseling competence. Ultimately, counselors need to be aware of how the assessment process may feel impersonal and strive to develop therapeutic rapport and positivity toward the assessment process.

CASE STUDY APPLICATION: EVA MARIE GARZA

The case of Eva Marie Garza provides an excellent opportunity to explore multicultural issues in assessment. Eva Marie is a 40-year-old Mexican American female suffering from issues related to anxiety, her marriage, and her career. A counselor working with Eva Marie may be remiss if Eva Marie's cultural issues and background were ignored. Eva Marie identified the move from Mission, Texas, to Atlanta, Georgia, as a difficult transition in her childhood. She recalled moving from a primarily Latino area of the country to being the only Latino family in the neighborhood. This, along with her father dying at an early age, may certainly be a factor related to her present-day anxiety.

Eva Marie mentioned her most important relationship is with her mother. As an individual who suffers from a rather unfulfilling marriage, counselors who are unfocused on the multicultural implications emanating from a matriarchal culture may inadvertently indicate that the most important relationship should be her marriage. Such a statement could be an ethical violation, as counselors are not to impose their values upon the client. "Counselors are aware of their own values, attitudes, beliefs, and behaviors and avoid imposing values that are inconsistent with counseling goals. Counselors respect the diversity of clients, trainees, and research participants" (American Counseling Association, 2005, pp. 4–5). The value of the relationship Eva Marie has with her mother is a cultural norm and should be respected and understood.

Another aspect of Eva Marie's marriage that should be considered is her long history of remaining in an unfulfilling marriage. Such an issue should be viewed from a multicultural context in which both Eva Marie's Mexican American background and Catholic faith discourage divorce. Counselors should be aware that religious diversity is an aspect of multicultural diversity (Levitt & Balkin, 2003). Eva Marie's upbringing, her relationships as an adolescent, and her notions about family appear heavily influenced by her faith. A counselor should note that the job that Eva Marie enjoyed most was related to a position as a bookkeeper with a Catholic church. Once again, a counselor should be aware of the cultural implications related to the issues and decisions Eva Marie made regarding her marriage and understand why Eva Marie persists in a rather unhappy and unfulfilling relationship.

Ultimately, a client such as Eva Marie should be viewed within the context of her culture. The aforementioned case study contains elements related to ethnicity, Latino/a culture, religion, and spirituality that should be explored within the context of the relevant treatment issues identified by the client and counselor. Counselors working with clients like Eva Marie may need to explore cultural issues with the client but also engage in additional learning and supervision opportunities to adequately address Eva Marie's issues with a degree of multicultural competence.

References

American Counseling Association. (2005). *ACA code of ethics.* Alexandria, VA: American Counseling Association.

American Educational Research Association, American Psychological Association, & National Council of Measurement in Education. (1999). *Standards for educational and psychological testing.* Washington, DC: American Educational Research Association.

American Psychiatric Association. (2000). *Diagnostic and statistical manual of mental disorders* (4th ed., text rev.). Washington, DC: Author.

Arredondo, P., Toporek, M. S., Brown, S., Jones, J., Locke, D. C., Sanchez, J., & Stadler, H. (1996). *Operationalization of the multicultural counseling competencies.* Alexandria, VA: AMCD.

Balkin, R. S. (2006). A reexamination of trends in acute care psychiatric hospitalization for adolescents: Ethnicity, payment, and length of stay. *Journal of Professional Counseling: Practice, Theory, and Research, 34,* 49–59.

Balkin, R. S., Miller, J., Ricard, R. J., Garcia, R., & Lancaster, C. (2011). Assessing factors in adolescent adjustment as precursors to recidivism in court-referred youth. *Measurement and Evaluation in Counseling and Development, 44,* 52–59. doi: 10.1177/0748175610391611

Beck, A. T., Steer, R. A., & Brown, G. K. (1996). *BDI-II manual.* San Antonio, TX: The Psychological Corporation.

Brabeck, M. M., Rogers, L. A., Sirin, S., Henderson, J., Benvenuto, M., Weaver, M., & Ting, K. (2000). Increasing ethical sensitivity to racial and gender intolerance in schools: Development of the Racial Ethical Sensitivity Test. *Ethics & Behavior, 10,* 119–137. doi:10.1207/S15327019EB1002_02

Canel-Çınarbaş, D., Cui, Y., & Lauridsen, E. (2011). Cross-cultural validation of the Beck Depression Inventory-II across U.S. and Turkish samples. *Measurement and Evaluation in Counseling and Development, 44,* 77–91. doi: 10.1177/0748175611400289

Cartwright, B. Y., Daniels, J., & Zhang, S. (2008). Assessing multicultural competence: Perceived versus demonstrated performance. *Journal of Counseling & Development, 86,* 318–322.

Chernin, J., Holden, J. M., & Chandler, C. (1997). Bias in psychological assessment: Heterosexism. *Measurement and Evaluation in Counseling and Development, 30,* 68–76.

Constantine, M. G. (2001). Multiculturally-focused counseling supervision: Its relationship to trainees' multicultural counseling self-efficacy. *The Clinical Supervisor, 20,* 87–98. doi:10.1300/J001v20n01_07

Constantine, M. G. (2002). Predictors of satisfaction with counseling: Racial and ethnic minority clients' attitudes toward counseling and ratings of their counselors' general and multicultural counseling competence. *Journal of Counseling Psychology, 49,* 255–263. doi:10.103//00222-0167.49.2.255

Constantine, M. G. (2007). Racial microaggressions against African American clients in cross-racial counseling relationships. *Journal of Counseling Psychology, 54,* 1–16. doi: 10.1037/0022-0167.54.1.1

Council for Accreditation for Counseling and Related Educational Programs. (2009). *2009 standards.* Alexandria, VA: Author.

Fangzhou, Y., & Patterson, D. (2010). Examining adolescent academic achievement: A cross-cultural review. *Family Journal, 18,* 324–327. doi:10.1177/1066480710372071.

Helms, J. E. (1992). Why is there no study of cultural equivalence in standardized cognitive ability testing? *American Psychologist, 47,* 1083–1101.

Jones, W. P., & Markos, P. A. (1997). Client rating of counselor effectiveness: A call for caution. *Journal of Applied Rehabilitation Counseling, 28,* 23–28.

Levitt, D. H., & Balkin, R. S. (2003). Religious diversity from a Jewish perspective. *Counseling and Values, 48,* 57–67.

Li, L. C., & Kim, B. S. K. (2004). Effects of counseling style and client adherence to Asian cultural values on counseling process with Asian American college students. *Journal of Counseling Psychology, 51,* 158–167. doi:10.1037/0022-0167.51.2.158

Reynolds, W. M. (2001). *Reynolds Adolescent Adjustment Screening Inventory.* Odessa, FL: Psychological Assessment Resources.

Rye, M. S., Loiacono, D. M., Folck, C. D., Olszewski, T. A. H., & Madia, B. P. (2001). Evaluation of the psychometric properties of two forgiveness scales. *Current Psychology: Developmental, Learning, Personality, Social, 20,* 260–277.

Sedlacek, W. E. (2004). *Beyond the big test: Noncognitive assessment in higher education.* San Francisco, CA: Jossey-Bass.

Sedlacek, W. E., & Kim, S. H. (1995). *Multicultural assessment.* ERIC Digest (ERIC Digest No.: EDO-CG-95-24).

Skiba, R. J., Knesting, K., & Bush, L. D. (2002). Culturally competent assessment: More than non-biased tests. *Journal of Family Studies, 11,* 61–78.

Vereen, L. G., Hill, N. R., McNeal, D. T. (2008). Perceptions of multicultural counseling competency: Integration of the curricular and the practical. *Journal of Mental Health Counseling, 30,* 226–236.

Walsh, W. B., & Betz, N. E. (2001). *Tests and assessment* (4th ed.). Upper Saddle River, NJ: Prentice-Hall.

Wohlgemuth, E. A. (1997). Walking the fine line between parsimony and oversimplification: Attempting to decrease bias in assessment. *Measurement and Evaluation in Counseling and Development, 30* (2), 77-81.

CHAPTER 9

Fundamentals of Intelligence Assessment

OBJECTIVES

After reading this chapter, you will be able to:

1. Understand historical and contemporary theories of intelligence.
2. Evaluate theoretical frameworks of intelligence and assessment instruments used to measure intelligence.
3. Identify benefits and challenges in intelligence testing.
4. Understand the nature of assessment reports that measure intelligence.
5. Apply intelligence testing to the case example.

DEFINING INTELLIGENCE: THEORIES AND MODELS

The assessment of intelligence is intertwined with the history of assessment, as discussed in Chapter 1. The separate investigation into individual differences by Galton and Wundt led to the advent of the first intelligence test by Alfred Binet in 1905 (Gregory, 2007). Further development for intelligence testing in the United States occurred when Lewis Terman revised Binet's scale, creating the Stanford-Binet Test in 1916. Although the Stanford-Binet Test was revised in 1937, David Wechsler, who became chief psychologist at Bellevue Psychiatric Hospital, was dissatisfied with the Stanford-Binet scale and developed a measure known at the time as the Wechsler-Bellevue Intelligence Test in 1939, which would later become the Wechsler Adult Intelligence Scale (WAIS).

Missing from these tests, however, was any prominent theory guiding their development. The first test of intelligence from Binet in 1905 preceded any predominant theories of intelligence. Moreover, later revisions and future tests were developed in a response to the Binet test and later Stanford-Binet test. A famous statement associated with defining intelligence was made by the psychologist, Edwin G. Boring (1923, as cited in Gregory, 2007), indicating that intelligence may be defined by whatever is being evaluated by intelligence tests. In other words, the intelligence test defines intelligence. Hence, the evolution of intelligence testing occurred without a theoretical framework for the construct being measured, which is quite a deviation from the standards of test validity used today. Thankfully, intelligence testing has evolved since the early 20th Century and many tests of intelligence may be identified with a theory. However, with multiple theories of intelligence come multiple definitions of intelligence. Today, there continues to be a lack of consensus regarding the definition of intelligence, and even, perhaps, an overreliance on instruments to define intelligence. This is analogous to the tail wagging the dog. Instruments measuring intelligence are used to define the construct (Esters & Ittenbach, 1999), which results in questions of validity of these measures. Without an operational definition, can a construct be truly measured? Yet, the numerous intelligence tests developed tend to correlate to each other, indicating that they are measuring a similar construct.

g Theory

The first theory of intelligence actually predates Boring's famous statement mentioned earlier. Charles Spearman (1904, 1927) developed the first theory of intelligence, known as *g theory*. Rather than define intelligence through the formulation of a theory, Spearman defined intelligence by correlations of numerous tests. To understand this very abstract concept, it is helpful to understand the role of factor analysis.

Keep in mind that Spearman was a pioneer in factor analysis, a statistical procedure widely used today to validate measures. Factor analysis is the process of identifying *latent variables*, variables that are not initially observed but can be identified by correlating scores on variables together to see if they have some common trait that can be identified. So, although intelligence cannot be observed, various tasks and traits can be observed (e.g., speak a foreign language, play a musical instrument, identification of differences, mathematical problem solving). The extent to which these behaviors show a relationship and can be grouped together is deemed a factor.

Spearman, therefore, theorized that measures of intelligence converge on a unitary factor, known as a *general factor* or *g*. However, Spearman also indicated that tests might measure specific factors that relate to *g*. In other words, a test could measure a single aspect of *g*, such as response time, which is only a specific factor of *g* and may have low correlations with other factors. Intelligence, according to Spearman, was based on two factors: *g*, or general intelligence, and *s*, or specific abilities (Edwards, 1994). Louis Thurstone, a contemporary of Spearman, also used factor analysis to establish primary mental abilities. Although Thurstone identified various primary mental abilities, only some of the abilities demonstrated moderate correlations to each other and were likely to be second-order factors of *g*, thereby corroborating Spearman's theory (Gregory, 2007): (a) verbal comprehension, (b) reasoning, (c) perceptual speed, (d) numerical ability, (e) word fluency, (f) associative memory, and (g) spatial visualization (Thurstone, 1938).

Such a definition, then, lends credibility to Boring's statement—the definition of intelligence is based on the correlation of the various tests used to measure intelligence. Two of the most prominent intelligence tests used today, the Stanford-Binet Intelligence Scales (SB5)—currently in its fifth edition—and the Wechsler Scales—which include a variety of scales but most commonly refer to the Wechsler Adult Intelligence Scale—IV (WAIS-IV), the Wechsler Intelligence Scale for Children—IV (WISC-IV), and the Wechsler Preschool and Primary Scale of Intelligence—IV (WPPSI), were initially (i.e., in their earlier editions) developed without a theoretical framework of intelligence. The development of the Binet scale—Measuring Scale of Intelligence—was developed in France, quite far from the initial theoretical underpinnings of Charles Spearman and his study on *g* theory. On the other hand, the first of Wechsler's scales, developed in 1939, was Wechsler's response to his dissatisfaction with the Stanford-Binet test, which he administered to Army recruits during WWI. Wechsler noticed individuals' deviations related to the intellectual capabilities that they supposedly indicated and their performance on the Stanford-Binet (Edwards, 1994). Wechsler was sent to study with Spearman and Pearson in 1918 and had the opportunity to study under Spearman and learn firsthand Spearman's *g* theory, wherein he concluded that Spearman's theory was overly simplistic. In turn, Wechsler formulated his own definition of intelligence from which the subsequent Wechsler scales were all derived: intelligence is the "global capacity to act purposefully, think rationally, and deal effectively with the environment" (Edwards, 1994, p. 1135). Although the lack of a theoretical framework tied to the initial development of both the Stanford-Binet and Wechsler scales is a legitimate criticism, the wide use and contribution of these instruments cannot be disputed. The scores from these tests appear quite valid in identifying individuals with developmental needs in education, placement, and services.

Hierarchical Models

Factor analysis serves as the dominant method of devising a theory of intelligence. As noted before, a legitimate criticism of this method is that the measures define the construct, as opposed to operationally defining a construct and developing a measure. This pattern of using correlated measures to define intelligence continued with Raymond Cattell (1963), but unlike Spearman who identified a single unifying factor (*g*), Cattell identified two factors: fluid intelligence, known as *gf*, and crystallized intelligence, known as *gc* (Brody, 2000; Gregory, 2007). Fluid intelligence refers to the ability of an individual to adapt to new situations or environments through learning and problem solving. Fluid abilities include flexibility, adaptability, and creative or unique approaches to problem solving. Such skills are less likely to be influenced by formal learning, education, and culture. Crystallized intelligence, however, is more culturally and educationally dependent and refers to the completion of a task or the ability to solve problems based on formal learning, such as learning that occurred through formal education or acculturation. Crystallized abilities include information typically measured through achievement testing, such as the ability to complete a math problem or mastery of some assigned material (Hunt, 2000; Kaufman, McLean, & Kaufman, 1995). Unlike crystallized intelligence, Cattell viewed fluid intelligence as a biologically influenced component that declined during the adult lifespan (Brody, 2000; Hunt, 2000). However, later research would indicate that both *gf* and *gc* are influenced through biological and cultural factors (Davidson & Downing, 2000) and may decline with age. Crystallized ability tends to peak in middle age and decline gradually, most likely from old age, whereas fluid ability tends to peak earlier in adulthood and decline steadily throughout the adult lifespan (Kaufman & Kaufman, 2004).

Gf-gc theory, along with Thurstone's work, was important in developing intelligence theory beyond a unitary concept supported by Spearman's *g* theory. John Horn, a student of Raymond Cattell, was instrumental in expanding *gf-gc* theory. Later derivations of the *gf-gc* model included a hierarchical structure with *gf* and *gc* at the top followed by additional components such as visual and auditory processing, processing speed, short-term and long-term memory, and sensory information (Davidson & Downing, 2000; Gregory, 2007).

Different opinions pervade regarding the extent to which *gf-gc* theory links to *g*. Esters and Ittenbach (1999) indicated that *gf-gc* theory provides strong statistical evidence that intelligence is not a unitary construct. However, John Carroll developed a three-stratum theory, which combines elements of *g* and *gf-gc*. Carroll analyzed over 460 datasets and developed a hierarchical structure with three levels, structured as a pyramid. At the top stratum is *g*, followed by the middle stratum, which consists of eight factors similar to Horn's of the *gf-gc* model: (a) fluid intelligence, (b) crystallized intelligence, (c) general memory and learning, (d) broad visual perception, (e) broad auditory perception, (f) broad retrieval ability, (g) broad cognitive speediness, and (h) processing speed. The middle stratum is also hierarchical; therefore, fluid intelligence had the highest correlation to the top stratum, *g*, whereas processing speed had the smallest correlation to *g*. The bottom stratum consisted of numerous specific abilities or skills (Davidson & Downing, 2000).

As mentioned before, the Wechsler scales and Stanford Binet were not developed according to a theoretical framework, but revisions of the instruments are aligned with *gf-gc* theory (Esters & Ittenbach, 1999), particularly for the Stanford-Binet, fifth edition. For example, the nonverbal or performance measures on the tests conform to fluid ability, which relies on adaptation and flexibility to solve problems—essentially a nonverbal skill; on the other hand, vocabulary, information, and computation conform to crystallized ability, such as information learned in a formal educational environment.

Numerous intelligence tests are available and may be more theoretically derived. For example, the Kaufman Brief Intelligence Test, 2nd edition (KBIT-2), was specifically designed to address fluid and crystallized intelligence. The K-BIT provides measures based on two domains: (a) Verbal domain, which is aligned with crystallized ability, and (b) Nonverbal domain, which is aligned with fluid ability. A more comprehensive review of the KBIT-2 is presented later in this chapter.

Contemporary Models of Intelligence

Up to this point, theories of intelligence were developed post hoc, or after the fact. Existing measures were used to derive theories. More contemporary theories are less reliant on measurement principles, such as factor analysis, with the idea that theory should be used to develop measures. With this in mind, Robert Sternberg developed the triarchic theory of intelligence. Sternberg rejected the unitary concept of intelligence, *g*, and sought to include information processing and cognitive functioning as a component of intelligence. On the positive side, Sternberg indicated that traditional measures of intelligence do not provide a complete picture, as intelligence has numerous components that cannot be assessed by a single measure. On the negative side, empirical evidence validating Sternberg's model is limited (Davidson & Downing, 2000; Gregory, 2007).

In triarchic theory, Sternberg (1985) identified three components of intelligence. *Componential intelligence* is the first component and consists of internal processes, often associated with information processing theory. These processes include (a) metacomponents, such as processes in problem solving (e.g., identifying a problem, defining a goal, selecting a strategy); (b) performance, which includes specific processes informed by metacomponents, such as making comparisons to generate a solution or justifying a decision;

(c) knowledge acquisition, which includes the ability to learn information. *Contextual intelligence* is the second component and involves applying componential intelligence to real-world problems through adapting (i.e., fitting into an existing environment) or shaping (i.e., changing an environment to suit personal needs). Experiential intelligence is the third component and involves the ability to deal with new and/or unique situations without clear direction and quickly transition from conscious to subconscious processes, known as *automatic processing* (Davidson & Downing, 2000; Gregory, 2007).

Sternberg's model of intelligence is both complex and esoteric. As mentioned before, the model is not empirically driven. However, the model is important for identifying the complex nature of intelligence and the numerous processes involved, which are quite difficult to measure.

Another contemporary model of intelligence is multiple intelligence theory, developed by Howard Gardner. Like Sternberg, Gardner rejected the unitary concept of intelligence and embraced models of intelligence that cannot be easily measured (Davidson & Downing, 2000). Another similarity to Sternberg is the absence of statistical analyses to validate the model. A distinctive aspect, however, was that Gardner established multiple intelligence theory through qualitative research, grounding theory based on the analysis of empirical data in "biology, neuropsychology, developmental psychology, and cultural anthropology" (Chen, 2004, p. 18). Gardner believed that naturalistic inquiry was the best measure of intelligence. Essentially, intelligence is best evaluated when observing real life.

According to Gardner's theory, eight intelligences were identified, with the first three representing abilities measured by traditional intelligence tests:

1. Linguistic: ability to use language to convey meaning and recall information.
2. Logical-mathematical: use symbols to convey relationships and apply logic to evaluate concepts.
3. Spatial: discern, change, and convert visual-spatial associations.
4. Musical: ability to comprehend and apply musical properties.
5. Bodily-kinesthetic: refers to physical skills, such as athletic abilities and coordination.
6. Intrapersonal: self-understanding of personal goals, emotions, strengths, and weaknesses.
7. Interpersonal: understanding of others' goals, feelings, and behaviors.
8. Naturalistic: understanding patterns found in natural environments (Davidson & Downing, 2000).

An important component in Gardner's multiple intelligence theory is that intelligence may be viewed in the context of an individual's strengths. For example, individuals who may struggle academically but show gifted athleticism may still be viewed as highly intelligent in specific areas related to Gardner's theory. A professional athlete, for instance, may excel in bodily-kinesthetic intelligence; a musician may excel in musical intelligence. However, a major criticism of multiple intelligence theory is the lack of statistical evidence to support this model.

Emotional Intelligence

Despite the lack of statistical evidence to support multiple intelligence theory, Gardner's assertion of interpersonal and intrapersonal intelligences was a major influence in the advent of emotional intelligence (EI). EI is a controversial construct, and similar to intelligence theory, includes competing models. Thus, defining EI is not straightforward but rather is based on the model employed. Furthermore, EI is a distinct construct of intelligence discussed so far, as the focus of EI is cognitive ability, and in some cases personality characteristics, that solely relate to emotions intrapersonally and interpersonally.

The mental ability model was based on the foundational work of Jack Mayer and Peter Salovey. Mayer and Salovey (1997) identified intelligence as the model suggests, through various abilities based on (a) perceiving and expressing emotion; (b) using emotion to think and make decisions; (c) labeling, analyzing, and understanding emotions, particularly complex feelings or mixed feelings; and (d) reflecting and regulating emotions.

The mental ability model is best measured by the Mayer-Salovey-Caruso Emotional Intelligence Test (MSCEIT), which provides four scores on each of the aforementioned areas and a total score. The instrument uses emotion-based problem-solving items. For example, a respondent might be asked to identify an emotion based on a picture or identify helpful emotions to solving a problem. Two scoring systems were developed for the MSCEIT. The first was based on a normative sample of 5000 participants. Respondents' scores are compared to a norm group. The second method of scoring is based on responses from a panel of 21 experts.

The mixed ability model was based on two prominent EI theorists, Daniel Goleman and Reuven Bar-on. Both view EI as a combination of mental ability and personality characteristics. Goleman identified five abilities/characteristics in EI: self-understanding of emotions, understanding of others' emotions, self-management, self-motivation, and relationship management. In contrast, Bar-on identified areas of interpersonal skills, intrapersonal skills, adaptability skills, stress management skills, and general mood, such as optimism and happiness (Mayer, Salovey, & Caruso, 2000). Both Goleman and Bar-on developed EI instruments that measure the respective components of their theories. Goleman developed the Emotional Competency Inventory (ECI), which measures self-awareness, self-management, social awareness, and social skills. Although the reliability estimates appear adequate, as well as the norming, validity evidence is limited (Watson, 2007). Bar-on developed the Emotional Quotient Inventory (EQ-I), which measures each of the five components of the aforementioned model and a composite score. The EQ-I uses a 5-point Likert-type scale ranging from (1) *very seldom or not true of me* to (5) *very often true of me or true of me.* Cox (2001) indicated adequate psychometric characteristics, but questioned the validity of the instrument because of the controversial nature of EI.

As mentioned before, the concept of EI was driven by Gardner's theory of multiple intelligences. Thus, the same problem that plagues multiple intelligence theory, the lack of statistical evidence, is a criticism in EI theory as well. Waterhouse (2006) was highly critical of both multiple intelligence theory and EI theory because of the lack of empirical evidence, conflicting multiple theories, and lack of predictive evidence. Although these instruments are popular, particularly in organizational settings, evidence is limited with respect to valid use and interpretation.

THREE COMMON INTELLIGENCE MEASURES

In this section we present an overview of three common intelligence tests: the Wechsler Adult Intelligence Scale—IV (WAIS-IV), Stanford-Binet Intelligence Scales, 5th edition (SB5), and the Kaufman Brief Intelligence Test—2nd edition (KBIT-2). These most recent revised measures have closer alignment with Carroll's expansion of *gf-gc* theory, as each

TABLE 9.1	Classification of Intelligence Scores		
Range of Standard Scores	SD Above/Below the Mean	Percentile	Category
131 or greater	+2.1 or greater	98th or higher	Upper extreme
116 to 130	+1.1 to +2	84th to 97th	Above average
85 to 115	−.9 to +1	18th to 84th	Average
70 to 84	−2 to −1	2nd to 16th	Below average
69 or below	−2 or less	less than 2nd	Lower extreme

provides an estimate of many of the aforementioned components of the model. Another common element is the use of subtests to estimate ability in specific types of intelligence and then to combine the scores from the scales to identify an overall measure of intelligence, commonly referred to as a Full Scale IQ (FSIQ). In each of the instruments, raw scores are transformed to standard scores consistent with the documented age of the participant. The standard scores range from 40 to 160 with a mean of 100 and standard deviation of 15. Different publishers established slightly different terminology to describe the classification ranges of intelligence. As a general rule, Table 9.1 provides classifications that may be used in score interpretation. Note that an individual who scores below 70 may have major deficits in intellectual functioning, while scores higher than 130 are indicative of individuals with very high intellectual functioning. However, as with any test, scores should never be used as a sole basis for diagnosis. For example, simply because a client scores 69 does not mean the client should be diagnosed with a developmental disorder. Rather, further assessment is needed. A score of 69 on the WISC-IV may indicate the need to assess the client using the Vineland Adaptive Behavior Scale—2nd edition, in order to provide more data in the diagnosis of a developmental disability.

Each of the tests measures various domains. For the SB5 and KBIT-2, the domains represent two broad categories: Verbal and Nonverbal. On the WAIS-IV, four broad categories are described. So, when identifying a composite score (e.g., FSIQ) based on the combined subscales, individual strengths and weaknesses may influence the total score. Hence, identification of differences in the various domains or indices is important. When large enough differences occur between domains or indices, strengths and deficits in cognitive functioning may be explained, which may reflect a difference in fluid versus crystallized intelligence (Kaufman & Kaufman, 2004). The score reports on these measures, as well as the manual, provide information to compare various scores and determine whether differences between domains or indices are large enough to be of concern. When notable differences are found between scores, such differences may be deemed *statistically significant*—that is, occurring outside the realm of chance.

Another important issue to consider is the role of standard error of measurement (*SEM*). Recall from Chapter 4 that the *SEM* accounts for error in the observed score and provides a band to which the respondent may likely score if retested. The instruments discussed in this section generally have a 4- to 5-point *SEM*. This becomes very pertinent when using scores for clients. In the above example, where a client has a FSIQ of 69, given the *SEM*, the client may range from 64 to 74. Categories, therefore, should be interpreted with caution, as in this case, the client would be somewhere between below average and the lower extreme. How this is communicated to a client or parent is extremely important.

WAIS-IV

The Wechsler scales, which include specific instruments for adults, children, and pre-school age, are among the most popular intelligence scales in the United States. Although differences may be noted between the WAIS-IV and the WISC-IV, an overview of the WAIS-IV will provide a general idea of how such tests may be used. Do keep in mind that with each revision of an instrument comes changes in administration and scoring. For example, previous versions of the WAIS used two subscales, Verbal and Performance. With the most recent edition of the WAIS-IV, four indices compose the FSIQ.

VERBAL COMPREHENSION INDEX. Three subtests and one supplemental subtest are included in measuring Verbal Comprehension. *Similarities* is a measure of verbal reasoning, which requires respondents to identify how two elements are alike. *Vocabulary* is a measure of understanding and verbal expression and requires respondents to define given words. *Information* is a measure of acquired knowledge, which is often addressed in formal education. *Comprehension* (supplemental) measures the ability to understand verbal abstractions, such as metaphors, through responses to open-ended questions. Much of what is measured in the Verbal Comprehension index may be considered as crystallized ability.

PERCEPTUAL REASONING INDEX. Three subtests and two supplemental subtests are included in measuring Perceptual Reasoning. *Block Design* measures visual and spatial reasoning but also requires motor skills in replicating a design shown on a page with blocks that are provided to the respondent. *Matrix Reasoning* is a nonverbal test in which the respondent must identify patterns and use spatial reasoning and logic. *Visual Puzzles* is a nonverbal test in which the respondent uses pattern identification, spatial reasoning, and pattern recognition. *Picture Completion* (supplemental) measures the ability to evaluate visual elements. *Figure Weights* (supplemental) is a measure of quantitative reasoning and the ability to make logical comparisons.

WORKING MEMORY INDEX. Two subtests and one supplemental subtest are included in measuring Working Memory. *Digit Span* measures concentration and working memory by asking respondents to repeat number sequences. *Arithmetic* is a measure of concentration and quantitative reasoning, as well as the ability to comprehend and express mathematical relationships. *Letter-number Sequencing* (supplemental) is similar to digit span and requires the respondent to sequence both numbers and letters.

PROCESSING SPEED INDEX. Two subtests and one supplemental subtest are included in measuring Perceptual Speed. These tests also require motor control. *Symbol Search* and *Coding* measure visual perception, motor speed, and mental speed through the identification of specified symbols, and in the case of Coding, the ability to copy the symbols quickly. *Cancellation* (supplemental) also measures visual-perceptual speed and requires respondents to mark specific symbols.

Tests that require motor control may not be appropriate for respondents with physical disabilities, so caution must be used in making decisions about which subtests to use and how the omission or accommodations of various tests affects the scoring and interpretation. The WAIS-IV is a strong, highly regarded instrument. The normative sample included 2200 individuals between ages 16 to 90. Reliability estimates are strong. Reliability estimates for scores among 13 age categories ranged between .71 to .96 for subtests, .87 to .98 for indices, and .97 to .98 for FSIQ. Numerous clinical studies and correlations with other measures indicate strong evidence of validity (Canivez, 2010).

SB5

The SB5, as mentioned earlier, is among the oldest and widely used intelligence instruments. The SB5 is appropriate for ages 2 to 85. Two primary domains are measured in the SB5: Verbal and Nonverbal. Within each domain are five subtests that measure a cognitive ability. The five cognitive abilities are similar in scope to what has been described earlier in this chapter: (a) Fluid Reasoning, (b) Knowledge, (c) Quantitative Reasoning, (d) Visual-spatial Processing, and (e) Working Memory.

Because the SB5 may be used across a wide age span (2 years to 85 years), the SB5 presents six levels (1–6) that may be used, with higher levels indicating increased difficulty. Both the Nonverbal domain and Verbal domain begin with a routing test. Examinees may begin on Levels 1–5, depending on how they perform on the routing test (D'Amato, Johnson, & Kush, 2005).

For the Nonverbal domain, the routing test occurs on the Object series/Matrices subtest, which measures fluid reasoning. Based on the performance on this subtest, the starting level on subsequent Nonverbal subtests is determined. For the rest of the Nonverbal domain, a subtest is paired with a cognitive ability. Knowledge may be measured by Picture Absurdities (Levels 4–6) and Procedural Knowledge (Levels 2–3); Quantitative Reasoning is a single scale for Levels 2–6; Visual-Spatial Processing may be measured by Form Patterns (Levels 3–6) or Form Board (Levels 1–2); Working Memory may be measured by Block Span (Levels 2–6) or Delayed Response (Level 1; D'Amato et al., 2005).

For the Verbal domain, the routing test occurs on the Vocabulary subtest, which measures Knowledge. Based on the performance on this subtest, the starting level on subsequent Verbal subtests is determined. For the rest of the Verbal domain, a subtest is paired with a cognitive ability. Fluid Reasoning may be measured by Verbal Analogies (Levels 5–6), Verbal Absurdities (Level 4) or Early Reasoning (Levels 2–3); Quantitative Reasoning is a single scale for Levels 2–6; Visual-Spatial Processing is a single scale entitled Position and Direction for Levels 2–6; Working Memory may be measured by Last Word (Levels 4–6) or Memory for Sentences (Levels 2–3; D'Amato et al., 2005).

The raw scores on each of the subtests may be converted to a standard score with a mean of 10 and standard deviation of 3. However, as mentioned before, domain scores for Verbal and Nonverbal IQ, as well as for FSIQ are converted to standard scores with a mean of 100 and standard deviation of 15. Like the WAIS-IV, manipulatives are included in the assessment, which may require accommodations to scoring for individuals with physical disabilities. The normative sample included 4,800 individuals between the ages of 2 to 85. Reliability estimates for scores on Verbal, Nonverbal, and FSIQ domains are very high (.95 to .98) and scores on subtests range from .84 to .89. Excellent validity evidence with other established measures (i.e., correlations with other measures), such as the Wechsler scales, is indicated in the manual (Roid, 2003).

KBIT-2

Two essential issues govern the use of the Wechsler scales and SB5. The instruments are complex and take longer to administer. In addition, because of their complex nature, they are generally regarded as Class C instruments, which means assessment professionals should have a high level of expertise in test interpretation. We advocate for specific training in intelligence testing to administer either the SB5 or Wechsler scales. In contrast, the KBIT-2 is a Class B instrument, although formal training in assessment, particularly related to working with children and their parents, is required.

The KBIT-2 is a brief measure designed to provide estimates of intelligence consistent with more established measures in a short period of time. As mentioned before, the KBIT-2 provides measures based on two domains: (a) Verbal domain, which is aligned with crystallized ability, and (b) Nonverbal domain, which is aligned with fluid ability.

The Verbal domain includes two subtests: Verbal Knowledge and Riddles. These subtests are designed to measure vocabulary, reasoning ability, and general information. Two types of items are evident in Verbal Knowledge, general information and vocabulary, which serve as the primary components to measuring crystallized ability (*gc*) in the Catell-Horn-Carroll theory (Kaufman & Kaufman, 2004). In Verbal Knowledge, the respondent is shown a series of pictures and the administrator says a word or asks a question. The respondent has to point to the picture or say the corresponding letter that either identifies what the word means or answers the question. In Riddles, a question is asked and the respondent is to provide a one-word response. For younger children (ages 4 to 6), pictures are used. The Riddles subtest evaluates knowledge of information and vocabulary. Similar to Verbal Knowledge, crystallized ability is assessed, but so is reasoning and logic.

The Nonverbal domain includes one subtest—Matrices, which is designed for problem solving that is more atypical or innovative and not necessarily taught in formal education (Kaufman & Kaufman, 2004). Hence, the Matrices subtest is more aligned with fluid ability. Matrices contain three separate sections; as the examinee moves through each section, the items get progressively more difficult. In the first section, the client is presented with a drawing in the middle of a page with a series of objects at the bottom of the page. The examinee must select the object that is conceptually related to the drawing. In the second section, a pair of objects or designs is presented, with one object/design on the left and a blank on the right. The examinee is given choices to select the object/design that fits on the right. In the third section, a square array of abstract figures is presented with a blank cell in the square. The examinee must select the appropriate object/design that fits the pattern. Along with problem solving and logic, this subtest also evaluates pattern recognition and visual-spatial ability.

A benefit of this instrument is the short administration time, compared to more intensive instruments, of 15 to 30 minutes. In the experience of these authors, the KBIT-2 can be very helpful when clients may have fallen through the system and lack any type of formal evaluation. For example, a client who has not been tested for special services from the school may be administered a KBIT-2 as a screen for intellectual functioning. Findings may be reported to the school (with consent) to build a case for more formal testing. In addition, the KBIT-2 may be useful when the counselor has concerns related to intellectual functioning because of the client's inability to adapt to new situations or understand cause and effect. Scores from the KBIT-2 may be helpful in identifying deficits in cognitive ability. Counselors should keep in mind that the KBIT-2 correlates strongly with more established measures, but lacks the breadth of information as a comprehensive intelligence test like the WAIS-IV, WISC-IV, or SB5.

TYPES OF INFORMATION DERIVED FROM OUR CASE STUDY WITH EVA MARIE

From the information presented in either of the case studies, a rationale for administering an intelligence test is not readily available. In order to provide a rationale to use intelligence testing for a case study presented in this text, we need to add some additional information to the case study of Eva Marie Garza. Recall that Eva Marie was a good student, as evidenced by her induction in the National Honor Society in sixth grade and remaining in the National Honor Society throughout high school. Eva Marie earned an associate's degree in accounting and never considered continuing postsecondary education toward a bachelor's degree.

Previously, Eva Marie had a job as a bookkeeper, which she enjoyed immensely, but she currently works as an assistant to the chief librarian at an elementary school. At 40 years old, Eva Marie may have over 20 years to invest in a career, but she may also lack some self-efficacy with respect to going back to school to earn a 4-year degree or more in order to enhance her career opportunities. Given Eva Marie's anxiety, she may feel that she lacks the capacity to succeed in additional training that would facilitate a career transition. Even with encouragement from a counselor and pointing out that her academic history was quite strong, Eva Marie may be resistant to and anxious about the idea of further education. Certainly, the pressure she places on herself to care for her mother and the unemotional relationship she has with her husband, as well as the depressive symptoms that accompany her anxiety and possible comorbid depression, Eva Marie likely engages in negative self-talk that would serve as discouragement for pursuing further education. For example, Eva Marie may tell herself, "I could never get a four-year degree at my age," "I am not that smart. I just worked hard, and I do not know if I can do that anymore," or "Even if I earned a 4-year degree, who would hire me?"

Often, clients like Eva Marie may benefit from a concrete, objective evaluation that could enhance her self-concept and provide information that could be used to encourage her to take some risks that may be beneficial. For this reason, the counselor may opt to administer a brief intelligence measure, such as the K-BIT-2. What follows is a score report based on an administration of the KBIT 2 to Eva Marie.

Eva Marie was administered the Kaufman Brief Intelligence Test-2 (KBIT-2) in order to provide Eva Marie general feedback about her intellectual capabilities. Administration of the KBIT-2 was within the guidelines of stated procedures, and results from this test may be viewed as a valid measure. The KBIT-2 is a brief measure of intelligence that may be used as a screen for intellectual functioning. The KBIT-2 correlates strongly with established measures of intelligence, such as the Wechsler Intelligence Scales.

Eva Marie's score report from the KBIT-2 indicated above average intellectual functioning. The Table 9.2 represents Eva Marie's scores on the KBIT-2.

As shown in Table 9.2, Eva Marie scored in the 79th percentile of the Verbal domain, placing her in the average range of intellectual functioning. The Verbal domain is a measure of crystallized ability, which generally reflects cognitive ability associated more with formal education. Eva Marie, therefore, ranks in the average range in her ability to identify and express verbal concepts, reason, and demonstrate knowledge of general information.

TABLE 9.2	Score Summary on the KBIT-2				
Scale	Raw Scores	Standard Scores	90% CI (SEM)	Percentile Rank	Descriptive Category
Verbal Domain	97	112	104–119	79th	Average
Verbal Knowledge	52				
Riddles	45				
Nonverbal Domain	44	125	116–132	95th	Above average
Matrices	44				
IQ Composite*		119	113–124	90th	Above average

*IQ Composite is the sum of the standard scores (112 + 125 = 237) and then transformed to a standard score (119).

> *Eva Marie scored in the 95th percentile of the Nonverbal domain, placing her in the above average range of intellectual functioning. The Nonverbal domain is a measure of fluid ability, which generally reflects reasoning and learning outside of acculturation and formal education. Eva Marie, therefore, shows strong ability in addressing novel problems that are not necessarily taught or trained.*
>
> *Although the difference between Eva Marie's Verbal and Nonverbal scores was notable and statistically significant (p < .05), the difference was not large enough to be considered infrequent or unusual. Eva Marie's IQ composite is 119, also placing her in the above average range and reflective of the top 10% of intellectual functioning given her placement in the 90th percentile.*
>
> *The purpose of this assessment was to provide Eva Marie objective information that she could use to decide whether or not she has the ability to pursue higher education at this age and stage of her life. Given Eva Marie's above average intellectual capacities, particularly as they relate to her reasoning ability and problem-solving ability with novel situations, she is likely a good candidate for further educational pursuits.*

References

Boring, E. G. (1923, June 6). Intelligence as the tests test it. *New Republic, 35*–37.

Brody, N. (2000).Theories and measurements of intelligence. In R. J. Sternberg (Ed.), *Handbook of intelligence.* New York, NY: Cambridge University Press.

Canivez, G. L. (2010). Review of the Wechsler Adult Intelligence Scale—4th edition. In R. A. Spies, K. F. Geisinger, & J. F. Carlson (Eds.), *The eighteenth mental measurements yearbook.* Lincoln, NE: Buros Institute of Mental Measurements. Retrieved from Mental Measurements Yearbook with Tests in Print database.

Cattell, R. B. (1963). Theory of fluid and crystallized intelligence: A critical experiment. *Journal of Educational Psychology, 54,* 1–22.

Chen, J. Q. (2004). Theory of multiple intelligences: Is it a scientific theory? *Teachers College Record, 106,* 17–23.

Cox, A. A. (2001). Review of the emotional Quotient Inventory. In B. S. Plake & J. C. Impara (Eds.), *The fourteenth mental measurements yearbook.* Lincoln, NE: Buros Institute of Mental Measurements.

D'Amato, R. C., Johnson, J. A., & Kush, J. C. (2005). Review of the Stanford-Binet Intelligence Scales, 5th edition. In R. A. Spies & B. S. Plake (Eds.), *The sixteenth mental measurements yearbook.* Lincoln, NE: Buros Institute of Mental Measurements.

Davidson, J. E., & Downing, C. L. (2000). Contemporary model of intelligence. In R. J. Sternberg (Ed.), *Handbook of intelligence.* New York, NY: Cambridge University Press.

Edwards, A. J. (1994). Wechsler, David (1896–1981). In R. J. Sternberg (Ed.), *Encyclopedia of intelligence* (Vol. 1, pp. 1134–1136). New York, NY: Macmillan.

Esters, I. G., & Ittenbach, R. F. (1999). Contemporary theories and assessments of intelligence: A primer. *Professional School Counseling, 2,* 373–376.

Gregory, R. J. (2007). Psychological testing: History, principles, and applications (5th ed.). Boston, MA: Allyn & Bacon.

Hunt, E. (2000). Let's hear it for crystallized intelligence. *Learning and Individual Differences, 12,* 123–129.

Kaufman, A. S., & Kaufman, N. L. (2004). *KBIT-2 manual: Kaufman Brief Intelligence Test,* 2nd edition. Minneapolis, MN: NCS Pearson.

Kaufman, A. S., McLean, J. F., & Kaufman, J. C. (1995). The fluid and crystallized abilities of White, Black, and Hispanic adolescents and adults, both with and without an education covariate. *Journal of Clinical Psychology, 51,* 636–647.

Mayer, J. D., & Salovey, P. (1997). What is emotional intelligence? In P. Salovey & D. Sluyter (Eds.), *Emotional development and emotional intelligence: Implications for educators* (pp. 3–31). New York, NY: Basic Books.

Mayer, J. D., Salovey, P., & Caruso, D. (2000). Models of emotional intelligence. In R. J. Sternberg (Ed.), *Handbook of intelligence.* New York, NY: Cambridge University Press.

Roid, G.H. (2003). *Stanford-Binet Intelligence Scale—5th Edition.* Itasca, IL: Riverside [Test battery, examiners manual, technical manual, Scoring Pro software, and interpretive manual].

Spearman, C. (1904). "General intelligence" objectively determined and measured. *American Journal of Psychology, 15,* 201–293.

Spearman, C. (1927).*The abilities of man.* New York: Macmillan.

Sternberg, R. J. (1985). *Beyond IQ: A triarchic theory of human intelligence.* Cambridge, UK: Cambridge University Press.

Thurstone, L.L. (1938). *Primary mental abilities.* Chicago, IL: University of Chicago Press.

Waterhouse, L. (2006). Multiple intelligences, the Mozart effect, and emotional intelligence: A critical review. *Educational Psychologist, 41,* 207–225. doi:10.1207/s15326985ep4104_1

Watson, T. S. (2007). Review of the Emotional Competency Inventory. In K. F. Geisinger, R. A. Spies, J. F. Carlson, & B. S. Plake (Eds.), *The seventeenth mental measurements yearbook.* Lincoln, NE: Buros Institute of Mental Measurements.

CHAPTER 10

Fundamentals of Achievement and Aptitude Assessment: Issues of Ability

OBJECTIVES

After reading this chapter, you will be able to:

1. Understand ability testing in the context of achievement and aptitude tests.
2. Identify strengths and limitations in ability testing.
3. Identify elements of sound test construction related to achievement tests.
4. Conduct and interpret item analysis.
5. Identify various characteristics of ability tests.
6. Understand the relationship between achievement, aptitude, and general cognitive ability.
7. Apply ability testing to the case example.

THE CONTEXT OF ACHIEVEMENT AND APTITUDE TESTING

Perhaps no other area of testing is more used or debated than achievement and aptitude testing. The mandate of high-stakes testing required in No Child Left Behind Act (NCLB, 2002) brought achievement testing and educational accountability to the forefront in education, requiring documentation and monitoring of pass rates, educational assessment and placement of students, graduation requirements, and access to postsecondary education. Federal and state governments use achievement and aptitude testing to address the aforementioned requirements.

However, the role of achievement and aptitude testing goes beyond educational testing. Companies, state and federal agencies, the military, and other entities use achievement and aptitude tests to establish the appropriateness, skills, abilities, knowledge, and potential of applicants. The use of these tests is not without controversy, as noted in Chapter 1 relating to the New Haven, Connecticut, firefighters. The utility of achievement and aptitude tests, along with the interpretation, meaning, and decisions made based on these test results, may have enormous repercussions. Counselors need to be aware of the inherent strengths and weaknesses of achievement and aptitude testing, in order to place the use of such tests in proper perspective.

DEFINING ACHIEVEMENT AND APTITUDE TESTING

Achievement testing refers to an examination over material that was learned or acquired. Unlike intelligence and aptitude tests, which are not aligned with a set of material introduced to the examinee, achievement tests are aligned with a curriculum or program. For example, states often develop their own statewide achievement tests that are aligned with the educational standards for each state, such as the Iowa Test of Basic Skills or the Florida Comprehensive Assessment Test. Other examples outside of the educational system could include state drivers' license examinations, in which participants have the option of taking a course, reading a manual, and taking the test. The key to achievement testing is that the individuals tested were exposed to the material previously. Examinees, in essence, have the opportunity to be prepared for such an examination.

Aptitude testing refers to measurement of a set or sets of abilities. In other words, aptitude should measure what individuals may be capable of achieving. Whereas achievement tests measure the acquisition of knowledge and skills in which the presentation of material was standardized or at least partially standardized, aptitude tests measure ability when the presentation of material is relatively unknown or uncontrolled. A helpful comparison may be to view achievement testing as measuring something that should be known versus aptitude testing predicting what an individual may be able to do (Anastasi & Urbina, 1997).

The distinction between achievement testing and aptitude testing in educational settings may become blurry. For example, a department of education for a given state may mandate a given curriculum for each grade level and the development of an achievement test to measure knowledge areas of the curriculum. However, the extent to which each student was exposed to the specific curricular areas and the manner in which exposure occurred might vary. Thus, educational achievement is difficult to measure given that a standardized test is employed to measure a nonstandardized procedure (i.e., teaching). The extent to which a test score is predictive of future performance may actually be tied to prior exposure to a set of material. For instance, when taking an achievement test, an examinee is likely exposed to vocabulary words that are less familiar. However, the ability to discern the meaning of such words may be more related to the amount of reading the examinee engages in, rather than some predetermined criteria. The lack of a standardized method for enriching vocabulary may reflect more aptitude than achievement. Moreover, the antithesis is also true. When presenting more complex vocabulary on an aptitude test, such as the ACT or SAT, previous education may play a role in an examinee's ability to correctly respond to an item or scale. Anastasi and Urbina (1997) recognized the loose definitions of achievement and aptitude testing and advocated for the term *ability testing* as a more appropriate description of the cognitive process being measured.

The viewpoint that achievement testing and aptitude testing may be more similar than different should not be overlooked. Recall in Chapter 4 the reference to the state of

Maine, in which the state adopted the use of the SAT as an achievement measure. The issue with this decision was the use of an aptitude test to measure achievement. However, an examination of current research, along with Anastasi and Urbina's (1997) assertion of achievement testing and aptitude testing being quite similar, actually may lend credibility to Maine's decision to use the SAT as a measure of achievement. However, such a decision would be beneficial only if such aptitude tests were strong measures of future academic performance beyond grade point average (GPA) and standardized achievement tests.

The argument of using standardized aptitude tests for college entrance was based on the idea that a standardized aptitude test would increase fairness related to admissions to postsecondary education institutions. "The idea of using such tests is based on the noble aim of leveling the playing field at school-leaving age so that access to higher education is not limited to those who have had access to greater educational resources during childhood" (Stringer, 2008, p. 55). For instance, making comparisons among students with respect to GPA may be unfair because of the lack of opportunities some students had. A student who graduated from a rural school district may have less access to advanced placement courses than a student from a metropolitan school district. An argument in favor of aptitude testing is that such a test would serve as an unbiased measure of potential student achievement in higher education.

However, Cimetta, D'Agostino, and Levin (2010) noted that modern aptitude tests, particularly since 1994, include more facets of educational achievement in order to give more weight to actual problem solving, as opposed to predicting readiness for the higher education learning environment. One could argue that these elements, readiness to learn and the ability to problem solve, are synonymous. Indeed, modern aptitude tests appear quite similar to achievement tests because of the focus on knowledge-related items, and both kinds of tests appear to contribute equally to predicting first-year college GPA, approximately 6% of the variance to the model; the largest predictor to first-year college GPA was high school GPA (Cimetta et al., 2010).

Although the effort to view students without biased measures is ethical and honorable, the reality is that such tests may fall short of this goal. Both achievement tests and aptitude tests may fail to measure noncognitive variables such as study skills and motivation (Stringer, 2008), realistic self-appraisal, positive self-concept, and preference for long-term goals (Sedlacek, 2004).

CHARACTERISTICS OF ACHIEVEMENT INSTRUMENTS

Achievement tests may be as various as the curricula intended to be measured. Achievement tests may measure a specific area, such as reading, or may be broader, encompassing many areas. Although the focus of achievement testing is on knowledge acquired or learned, achievement testing is also used to address learning proficiency (as required by NCLB) and as evidence to determine if additional educational services are needed. For example, achievements tests may serve as evidence of some type of learning disability or dyslexia if a student tests at level in mathematics but markedly lower in vocabulary.

Achievement tests may fall into different categories. Keep in mind the description of an achievement test includes the focus on material introduced in a standardized or partially standardized fashion. However, the nature of standardization is that each individual is exposed to the same conditions for learning and evaluation. So, although exposure to material may be regimented, the process of teaching the material and evaluating the acquired learning may not necessarily be standardized. In the forthcoming discussion, nonstandardized and standardized measures of achievement are discussed.

Teacher-Created Examinations

Perhaps the most widely used nonstandardized examination procedure comes from educators who develop examinations to assess the extent to which individuals learned material presented to them. Although the content of courses, and even materials for a course (e.g., textbook) may be aligned with a larger curriculum, class examination occurs as an independent process. Two instructors teaching the same course may use different assessments to identify student learning. Clearly, the process of standardizing measures of achievement for teaching a variety of courses in numerous settings and various learning environments would be unfathomable. However, without a standardization procedure, how can educators and evaluators measure achievement in a fair manner? Anastasi and Urbina (1997) identified a three-step process to test development that may increase test fairness while simultaneously forgoing a formal standardization procedure: (a) test design, (b) item development, and (c) item analysis.

TEST DESIGN   Designing a test to cover appropriate content requires planning. Test developers need to make sure that the content is aligned with the material presented and is assessed at a variety of cognitive levels. For example, items may be developed to ascertain the degree to which test-takers recall information or may reflect higher order thinking in terms of the ability to apply or evaluate information. When designing a test, developers may wish to consider the degree to which items reflect recall, which may consist of easier items, versus items that reflect more complex cognitive tasks (e.g., analysis and evaluation). One method of identifying the complexity of an item is to create items aligned with both content presented and cognitive domains associated with Bloom's taxonomy.

Bloom (1956) identified six cognitive domains: (a) knowledge, (b) comprehension, (c) application, (d) analysis, (e) synthesis, and (f) evaluation. A team of cognitive psychologists led by Lorin Anderson revised Bloom's cognitive domains. The revised version changed the six major categories from nouns to verbs and changed some of the terminology. Most notably, creating, formerly known as synthesis, was moved to a higher level of evaluating. Thus, the ability to generate something new was seen as a more complex task than evaluating what is currently known or present. The revised taxonomy is as follows: (a) remembering, (b) understanding, (c) applying, (d) analyzing, (e) evaluating, and (f) creating (Anderson & Krathwohl, 2001).

Using the revised cognitive domain categories, test developers should consider the extent to which an item requires the examinee to employ a lower level cognitive task (e.g., remembering) versus a higher level cognitive task (e.g., evaluating). Furthermore, consideration of the development of items that measure the aforementioned cognitive domains is important. Essay exams are useful in measuring a variety of cognitive domains, but the uniformity of evaluating answers, as well as the time necessary to evaluate responses, does not always lend to this method as appropriate or useful. Multiple-choice items may be developed to assess both lower level and higher level cognitive tasks, whereas other methods, such as matching or short answer, may focus more on the lower level cognitive categories.

Such preparation should result in a blueprint for the prospective test. From this plan, test developers may ensure that (a) the appropriate content is covered and (b) a balance between lower level and higher level cognitive categories is reflected. Keep in mind, tests that are weighted toward higher level cognitive categories may be perceived as difficult, whereas tests that are weighted toward lower level cognitive categories may be perceived as easy.

ITEM DEVELOPMENT The process of creating a blueprint for the test is essential for developing test items. Test developers should align items with the appropriate content and cognitive category to be evaluated. Item type should be considered carefully. Items may be open-ended, such as short answer or essay, or items may be closed-ended, such as multiple choice.

Although multiple-choice items appear to be quite popular because of their simplicity in grading, test developers should be cautious. Creating appropriate items that are clear, content aligned, and evenly distributed among the cognitive categories being assessed is pertinent to developing a valid measure. Multiple-choice tests or items can be difficult and time-consuming to develop but can be useful in assessing a variety of cognitive domains and result in rather reliable scores.

In addition to multiple-choice items, other item types to consider in test construction include true–false items, matching, short answer, and essay tests. Although true–false items are easier to score, the items are often less reliable. Short-answer and essay questions also are less reliable, in addition to taking more time to score. However, such items may be more appropriate for the cognitive domain being measured. For example, matching items may be helpful in measuring remembering, whereas essays may be more appropriate for measuring evaluating and creating.

ITEM ANALYSIS Previously addressed briefly in Chapter 6, item analysis is a process by which items can be evaluated according to difficulty and discrimination. Recall that item difficulty refers to the percentage of respondents that answer an item correctly:

$$P - \frac{C}{N}$$

where P refers to the item difficulty, C refers to the number of respondents answering the item correctly, and N refers to the total number of respondents. If 20 students take an exam and 8 individuals answer an item correctly, then $P = .40$ or 40% of the students answered the item correctly. Thus, a higher P indicates an easier item, and a lower P indicates a more difficult item.

Certainly, item difficulty can lend information about the easiness of an item and overall test. However, item difficulty alone is not sufficient in addressing whether an item should be kept and counted on an exam or removed. Evaluating item discrimination can be helpful in addressing the value of an item. Item discrimination provides for each item an index to compare how individuals who did well on the test compared to individuals who had a weaker performance on the test. In item discrimination, tests scores are divided into three groups: the upper groups consisting of the top 27% of scores, the lower group consisting of the bottom 27% of scores, and the middle group, which consists of everyone else and is generally not used in the discrimination index. Wiersma and Jurs (1990) suggested that the upper and lower 27% of scores is usually sufficient to differentiate between two groups while providing the necessary sample size for analysis. Once the scores are divided among the three groups, the discrimination index, D, can be computed as follows:

$$D = \frac{U_C}{n_U} - \frac{L_C}{n_L}$$

where U_C refers to the number of individuals who answered the item correctly in the upper group, L_C refers to the number of individual who answered the item correctly in the lower group, n_U refers to the number of individuals in the upper group, and n_L refers to the number of individuals in the lower group.

For example, a teacher administers an exam to 28 students. From the 28 students, the top and bottom eight scores approximately will compose the upper and lower groups, respectively. In the bottom 27%, two students made the same lowest score, so nine scores were in the lower group and eight scores were in the upper group. From eight students in the upper group, six students answered the item correctly. In the lower group consisting of nine students, three students answered the item correctly. So, using the formula above:

$$D = \frac{6}{8} - \frac{3}{9} = .42$$

Thus, 75% of individuals in the high group answered the item correctly, and 33% of individuals in the low group answered the item correctly. Generally, a discrimination index of .35 or higher is indicative of a higher quality item, whereas item discrimination below .20 is indicative of a less useful item (Hopkins, 1998). Therefore, this example is indicative of an item with rather strong discrimination. In other words, the majority of individuals in the high group know the material this item tests, but the majority of the individuals in the lower group do not. Along with item difficulty, a teacher can glean some important information related to this item:

1. To some degree, this item distinguishes well between students who understand the material this item represents and students who have less understanding.
2. An item of this nature may have a higher level of difficulty (depending on how well the middle group performed, as they were not included in computing item discrimination). Simply because an item is difficult does not make it a bad item, especially if students who have learned the material perform better on this item than students who have lesser understanding of the material.
3. The teacher has feedback on which items, and possibly what material, students may struggle with in the class.

So, when is an item bad? A bad item is evident when the discrimination index is lower than .20 and the item difficulty is low. For example, assume 20% of a class correctly answers an item, and the discrimination index is .15. This is indicative of an item in which both the higher and lower groups performed similarly and the vast majority of students (80%) answered the item incorrectly. When an item is both difficult and does not discriminate, the evaluator learns that either (a) the item is poorly written and should be discarded or (b) more time should be spent on this material, as the class appeared to struggle with this information.

Keep in mind that a discrimination index of .00 refers to a situation where equal percentages of students in the higher and lower groups answered the item correctly. This may happen on an extremely difficult item, in which a majority of students answer incorrectly as just noted, or this may occur with very easy items that all students answer correctly. For example, when material is taught well or the cognitive domain being tested is relatively low, such as remembering, a greater percentage of students may answer the item correctly. When the percentage of individuals answering the item correctly is high, and the item discrimination is near .00, such an item is relatively easy.

Another possibility is for a discrimination index to be negative (e.g., $D = -.20$). This occurs when a higher percentage of students in the lower group correctly answer an item than do students who performed well on the test. With respect to an item on a test, when the lower performing students outperform students who scored higher on the test, the item should be discarded, as the results are likely because of guessing and/or a poorly worded item.

Key to this discussion is the need for counselors, particularly those who work in academic settings and/or serve in areas of program evaluation and training, use proper procedures in developing test items. School counselors can provide in-services to teachers in terms of developing appropriate classroom tests and evaluating the items they use. Although item analysis is an essential component to creating tests and measuring progress, most preservice teachers are not exposed to this process in their training. Furthermore, counselors may serve as consultants and evaluators to agencies and organizations and develop proper instruments that reflect training or information related to an agency or organization.

TYPES OF ABILITY TESTING

The nature and purpose of various tests may differ, and therefore so do the areas tested. The next section addresses common areas of achievement and aptitude testing with brief descriptions of each area. As noted previously, Cimetta et al. (2010) documented the increased similarities between modern aptitude tests and achievement tests in educational environments. Therefore, the term *ability testing* encompasses relevant aspects of both achievement and aptitude testing.

Ability tests are administered in individual and group formats, often depending on the function and purpose of the test. Group administrations may be used to gauge learning outcomes. For example, states administer achievement tests to determine accountability for a teachers, schools, and districts, as well as use scores to address placement and measure achievement of set standards aligned with the curriculum. Colleges and universities use group-administered aptitude tests in the selection process of potential students. Individual administrations, on the other hand, may be used for diagnostic purposes, such as evaluating abilities or assessing for learning disabilities. Once again, the distinction between achievement tests and aptitude tests may be blurred; what is pertinent to counselors is the nature of the assessment and the evidence of the consequences of testing. For example, using a state achievement test to evaluate for learning disabilities would be inappropriate, even though many assessment professionals use achievement tests as evidence to determine the presence of a learning disability. Essentially, counselors need to be aware of what tests were administered and how they were used in evaluating a client/student. When assessments are used for diagnostic purposes, counselors should be aware that a single measure only serves as evidence and should never be used as a sole indicator related to the presence or absence of a diagnostic condition. Finally, individual ability measures, particularly related to achievement, should be viewed with caution. Whereas a state achievement test may be created by professionals who can align the test with a state curriculum, such a feat would be impossible with individual achievement tests normed on a national basis. This begs the question, how can a person be held accountable for knowledge not included in an organized curriculum? An argument can be made that national norms were used to gauge performance on each item, thereby identifying the items as appropriate.

Rather than catalog and describe a variety of individual and group measures of ability, the following sections will highlight some commonalities across widely used individual and group ability measures. Additional in-depth reviews of instruments may be found in the *Mental Measurements Yearbook* (described in Chapter 6).

Common Characteristics in Ability Assessment Instruments

Individual ability assessments use an array of subtests designed to facilitate diagnosis of learning disabilities, identification of gifted and talented students, and/or direction related to placement and planning of individuals in a variety of educational or vocational settings. These tests often include elements of verbal reasoning and mathematical reasoning.

Verbal reasoning is a term that is often used in aptitude testing, but generally refers to a global process that includes reading comprehension, vocabulary, and analysis of meaning, structure, or grammar of words, sentences, and passages. Traditionally, reading comprehension referred to the ability of an individual to discern, interpret, or understand the meaning of a written passage (Harris & Hodges, 1995). However, different tests may expand the definition of reading comprehension. For example, respondents may be asked to draw conclusions about a passage, identify strengths and weaknesses, and/or establish relationships.

Sight vocabulary includes items that evaluate the respondent's ability to identify words without context or use of phonetic techniques/devices (Harris & Hodges, 1995). For example, in the Wide Range Achievement Test (WRAT-4), respondents may be asked to read a series of words in order to evaluate recognition of more easily identifiable words. *Spelling* is a common scale on many achievement tests, often measured by the test examiner saying the word and the respondent attempting to spell the word. In other tests, a word may be presented that is misspelled and the respondent is required to note the misspelling. *Writing* tests on achievement and aptitude measures are somewhat complex because of the lack of standardization in measuring writing skills. Scoring for writing tests may include raters or computer programs. Scores may be based on content, grammar, structure, and complexity. Such measures may be ascertained by sentence length and the use of different sentence structures. Although some tests include an optional writing section, other tests, particularly in areas of achievement for schools, require writing tests.

Individual ability measures like the *Wide Range Achievement Test,* 4th Edition (WRAT-4) and the Wechsler Individual Achievement Test, Third Edition (WIAT-III) employ a variety of verbal reasoning measures, which, depending on the grade level of the child, may or may not be included in a verbal reasoning composite score. For example, the WRAT-4 includes three verbal reasoning subtests: word reading, sentence comprehension, and spelling. However, only word reading and sentence comprehension was included in the reading composite score. The WIAT-III is more complex, with up to 11 subtests used to compile five verbal reasoning composite scores: oral language, total reading, basic reading, reading comprehension and fluency, and written expression.

Mathematical reasoning refers to quantitative skills in methods, analysis, deduction, and inference (Steen, 1999). Therefore, what one test references as mathematical reasoning may be quite different from how another test presents mathematical reasoning. Although the term *mathematical reasoning* may imply a subtest on an aptitude measure, scores related to mathematical reasoning may correlate with scores related to math achievement, as evidenced by the relationship of the Differential Aptitude Test to other achievement measures (Hattrup, 1995). Essentially, mathematical reasoning may imply a variety of processes, from simple computation and procedural steps to complex tasks and applications of proofs and estimation that use more concrete skills as well as intuition. *Math calculation* refers to processes and strategies involved in computation of numerical operations. These types of items involve solving numerical problems using arithmetic operations. Some achievement tests, such as the WRAT-4, and aptitude tests, such as the Armed Services Vocational Aptitude Battery (ASVAB), time this subtest, so the evaluation may contain both speed and power elements. *Applied math skills/word problems* refer to items that require comprehension, application, and reasoning skills, which may include computation as well. In these items, examinees may be required to interpret meaning and draw inferences from what is written in order to answer the item. Hence, verbal reasoning skills are an integral component to applied math skills/word problems, so the conceptualization that verbal reasoning and mathematical reasoning are separate and distinct constructs may be unsubstantiated because of the reliance of verbal reasoning to perform many applied problems in mathematics.

What to Report

In addition to raw scores, standard score conversions, percentiles, and confidence interval measures based on standard error of measurement, score reports on achievement tests often provide information related to significant differences related to subscale scores. For example, the WIAT-III provides extensive data related to each subscale, as well as a composite summary, as noted in Figure 10.1. Qualitative descriptions accompany the scores in order to provide perspective of how the client's score may be compared to the general population.

In Figure 10.1, the standard score (third column) is based on a mean of 100 and standard deviation of 15. The qualitative description is based on the percentile rank (fifth column) related to the standard score. Note that a score marked as "Average" would fall between −1 and +1 standard deviation, or between 85 and 115. Scores identified as below average fall between −1 and −2 standard deviations, or between 70 and 84. Scores below 70 would therefore be at −2 standard deviations or below (see Figure 10.2). Another import facet of the summary table is the 95% confidence interval (fourth column). Recall from Chapter 4 that the *SEM* provides a less rigid interpretation by accounting for the error in the observed score. In other words, keep in mind that the score on a test is representative of a performance at a single point in time and therefore may not be

Age Based Scores

Subtest	Raw Score	Standard Score	95% Confidence Interval	Percentile Rank	Normal Curve Equiv.	Stanine	Grade Equiv.	Age Equiv.	Growth Score
Listening Comprehension	—	93	80–106	32	40	4	6.2	11:2	530
Reading Comprehension	21*	85	74–96	16	29	3	2.5	8:0	493
Math Problem Solving	49	89	81–97	23	35	4	6.1	11:0	566
Sentence Composition	—	53	43–63	0.1	<1	1	1.0	6:0	457
Word Reading	35	77	71–83	6	18	2	3.2	8:8	503
Essay Composition	—	80	70–90	9	22	2	3.4	8:4	499
Pseudoword Decoding	29	92	87–97	30	39	4	5.4	10:0	519
Numerical Operations	35	96	87–105	39	44	4	7.2	12:4	610
Oral Expression	—	93	80–106	32	40	4	6.3	11:7	533
Oral Reading Fluency	105*	107	100–114	68	60	6	9.0	15:0	557
Spelling	25	83	76–90	13	26	3	4.7	9:8	554
Math Fluency—Addition	43	113	102–124	81	68	7	12.7	17:0–19:11	778
Math Fluency—Subtraction	42	120	110–130	91	78	8	>12.9	>19:11	855
Math Fluency—Multiplication	29	102	92–112	55	53	5	7.5	13:4	719

— Indicates a subtest with multiple raw scores (shown in the Subtest Component Score Summary).

* Indicates a raw score that is converted to a weighted raw score (not shown).

† Indicates that a raw score is based on a below grade level item set.

FIGURE 10.1 Example of a Composite Score Summary for the WIAT-III

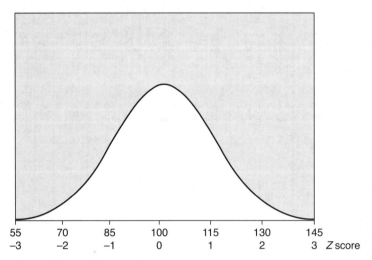

55	70	85	100	115	130	145	
−3	−2	−1	0	1	2	3	*Z* score

FIGURE 10.2 Interpretation of Standard Scores

representative of the true score. The issue of the difference between the true score versus the observed score is accounted for by using a 95% confidence interval, suggesting that the true score lies somewhere within the band that includes the observed score.

Some score reports provide information related to differences between subscale scores. The WRAT-IV uses a standard score comparison table (see Figure 10.3) to differentiate between various subscale scores. Note that once the score difference is calculated, statistical significance between the scores can be noted. Appendices in the test manual provide this information. Assessment professionals should focus on more conservative

Score Comparisons > = < (circle one)	Score Difference	Significance Level	Prevalence in Standardization Sample
Word Reading ☐ > = < ☐ Sentence Comprehension		ns .15 .10 .05 .01	>25% 25% 20% 15% 10% 5% 1%
Word Reading ☐ > = < ☐ Spelling		ns .15 .10 .05 .01	>25% 25% 20% 15% 10% 5% 1%
Word Reading ☐ > = < ☐ Math Computation		ns .15 .10 .05 .01	>25% 25% 20% 15% 10% 5% 1%
Sentence Comprehension ☐ > = < ☐ Spelling		ns .15 .10 .05 .01	>25% 25% 20% 15% 10% 5% 1%
Sentence Comprehension ☐ > = < ☐ Math Computation		ns .15 .10 .05 .01	>25% 25% 20% 15% 10% 5% 1%
Spelling ☐ > = < ☐ Math Computation		ns .15 .10 .05 .01	>25% 25% 20% 15% 10% 5% 1%

FIGURE 10.3 Standard Score Comparison Table for the WRAT-IV

significance levels (e.g., .05, .01) for interpretation purposes. The last column in Figure 10.3 indicates the likelihood of such differences occurring.

Noted differences between specific subscale scores, such as math reasoning and verbal reasoning, may shed light on possible learning deficits. For example, persistent differences between lower scores on word reading, sentence comprehension, and spelling when compared to math computation may indicate learning deficits with respect to verbal reasoning.

GROUP-ADMINISTERED ABILITY ASSESSMENT

Group-administered ability assessments are used in a variety of settings, providing information to address accountability, understanding of preestablished standards, vocational placement, and potential. States across the country rely on standardized tests to address learning outcomes in schools. Higher education relies on group-administered ability assessments to make decisions related to placement in higher education. In addition, agencies/organizations may use ability assessments for job placement, promotion, and hiring.

High-Stakes Testing

Perhaps more than any other test, group achievement tests in education tend to be the most publicized and utilized ability assessment instrument. Although the use of group ability assessments in schools preceded NCLB (2002), achievement testing was mandated by NCLB, thereby pushing education toward accountability and high-stakes testing. But what are the effects of such tests and testing practices in counseling? What do counseling professionals need to know about these tests and how the scores are used?

The implications of high-stakes testing—as a general practice by schools, agencies, and organizations—are serious, affecting clients, students, employees, administrators, and job seekers. High-stakes testing may be used to determine if a student, school, or school district meets a minimum standard, an employee receives a promotion, an individual meets requirements for a job, or a program receives funding. Specific to education, students may be denied a diploma or grade promotion, teachers may be denied merit, and schools/school districts may be denied funding.

In 2004, the American Counseling Association (ACA) released a position statement related to high-stakes testing. In the position statement, ACA recommended guidelines for high-stakes testing and indicated support for using high-stakes testing as a measure of accountability in education and program evaluation. "Essentially, high stakes testing should contribute to motivation and implementation of student learning, instructional effectiveness, and effective policy decisions about distribution of resources" (p. 1). ACA addressed 10 principles in the position statement: (a) alignment, (b) multiple measures, (c) impact, (d) opportunity to learn, (e) availability of remediation, (f) resources, (g) development of tests, (h) usefulness, (i) validity of scores for diverse populations, and (j) policies and applications.

The guidelines from the ACA position statement provide counselors with important information related to practical and ethical issues in high-stakes testing. Several of the principles outlined in the ACA policy statement address curriculum alignment. Alignment, as mentioned previously, refers to the extent to which the content of the exam is matched with the curriculum taught within a program. Within this alignment, examinees must have adequate and equivalent opportunities to learn the material along with the relevant resources required to address learning and, if necessary, remediation. In particular, individuals who fail to meet a minimum standard should be afforded the opportunity to remediate and rectify the situation. In addition, services should be offered to assist in remediation.

Another important element of the ACA (2004) position statement is related to validity evidence of the high-stakes testing. Recall that validity refers to the appropriateness of how test scores may be used. High-stakes testing not only uses instrument with strong psychometric properties (e.g., reliable scores, strong internal structure and relationship to other variables, appropriate content and response processes), but the appropriateness for testing with diverse populations (e.g., disabilities, English as a Second Language students) should be investigated, reported, and addressed in interpretation. Test scores should be interpreted accurately in understandable terms for professionals, parents, examinees, and stakeholders.

How high-stakes testing is ultimately used should be carefully analyzed on an ongoing basis to avoid adverse ramifications toward the application of the results. Counselors should be aware that no single measure stands alone. High-stakes testing can affect individuals and large groups/organizations. Multiple measures should be used in making decisions that can influence the future standing of individuals or groups. Individuals who create policies for high-stakes testing are responsible for ensuring the consequences of the test are aligned with the stated purpose and that such policies are published and distributed to examinees and stakeholders. High-stakes testing can affect an entire system. For example, the results of high-stakes testing can have deleterious consequences for students, teachers, school administrators, and districts. Appropriate professionals and stakeholders should be involved in the formation of policies regarding high-stakes testing to ensure the use of appropriate ethical and legal processes.

Common Group-Administered Ability Assessments

As mentioned previously, the shared qualities between achievement and aptitude testing make differentiation between the two types of tests difficult to distinguish. Perhaps one theoretical distinction, however, is the supposed alignment between curriculum standards and achievement testing. Hence, achievement tests are often the tool of choice in complying with NCLB (2002) policies. States often employ or create their own measures to comply with specific standards set forth by each state's department of education. In most cases, therefore, each state adopts its own group-administered achievement measure. Perhaps one of the most widely used and formative achievement measures is the Iowa Test of Basic Skills (ITBS). The ITBS was published in 1955 (Engelhard, 2007), although initial development goes back another 20 years prior. Engelhard summarized, "[T]he ITBS is as good it gets for users requiring a comprehensive, norm-referenced achievement test battery for elementary school students (Grades K to 8)" (paragraph 18).

A review of the ITBS can be helpful in understanding the common group-administered achievement test. The test was designed to provide teachers with data for making student-centered decisions, provide parents and students with a measure of educational progress, and evaluate student progress with a content-aligned curriculum. The content areas tested on the ITBS vary by level and the type of desired information. The level of the test refers to Levels 5 (beginning at kindergarten) through 14. Riverside Publishing, which publishes the ITBS at the time of this writing, provides a breakdown of the instrument, which consists of three batteries listed from most extensive to least extensive: the complete battery, the core battery, and the survey battery. The entry levels (Levels 5 and 6), consist of the following tests for the complete battery: Vocabulary, Word Analysis, Listening, Mathematics, Word Reading, and Reading Comprehension. Each of these tests are untimed and read aloud by the teacher, with the exception of the reading test. In Levels 7 and 8, the complete battery consists of the following tests: Vocabulary, Word Analysis, Reading, Listening, Language, Word Concepts, Math Problems, Math Computation, Social Studies, Science, and Sources of Information. With the exception of vocabulary and reading, all of the tests at these levels are orally administered and all tests at these levels and beyond are timed. In Levels 9 through 14, the complete battery consists of the following tests: Vocabulary, Reading Comprehension, Language, Math, Social Studies, Science, and Sources of Information (Riverside Publishing, 2010).

Similarities between individually administered achievement measures and group-administered achievement measures, such as the ITBS, should be noted. Specifically, areas related to mathematical and verbal reasoning in individually administered achievement tests were addressed in the ITBS and other group administered ability measures [e.g., Arizona's Instrument to Measure Standards (AIMS)].

Group-administered ability instruments may be designed to predict performance, identify strengths and weaknesses, and/or measure skills/abilities in key areas. These tests may be referred to as aptitude tests. Although both achievement tests and aptitude tests are ability measures that may assess strengths and weaknesses in key areas, aptitude measures are not necessarily aligned with a curriculum. Moreover, the categorization of such tests is confusing as a result of such seminal published works like the *Mental Measurements Yearbook* (MMY). As examples of various aptitude measures follow, be aware of the MMY categorization of the measure and why confusion regarding ability measures persists.

Common measures of job performance include the Differential Aptitude Test (DAT) and the ASVAB. The DAT is for Grades 7 through 12 and adults and is designed to measure essential domains relevant to job performance based on general cognitive ability (e.g., verbal reasoning, numerical reasoning), skills (e.g., spelling, language use, perceptual speed and accuracy), and perceptual ability (abstract reasoning, mechanical reasoning, space relations). Although the publisher, Pearson Assessments, indicates that the focus of the instrument is to predict job performance, the MMY lists the DAT as an achievement test.

The ASVAB is listed as an intelligence and general aptitude measure in the MMY and administered to high school and young adult populations. The ASVAB includes eight subtests: General Science, Arithmetic Reasoning, Word Knowledge, Paragraph Comprehension, Mathematics Knowledge, Electronics Information, Auto and Shop Information, and Mechanical Comprehension. The ASVAB uses a subscale, the Armed Forces Qualifications Test, comprised of scores from Word Knowledge, Paragraph Comprehension, Arithmetic Reasoning, and Math Knowledge, to determine military service qualification.

Aptitude measures are very popular in educational settings related to college admissions (e.g., SAT, ACT) and admission to graduate studies (e.g., GRE, Law School Admission Test [LSAT], Medical College Admission Test [MCAT], Graduate Management Admission Test [GMAT]). The idea is that these tests are helpful in predicting success in postsecondary education. As a general rule, these tests emphasize verbal reasoning, mathematical reasoning, and writing. Variations do exist among the measures. For example, the SAT evaluates critical reading, mathematics, and writing. The ACT evaluates English, mathematics, reading, and science and includes an optional writing test. Although differences may exist between the measures, the SAT and ACT both attempt to address the same issue—how might a student perform in college? Dorans (1999) noted that ACT composite scores were strongly correlated with SAT Verbal and Mathematical reasoning scores ($r = .92$).

The use of college and graduate entrance examinations is an ongoing debate. The noted bias of these instruments is well documented, and the need to incorporate multiple measures to address entrance into academic programs cannot be overstated (Cimetta et al., 2010; Sedlacek, 2004; Stringer, 2008). Referring back to Cimetta et al. (2010), aptitude test scores account for only 6% of the variance in freshman year GPA. This is only slightly higher than the recommended 4% for a minimum level of practical significance (Ferguson, 2009). So, more seems to be unknown about predictors of college and postgraduate success than what is actually known.

Individuals who perform well on achievement measures also tend to perform well on aptitude measures and intelligence measures. A series of studies by Frey and Detterman (2004) and Koenig, Frey, and Detterman (2008) evaluated the relationship between SAT scores and IQ scores and ACT scores and IQ scores, respectively. Relationships between aptitude measures (SAT/ACT) and various IQ tests (i.e., California Test of mental Maturity, Otis-Lennon Mental Ability Test, Lorge-Thorndike Intelligence Test, and Henmon-Nelson Test of Mental Maturity) correlated between .55 and .82. Thus, aptitude and achievement measures not only correlate highly with each other but also correlate highly with general cognitive ability, also known as intelligence. In fact, both achievement and aptitude tests may be considered measures of crystallized ability (*gc*, see Chapter 9). Roberts et al. (2000) states that the ASVAB is truly a measure of crystallized intelligence (*gc*), thereby measuring facets of formal education and acculturated learning. The true value of ability testing is difficult to ascertain.

TYPES OF INFORMATION DERIVED FROM OUR CASE STUDY WITH EVA MARIE

To apply the information on ability testing, the case study of Eva Marie Garza will be used. Recall that Eva Marie was an "A" student who was in the National Honor Society from sixth grade throughout high school. Upon graduation, she attended community college and received her associate's degree in accounting. Eva Marie had a long history of anxiety and indicated school was especially anxiety provoking. From an early age, Eva Marie admitted she would run into her parent's room at 4 A.M. and demand to be taken to school because she feared being late and failing. "I was always so nervous I would flunk classes that I studied very hard."

At the present time, Eva Marie works as a librarian assistant and expressed extreme job dissatisfaction. She felt valued in her previous bookkeeping work. A counselor may opt to administer the DAT to Eva Marie. Eva Marie presents as a capable, intelligent individual with a strong academic history. The DAT may be helpful in assessing strengths and weaknesses that could lead to a new career path or opportunity. A DAT summary report (see Table 10.1) provides scale scores and percentiles based on the standard score.

TABLE 10.1 Summary of DAT Scores for Eva Marie Garza	
Scale	Percentile
Verbal Reasoning	60
Numerical Reasoning	90
Abstract Reasoning	95
Perceptual Speed/Accuracy	99
Mechanical Reasoning	55
Space Relations	90
Spelling	40
Language Usage	75
Educational Aptitude	65

Eva Marie was in the average range for Verbal Reasoning, Mechanical Reasoning, Spelling, and Educational Aptitude. She was above average in language use and excelled in numerical reasoning, abstract reasoning, perceptual speed/accuracy, and space relations. Eva Marie's high score in Abstract Reasoning, along with her scores in Verbal Reasoning and Educational Aptitude, are indicative of an individual who would do well in further education and training. Eva Marie shows potential for the capacity to work in more technical fields (e.g., computer programming, software engineer, science and engineering, architecture) given her high scores in abstract reasoning and space relations. In addition, her very high Numerical Reasoning and Perceptual Speed/Accuracy scores indicate why accounting and bookkeeping seemed to be natural fits. Hence, a career counselor may work with Eva Marie to either further her education and career in these areas, or given her present anxiety, assist her in finding a position more relevant to her strengths.

References

American Counseling Association. (2004). The American Counseling Association (ACA) position statement on high stakes testing. Retrieved from http://www.counseling.org/aboutus/

Anastasi, A., & Urbina, S. (1997). *Psychological testing* (7th ed.). Upper Saddle River, NJ: Prentice Hall.

Anderson, L. W., & Krathwohl, D. R. (Eds.). (2001). *A taxonomy for learning, teaching and assessing: A revision of Bloom's taxonomy of educational objectives: Complete edition*. New York, NY: Longman.

Bloom B. S. (1956). *Taxonomy of Educational Objectives, Handbook I: The Cognitive Domain*. New York, NY: David McKay.

Cimetta, A. D., D'Agostino, J. V., & Levin, J. R. (2010). Can high school achievement tests serve to select college students? *Educational Measurement: Issues and Practice, 29,* 3–12.

Dorans, N. J. (1999). *Correspondences between ACT™ and SAT® I scores*. New York: College Entrance Examination Board. Retrieved from http://research.collegeboard.org/sites/default/files/publications/2012/7/researchreport-1999-1-correspondences-between-act-sat-i-scores.pdf

Engelhard, G. (2007). [Review of the Iowa Test of Basic Skills®, Forms A and B]. In K. F. Geisinger, R. A. Spies, J. F. Carlson, & B. S. Plake, (Eds.), *The seventeenth mental measurements yearbook*. Lincoln, NE: Buros Institute of Mental Measurements.

Ferguson, C. J. (2009). An effect size primer: A guide for clinicians and researchers. *Professional Psychology:*

Research and Practice, 40, 532–548. doi:10.1037/a0015808

Frey, M. C., & Detterman, D. K. (2004). Scholastic assessment or g? The relationship between the Scholastic Assessment Test and general cognitive ability. *Psychological Science, 15,* 373–377.

Harris, T. L., & Hodges, R. E. (1995). *The literacy dictionary: The vocabulary of reading and writing.* Newark, DE: International Reading Association.

Hattrup, K. (1995). [Review of the Differential Aptitude Tests—Fifth Edition]. In J. C. Conoley & J. C. Impara (Eds.), *The twelfth mental measurements yearbook* (pp. 1103–1104). Lincoln, NE: Buros Institute of Mental Measurements.

Hopkins, K. D. (1998). Educational and psychological measurement and evaluation (8th ed.). Boston, MA: Allyn & Bacon.

Koenig, K. A., Frey, M. C., & Detterman, D. K. (2008). ACT and general cognitive ability. *Intelligence, 36,* 153–160.

No Child Left Behind (NCLB) Act of 2001, Pub. L. No. 107-110, § 115, Stat. 1425 (2002).

Riverside Publishing. (2010). *Iowa Tests of Basic Skills*® *(ITBS*®*) Forms A, B, and C.* Retrieved from http://www.riversidepublishing.com/products/itbs/details.html

Roberts, R. D., Goff, G. N., Anjoul, F., Kyllonen, P. C., Pallier, G., & Stankov, L. (2000). The Armed Services Vocational Aptitude Battery (ASVAB): Little more than acculturated learning (Gc)!? *Learning and Individual Differences, 12,* 81–103.

Sedlacek, W. E. (2004). *Beyond the big test: Noncognitive assessment in higher education.* San Francisco, CA: Jossey-Bass.

Steen, L. A. (1999). Twenty questions about mathematical reasoning. In L. Stiff (Ed.), *Developing mathematical reasoning in grades K-12* (pp. 270–285). Reston, VA: National Council of Teachers of Mathematics.

Stringer, N. (2008). Aptitude tests versus school exams as selection tools for higher education and the case for assessing educational achievement in context. *Research Papers in Education, 23,* 53–68.

Wiersma, W., & Jurs, S. G. (1990). *Educational measurement and testing* (2nd ed.). Boston, MA: Allyn & Bacon.

CHAPTER 11

The Multiaxial System, Common Axis I and II Disorders, and the MMPI and MMPI-2-RF

OBJECTIVES

After reading this chapter, you will be able to:

1. Explain what the *Diagnostic and Statistical Manual* (DSM) is, how the five clinical axes are helpful when assessing clients, what each axis describes, how personality disorders are recorded, and how to write a DSM diagnosis.

2. Understand the basic validity and clinical scales of the widely used Minnesota Multiphasic Personality Inventory—2 (MMPI-2).

3. Explain the MMPI-2 standardized use of two- and three-point codes.

4. Describe the Minnesota Multiphasic Personality Inventory—2—Restructured Form (MMPI-2-RF), including Validity, Higher-Order, Restructured Clinical, Internalizing, Externalizing, Interpersonal, and Personality Psychopathology Five scales.

5. Provide narrative reviews of Robert's and Eva Marie's MMPI-2 and MMPI-2-RF scores.

OVERVIEW

This chapter will explain the DSM and its composition of five axes. Furthermore, readers will learn how the DSM's five clinical axes are used to ensure a thorough assessment process. The chapter will also provide an overview of the grandfather of all personality tests, the MMPI-2, and its restructured version, the MMPI-2-RF. Readers will gain an understanding of the MMPI-2's basic validity and clinical scales and two- and three-point codes as well as the MMPI-2-RF's Validity, Higher-Order, Internalizing, External-izing, Interpersonal, and Personality Psychopathology Five scales. For demonstration purposes, the chapter will provide test profiles and narrative reports for Mr. Robert Jones and Ms. Eva Marie Garza.

THE DSM

Potential DSM Benefits

Students enrolled in the authors' graduate courses often ask, "Why do I need to know assessment or the DSM? How will these courses help me?" Many do not readily comprehend the significant benefits of the assessment process or using the DSM to attain an accurate diagnosis. Some are concerned about "spying on clients" via the assessment experience or "labeling clients" with DSM diagnoses. Others are concerned that assigning a DSM diagnosis "overpathologizes" people. Instead, we believe appropriate assessment facilitates accurate DSM diagnosis and therefore promotes effective counseling practices that benefit clients.

Counselors skilled in assessment and basic DSM comprehend their clients' presenting symptomatology and understand how to use diagnosis as a means to ensure treatment efficacy. This is accomplished via continuous assessment (Vacc, 1982). These counselors continually assess their clients' current symptom levels and compare the severity of these symptoms to previous levels as well as established DSM criteria. Thus, counselors constantly track clients' counseling progress. Should insufficient progress occur, counselors investigate changing techniques or adding treatment options.

For example, a client diagnosed with major depression and failing to adequately respond to talk therapy may be referred to a psychiatrist to determine if psychotropic medications are warranted. If the client has been taking antidepressants and actively invested in counseling, the counselor might obtain a release of confidential information. This will allow the counselor to speak with the prescribing psychiatrist to determine if a change in antidepressant dosage or change in medications may be helpful. Hence, a client who continues to have the same degree of depressed symptomatology after 2 months of using antidepressants known as selective serotonin reuptake inhibitor (SSRI) medications (e.g., Prozac, Zoloft, Lexapro) and actively participating in counseling may be prescribed a different type of antidepressant known as a tricyclic antidepressant (e.g., Tofranil, Elavil, Sinequan). Concomitantly, the counselor may wish to investigate different treatment modalities (e.g., group or family counseling), or the use of different counseling theories (e.g., Rational Emotive Behavioral Therapy, cognitive-behavioral therapy) or techniques (e.g., the empty chair, visualizations, metaphors) to determine what works best to lessen or eliminate the client's depressive symptoms. None of this could occur without skilled and continuous counselor assessment and diagnosis.

When treatment is progressing well, counselors' skilled in assessment ensure the continuation of counseling techniques noted as helpful by clients. Further, these same identified helpful techniques can be used by counselors to help clients affectively respond to stressors in other areas of their lives. In other words, if clients report the use of Rational Emotive Behavioral Therapy's "Activating Event, Beliefs, Consequences" (A-B-C), a technique helpful in reducing depressed feelings, counselors will likely wish to replicate this technique in other areas noted by the client as stressful. Here, the A-B-C technique could be used to help the client related to job, interpersonal relationships, and parenting concerns.

Skilled DSM assessment and diagnosis also helps clients obtain necessary counseling services. Since the mid-1990s, managed care has used standardized treatment protocols. Clients experiencing similar symptoms are assigned to diagnostic related groups (DRGs). DRGs cluster clients diagnosed with the same conditions (e.g., generalized anxiety disorder) and symptom severity levels (e.g., mild, moderate, or severe symptoms). Managed care typically uses DRGs to dictate the specific evidenced-based counseling theories counselors are required to use if they wish reimbursement from the managed care entity (e.g., cognitive-behavioral therapy, brief strategic family therapy) and the counseling modality (e.g., group counseling). In addition, the number of preauthorized treatment sessions is standardized by client-assigned DRG. Counselors skilled in both assessment and DSM diagnosing increase the likelihood their clients will be included in the most appropriate DRG. This increases the probability that managed care will preauthorize an appropriate number of client-needed counseling sessions and increased treatment care levels for important services such as case management, inpatient psychiatric hospitalization, or medical detoxification. Correct DSM diagnoses ensure correct DRG assignment. This is especially important when clients present with severe symptomatology.

Clients who are inaccurately assessed and diagnosed often are assigned to less severe DRGs. Thus, they are preauthorized for fewer sessions and do not have access to many important services. Therefore, they may opt out of entering treatment because of projected out-of-pocket financial costs or may discontinue counseling prematurely, because the DRG they were assigned has reduced benefits.

Not only is correct DRG placement important for clients, but also for counselors as well. Many counselors working in private practice settings petition to serve on local mental health provider panels. The benefits of serving on mental health provider panels include a steady flow of referred clients, a guaranteed per session charge (e.g., $80 per hour), and a set number of treatment sessions based on the client's DRG placement. However, these counselors often must agree to capitation clauses. Capitation clauses typically indicate that if clients require more treatment sessions than allotted within the client's corresponding DRG, either the reimbursement charge will be less or the counselor will need to provide services without reimbursement. In either situation, the counselor absorbs the additional financial costs. Given that the counselor's initial assessment and diagnosis determines the DRG the client is assigned, one quickly understands the importance of accurate assessment and diagnosis.

The DSM Multiaxial Assessment

The DSM's multiaxial system ensures that counselors minimally assess clients according to five specific domains. These domain areas are called "axes." This assessment investigates potential interactions or synergy between the client's voiced concern and major areas such as the client's general medical condition and social interactions. Specifically, the assessment and diagnosis process promotes a thorough understanding of what contributes to or influences the client's voiced concerns. This understanding helps counselors develop thorough and encompassing treatment plans that increase the probability of successful treatment. These five axes include (American Psychiatric Association [APA], 2000, p. 27):

Axis I	The presenting clinical disorders or conditions which are the primary focus of clinical attention
Axis II	Personality disorders or mental retardation
Axis III	General medical conditions
Axis IV	Psychosocial and environmental problems or concerns
Axis V	A global functioning assessment

Thus, clients voiced concerns specific to anxiety are assessed according to the DSM anxiety disorders classification that includes anxiety-related disorders such as generalized anxiety disorder, panic disorder, agoraphobia, and posttraumatic stress disorder. Concomitantly, their anxiety is viewed within the context of their life's corresponding DSM axes. Hence, counselors using the DSM apply the multiaxial system to assess clients according to the following: (a) presenting concerns or clinical disorders as well as other areas of concern that clients may not readily divulge such as addictive behaviors, marital problems, or depressive symptoms; (b) personality disorders or mental retardation that may be related to or influencing presenting concerns; (c) general medical conditions, especially medical factors that may contribute or influence voiced concerns (e.g., low thyroid, cancer, diabetes, amyotrophic lateral sclerosis [ALS] disease); (d) psychosocial and environmental problems that may engender stressors related to the client's noted presenting concerns such as anxiety or depression; and (e) overall functioning level. The intent is to secure the most complete and accurate picture of clients and their concerns via the multiaxial system and DSM diagnosis.

Some essential multiaxial system diagnostic features warrant discussion. For example, sometimes it is impossible to make an adequate diagnostic determination within a single, 50-minute interview. This is especially true when clients present with one or more of the following: (a) severe symptoms such as anxiety, hallucinations, or depression; (b) overwhelming chaos in multiple life areas (e.g., interpersonal relationships, employment, finances); (c) limited intelligence; (d) acute physical needs (e.g., cancer, HIV); (e) polysubstance dependence; and (f) pressing legal issues that may either cause incarceration or influence sentencing determinations, terminate parental custody of children, or result in significant financial hardship.

Should counselors be unable to make an immediate Axis I disorder determination and need to defer an Axis I diagnosis, they merely indicate "V799.9 Diagnosis or Condition Deferred on Axis I" (APA, 2000). This simply indicates inadequate information has been thus far obtained by the counselor to make an informed and accurate Axis I determination. Such was the case with Eva Marie. As previously mentioned, she was so anxious in the first assessment interview that the counselor could not fully comprehend her presenting symptomatology. Thus, he would have denoted V799.99 on Axis I and Axis II of Eva Marie's diagnostic report following their first meeting. However, after his second meeting with Eva Marie, he was able to gather sufficient information to accurately diagnosis her multiple presenting Axis I disorders (i.e., generalized anxiety disorder, partner relational problem, and phase of life problem). Note, however, that deferred diagnoses should not continue indefinitely. Contrary to some guarded counselors who inappropriately continue a deferred diagnosis until treatment conclusion, an accurate diagnosis should be presented as early in the assessment and treatment process as possible. In most cases, a clear diagnosis will be noted within one to three clinical interview meetings.

Many times clients will fulfill either an Axis I disorder (e.g., major depression, single episode) or an Axis II disorder (dependent personality disorder). This was the case with Eva Marie. She was diagnosed with multiple Axis I disorders but fulfilled no Axis II disorders. When multiple Axis I disorders occur, counselors use the DSM notation V71.09 on the diagnosis absent axis (APA, 2000). Hence, in Eva Marie's case her absence of an Axis II diagnosis resulted in a notation of "V71.09 No Diagnosis or Condition on Axis II." Conversely, if Eva Marie would have fulfilled only the Axis II diagnosis of antisocial personality disorder with no Axis I disorders being fulfilled, her Axis I would denote "V71.09 No Diagnosis or Condition on Axis I."

Multiple Axis I diagnoses are presented in descending order. Thus, the most pressing diagnosis is reported first and the least pressing diagnosis is reported last (APA, 2000, p. 27). In Eva Marie's case, her most pressing concern is the overwhelming anxiety she has experienced. This anxiety continues to negatively intrude on most every aspect of her life. Thus, her most pressing disorder (generalized anxiety disorder) is listed first. Her next most pressing disorder (partner relational problem) is her marital dissatisfaction. It is listed second on the descending diagnosis disorder list. Moreover, her least pressing Axis I disorder (phase of life problem) is listed last.

Similar to the descending order used on Axis I, Axis II disorders are also ranked using the descending order system. Again, the most pressing Axis II disorder is placed first with a descending list of personality or mental health disorders positioned underneath. If descending Axis II disorders are listed, this is typically either with the first denoted as being mental retardation and the second being a single personality disorder. In the authors' entire careers, they have never had a client fulfill more than either mental retardation or a single personality disorder on Axis II. Thus, depending on the type of practice, agency, treatment center, or school where employed, it is unlikely that counselors will experience clients with more than one Axis II disorder noted.

Dual diagnosis is a term used by many within the mental health professions to denote clients who present with comorbid or cooccurring diagnoses. In other words, these clients fulfill the diagnostic threshold for two separate DSM disorders. Frequently, clients will present with both an Axis I and an Axis II disorder. Robert is a prime example. His alcohol abuse fulfills an Axis I alcohol dependence diagnosis while his cooccurring Axis II disorder is antisocial personality disorder. However, dual diagnosis can indicate someone who has two Axis I diagnoses (e.g., alcohol dependence and major depression) or two Axis II diagnoses. There exist two critically important issues when discussing dual diagnosis or multiple diagnoses. First, both diagnoses must be clinically significant and warrant a clear treatment focus. Second, both diagnoses must fulfill their criteria independently from the other. In Robert's case, his antisocial behaviors (e.g., lying for personal gain, arguing with persons in authority, and his socially amoral behaviors) occur both while he is under the influence of alcohol and when he is not under the influence of alcohol. If Robert's antisocial behaviors occurred only when he was under the influence, he likely would not qualify for this Axis II antisocial personality disorder diagnosis.

Axis I and Axis II personality disorders differ in that Axis II personality disorders are a result of the individual client's personality—a rigid, enduring, and inflexible way of interacting with others (Millon, 1981). O'Connor (2008) sums Axis II personality disorders best when he states,

> Unlike most Axis I disorders, the PDs [Personality Disorders] on Axis II are more chronic, ingrained, resistant to change, and bearable by those who have them. People do not suddenly become ill with a PD and seek help. Rather, individuals with PDs feel normal and at home with their conditions because their disordered personalities and self-concepts are all they know and remember. They often value the very habits and features in themselves that are troublesome for others. (p. 438)

Axis II personality-disordered persons usually create emotional distress for others. Typically, their maladaptive ways of behaving and interacting with others, as well as their dysfunctional ways of living and experiencing life, provoke and wear on others—especially over time within relationships (e.g., work, dating). This then results in sanctions towards or hardships on the personality-disordered persons and their maladaptive and enduring inner experiences.

Approximately 2.7 million Americans or roughly 9% of the U.S. population fulfill Axis II personality disorder criteria (Lenzenweger, Lane, Loranger, & Kessler, 2007). Their personality disorders are separated into three distinct clusters (APA, 2000, p. 685). The first cluster includes persons who present as odd or eccentric (p. 685). This cluster includes paranoid, schizoid, and schizotypal personality disorders. Another cluster includes persons who frequently present as anxious or fearful and includes avoidant, dependent, and obsessive-compulsive personality disorders (p. 685). The third cluster includes the Antisocial, borderline, histrionic, and narcissistic personality disorders (p. 685). This cluster contains the three personality disorders most frequently treated by the authors and their supervisees—borderline, antisocial, and narcissistic personality disorders.

The authors trust this description of the DSM five clinical axes and common Axis I and Axis II personality disorders have helped demonstrate the diagnostic process and promoted greater understanding regarding these commonly experienced disorders. Next, the authors will describe one the most commonly used personality inventories and its restructured form. They will further integrate your new knowledge regarding the aforementioned Axis I clinical and Axis II personality disorders and describe how such disorders may present via two established personality inventories.

THE MMPI-2 AND MMPI-2-RF: WHY DESCRIBE THE MMPI-2 AND MMPI-2-RF?

There are many personality assessment instruments available to counselors who have completed the necessary corresponding course work and supervision related to these specific instruments. However, the authors have carefully considered and selected two instruments to describe within this chapter. These include the MMPI-2 and the MMPI-2-RF. Reasons for their inclusions are simple. First, the MMPI-2 is one of the most thoroughly reviewed and researched personality instruments on the market today. Second, the MMPI-2 is one of the most frequently utilized personality instruments used by counselors and the personality instrument most often identified by counseling professionals as the assessment instrument counselors should receive training in (Bubenzer, Zimpfer, & Mahrle, 1990; Juhnke, Vacc, Curtis, Call, & Paredes, 2003; Watkins, Campbell, & McGregor, 1988; Wise, Streiner, & Walfish, 2010). Third, although the MMPI-2-RF is newer, established, counseling practitioners in the field with whom the authors spoke continue to use the MMPI-2 more frequently than the MMPI-2RF. Fourth, both the MMPI-2 and MMPI-2-RF have clinical scales and supplemental scales deemed important by the authors. Specifically, the MMPI-2 and MMPI-2-RF provide a broad-spectrum view of both the person's personality and symptomatology. As noted in the earlier section of this chapter, given the many commonly occurring Axis I clinical disorders and Axis II personality disorders, it is imperative that counselors use personality instruments that can provide a "full view" of the client and her presenting concerns.

General MMPI-2 Overview

The MMPI-2 is composed of 567 true–false items and was restandardized by Butcher, Dahlstrom, Graham, Tellegen, and Kaemmer (2001). The MMPI-2 was developed for clients 18 years of age and older with a fifth-grade reading level (Pearson, 2011a). The instrument takes approximately 60 to 90 minutes to complete and can be ordered directly from Pearson at 1-800-627-7271.

MMPI-2 Reliability and Validity

No psychological instrument known to the authors has perfect reliability and validity, and no instrument is without both supporters and critics. With this said, it is clear that the MMPI-2 revised in 2001 is not without both (Drayton, 2009; Sellbom & Ben-Porath, 2005; Sellbom, Ben-Porath, Lilienfeld, Patrick, & Graham, 2005; Vacha-Haase, Tani, Kogan, Woodall, & Thompson, 2001). In a perfect world, the personality instrument used by counselors would precisely indicate each client's presenting concerns, symptoms, personality, healthy functioning, and any attempts to distort findings either in a favorable or negative manner. Combining assessment instruments with a thorough and continuous client and significant others clinical interview process, as well as filtering all with the counselor's clinical judgment and clinical supervision, is the very best way to ensure the most accurate assessment (Juhnke, 2002).

Taking the above into consideration, the authors believe the MMPI-2 provides adequate reliability and validity qualities. In one of the most recent and thorough reliability reviews of the revised MMPI-2 to date, Wise, Streiner, and Walfish (2010) found 1-week test–retest reliability for the MMPI-2 scales surpassed the .70 level on all but one scale for males (scale Paranoia [Pa]) and all but six scales for females (scales Psychopathic Deviate [Pd], Pa, Psychasthenia [Pt], Schizophrenia [Sc], Hypomania [Ma], and RC3 [Antisocial Behavior]). Interestingly, the authors of that review state,

> If the MMPI-2 is taken as the "gold standard," in light of longevity, accumulated research base, and frequency of use, it is clear that it will need to continue to build on the tradition set by the newer Content and RC scales (Wise et al., 2010, p. 251).

Concomitantly, the MMPI-2 appears to have satisfactory construct validity (Sellbom & Ben-Porath, 2005).

MMPI-2 Scales

The revised MMPI-2 has 9 Validity Scales, 5 Superlative Self-Presentation Subscales, 10 Clinical Scales, 9 Restructured Clinical (RC) Scales, 15 content Scales, 27 Content Component Scales, 20 Supplementary Scales, and 31 Clinical Subscales (Harris-Lingoes and Social Introversion Subscales; Pearson, 2011a). Clearly one needs advanced clinical assessment training to administer the MMPI-2 and all of its available scales. However, for the purposes of this book, the authors will provide a brief overview of the scales and describe Robert's MMPI-2 profile.

VALIDITY AND CLINICAL SCALES

The MMPI-2 Validity Scales are akin to the engine that pulls the train. They establish the foundation for the interpretation of clinical and supplemental scales commonly relevant to Alcohol and Other Drug (AOD) abusing clients. These scales provide counselors vital information related to their clients' endorsements. Specifically, the Validity Scales indicate if the client appears to be responding truthfully or randomly to the question stems. The Validity Scales further indicate whether the client's endorsements appear suspect or invalid.

The revised MMPI-2 includes 10 Validity Scales. Specifically, the validity scales are composed of the following scales: (a) Cannot Say Scale (?), (b) Variable Response Inconsistency Scale (VRIN), (c) True Response Inconsistency Scale (TRIN), (d) Infrequency Scale (F), (e) Back F Scale (Fb), (f) Infrequency-Psychopathology Scale (Fp), (g) Symptom Validity Scale (FBS), (h) Lie Scale (L), (i) Correction Scale (K), and (j) Superlative Self-Presentation Scale (Pearson, 2011a). These scales are evaluated both individually and in unison to determine whether it appears clients were invested and appropriately responded to assessment question stems.

For example, the Cannot Say Scale indicates the number of items that clients did not respond to. In other words, this scale suggests both the items that were left blank and whether it appears clients were cooperating in the assessment process. Thus, a client who failed to endorse a significant number of items would end with a suspect or invalid test because of the number of non-endorsed question stems. Conversely, if a client responded to all items except two, it would be important to determine what these questions were about. Was there a central theme to the omitted questions? Were the questions specific to depression, anxiety, grandiosity, hallucinations, or violence? If so, it would be important to follow up with the client to determine what about these questions resulted in the client's failure to endorse a response and what clinical responses might be warranted.

In addition, instead of simply looking at each scale individually, the Validity Scales are also viewed in unison. This provides a more complete picture of the client's investment in the assessment process. Thus, individual Validity Scales like the Cannot Say Scale (?) are reviewed in light of the other Validity Scales such as the Lie Scale (L) and the Correction Scale (K). Here, the Lie Scale indicates the client's ability to present him- or herself in a truthful, balanced manner. Clients endorsing an unusually high number of items on this scale are likely attempting to present themselves in a most positive light and are denying the presence of even minor flaws. Clients endorsing such a high number of positive items may be defensive or may present with a high degree of religiosity. On the other hand, the Correction Scale indicates the degree of symptomatology or lack thereof endorsed by the client. Here, high Correction Scale scores may suggest an absence of symptoms or problems or defensiveness. In other words, these clients are suggesting they have no reason for participating in counseling and life is going exceptionally well. Two ways of using the Correction Scale to potentially identify persons attempting to present themselves in an overly positive manner are to evaluate scale combinations. For example, when both the Lie and Correction Scales have relatively high scores and the Infrequency Scale (F) has a relatively low score, this suggests the client has endorsed items in a fashion similar to those who are attempting to present themselves in an overly positive manner. Conversely, clients admitting significant problems will score low on the Correction Scale. These low-scoring clients may be crying for help. As in the case with elevated Infrequency Scale scores, clients entering treatment and facing significant interpersonal, legal, and environmental stressors such as jail time, divorce, and job loss may endorse few if any positives in their lives.

Hence, it quickly becomes apparent that counselors reviewing the MMPI-2 Validity Scales can best judge how the client approached the test-taking experience by looking at both the individual Validity Scales and their configurations in unison. For example, in the case of Robert, his Validity Scale scores will indicate a higher than expected Correction

Scale score and a lower Infrequency Scale score. Thus, when taking the MMPI-2, Robert was attempting to present himself in a most favorable light—a kind, caring, law-abiding citizen vis-à-vis a deceitful, irresponsible, aggressive, alcohol abusing thief who lacks remorse and compunction for how he treats others and who is facing trial for stealing from his employer and being found in possession of stolen property in excess of $100,000. As you will recall, Robert reported his attorney encouraged him to begin counseling. There is a high probability that Robert's attorney encouraged Robert to enter counseling so the attorney could declare to the Judge that Robert had voluntarily entered into counseling and sought help for his behaviors. Stated differently, there exists a high probability that Robert's legal counsel and Robert have an agenda specific to Robert's entering treatment. The MMPI-2 Validity Scales will likely identify such an agenda.

Clinical Scales

The MMPI-2 contains 10 clinical scales. These include (a) Hypochondriasis, (b) Depression, (c) Hysteria, (d) Psychopathic Deviate, (e) Masculinity-Femininity, (f) Paranoia, (g) Psychasthenia, (h) Schizophrenia, (i) Hypomania, and (j) Social Introversion (Pearson, 2011a). Many times, these scales are referred to by the numbered order in which they are depicted on the clinical profile sheet. Thus, The One Scale is Hypochondriasis, The Two Scale is Depression, The 10 Scale is Social Introversion, and so forth.

THE ONE SCALE: HYPOCHONDRIASIS   This scale denotes bodily aches, pains, and general physical concerns. Clients who score high on this scale are endorsing a significant number of somatic concerns and symptoms and may tend to use these complaints for attention or secondary gains (e.g., being relieved of charges as a result of their physical complaints). Clients endorsing few items on this scale indicate a lack of physical alignments and likely are healthy, younger clients (e.g., 18 years of age) who truly are in the prime of their lives.

Before we move on to the next clinical scales, consider this question, "Whom would you anticipate would have at least a moderately elevated One Scale score, Robert or Eva Marie?" Although Robert may have some anxiety about his upcoming court arraignment and possible jail sentence, the authors believe that Eva Marie is far more likely to endorse more hypochondriasis items than Robert. Given Eva Marie's constant state of anxiousness and heightened anxiety in interactions with others, along with her current life dissatisfaction specific to living with a spouse reported as "absent" and "emotionless," working in a job she finds less than rewarding, and living with her mother whom she reports bosses Eva Marie around and refuses to allow Eva Marie appropriate, age-related authority and independence, one would anticipate that Eva Marie would have some elevation on this scale.

THE TWO SCALE: DEPRESSION   As the name implies, the Two Scale indicates depressive symptomatology endorsed by the client. Clients spiking this scale with an extremely high score may be making a "cry for help." This could be a naïve or highly dependent client whose spouse left him or someone who may be so overwhelmed that she is suicidal and seeking immediate help to prevent her planned suicide. Thus, the presence of suicidal ideation and intent should be assessed with clients indicating highly depressed feelings on this scale and appropriate interventions should be implemented to insure safety.

Interestingly, someone like Eva Marie may well demonstrate a moderate elevation on the Two Scale. Although Eva Marie's primary presenting concern is her marked anxiety, she may have a moderately elevated Two Scale, because she feels sad, unhappy, disheartened, depressed, sorrowful, and possibly even despondent about her less than favorably perceived marriage. Her marriage has not brought about the support, nurturance, and love that she anticipated. Eva Marie also reports she "hates" her job and returned to Texas because "as an only child, I have to take care of my mother." Thus, she perceives she left a job she enjoyed in Atlanta, now has a job that she perceives as less rewarding, and she and her husband are living with her mother in Eva Marie's grandmother's former home, because Eva Marie and her husband reportedly do not have sufficient monies to live independently of her mother. Given all of this, one would be surprised if Eva Marie did not have at least some elevation on the Two Scale.

THE THREE SCALE: HYSTERIA   Clients scoring high on this scale tend to demand attention from others, act immaturely and selfishly, and report broad and vague physical complaints. Often, they will initially present as socially able, talkative, and flamboyant. However, as others begin to know them, those who score high on the Three Scale will frequently be perceived as shallow and self-centered, and their once perceived alluring qualities will vaporize as their noxious personality characteristics become more obvious.

THE FOUR SCALE: PSYCHOPATHIC DEVIATE   This is a critical scale for counselors to understand. Those scoring moderately high to high on the Four Scale endorse items in a fashion similar to persons who tend to act illegally, steal, lie, and use other people for personal gain without remorse for their behaviors. In general, those scoring moderately high to high on the Four Scale often present as adventure seeking, impulsive, rebels, who have difficulties with those in authority. Often, they will be substance abusing, self-centered, and unconcerned with the potential negative effects their behaviors will have on innocent others or dangerous and foolish behaviors such as drinking and driving. This scale is often correlated with antisocial personality disorder.

Given these descriptions and your knowledge of both Eva Marie and Robert, whom do you believe would be more likely to have an elevated Four Scale score? Robert is the correct answer. He presents as a full-fledged, high Four Scale endorsing client. This scale also matches his primary Axis II personality disorder—antisocial personality disorder. However, be careful to remember that not every Axis II antisocial personality disordered person will present as a beer-guzzling, black leather jacket wearing, chopper-riding hellion with a beard, tattoos, and a sawed-off shotgun. Such stereotypical, antisocial personality disordered persons are relatively easy to spot when they are locked in the backseat of a police car after fighting multiple patrons and police officers at the local bar. Less obvious, however, are those who endorse a significant number of Four Scale items who may present on cursory glance as respectable coaches, prominent business persons, bankers or financial brokers, college or school administrators, physicians, dentists, lawyers, or politicians, but who may repeatedly lie, steal, or place others in physical, social, emotional, or financial jeopardy without concern or compunction. These are persons like the famed Bernard Madoff. He is a former NASDAQ chair who presented as a highly respectable investment securities company owner. Yet, unbeknownst to millions, Madoff operated the largest Ponzi scheme in American history. These antisocial personality disorder persons are often far less discernable to the general population. However, the results of their psychopathology can be just as severe and dangerous as the stereotypical Hell's Angel biker.

THE FIVE SCALE: MASCULINITY-FEMININITY This scale relates to stereotypical gender role affiliation. For example, higher scoring males may present with greater aesthetic interests than the general population of males within the United States while lower scoring males may present with a type of John Wayne persona. The later may perceive themselves as robustly masculine and enjoy stereotypical masculine roles, recreation, and interests (e.g., football, NASCAR). High-scoring females may work in nonstereotypical female work roles (e.g., auto mechanic). They may further present as highly self-confident and competitive. Lower scoring females may fit the stereotypical "Southern Belle" profile of robustly embracing traditionally accepted feminine roles and interests (J. Oldz, personal communications, February 7, 1990). This scale no longer is truly perceived by most experienced mental health professionals as a true clinical scale. Instead, most perceive this scale as possibly providing further information regarding the client but without the psychopathology suggested in outdated DSM diagnoses.

THE SIX SCALE: PARANOIA This scale is specific to paranoia and trust. Persons scoring high on this scale may present with peculiar thinking. They may be paranoid and distrustful of others. Extremely high scores may suggest someone who presents with active delusions or hallucinations. However, it seems highly unlikely that a person presenting with robust delusions or vividly active hallucinations would be able to fully complete the MMPI-2's 567 questions. Thus, in extreme scoring cases, the authors would question the veracity of the responses and likely view the results as suspect.

THE SEVEN SCALE: PSYCHASTHENIA Clients with moderately high and higher Seven Scale scores typically present as excessively anxious and worried. Many will report they are unable to focus or concentrate and may have physical complaints of fatigue or exhaustion. They are often identified by others as extremely well organized, meticulous, and perfectionist. Frequently, they are highly self-critical and lack self-confidence. Some may attempt to self-medicate using substances like cannabis to reduce their anxiety and worry. In addition, some high scorers may qualify as obsessive compulsive disordered. Based on Eva Marie's excessive and unfounded anxiousness and worry, we would anticipate that she would have a moderate to high Seven Scale score.

THE EIGHT SCALE: SCHIZOPHRENIA Clients with high scores on the Eight Scale may well be endorsing psychotic experiences that could include florid hallucinations. Similar to the description of robust Scale Six scores, clients with high scores on this scale would likely have difficulty remaining focused on a standardized assessment instrument composed of so many questions. More likely, robustly high scores are indicative of clients making a cry for help. In other words, floridly psychotic clients would be so confused, it is unlikely that they could actually complete the 567 MMPI-2 questions. Thus, it is far more likely that a client scoring in this fashion is making a deliberate cry for help or seeking to present him- or herself with florid delusions and hallucinations.

THE NINE SCALE: MANIA This scale describes manic behaviors or episodes. Clients with high scores may qualify for bipolar disorder and may present as grandiose with pressured speech and a history of inpatient hospitalizations. Nonbipolar-disordered clients with moderate to moderately high scores will typically present as impulsive, flamboyant, socially confident, and gregarious. Given this scale's descriptors, how would you anticipate Robert and Eva Marie would score? Although Robert's score would not be expected to be excessively high, his self-confidence and outgoing demeanor would likely suggest that he would have at least moderate to moderately high scores on this scale. The opposite is true for Eva Marie. Given Eva Marie does not present as overly self-confident, flamboyant, outgoing, and gregarious, and given her preferred occupation within accounting, one would anticipate she would endorse fewer items on this scale and have a lower Nine Scale score.

THE TEN (ZERO) SCALE: SOCIAL INTROVERSION   This scale measures the degree to which a client interacts with others and feels socially comfortable. Clients scoring high on this scale typically are uncomfortable in social situations and prefer to be alone or with a limited number of very close and trusted friends. Social interactions are often very difficult for these clients as they are often extremely shy and have difficulty voicing themselves. Concomitantly, they often feel anxious, acquiesce easily, and lack energy. Those scoring low on this scale frequently are perceived as outgoing, extroverted clients who interact freely with others. Often they are perceived as brazen or audacious.

Given Robert and Eva Marie's personality characteristics, we would anticipate that Robert and Eva Marie's Nine and Ten Scale scores would reflect divergent congruence. In other words, Robert's and Eva Marie's Nine and Ten Scales would be opposite of one another. Thus, Robert's Nine Scale score would be moderate to moderately high and Robert's Ten Scale would be low. That is because Robert knows how to interact with others socially, feels socially comfortable with others, and is relatively gregarious. This combination of personality characteristics matches what one would expect from a salesperson.

The opposite would be true of Eva Marie. Her Nine Scale would likely be low and her Ten Scale would be high. This would reflect Eva Marie's discomfort around others, her fulfilled generalized anxiety disorder criteria, and her preference for interacting with one or two family members or friends vis-à-vis persons with whom she is unfamiliar.

Code Types

When two or more clinical scales are elevated above typical scores endorsed by the general population sample used to norm the MMPI-2, counselors can use the client's two or three highest scale scores to indicate "two-point" or "three-point" code types. Specifically, these two- and three-point codes provide more information than merely reviewing each scale separately. For example, should a client's Two Scale (Depression) be elevated above the general response threshold and be the highest score on the client's MMPI-2, and the client's second highest score be elevated above the general response threshold and be on the Four Scale (Psychopathic Deviate), the counselor would indicate the client had a "2-4" code type. Should the client's third highest score be the Six Scale (Paranoia), and if this third highest score was above the general response threshold, the client would have a three-point code (i.e., "2-4-6" code type). This code would suggest the client would have (a) both depression and anxiety but with more anxiety than depression, (b) resentment, and (c) feelings of dependence and a strong need for affection from others (Nichols, 2001). Many of the most commonly occurring Axis I clinical diagnoses and Axis II personality diagnoses listed earlier in the chapter have a corresponding two- or three-point code. However, not all high clinical scale scores result in two- or three-point code types. Most code types, and especially two-point code types, are interchangeable. In other words, the order of the highest and second highest scores has the same implications. For example, the previously noted 2-4 code type is often indicated as the 2-4/4-2 code type. Thus, no matter if the client's highest scale score was two or four, the general information regarding the client is similar. In addition, should the first and second elevated clinical scales be equal, the results would be used similarly (e.g., 2-4/4-2 code type).

PSY-5 and Supplementary Scales

The MMPI-2 has numerous additional scales that can be purchased and used for specific populations and presenting or suspected concerns. These include the Personality Psychopathology Five Scales (PSY-5; Aggressiveness, Psychoticism, Disconstraint, Negative Emotionality/Neuroticism, and Introversion/Low Positive Emotionality), Broad Personality Characteristics (Anxiety, Repression, Ego Strength, Dominance, and Social Responsibility), Generalized Emotional Distress (College Maladjustment, Post-Traumatic Stress Disorder—Keane, and Marital Distress), Behavioral Dyscontrol (Hostility, Overcontrolled Hostility, MacAndrew—Revised, Addiction Admission, and Addiction Potential), and Gender Role (Gender Role—Masculine, and Gender Role—Feminine).

The second author has found these scales of significant value—especially when counseling within his specialty addictions area (Juhnke, 2002). For example, when assessing or counseling addicted clients and their families, Juhnke uses the MacAndrew Alcoholism Scale—Revised (MAC-R), the Addiction Potential Scale (APS), and the Addiction Acknowledgment Scale (AAS) MMPI-2 Supplementary Scales. Employing clinical interviews with the clients and their significant others in conjunction with these MMPI-2 Supplementary Scales provides the necessary information to make an extremely thorough and accurate diagnosis (Juhnke, 2002).

Here, for example, Juhnke (2002) uses the MAC-R to provide general information regarding the client's AOD use as well as addictive behaviors such as gambling. Given that most MAC-R items are not openly transparent or obvious, most clients do not realize the items are specific to their potential addictions. Thus, Juhnke has found that even guarded, AOD-abusing clients typically score in a relatively similar manner to those who openly admit their AOD abuse on the MAC-R. Higher scores on the MAC-R Scale are indicative of AOD-abusing clients and a corresponding abuse or dependence DSM diagnosis. However, it should be noted that clients endorsing a significant number of MAC-R scale items may simply be clients who are similar in personality to AOD-abusing clients (e.g., extroverted, confident) and may not actually be addicted. In other words, although AOD is exceptionally common among clients with such personalities, such endorsements do not mean that the client is addicted. This is why it is especially important to include client and significant other interviews when making any diagnosis.

As mentioned, Juhnke uses two other MMPI-2 Supplementary Scales along with the MAC-R. These include the APS and the AAS. The APS assesses the presence of personality factors that suggest potential for addiction and addictive behaviors. Like the MAC-R, the APS scale items are not transparent. Juhnke has found that some clients who are not assessed as AOD abusing on the MAC-R are positively assessed on the APS. The AAS scale items are different. They are highly transparent and query the client regarding specific AOD-related questions. Together, these MMPI-2 Supplementary Scales are helpful in supporting the counselor's clinical judgment and can be used to help establish a valid and useful diagnosis.

Restructured Clinical Scales

The MMPI-2 extended score report provides 10 Restructured Clinical Scales. The first of these scales is Demoralization (RCd-dem) and includes feelings of overall discouragement and general emotional discomfort. Second is Somatic Complaints (RC1-som). As you will note, RC1 correlates to the original MMPI's Scale One. This scale reports physical complaints and the client's attention to bodily concerns. The former MMPI original Scale Two, Depression, is now the Low Positive Emotions (RC2-lpe) Scale. This scale continues to focus on depression, low energy, and indecisiveness. The RC Scale Cynicism (RC3-cyn) is no longer related to the former MMPI original scale Hysteria. Instead, this restructured clinical scale reports how the client perceives others in general (e.g., untrustworthy, uncaring). The new RC4 Antisocial Behavior (asb) Scale focuses more purely on the core of antisocial behaviors than the previous Psychopathic Deviate Four Scale. This new scale reflects measures of aggressiveness and one's tendency to deceive and cheat for personal gain. The new Ideas of Persecution (RC6-per) Scale specifically measures persecutory ideation. The restructured clinical scale Dysfunctional Negative Emotions (RC7-dne) basically reviews negative emotions like anxiety, irritability, and intrusive thoughts. The Aberrant Experiences (RC8-abx) Scale measures hallucinations and delusions. Finally, the Hypomanic Activation (RC9-hpm) Scale measures hypomania and mania. It reports things like racing thoughts, excitement, and poor impulse control (Pearson, 2011a). The developer of the RC Scales, Auke Tellegen, by making these new scales, restructured the MMPI-2, greatly enhancing it. His intent was to psychometrically improve the original MMPI Clinical Scales that clinicians were already familiar with (Pearson, 2011a). In essence, Tellegen took the primary central psychopathology of each of the original MMPI Clinical Scales and used the entire MMPI-2 item pool to develop corresponding scales that better matched the underlying psychopathology affiliated with the new scales.

ROBERT'S MMPI-2 PROFILE

Now that we have discussed the MMPI-2, let's take a look at Robert's MMPI-2 Profile.

We will begin with a brief review of Robert's Validity Scale Profile (see Figure 11.1). The Variable Response Inconsistency Scale (VRIN) and True Response Inconsistency Scale (TRIN) scales measure inconsistency in responses. Given that Robert's VRIN and TRIN endorsements fall between T scores of 50 and 65, it appears that Robert responded to the question stems in a manner consistent with most MMPI-2 test takers. Therefore, it appears Robert's endorsements are interpretable specific to him being consistent in his responses. Next, when reviewing Robert's endorsements on the F, Fb, and Fp scales, things get a little more interesting. These scales represent "Infrequency" or what used to be termed "Faking Bad." Typical mean scores on the Infrequency scales should be between 50 and 65. Scores 65 and higher suggest someone is endorsing significant psychopathology levels. Scores in excess of 80 are suggesting someone may well be overreporting psychopathology. Persons scoring very high on these scales may be attempting to endorse severe levels of psychopathology (e.g., depression, anxiety, hallucinations) in an attempt to either be hospitalized or, if a lawsuit is involved, to suggest they have been

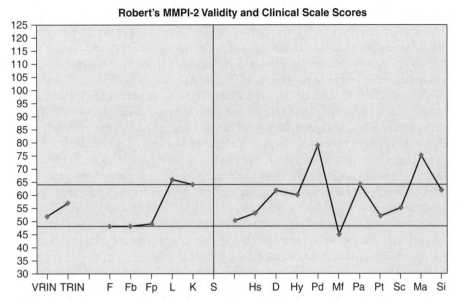

FIGURE 11.1 Robert's MMPI-2 Validity and Clinical Scale Scores. Abbreviations: VRIN=Variable Response Inconsistency Scale; TRIN=True Response Inconsistency Scale; F=Infrequency Scale; Fb=Back Infrequency Scale; Fp=Infrequency-Psychopathology Scale; L=Lie Scale; K=Correction Scale; Hs=Hypochondriasis Scale; D=Depression Scale; Hy=Conversion Hysteria Scale; Pd= Psychopathic Deviate Scale; Mf=Masculinity-Femininity Scale; Pa=Paranoia; Pt=Psychasthenia; Sc=Schizophrenia; Ms=Hypomania Scale; Si=Social Introversion Scale

emotionally traumatized by an event or experience. This clearly is not the case with Robert. He has responded to the instrument by endorsing fewer psychopathic symptoms than the general population and his scores are just below the typical threshold of 50. Might there be a reason for Robert's underresponding?

Before we answer that question, let's continue investigating his other Validity Scale Scores. Next, we look at Robert's L Scale. He has endorsed himself as more virtuous than the average MMPI-2 test taker. Specifically, his score is just above the high typical threshold score of 65. Concomitantly, his K and S scales are at or near the top of the typical response range for MMPI-2 test takers. This combination of responses, when viewed in unison, may suggest someone who is highly virtuous with many strong religious morals and traditional values. Does this match Robert's clinical presentation and the information we gathered from his clinical interview? It does not. Thus, based on Robert's endorsements that appear to suggest that he has fewer psychological concerns than most and he has extremely high personal ethics, the authors would believe Robert is attempting to present himself in a most favorable light. In other words, when Robert goes to court, he likely wants the counselor to interpret the MMPI-2 results as suggesting Robert as an unjustly accused, honest, hard-working, decent, law-abiding citizen who would never steal heavy-duty road equipment from his former place of employment. In fact, Robert would like his MMPI-2 endorsements to suggest that he is the kind of outstanding citizen who was probably painting, repairing, and improving the heavy-duty equipment housed on his property before he returned it to his former employer.

Now let's review Robert's MMPI-2 Clinical Scales. Typically, the authors find when a client like Robert endorses high correction scores on K and S, the actual psychopathology levels will be higher than indicated on the MMPI-2 Clinical Scales. Stated differently, higher K and S scores reduce the reported pathology levels on the clinical scales. Thus, moderately depressed or anxious clients will appear as only slightly depressed or anxious on their profiles. Robert's One Scale: Hypochondriasis is unremarkable. According to this profile, his endorsed items place him in the low average range. Interestingly, Robert's Two Scale: Depression, although falling within the higher end of the normal range, suggests that Robert might be experiencing a twinge of sadness or anxiety. This is less likely a result of remorse or compunction for unlawful behaviors and more likely a twinge of sadness that he was caught. This Two Scale may increase if he is convicted for crimes. Again, the identified "sadness" will likely not be related to compunction for stealing. Instead, these scores would likely reflect his "sadness" that he has to do jail time. Stated differently, Robert, if convicted and required to enter prison and pay a hefty fine, will feel more depressed that he will have lost his freedom and has to pay his "hard-earned" money than feel sad that he had violated the rights of others.

Robert's Three Scale: Hysteria, is relatively unremarkable and falls within the high side of the normal range. Based on the authors' experiences with persons qualifying for antisocial personality disorder, this tad higher score well within the normal range may be related to Robert's rather flamboyant, socially skilled, and talkative mannerism. However, Robert's Four Scale: Psychopathic Deviate is quite remarkable. This is his highest clinical score along with his Nine Scale: Mania. This elevated Four Scale by itself would suggest that Robert has endorsed items in a fashion similar to persons fulfilling criteria for antisocial personality disorder. Specifically, this suggests that Robert likely tends to take advantage of others, engage in unlawful behaviors, and be self-centered. Further, the elevated Four Scale indicates that Robert is likely adventure seeking, impulsive, and has difficulties with authority figures. However, when one looks at both Robert's elevated Four Scale and his elevated Nine Scale: Mania it would suggest that Robert is rebellious, disinhibited, socially skilled and charming. He understands how to gain peoples' trust and then exploit that trust or use information divulged by those who trusted the "charming guy" to later intimidate others. In addition, he has a sense of personal entitlement. Thus, he likely feels he is "better" or "superior" to others and uses his gift of charm and wit to support his feelings of entitlement. The 4-9 two-point code also suggests he is impulsive, manipulative, and can become hostile when he perceives either real or imagined threats. Of course, one should never diagnosis someone as fulfilling antisocial personality disorder merely on an elevated Four Scale on the MMPI-2 or any instrument. However, when we consider Robert's MMPI-2 scores in light of his previous clinical interview with the counselor and Robert's reported history, the antisocial personality disorder certainly appears to be a viable diagnosis.

Some might simply overlook Robert's lower than normal Five Scale: Masculinity-Femininity. However, the authors' believe comment is warranted. This lower than normal score suggests that Robert likely presents as robustly masculine. He clearly is acculturated into presenting like a "man's man" and likely uses this persona to both gain acceptance and later to intimidate others.

Regarding Robert's Scale Six: Paranoia, his two highest Clinical Scale scores are 4 and 9. As previously mentioned, Robert qualifies for a 4-9 two-point code and has been diagnosed with antisocial personality disorder. Interestingly, there exists a 4-6 two-point code. However, Robert does not qualify for the 4-6 code, because of his robustly higher and clinically significant 4-9 scores. Although the authors' are unaware of a 4-9-6 three-point code, discussion of Robert's 4-9-6 scoring is warranted. The authors believe Robert's elevated Scale Six likely is at least partly influenced by his pending court arraignment and possible upcoming court sanctions. Honestly, who wouldn't be at least slightly vigilant or anxious not knowing what others will be doing "to you" based on one's upcoming court case? Four to six two-point coded persons typically blame others for their problems and brood about their situation. Our strong suspicion is that Robert is in fact doing the same thing, and although he typically can contain his anger, as the stress builds he likely may struggle with his anger containment.

Next is Robert's Seven Scale: Psychasthenia. Folks who typically present as anxious and worried often have higher scores on this scale. Robert's score is in the low normal range. Given his personality, instead of acting or being anxious, his previous scores suggest he is a "man's man," has the ability to influence others via his significant charm and social skills, and to intimidate others whenever necessary. Thus, his lower-normal range score makes sense. Why be anxious when he can control others via his conning and intimidating behaviors? In addition, regarding the Seven Scale, higher scores may suggest persons who are anxious regarding their milieu. Thus, they often attempt to reduce their anxiety by being highly organized, meticulous, and perfectionist. Robert, on the other hand, is likely impulsive and spontaneous. He may not fully think things out before acting. Hence, his lower-normal range seems logical and supportive of his other MMPI-2 scores and clinical presentation.

Although Robert's Eight Scale: Schizophrenia score is in the middle of the normal range and unremarkable, his Nine Scale: Mania is far above the normal range and clinically significant. Given that Robert denies hallucinations and during his clinical interview he was oriented times three (i.e., person, place, time), engaging, and socially confident, his higher score does not indicate that he is in a manic phase of bipolar disorder or schizophrenic. Instead, the authors believe Robert's scores simply reflect his egocentric energy, flamboyant and outgoing personality, and social confidence. This seems supported by Robert's 10 Scale: Social Introversion as well. High scores on this scale would suggest persons who are uncomfortable around others. This clearly is not the case with Robert. He thrives on "the con" and being the center of attention for personal gain.

After reviewing the client's Validity Scores and individual Clinical Scores, we would typically look for two- or three-point codes. In this case, the authors have already discussed Robert's 4-9 two-point code with his antisocial personality disorder diagnosis. However, if the Supplemental or Other Scores via the Extended MMPI-s Report had been purchased, a review of these scores would be helpful. In Robert's case, because of the counselor's Axis I clinical diagnosis of alcohol dependence for Robert and the high probability that the counselor may be asked to either author a letter regarding his clinical findings to the court or testify in court, he may be particularly interested in the Supplemental Addictions Scale such as the MAC-R, APS, and AAS as well as the additional PSY-5 Scale. Specifically, the results of Robert's endorsements on these scales could be used to supplement the counselor's diagnosis of Robert to the court. Thus, if the MAC-R, APS, and AAS supported the counselor's alcohol dependence diagnosis, Robert's legal counsel couldn't merely call the counselor's clinical judgment into question. The counselor would say that his findings were supported by Robert's MAC-R, APS, and AAS scores, as well as the MMPI-2's overall findings. Conversely, should the counselor's clinical diagnosis not align with the MAC-R, APS, and AAS, the counselor should reevaluate the assigned diagnosis to make certain the diagnosis remains the most accurate for Robert. If after reevaluation of the clinical assessment interview and the MAC-R, APS, AAS, and MMPI-2 findings, the counselor believes a diagnosis change is warranted, he should do so. However, if after reevaluation the counselor believes the initial clinical diagnosis was in fact the most accurate, he should be able to explain why the diagnosis assigned is the most accurate diagnosis and how Robert's endorsements may have reflected either something different or influenced the scoring in a particular manner.

Think for a moment. Had you been Robert's counselor and assigned an Axis I clinical diagnosis of alcohol dependence after a very thorough clinical assessment interview with Robert and one or more of his significant others, and yet Robert's MMPI-2 scores, including his MAC-R, APS, and AAS scores, have suggested something different, where might you first begin to look on the MMPI-2 to explain why Robert's MMPI-2 did not assess him as fulfilling your assigned diagnosis? You would begin by reviewing his Validity Scale Scores. Specifically, if Robert's combination of F scores were very low and his K and L scores were very high, it would suggest that Robert's profile might be invalid and that he may have been attempting to present himself in a very positive and virtuous manner. If this was not the case, are you certain it was Robert who completed the MMPI-2? On occasion, the second author has known of counselors who gave clients assessment instruments to complete at home or in the waiting room lobby. Sometimes the returned instruments were highly suspect. You should always have the client complete the MMPI-2 in the counselor's office without others' potential input into question stems.

Remember, any assessment instrument should be viewed as augmenting the counselor's diagnosis. Stated differently, the counselor's clinical judgment always trumps the assessment instrument's outcome. The counseling professional is the one who diagnoses the client. Assessment instruments do not diagnose clients. Instead, they merely support the counselor's diagnosis of the client or provide additional information that may warrant further investigation and reevaluation of the final diagnosis. Should the counselor's diagnoses seem to frequently be at odds with assessment instrument outcomes, clinical supervision should be helpful. Here, the clinical supervisor can help the counselor better understand the incongruence and help ensure that the most accurate diagnosis is used.

GENERAL MMPI-2-RF OVERVIEW

Ben-Porath and Tellegen (2008) developed the MMPI-2-RF. This instrument is a revised version of the MMPI-2. Thus, there exist similarities between the two instruments. The intent of this description is to highlight some of these differences. This said, one of the most evident differences between the MMPI-2 and the MMPI-2-RF is instrument length. Specifically, the MMPI-2-RF is significantly shorter. The MMPI-2-RF is composed of only 338 true–false items. These same questions were used in the MMPI-2. However, the MMPI-2-RF restructured the questions and eliminated over 200 MMPI-2 questions. The result is an instrument with scoring based on 50 scales. Ben-Porath and Tellegen, 2008 (p. 1) reported the instrument was designed to be a "broad-band instrument intended for use in a variety of settings" (Ben-Porath & Tellegen, 2008, p. 1). The MMPI-2-RF was developed for persons 18 years of age and older, and was first published in 2008 (Pearson, 2011b). The MMPI-2-RF requires a fifth-grade or higher reading level. The anticipated completion time for MMPI-2-RF is 35 to 50 minutes, and it can be administered via paper-and-pencil test, CD, or computer administration (Pearson, 2011b). Pearson states, "The

MMPI-2-RF provides a valuable alternative to the MMPI-2 test, not a replacement....The MMPI-2-RF aids clinicians in the assessment of mental disorders, identification of specific problem areas, and treatment planning in a variety of settings" (Pearson, 2011b). Pearson indicates purchasers must qualify at the "C-Level" (Pearson, 2011b). The MMPI-2RF can be ordered directly from Pearson at 1-800-627-7271.

MMPI-2-RF Reliability and Validity

One-week test–retest coefficients for the MMPI-2-RF validity scales based on the MMPI-2 normative sample ranged between .40 and .84 for men and women with an internal consistency (alpha) for men between .37 and .69 and for women .20 to .71 (Tellegen & Ben-Porath, 2008, p. 23). Regarding Clinical Scales, Tellegen and Ben-Porath (2008, p. 32) state,

> With the exception of the original Clinical Scales, no other MMPI or MMPI-2 scales have been as extensively validated against a variety of criteria in as broad a range of settings as have the MMPI-2-RF scales.

The MMPI-2-RF Technical Manual (Tellegen & Ben-Porath, 2008) is filled with a plethora of assorted tables supporting their claim.

MMPI-2-RF Scales

The MMPI-2-RF has nine Validity Scales and 42 Substantive Scales. MMPI-2-RF Validity Scales include the following: (a) Variable Response Inconsistency (random responding), (b) True Response Inconsistency (fixed responding), (c) Infrequent Responses (responses that are atypical from the main sample of responses), (d) Infrequent Psychopathology Responses (responses that are atypical in psychiatric populations), (e) Infrequent Somatic Responses (responses atypical in medical populations), (f) Symptom Validity (bodily and cognitive complaints often associated with overreporting), (g) Response Bias Scale, (h) Uncommon Virtues (infrequently reported moral thinking or behaving), and (i) Adjustment Validity (proclamation of good psychological functioning associated with under reporting) scales (Pearson, 2011b; Tellegen & Ben-Porath, 2008, p. 6).

Tellegen and Ben-Porath (2008, p. 16) also created three Higher-Order Scales that are included in the MMPI-2-RF. These are broad areas and include Emotional/Internalizing Dysfunction (problems specific to mood and affect), Thought Dysfunction (disordered thinking), and Behavioral/Externalizing Dysfunction (problems resulting from undercontrolled behaviors (Tellegen & Ben-Porath, 2008, p. 6). The intent behind these Higher-Order Scales was to establish a set of narrowly focused measures that are clinically meaningful and serve an integrative function (Tellegen & Ben-Porath, 2008, p. 16).

Unlike the MMPI-2, the MMPI-2-RF does not use the 10 Clinical Scales. Instead, the MMPI-2-RF uses only the Restructured Clinical Scales. As you will remember from the earlier MMPI-2 description, the Restructured Clinical Scales include (a) Demoralization (general life dissatisfaction and unhappiness), (b) Somatic Complaints (vague bodily complaints), (c) Low Positive Emotions (a lack of positive emotional responsiveness), (d) Cynicism (overall distrust and low opinion of others), (e) Antisocial Behavior (rule breaking and irresponsible behaviors), (f) Ideas of Persecution (perceptions that others are out to harm the client), (g) Dysfunctional Negative Emotions (anxiety, anger, irritability), (h) Aberrant Experiences (atypical thinking or perceptions), and (i) Hypomanic Activation (overactivation, aggression, impulsivity, and grandiosity; Ben-Porath & Tellegen, 2008, p. 6).

Internalizing Scales in the MMPI-2-RF are specific to the client's internalized experiences and perceptions. These include the following: (a) Suicidal/Death Ideation (direct reports of suicidal ideation and recent attempts), (b) Helplessness/Hopelessness (perceptions that goals are unattainable and problems will never be resolved), (c) Self-Doubt (a lack of confidence and feelings of uselessness), (d) Inefficacy (perceptions of self-inefficaciousness and indecisiveness), (e) Stress/Worry (rumination and focus on disappointments and time pressure stressors), (f) Anxiety (pervasive anxiety, frights, and frequent night terrors), (g) Anger Proneness (becoming easily angered and impatient), (h) Behavior-Restricting Fears (fears that stop or truncate daily activities), and (i) Multiple Specific Fears (fears of blood, fire, thunder, and so forth; Ben-Porath & Tellegen, 2008, p. 6). Conversely, Externalizing MMPI-2-RF Scales are experiences within the external environment. These Externalizing Scales include (a) Juvenile Conduct Problems (difficulties at school and home or stealing), (b) Substance Abuse (current and past alcohol and drug abuse), (c) Aggression (physically aggressive and violent behaviors), and (d) Activation (heightened excitation and energy level; Ben-Porath & Tellegen, 2008, p. 7).

Interpersonal Scales on the MMPI-2-RF include (a) Family Problems (conflictual family relationships), (b) Interpersonal Passivity (unassertiveness and submissiveness), (c) Social Avoidance (not enjoying and avoiding social experiences), (d) Shyness-Bashful (feeling inhibited and anxious in social contexts), and (e) Disaffiliativeness (disliking people and disliking being around others; Ben-Porath & Tellegen, 2008, p. 7). In addition, the MMPI-2-RF uses the PSY-5. Ben-Porath and Tellegen (2008, p. 58) state, "The MMPI-2-RF PSY-5 Scales are updated versions of the five MMPI-2 scales…all five scales both low and high scores are interpretable as such." Thus, the MMPI-2-RF uses updated PSY-5 Scales in comparison to the MMPI-2 and the term "low" reflects either an absence or limited presence of the corresponding scales' psychological construct and "high" reflects significant presence of the corresponding scales' psychological construct.

EVA MARIE'S MMPI-2-RF PROFILE

The review of the MMPI-2-RF will be somewhat similar to the MMPI-2 described with Robert. We will start with the Validity Scales. The Validity Scales set the stage. If they suggest the test taker endorsed a suspect or invalid test, the other scales provide little if any relevant information. Once it is determined that the test taker endorsed the MMPI-2-RF in a fashion similar to others who were invested in the assessment process, we can review important other scales. When the authors review MMPI-2-RF scores, they review Higher-Order Scales first. This provides a broad interpretation of the client's overall functioning and the types of chief presenting issues. Next, the authors review the Restructured Clinical Scales and PSY-5. These scales provide a more in-depth description of the client's chief presenting concerns and personality characteristics. This is followed by a review of the Internalizing, Externalizing, and Interpersonal scales. Finally, they review the Specific Problem Scales and if warranted Interest Scales.

Now let's look at Eva Marie's Validity Scale Scores contained within Figure 11.2.

We first start with Eva Marie's VRIN-r Scale score, 38. High scores on the VRIN-r make the test uninterpretable, because the test taker had excessive response inconsistency. In Eva Marie's case, we visually see that her 38 score is below the marked 50 point line and is low. This suggests that Eva Marie endorsed question responses in a consistent manner and the test is interpretable. Next, we review Eva Marie's TRIN-r score, 57. Again, Eva Marie

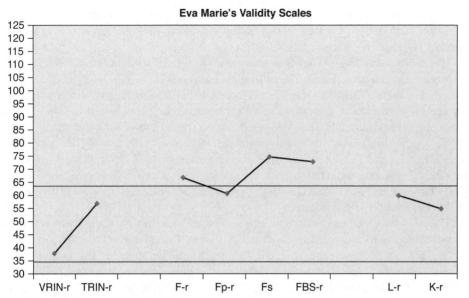

FIGURE 11.2 Eva Marie's Validity Scales. Abbreviations: VRIN-r Variable Response Inconsistency; TRIN-r=True Response Inconsistency; F-r=Infrequent Responses; Fp-r=Infrequent Psychopathology Responses; Fs=Infrequent Somatic Responses; FBS-r=Symptom Validity; L-r=Uncommon Virtues; K-r=Adjustment Validity

endorsed responses in a manner that suggests the test is interpretable. Had she scored excessively high or low on this scale, her endorsements would have suggested that she intentionally attempted to misrepresent herself and the test would be uninterpretable. Eva Marie scored 67 on the F-r. This is a low score. It suggests that Eva Marie did not overreport her complaints. Extremely high scores over 120 would suggest that even if presenting with severe psychological difficulties, the test taker is overreporting an excessive number of infrequent responses (Ben-Porath & Tellegen, 2008, p. 26). The same is true with Eva Marie's Fp-r, Fs, and FBS-r Scale scores. Her respective low scores of 61, 75, and 73 all suggest that Eva Marie did not overreport her symptoms or psychopathology. The opposite problem of overreporting psychological symptoms is underreporting. Here, the client attempts to minimize psychological problems or present him- or herself in a most favorable light. Eva Marie's scores on scales designed to identify underreporting, L-r and K-r, are low (i.e., 60 and 55). Thus, based on Eva Marie's Validity Scale scores it appears that Eva Marie was invested in the test-taking process, consistent in her responses, and approached the test in an honest and forthright manner. In nonprofessional terms, she did not attempt to "Fake Good" or "Fake Bad." The result is an interpretable and valid appearing test.

HIGHER-ORDER SCALES

Higher-Order Scales demonstrate "clinically important individual variations in the basic domains of affect, thought, and action" (Ben-Porath & Tellegen, 2008, p. 32). Stated differently, these Higher-Order Scales provide an overview of the client's general functioning according to affect, thought, and action. Although individual RC Scales may identify greater levels of psychopathology or functioning, the Higher-Order Scales provide a general idea of what major area(s) the client is experiencing psychological distress or difficulties in. The first scale that we review is the Emotional/Internalizing Dysfunction (EID) Scale. Here, Eva Marie scores a moderately high score of 77.

Her score suggests she clearly is experiencing significant emotional distress. A score of 80 would indicate that the degree of distress experienced would likely be perceived by the client as a crisis. Thus, her score is very close to "crisis levels." Her score suggests she likely feels overwhelmed, pessimistic about the future, helpless to change the emotional feelings she is experiencing, and depressed. Given the length of time Eva Marie has been remaining in her unsatisfactory relationship with her spouse, living with her spouse in her mother's home, and the length of time she has experienced her reported anxiety, her moderately high, but not crisis, score seems logical. Stated differently, she likely has become familiar and accustomed with the psychological distress because of the length of time she has had these experiences.

The next two Higher-Order Scales to review include the Thought Dysfunction Scale and the Behavioral/Externalizing Dysfunction Scale. Eva Marie scores low on both (45 and 32). Her low score on the Thought Dysfunction Scale suggests she is thinking logically and coherently. In other words, she does not present with psychotic features. Concomitantly, her Behavioral/Externalizing Dysfunction Scale Score (32) suggests she is unlikely to be violent, abuse alcohol or other drugs, or have poor impulse control. Stated differently, Eva Marie demonstrates significant impulse control and is likely an outstanding citizen who strictly follows expected social norms and rules. Just as an aside, and given your knowledge of Robert, would you anticipate Robert would score "high" or "low" on the Behavioral/Externalizing Dysfunction Scale? He would score "high." Robert's high score would suggest that he had poor impulse control.

RESTRUCTURED CLINICAL SCALES

Next, the authors move to the Restructured Clinical Scales (Figure 11.3) and start with the Demoralization Scale (RCd). The Demoralization Scale indicates the client's general life unhappiness and dissatisfaction. Given your knowledge of Eva Marie from the clinical interview and her diagnosis, would you anticipate her score would be low or high on this scale? In other words, would you believe Eva Marie has general happiness and life satisfaction (low score) or do you believe she has general unhappiness and life dissatisfaction (high score)? Eva Maria actually scores at the lowest end of the "high" score with an 80.

This suggests she is experiencing robust emotional turmoil in her life, she is feeling overwhelmed, and she is extremely dissatisfied. As we review the remainder of the Restructured Clinical Scales, we will use Eva Marie's Demoralization Scale as a backdrop to help keep the individual scale scores in perspective.

As an aside and given Eva Marie's score is high, the counselors will also need to review her Suicide Scale and minimally query Eva Maria about possible suicidal ideation or intent. The counselor would also provide a 24-hour helpline number she can call should she feel overwhelmed, ask how she would kill herself if she intended to, and remove or eliminate the suicide instrument (e.g., gun) from her immediate environment. Then, the counselor would document within her case notes Eva Marie's responses, the counselor's responding interventions, and Eva Marie's agreement to the same, or involuntary hospitalization or other necessary least restrictive environment (Juhnke, Granello, & Granello, 2010; Juhnke, Juhnke, & Hsieh, 2012).

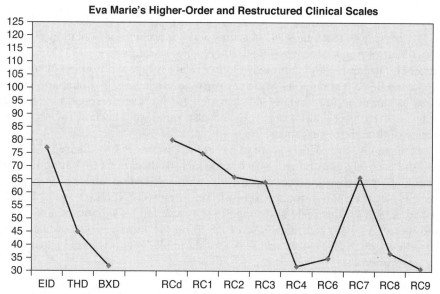

FIGURE 11.3 Eva Marie's Higher Order and Restructured Clinical Scales. Abbreviations: EID=Emotional/Internalizing Dysfunction; THD=Thought Dysfunction; BXD=Behavioral/ Externalizing Dysfunction; Rcd=Demoralization; RC1=Somatic Complaints; RC2=Low Positive Emotions; RC3=Cynicism; RC4=Antisocial Behavior; RC6=Ideas of Persecution; RC7= Dysfunctional Negative Emotions; RC8=Aberrant Experiences; RC9=Hypomanic Activation

At this point in the MMPI-2-RF review process, we will complete the review of each of the remaining Restructured Clinical Scales. Because this was also demonstrated in the MMPI-2 review, the authors will provide only a succinct review here. If you review Figure 11.3 and Eva Marie's individual Restructured Scale Scores, you will find that Eva Marie presents with a score of 75 on the Somatic Complaints Scale (RC1). This is a moderately high score and suggests that Eva Marie may well complain of headaches, gastrointestinal problems, or other physical complaints related to her anxiety and distress. Her Low Positive Emotions Scale (RC2) has a high score (66). This reflects her overall pessimism that things will improve, that she likely is socially introverted and socially disengaged from others. It further suggests that she lacks energy and may qualify for a disorder such as major depression. Eva Marie's Cynicism Scale (RC3) score is 64. This score is a moderate score and just one point from a high score. Persons with similar scores may feel alienated from others and possibly distrustful of others. Eva Marie's Antisocial Behavior Scale (RC4) should not surprise us. Her 32 score is far below average and suggests that she likely has not participated in criminal activity, that she does not endorse items similar to those who are diagnosed with antisocial personality disorder, and that her endorsements do not appear to reflect past or present substance-abusing behaviors. Eva Marie does not appear to have persecutory, paranoid delusions, or psychotic features as evidenced by her respective low scores of 35 and 37 on her Ideas of Persecution Scale (RC6) and Aberrant Experiences Scale (RC8). However, her dysfunctional Negative Emotions Scale (RC7) score of 66 is high and suggests she may excessively worry, be guilt prone, and self-critical; her low Hypomanic Activation Scale (RC9) score (31) suggests she has below expected activation and engagement within her environment.

PSY-5

Figure 11.4 provides Eva Marie's PSY-5 scores and a graphic representation of her scores. Here, Eva Marie's Aggressiveness—Revised (AGGR-r) Scale score is 35. This score suggests Eva Mare is passive and submissive in her relationships with others, whereas scores above 65 are reflective of persons who are overly assertive, socially dominant, and viewed by others as domineering—clearly not a match for Marie's personality. Her Psychoticism—Revised (PSYC-r) scale score is 32 and also quite low. Such a low score suggests an absence of thought disturbances.

Concomitantly, Eva Marie's score of 34 on the Disconstraint—Revised (DISC-r) Scale suggests she is overly constrained in her behaviors. High scores of 65 and above on this scale would suggest that one acts impulsively, and is sensation seeking. The next PSY-5 scale is the Negative Emotionality/Neuroticism—Revised (NEGE-r) Scale. Eva Marie's score of 66 is high on this scale and suggests she experiences significant anxiety, insecurity, and worry. As well, Eva Marie's score of 70 on the Introversion/Low Positive Emotionality—Revised (INTR-r) Scale suggests Eva Marie likely avoids social situations and is socially introverted.

Internalizing, Externalizing, and Interpersonal Scales

Although some may argue that the review of these scales should be reviewed before the PSY-5, the authors find it helpful to review these Internalizing, Externalizing, and Interpersonal scales (Figure 11.5 and Figure 11.6) after the PSY-5. This review starts with the Internalizing scale Suicidal/Death Ideation (SUI).

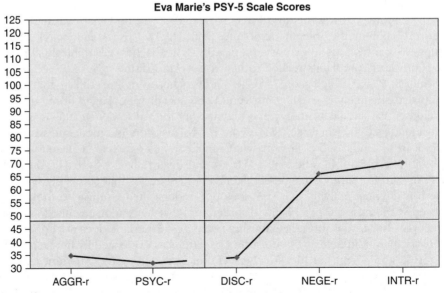

FIGURE 11.4 Eva Marie's PSY-5 Scale Scores. Abbreviations: AGGR-r=Aggressiveness—Revised; PSYC-r=Psychoticism—Revised; DISC-r=Disconstraint—Revised; NEGE-r=Negative Emotionality/Neuroticism—Revised; INT-r=Introversion/Low Positive Emotionality—Revised

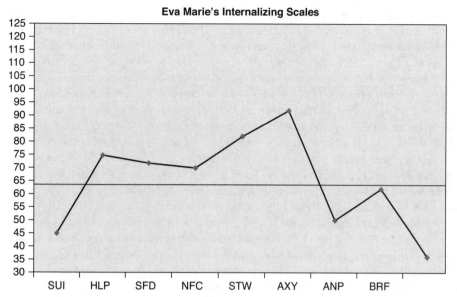

FIGURE 11.5 Eva Marie's Internalizing Scales. Abbreviations: SUI=Suicidal/Death Ideation; HLP=Helplessness/Hopelessness; SFD=Self-Doubt; NFC=Inefficacy; STW=Stress/Worry; AXY=Anxiety; ANP=Anger Proneness; BRF=Behavior-Restricting Fears

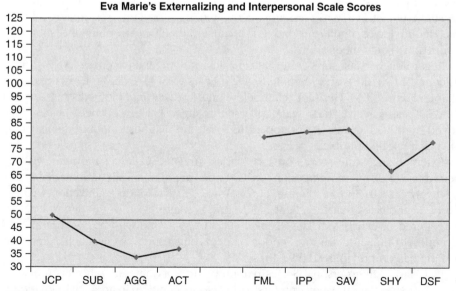

FIGURE 11.6 Eva Marie's Externalizing and Interpersonal Scale Scores. Abbreviations: JCP=Juvenile Conduct Problems; SUB=Substance Abuse; AGG=Aggression; ACT=Activation; FML=Family Problems; IPP=Interpersonal Passivity; SAV=Social Avoidance; SHY=Shyness; DSF= Disaffiliativeness

As previously mentioned, this is an important scale to investigate given Eva Marie's elevated Demoralization Scale score. Interestingly, Eva Marie scores low (45) on the Suicidal/Death Ideation Scale. Thus, she endorses few if any items suggesting either suicide or death intent. Going back to Eva Marie's clinical interview, she stated significant religiosity and her mother's strong "Catholic" presence. Although it is not impossible for those with significant religiosity or from Catholic backgrounds (or any other religious backgrounds) to commit suicide, Eva Marie seems to take pride and comfort in her religious upbringing. Because suicide is broadly believed to be a sin of commission within most religions, Eva Marie may perceive that suicide is an unacceptable behavior that would result in eternal banishment to Hell. This may well reflect why her Suicidal/Death Ideation Scale is low. Whatever the reason for her low Suicidal/Death Ideation Scale score, the counselor should follow the suicide assessment and intervention protocol described earlier, to ensure that Eva Marie is safe and knows how to contact help, should she begin to experience suicidal ideation.

Eva Marie's endorsements on the Helplessness/Hopelessness (HLP) Scale are in the moderate middle (75; Figure 11.5). Persons endorsing similar items feel hopeless and pessimistic regarding their future, and often believe they cannot be helped. This appears to be a solid match to Eva Marie's clinical presentation. Concomitantly, Eva Marie's Self-Doubt (SFD) scale score of 72 suggests she experiences self-doubt, lacks self-confidence, and feels useless. It further suggests that she is prone to rumination and intropunitive thinking (Ben-Perth & Tellegen, 2008, p. 48). Eva Marie's Inefficacy (NFC) Scale score of 70 and her Stress/Worry (STW) Scale score of 82 suggest she is predominantly passive, indecisive, inefficacious, prone to worry, and overly reactive to perceived stressful situations; she may ruminate on worrisome or stressful events (Ben-Perth & Tellegen, 2008, p. 48).

As one would expect, Eva Marie's Anxiety (AXY) Scale is in the moderately high area (92) and is eight points from a high score (Figure 11.5). This scale is congruent and supports other MMPI-2-RF scales specific to anxiety and anxious behaviors. The Anxiety Scale suggests that Eva Marie reports anxious feelings and endorses anxiety-related concerns. Her anxiety is significant enough to cause difficulties sleeping, and she may benefit from antianxiety medications.

Regarding her last three Internalizing Scales—Anger Proneness (ANP), Behavior-Restricting Fears (BRF), and Multiple Specific Fears (MSF)—Eva Marie's scores are unremarkable (Figure 11.5). Her scores fall below noted psychopathology distress levels at 50, 62, and 36, respectively. Thus, Eva Marie's scores suggest she rarely becomes impatient or annoyed by others and does not appear to fulfill the diagnostic requirements for agoraphobia or a specific phobia.

Externalizing Scale scores on Eva Marie's Juvenile Conduct Problems (JCP), Substance Abuse (SUB), and Aggression (AGG) scales are all clinically unremarkable and are respectively 50, 40, and 34 (Figure 11.6). However, Eva Marie's Activation (ACT) Scale score of 37 indicates that the client has below-average levels of energy and potentially may feel tired or exhausted. This seems logical of someone who has been anxious for a long period of time and who has endorsed items suggesting physical aches and pains as Eva Marie has on previous MMPI-2-RF scales.

Eva Marie's Interpersonal Scales paint a picture of someone who has robust family relationship stressors and who prefers to be alone rather than in social situations. Her Family Problems (FML) Scale score is 80 (Figure 11.6). This score further suggests that Eva Marie feels unsupported and unappreciated by family members, and she believes family members cannot be fully trusted.

The Family Problems Scale further suggests family conflict and blaming of family members for Eva Marie's difficulties. Eva Marie's Interpersonal Passivity (IPP) Scale score of 82 suggests she is unassertive, fails to stand up for herself, and is unlikely to take charge of situations. This score is supported by Eva Marie's Social Avoidance (SAV) Scale, her Shyness (SHY) Scale, and her Disaffiliativeness (DSF) Scale sores that are 83, 67, and 78, respectively (Figure 11.6). These combined scale scores suggest that Eva Marie is introverted and shy, dislikes social events, is easily embarrassed, and is uncomfortable around others.

DISCUSSION

This chapter reviewed the DSM five clinical axes, characteristics of DSM Axis I Clinical Disorders and Axis II Personality Disorders, the MMPI-2, and the MMPI-2-RF. The types of scales used by both the MMPI-2 and MMPI-2-RF have been discussed. Finally, the chapter has provided narrative reviews of Robert's and Eva Marie's MMPI-2 and MMPI-2-RF scores.

References

American Psychiatric Association. (2000). *Diagnostic and statistical manual of mental disorders* (4th ed., text rev.). Washington, DC: Author.

Ben-Porath, Y. S., & Tellegen, A. (2008). *MMPI-2-RF: Manual for administration, scoring, and interpretation.* Minneapolis, MN: University of Minnesota Press.

Bubenzer, D. L., Zimpfer, D. G., & Mahrle, C. L. (1990). Standardized individual appraisal in agency and private practice. *Journal of Mental Health Counseling, 12,* 51–66.

Butcher, J. N., Dahlstrom, W. G., Graham, J. R., Tellegen, A., & Kaemmer, B. (2001). *MMPI2: Minnesota Multiphasic Personality Inventory 2 manual for administration and scoring.* Minneapolis, MN: University of Minneapolis Press.

Drayton, M. (2009). *The Minnesota Multiphasic Personality Inventory—2 (MMPI-2). Occupational Medicine, 59*(2), 135–136.

Juhnke, G. A. (2002). *Substance abuse assessment: A handbook for mental health professionals.* New York, NY: Brunner-Routledge.

Juhnke, G. A., Granello, D. H., & Granello, P. F. (2010). *Suicide, self-injury, and violence in the schools: Assessment, prevention, and intervention strategies.* Hoboken, NJ: John Wiley & Sons.

Juhnke, G. A., Juhnke, G. B., & Hsieh, P. (2012). SCATTT: A suicide intervention plan mnemonic for use when clients present suicide intent. Retrieved October 16, 2012, from http://www.counseling.org/Resources/Library/VISTAS/vistas12/Article_34.pdf

Juhnke, G. A., Vacc, N. A., Curtis, R. C., Coll, K. M., & Paredes, D.M. (2003). Assessment instruments used by addictions counselors. *Journal of Addictions & Offender Counseling, 23,* 66–72.

Kessler, R. C., Chiu, W. T., Demler, O., & Walters, E. E. (2005). Prevalence, severity, and comorbidity of twelve month DSMIV disorders in the National Comorbidity Survey Replication (NCSR). *Archives of General Psychiatry. 62,* 617–627.

Lenzenweger, M. F., Lane, M. C., Loranger, A. W., & Kessler, R. C. (2007). DSM-IV personality disorders in the National Comorbidity Survey Replication. *Biological Psychiatry, 62,* 553–564.

Millon, T. (1981). *Disorders of Personality: DSM-III Axis II.* New York, NY: Wiley—Interscience.

Nichols, D. S. (2001). *Essentials of MMPI-2 Assessment.* New York, NY: Wiley.

O'Connor, B. P. (2008). Other personality disorders. In M. Hersen & J. Rosqvist (Eds.), *Handbook of psychological assessment, case conceptualization and treatment* (Vol. 1; pp. 438–462). Hoboken, NJ: Wiley.

Pearson (2011a). MMPI-2. Retrieved from http://psychcorp.pearsonassessments.com/HAIWEB/Cultures/en-us/Productdetail.htm?Pid=MMPI-2

Pearson. (2011b). MMPI-2-RF retrieved from http://www.pearsonassessments.com/HAIWEB/Cultures/en-us/Productdetail.htm?Pid=PAg523&Mode=summary

Sellbom, M., & Ben-Porath, Y. S. (2005). Mapping the MMPI-2 restructured clinical scales onto normal personality traits: Evidence of construct validity. *Journal of Personality Assessment, 85,* 179–187.

Sellbom, M., Ben-Porath, Y. S., Lilienfeld, S. O., Patrick, C. J., & Graham, J. R. (2005). Assessing psychopathic personality traits with the MMPI-2. *Journal -of Personality Assessment, 85,* 334–343.

Tellegen, A., & Ben-Porath, Y. S. (2008). *MMPI-2-RF: Technical manual.* Minneapolis, MN: University of Minnesota Press.

Vacc, N. A. (1982). A conceptual framework for continuous assessment of clients. *Measurement and Evaluation in Guidance, 15,* 40–48.

Vacha-Haase, T., Tani, C. R., Kogan, L. R., Woodall, R. A., & Thompson, B. (2001). Reliability generalization: Exploring reliability variations on the MMPI/MMPI-2 validity scale scores. *Assessment, 8,* 391–401.

Watkins, C. E., Jr., Campbell, V. L., & McGregor, P. (1988). Counseling psychologists uses of and opinions about psychological tests: A contemporary perspective. *Counseling Psychologist, 16,* 476–486.

Wise, E. A., Streiner, D. L., & Walfish, S. (2010). A review and comparison of the reliabilities of the MMPI-2, MCMI-III, and PAI presented in their respective test manuals. *Measurement and Evaluation in Counseling and Development, 42,* 246–254.

CHAPTER 12

Fundamentals of Career Assessment

OBJECTIVES

After reading this chapter, you will be able to:

1. Identify various constructs related to career assessment.
2. View career assessment as a multifaceted assessment process, including assessment of personality, interests, values, and abilities.
3. Become familiar with a variety of assessment tools.
4. Understand Holland's RIASEC model and its relation to personality, interests, and values.
5. Identify how career assessment constructs can be used with clients and applied to our case studies.
6. Become familiar with the O*NET system.
7. Identify strengths and weaknesses in using technology in the career assessment process.

The purpose of this chapter is to provide an overview of assessment in career counseling. Foundations of career counseling are beyond the scope of the chapter. Rather, we will focus on how career assessment may provide valuable information for guiding career counseling and overall wellness of clients served in multiple settings such as schools, agencies, organizations, and practices.

WHAT IS CAREER ASSESSMENT?

The foundation of career counseling was based on career assessment. Frank Parsons, considered the founder of vocational guidance and the counseling movement, identified the assessment of traits as the primary component to selecting a career (Sharf, 2010). Examples of common career traits include personality, interests, values, and abilities.

Career assessment, therefore, is a process in which counselors work with clients to gain a composite framework of personality, interests, values, and abilities to facilitate career counseling and foster a career identity. Counselors use career assessment to assist clients with career exploration, selection, and/or adjustment to new career settings.

Counselors recognize that career development begins in childhood and advocate a lifespan development approach to understanding one's career (e.g., Super, 1990). Therefore, career assessment may also begin in the formative years, yet extant research on career assessment in childhood is limited (Schultheiss & Stead, 2004). Schultheiss and Stead hypothesized that addressing career development in childhood (e.g., fourth grade) could provide information to counselors related to effective problem solving and decision making. The purpose in assessing career development at an early age is not to influence career choice but rather to use career assessment to promote goal setting, achievement, and academic success.

Through matriculation of middle school and high school, career assessment may incorporate models that integrate interests, personality, abilities, and values (Armstrong & Rounds, 2010). Career assessment at this stage may influence individuals' decisions on postsecondary education, training, and vocational placements. During this phase of career assessment, individuals may explore how their interests, values, and abilities relate to goal setting and future career choice. For example, Super (1990) encouraged younger adolescents to focus on identification of careers and awareness of one's own attributes. Older adolescents and young adults may be exposed to a wider variety of career assessment strategies that may be important to career decision making. For example, the Armed Services Vocational Aptitude Battery (ASVAB), college entrance examinations, various state achievement tests, and potential interest, ability, and values inventories (e.g., Strong Interest Inventory, Occupational Information Network [O*NET] instruments) may be administered or made available through guidance counselors.

Throughout adulthood, career assessment may be integral for clients who wish to explore different career opportunities or options, transition between or within a career, identify career needs or placement opportunities, or transition because of developmental needs. Such examples may include individuals who simply wish to change careers, realizing that their current career is less satisfying, to individuals who served in the armed forces and are transitioning to civilian life, or to a new phase such as semiretirement or retirement. In addition, career assessment may be helpful in identifying issues related to career satisfaction and work–life balance.

ELEMENTS OF CAREER ASSESSMENT

Personality, interests, values, and abilities are all relevant constructs to career assessment. Each of these facets of career assessment will be addressed, along with the implication to career assessment. Previously in Chapter 10, we discussed the assessment of ability, addressing various types of instruments categories such as achievement and aptitude measures. Tests such as the ASVAB and DAT, as well as various achievement tests, may be used to identify strengths and challenges for individuals seeking to begin, transition to, or advance in new career opportunities. Many of these tests emphasize various cognitive capacities, such as mathematical reasoning and verbal reasoning.

Evaluation of a single construct provides a limited approach to career assessment. We advocate for a multifaceted approach to career assessment that integrates abilities, interests, values, and personality into a comprehensive profile. One extremely helpful resource, discussed in a greater degree in the following sections, is the O*NET system. O*NET is a comprehensive assessment system funded by the U.S. Department of Labor/Employment and Training Administration (n.d.a). At the time of this writing, information on the O*NET system can be found on the following O*NET Resource Center Web site: http://www.onet-center.org/usingOnet.html. From the Web site, counselors can access and facilitate a variety of career exploration tools, including assessment instruments for career exploration and various occupational support and information materials for a variety of populations.

Interests and Personality

Perhaps the most widely used personality theory tied to career assessment is Holland's model of career interest based on personality theory. For this reason, it is difficult to address issues of personality assessment and interest assessment separately when discussing career assessment. The reason is that Holland's theory incorporates issues of personality in respect to career choice. Holland believed that individuals would experience higher degrees of congruence when an individual's personality is matched with the occupational environment. In other words, a large degree of life satisfaction rests in the idea that an individual's personality should be aligned with the career vocation s/he chooses.

THE RIASEC MODEL   Holland (1973, 1985, 1997) outlined a model of six personality types aligned with corresponding vocational environments in a hexagonal model that would attribute similar and dissimilar work environments for each personality type. The model incorporates six personality types, known as the RIASEC model: realistic, investigative, artistic, social, enterprising, and conventional. Figure 12.1 provides a visual representation of the model.

In Figure 12.1, personality types adjacent to each other share similar characteristics (e.g., enterprising and social), whereas personality types directly opposite (e.g., enterprising and investigative) share fewer characteristics. What follows is a description of each of the personality types.

REALISTIC   Individuals who fit this personality type often engage in hands-on activities. Such work may involve using tools or machinery in a variety of environments (e.g., forestry, farming, construction, maintenance).

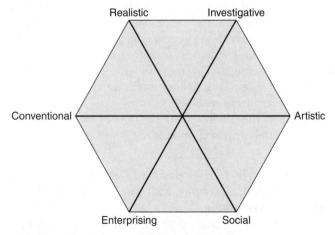

FIGURE 12.1   Holland's Code (RIASEC Model)

INVESTIGATIVE   Individuals who are investigative prefer careers that require problem solving and fact-finding. Such individuals prefer to address issues mentally, rather than physically. Researchers in a variety of settings, engineers, and detectives are a few examples that fit this personality type.

ARTISTIC   This type of individual often prefers vocations that require creative elements or expertise. Although the arts (e.g., musician, artist, writer) are a natural fit for this personality type, areas of counseling, education, and architecture also serve as examples of the artistic type. People who ascribe to this personality type may be individuals who work well with forms, patterns, and diagrams.

SOCIAL   Occupations in the social realm involve working with others in some capacity. These often include positions in the service and healthcare industries. Counselors and educators also fit this description quite well.

ENTERPRISING   Individuals who fit this profile often prefer vocations that require leadership and decision making. Such individuals are not adverse to risk taking. People who enter the business professions or move into leadership within an agency or organization often fit this personality type.

CONVENTIONAL   Individuals who fit this personality type may excel in working with details and prefer routines. Although this personality type often is associated with bookkeeping, other potential vocations include such jobs as accountant, pharmacist, and research analyst.

Because of the prevalent nature of Holland's theory, also referred to as Holland's codes, a number of assessment batteries and career assessment resources were developed using this theoretical framework. Common assessment batteries include the Strong Interest Inventory (SII), Self-Directed Search (SDS), and the O*NET Interest Profiler (IP).

The SII is considered to be among the best interest inventories on the market (Layton, 1995). The purpose of the SII is to match individuals across a wide range of occupations based on the individual's interests as operationally defined using Holland's codes. Hence, individuals are matched with occupations that may appear congruent to their interests (Kelley, 2010). The SII takes approximately 40–45 minutes to administer and is specifically geared toward ages 16 and older. Therefore, the SII is not appropriate for exploring career interests in early developmental stages. One advantage of the SII is that it may be used for group administrations, thereby making the SII an effective tool for group guidance in school settings. The psychometric properties of the instrument are sound, and the instrument has a long history with ongoing updates and renorming that encourage comprehensive, current results.

The SDS is similar to the SII in that the SDS uses the RIASEC model to facilitate career exploration. The SDS is a psychometrically sound instrument with the following added benefits:

- The SDS was developed by John Holland, who created the RIASEC model.
- The SDS was developed to comply with assessment guidelines of the National Career Development Association.
- The SDS includes multiple forms that can be used with professional-level employees, such as adults in career transition, and younger adolescents (ages 11 and above),

students, and adults with limited reading levels (Brown, 2001). An advantage of the SDS is that career booklets are provided with each of the forms to assist with career exploration activities.

The O*NET IP is part of a comprehensive assessment system operated by the United States Department of Labor/Employment and Training Administration described earlier in this chapter. Similar to the SII, the IP uses the RIASEC model. The IP can be accessed in two forms from the O*NET Resource Center. Individuals may download the test manual and test form to administer or self-administer. A computerized version, referred to as the CIP, is also available. The test form and computerized version are identical, containing 180 items that match occupations with career interests. The psychometric characteristics of the IP are strong; with the added flexibility of materials being accessible online and free to the user, the IP is an excellent resource for counselors to use with clients or for individuals to use the assessment forms and additional employment/vocational resources. One of the advantages to using the CIP is the wealth of resources presented at the end of the administration. Upon completing the 180 items, the user receives scores and a Holland code from the RIASEC personality types to identify potential jobs that match the user's interests. In addition, the user is asked to identify the amount of training and education he or she has at present or to search for jobs that would require some additional training. Job zones are provided for the following areas:

1. Little or no preparation
2. Some preparation, such as previous work experience, vocational training, a high school diploma or associate's degree
3. Medium preparation, such as on-the-job training, previous work experience, an associate's or bachelor's degree
4. Considerable preparation, such as a bachelor's degree or 2 to 4 years' work experience
5. Extensive preparation, such as a graduate degree and extensive training in a specific area

One limitation of the O*NET system is the required skill needed to search through the abundance of materials in the O*NET Resource Center. Skills in using the Internet can be overwhelming for clients who have limited exposure to technology and the Internet.

Holland (1997) identified personality and interest as a unified construct. Counselors can be helpful in facilitating clients to seek out work environments that fit their personality type. Thus, through the use of assessment batteries that identify career interests according to Holland's codes (i.e., RIASEC), individuals may achieve greater career self-efficacy and self-actualization. In addition to Holland's codes, other personality theories and measures are used frequently in career assessment. Specifically, the Myers-Briggs Personality Type Indicator (MBTI) and instruments related to the five-factor model of personality (e.g., NEO Personality Inventory—Revised [NEO-PI-R], Adjective Checklist) are used frequently for career assessment.

The MBTI is a popular personality instrument used in various capacities, such as individual counseling; couples, marriage, and family counseling; and task groups in organizations. The MBTI uses Jungian theory of personality to categorize individuals into specified categories. Using four categorical dyads, individuals may be classified along the following:

- Introversion—Extroversion
- Sensing—Intuition

- Thinking—Feeling
- Judging—Perceiving

As a result of the multifaceted uses for the MBTI, applications to career assessment may appear to be a natural fit. Katz, Joyner, and Seaman (1999) evaluated college students and found the MBTI to be as helpful as the SII in making career decisions. Katz et al. recommended joint administration of the MBTI and SII to facilitate career choices in college students. However, correlations between MBTI personality types and the RIASEC categories are low (Pulver & Kelly, 2008), which may indicate that although the two instruments together may provide a more comprehensive profile of the individual, using the MBTI in lieu of the SII is not advisable.

The five-factor model of personality (FFM) is a well-defined, highly researched personality theory that identifies five aspects of personality: openness, conscientiousness, extraversion, agreeableness, and neuroticism. Openness refers to someone who may be receptive, accommodating, and/or amenable to new ideas and situations. Conscientiousness may refer to one who is responsible and persistent. Individuals who fit this description may plan ahead in order to achieve. Extraversion refers to individuals who are sociable, amiable, and willing to assert their thoughts and points of view to others. Agreeableness refers to individuals who may be trustworthy, cooperative, and caring. Neuroticism may refer to individuals prone to negative affective states, such as feelings of hostility, fear, depression, anxiety, or negative self-evaluation (McCrae & Costa, 1992). The personality dimensions of the FFM tend to be predictive of career self-efficacy and achievement orientation, particularly with respect to individuals who are extraverted and conscientious (Reed, Bruch, & Haase, 2004). Similar to limitations of the MBTI, the correlations between the RIASEC personality model and the FFM are not overwhelmingly strong (Nauta, 2004), thereby reiterating caution in using such personality measures in lieu of interest inventories.

An additional limitation of such personality tests that do not specifically address the RIASEC model is that career exploration tools are not inherently developed to address other personality types at this time. Instruments such as the SII and IP use the RIASEC model and include an abundant number of resources (e.g., O*NET Resource Center) that can be used to facilitate career exploration.

Values

Values within the context of career assessment refer to the subjective importance and meaningfulness of activities in work and the work environment (Smith & Campbell, 2008). Smith and Campbell further ascribed to the belief that work values are more tied to "standards or goals" (p. 41). Career interests may be viewed as means to pursue goals or objectives, which are identified through values. In this respect, career interests emanate from career values. Work values may be assessed through the identification of individuals' personal values, referred to as "person-based" assessment, or through identifying values that may be descriptive of various work environments, referred to as "occupation-based" assessment (Smith & Campbell, 2008, p. 41).

A popular person-based assessment is the Minnesota Importance Questionnaire (MIQ). The purpose of the MIQ is to evaluate adjustment toward work, operationally defined as the extent to which an individual's needs and realization of rewards are met through work (Layton, 1992). To achieve this goal, the MIQ measures 20 psychological needs across six fundamental values: (a) achievement, (b) autonomy, (c) altruism, (d) comfort, (e) safety, and (f) status. Although the MIQ exhibits adequate psychometric properties, one limitation is that the instrument is designed for individuals 16 years and older. Therefore, the MIQ is not appropriate for evaluating work values prior to the later high school years.

Aligned with the MIQ, the Minnesota Job Description Questionnaire (MJDQ) is an occupation-based assessment. The MJDQ uses statements aligned with the 20 psychological needs of the MIQ to describe the types of reinforcement [referred to as occupational reinforcement patterns (ORPs)] from various occupational environments (Zedeck, 1978). Counselors can use client responses on the MJDQ to address alignment with client responses on the MIQ. In this regard, the MJDQ is not an independent assessment but functions as an addition to a comprehensive assessment system with the MIQ. Similar to the MIQ, the MJDQ has strong psychometric characteristics and is appropriate for use with older adolescents and adults. An additional limitation is that counselors need to adopt the system of assessment (i.e., use the MIQ) to make use of the MJDQ.

Similar to what O*NET did with the IP, O*NET created two work values inventories based upon the MIQ and MJDQ: the Work Importance Locator (WIL) and the Work Importance Profiler (WIP). The instruments are the same, with the exception that the WIP is a computer-based administration and the WIL is a card-sort administration and hand-scored instrument (Smith & Campbell, 2008). Similar to the MIQ and MJDQ, the WIL and WIP assess six work values across 20 psychological needs. The U.S. Department of Labor/Employment and Training Administration provided the following work values and psychological needs:

1. *Achievement* —refers to individuals who value attaining results and using their strengths, resulting in feelings of accomplishment. Corresponding psychological needs are *ability utilization* and *achievement*.
2. *Independence* —refers to individuals who value making decisions and working autonomously. Corresponding psychological needs are *creativity, responsibility,* and *autonomy*.
3. *Recognition* —refers to individuals who value advancement and potential to serve as a leader. Such individuals may value positions that garner prestige. Corresponding psychological needs are *advancement, authority, recognition,* and *social status*.
4. *Relationships* —refers to individuals who value providing service to others and working with colleagues in a noncompetitive environment. Corresponding psychological needs are *co-workers, moral values,* and *social service*.
5. *Support* —refers to individuals who value management that advocates, validates, and encourages employees. Corresponding psychological needs are *company policies, supervision over personnel,* and *technical expertise*.
6. *Working conditions* —refers to individuals who value job security and a good working environment. Corresponding psychological needs are *activity, compensation, independence, security, variety,* and *working conditions* (U.S. Department of Labor/Employment and Training Administration, n.d.b,O*NET OnLine, http://www.onetonline.org/find/descriptor/browse/Work_Values/).

Both the WIL and WIP require the individual to sort through 20 psychological needs that apply to the six corresponding values. Individuals will have the option of identifying the importance of each need from a scale of 1 (*least important*) to 5 (*most important*).

Only four cards can be identified under each scaled score (e.g., four needs identified as *most important* [5], four needs identified as *important* [4]). As each psychological need reflects a value, a score for each value will be tallied. The top two values indicate job categories to be explored. Similar to the CIP, when the WIP is used in conjunction with the CIP, users can identify the match between their interests and values in order to identify jobs that are aligned with both constructs. In addition, the user can search through various job zones described earlier in the chapter to identify required training for particular jobs. Hence, training, interests, and values can all be integrated in the O*NET system to provide a comprehensive profile of the client.

O*NET offers the Ability Profiler (AP) as an additional measure. The AP measures nine job-related abilities, including (a) verbal ability, (b) arithmetic reasoning, (c) computation, (d) spatial ability, (e) form perception, (f) clerical perception, (g) motor coordination, (h) finger dexterity, and (i) manual dexterity. The AP includes components that cannot be provided online for the finger dexterity and manual dexterity subtests. In addition, the instrument requires timed tasks. An administrator with training is necessary for this instrument, and additional scoring materials need to be purchased. For these reasons, the AP is less user-friendly than other instruments offered through O*NET.

ISSUES IN COMPUTERIZED CAREER ASSESSMENT

Many publishing companies take advantage of technology to facilitate assessment, especially with respect to scoring and interpretation profiles. Career assessment, by comparison, includes far more resources, probably because the U.S. government dedicated significant resources to developing career assessment and exploration tools through the Department of Labor. As with any computerized assessment process, interpretations may be generated through the software and therefore lack a human element to interpretation. Hence, when counselors rely solely on computer output to evaluate clients, information garnered through clinical interviews, subsequent sessions, and/or additional assessment measures may not be reflected in the computerized profiles. Career assessment may complicate this process further with the multitude of resources all individuals have access to regardless of training. For example, the O*NET system includes sophisticated measures that are not readily understood without training. Although a layperson could investigate the limited information on the RIASEC model or work values, having a theoretical understanding of how the O*NET system was developed and applied is helpful. More important is the issue of how clients will use career assessment to make decisions. Because of the amount of information presented, counselors should take considerable time to process with the client the results of various assessments. Issues that the counselor can facilitate include the amount of training the client has and is willing to obtain in order to advance or transition to a new career. Such information is important in successfully working through the O*NET system.

Counselors who use the computerized career assessments may need to provide training to clients with respect to how clients can navigate through the O*NET system. We offer the following suggestions to assisting counselors in using this career assessment process:

1. Counselors should become familiar with the O*NET system by self-administering the assessment instruments, particularly the CIP and WIP. Once the assessment is completed, the system produces results and provides search strategies for identifying potential career options.

2. One benefit of the O*NET system is that the client can self-administer the assessments at home. However, for the counselor to be able to process the information from the assessments, the output produced from the assessments would be helpful. Clients may need assistance in identifying important personality interests or values versus less pertinent personality interests or values.

3. Because of the opportunity to engage in career exploration after the completion of the assessment(s), administration, scoring, and subsequent career exploration activities might be best facilitated with the counselor present.

4. The scoring system for the assessment instruments, although available to the client in the user's manuals, tends to be rather technical. Ethical administration, scoring, and interpretation of measures depend on the counselor's knowledge of administration, scoring, and interpretation processes. Counselors should review the user manuals provided.

5. Clients who are less familiar with technology may find this process intimidating. Procedures to administer the instruments in the counselor's office may be necessary. In addition, use of the O*NET system requires downloading of necessary software, so a level of technology literacy is necessary.

The use of career assessment processes through the Internet provides an opportunity and accessibility for assessment tools that is unprecedented in other assessment areas. Counselors should be cautious with such technology because of the potential of unstandardized administrations being undertaken. The assessment tools provided through O*NET are useful and valid when used appropriately. However, the potential for confounding results through overreliance on individual client administration is apparent and should be addressed when training the client to use the materials appropriately.

TYPES OF INFORMATION DERIVED FROM OUR CASE STUDY WITH EVA MARIE GARZA

To provide an overview of career assessment and the application of the concepts presented in this chapter, we will focus on administration of the CIP and WIP with Eva Marie Garza. To facilitate interpretation of Eva Marie's career assessment profile, we present information from the user's manual of the CIP and WIP that may be accessed from the O*NET Resource Center Web site.

The CIP was developed to be parallel to the hand-scored administration of the IP. Recall that the goal of the CIP (and IP) is to evaluate personality interests based on the RIASEC model. The CIP includes 180 items. There are 30 items that represent each of the personality interests (Realistic, Investigative, Artistic, Social, Enterprising, Conventional). Each item includes a work task in which the client responds with *Like or Dislike*. If the client is unsure, he or she can click on a question mark as a third option. The CIP is scored through the software and results are presented to the client. The client receives a score in each of the six areas of the RIASEC model. For each of the 30 items endorsed on a particular subscale, a point is recorded for that subscale. For example, if a client marks *Like* for an item that is matched with Conventional, then one point is recorded for Conventional. No points are scored for an item marked otherwise. So, with 30 items for each subscale, the maximum score for each subscale is 30. The top three scores represent the client's Holland code. Once a score report is produced and a Holland code is put forward, the client is presented with job zones matching the Holland code and the amount of training he or she wishes to consider for a career. Clients can search through particular vocations that match their interests.

The Work Interest Profiler (WIP) includes two tasks. The first task is to rank work needs, described earlier as psychological needs. Five different needs are presented at one time. The client ranks each of the needs, starting with the most important to the least important. This process is repeated across 21 screens with each need appearing several times in order to compare and rank each need across all other needs. Once the client completes the 21 screens, the second task requires the client to rate work needs. On a single page, 21 statements appear and the client provides a *Yes* or *No* response to indicate whether a particular work need is important to him or her. From these two tasks, the computer generates scores for each of the six work values: (a) achievement, (b) independence, (c) recognition, (d) relationships, (e) support, and (f) working conditions. The score report may fit one of three categories. A *differentiated* score report occurs when at least one work value is positive and different from the other work values. A *negative* score report occurs when all work value scores are below zero. In this case, the client receives a notification indicating that the work values being measured on this instrument do not appear pertinent to the client. An *undifferentiated* score report occurs when no work value appears more or less important than other work values. In this case, a notification is generated to indicate this to the client. So, it is possible that the results from the WIP contribute little to clients' understanding of work values and the influence on career choice. However, it is also possible that the results from the WIP can be integrated with the CIP results to provide a rather comprehensive profile of the client.

Below is a description of Eva Marie's score report on the CIP and WIP.

Eva Marie Garza is a 40-year-old Latina female who presents with a history of anxiety and depression. Based on a clinical interview with Eva Marie, some maladjustment is evident from dissatisfaction with her career. Eva Marie earned an associate's degree and worked previously as a bookkeeper, first for a Catholic church, and then for a local drug store. Eva Marie reported being "good with numbers" and that bookkeeping gave her a "sense of purpose." Eva Marie described her previous boss at the drug store as someone who valued her work, and she took pride in her job. When Eva Marie relocated to San Antonio, she was unable to obtain a bookkeeping position and now works as an assistant to the librarian at an elementary school. Eva Marie dislikes her current position but enjoys the opportunity to make decisions.

Eva Marie was administered the Computerized Interest Profiler (CIP) and the Work Importance Profiler (WIP). Administration of the CIP and WIP was within the guidelines of stated procedures, and results from this test may be viewed as a valid measure. Eva Marie's score report from the CIP indicated a Holland code of CSA (Conventional, Social, Artistic) with the following scores:

Realistic: 0
Investigative: 0
Artistic: 3
Social: 5
Enterprising: 2
Conventional: 14

The Artistic trait was quite low and comparable to Enterprising, indicating that emphasis on job interests should focus more so on Conventional characteristics and some Social characteristics. Eva Marie had a differentiated score report on the WIP, identifying Relationships and Achievement as her most pertinent work values as indicated in the score report below:

Achievement: 1.4
Support: 0.2
Recognition: 0.8
Relationships: 1.5
Working Conditions: 0
Independence: 0.4

The score reports from the CIP and WIP fit the information from Eva Marie's clinical interview quite nicely. Individuals described as Conventional tend to enjoy routines and prefer working with data and details. In addition, Eva Marie's desire to work with tasks that help people or are important to an organization fit nicely with the Social personality interest, as well as the Relationship work value. In addition, Eva Marie's desire to feel productive and use her skills (such as working with numbers) contributes to the Achievement work value.

When exploring potential career options, Eva Marie may want to consider whether she wants to explore career options with her current training or whether she is willing to obtain additional training. Although bookkeeping was an immediate fit, given her Conventional personality interest that fit her work values, 36 potential occupations were listed from the O*NET database. Some of these diverse positions include travel agents and ticket agents, statistical assistants, emergency dispatchers, customer service representatives, and municipal clerks. If Eva Marie is open to additional training, other job opportunities may include medical secretary or technician, legal secretary, city planning aide, licensing examiners and inspectors, title examiners or abstractors, or court clerk. Eva Marie should be encouraged to explore both a current job that matches her interests and values, as well as the potential to secure additional training/education to pursue a new career. Such a transition, while stressful, may improve her self-concept and decrease her stress, which in part stems from an unfulfilling career.

The above report may accompany a psychological report or stand alone as a career assessment report. What is important is that the client obtains a sense of validation, hope, and self-efficacy from the process. In other words, if a client is experiencing maladjustment from dissatisfaction with work, the prospect of exploring new opportunities and options may be both empowering and fulfilling. Individuals may spend an inordinate amount of time in career-related activities. Thus, the importance of addressing career and assessing career satisfaction can be a major component to address the overall well-being of clients.

References

Armstrong, P. I., & Rounds, J. (2010). Integrating individual differences in career assessment: The Atlas Model of Individual Differences and the Strong Ring. *The Career Development Quarterly, 59,* 143–153.

Brown, M. B. (2001). Test review of the Self-Directed Search. In B. S. Plake & J. C. Impara (Eds.), *The fourteenth mental measurements yearbook.* Lincoln, NE: Buros Institute of Mental Measurements.

Holland, J. L. (1973). *Making vocational choices: A theory of careers.* Englewood Cliffs, NJ: Prentice Hall.

Holland, J. L. (1985). *Making vocational choices* (2nd ed.). Englewood Cliffs, NJ: Prentice Hall.

Holland, J. L. (1997). *Making vocational choices: A theory of vocational personalities and work environments* (3rd ed.). Odessa, FL: Psychological Assessment Resources.

Katz, L., Joyner, J. W., & Seaman, N. (1999). Effects of joint interpretation of the *Strong Interest Inventory* and the *Myers-Briggs Type Indicator* in career choice. *Journal of Career Assessment, 7,* 281–297. doi:10.1177/106907279900700306

Kelly, K. R. (2010). Test review of the Strong Interest Inventory. In R. A. Spies, J. F. Carlson, & K. F. Geisinger (Eds.), *The eighteenth mental measurements yearbook.* Lincoln, NE: Buros Institute of Mental Measurements.

Layton, W. L. (1992). Test review of the Minnesota Importance Questionnaire. In J. J. Kramer & J. C. Conoley (Eds.), *The eleventh mental measurements yearbook.* Lincoln, NE: Buros Institute of Mental Measurements.

Layton, W. L. (1995). Test review of the Strong-Campbell Interest Inventory. In J. C. Conoley & J. C. Impara (Eds.), *The twelfth mental measurements yearbook.* Lincoln, NE: Buros Institute of Mental Measurements.

McCrae, R. R., & Costa, P. T. (1992). Discriminant validity of NEO-PI-R facet scales. *Educational and Psychological Measurement, 52,* 229–237.

Nauta, M. M. (2004). Self-efficacy as a mediator of the relationships between personality factors and career interests. *Journal of Career Assessment, 12,* 381–394. doi:10.1177/1069072704266653

Pulver, C. A., & Kelly, K. R. (2008). Incremental validity of the *Myers-Briggs Type Indicator* in predicting academic major selection of undecided university students. *Journal of Career Assessment, 16,* 441–455. doi:10.1177/1069072708318902

Reed, M. B., Bruch, M. A., & Haase, R. F. (2004). Five factor model of personality and career exploration. *Journal of Career Assessment, 12,* 223–238.doi:10.1177/1069072703261524

Schultheiss, D. E. P., & Stead, G. B. (2004). Childhood Career Development Scale: Scale construction and psychometric properties. *Journal of Career Assessment, 12,* 113–134. doi: 10.1177/1069072703257751

Sharf, R. S. (2010). *Applying career development theory to counseling.* Belmont, CA: Brooks/Cole, Cengage Learning.

Smith, T. J., & Campbell, C. (2008). The relationship between occupational interests and values. *Journal of Career Assessment, 17,* 39–55. doi:10.1177/1069072708325740

Super, D. E. (1990). A life-span, life-space approach to career development. In D. Brown, L. Brooks, & Associates (Eds.), *Career choice and development* (2nd ed., pp. 197–261). San Francisco, CA: Jossey-Bass.

U.S. Department of Labor/Employment and Training Administration. (n.d.a). O*NET Resource Center. Retrieved from O*NET Resource Center Web site: http://online.onetcenter.org/

U.S. Department of Labor/Employment and Training Administration. (n.d.b). Work Values. Retrieved from O*NET OnLine Web site: http://www.onetonline.org/find/descriptor/browse/Work_Values/

Zydeck, S. (1978). Test review of the Minnesota Job Description Questionnaire. *The eighth mental measurements yearbook.* Lincoln, NE: Buros Institute of Mental Measurements.

CHAPTER 13

Marriage, Substance Abuse, and Suicide Assessment

OBJECTIVES

After reading this chapter, you will be able to:

1. Describe the Marital Satisfaction Inventory—Revised and understand how Eva Marie and her husband view their marriage, based upon their scores.

2. Explain the major Substance Abuse Subtle Screening Inventory—3 scales and determine if a client's scores suggest he is attempting to cover up his alcohol use by endorsing items in a more favorable manner.

3. Understand the Alcohol Use Inventory and be able to logically compare and contrast the Substance Abuse Subtle Screening Inventory—3 and the Alcohol Use Inventory.

4. Describe the Suicide Probability Scales and determine if a client is at high or low risk of suicidal behaviors.

5. Identify the Suicide SCATTT mnemonic's six phases and describe how to use the assessment with clients perceived to be at imminent risk.

OVERVIEW

Over the years, the authors have found the need to use many different psychological assessment instruments. Three clinical areas that the authors and their supervisees frequently use assessment instruments for include marital and couples counseling, addictions counseling, and suicide prevention and intervention. Thus, the authors will review the assessment instruments they actually use specific to these clinical areas. Each clinical assessment instrument will be described by its scales and intended purposes. In addition, the chapter includes the Suicide SCATTT mnemonic. This mnemonic is used immediately after a client has been assessed to be at significant suicide risk. It is intended to both protect the suicidal client and provide counselors a six-phase plan of what to do between making the suicide assessment and moving the suicidal client to a least restrictive and protective environment. Robert Jones and Eva Marie Garza's clinical vignettes will be used throughout the chapter to demonstrate the instruments.

MARITAL SATISFACTION INVENTORY—REVISED (MSI-R)

General MSI-R Overview

The authors have found the MSI-R to be a user-friendly assessment instrument that has exceptional utility for counselors treating client couples. The instrument was created to help identify "the nature and extent of relationship distress with couples considering or beginning conjoint therapy" (Snyder, 1997, p. 1). The instrument can be used with traditional or nontraditional couples (Western Psychological Services [WPS]; 2012). The MSI-R provides clear indications of the couples' individual and joint perceptions of their marriages, including challenges that may warrant immediate attention. These comprise 11 separate marital interaction dimensions, including Affective Communication, Role Orientation, Problem-Solving Communication, Aggression, Family History of Distress, Time Together, Dissatisfaction with Children, Disagreement about Finances, Conflict over Child Rearing, Sexual Dissatisfaction, and Global Distress (WPS, 2012). Concomitantly, the instrument provides information regarding the couples' perceptions of their children and the couples' parenting.

The MSI-R is comprised of 150 question stems with corresponding "True" and "False" response options (WPS, 2012). Childless couples complete Questions 1 through 129. Couples with children complete all 150 question stems. These last 21 questions deal specifically with perceptions related to the couple's children and parenting (e.g., disciplining, child-rearing workloads; Juhnke, 2002). A combination of 13 or more unmarked or "double-marked" responses (where the respondent endorsed both True and False responses) suggests the profile to be "unscorable" (Snyder, 1997, p. 6). According to Snyder, persons taking the instrument "should be instructed to respond to the inventory items *separately and without collaboration*" (p. 6). Thus, completing the MSI-R is not a project the couple completes together. Instead, each partner takes the instrument independently. The instrument takes approximately 25 minutes to complete and requires a sixth-grade reading level (p. 1). The MSI-R was developed for persons 16 years of age and older (D. Snyder, personal communications, September 27, 2005) and can be directly ordered from Western Psychological Services 1 (800) 648-8857.

MSI-R Reliability and Validity

Test–retest reliability coefficients ranged between .74 and .88 with a mean coefficient of .79 (excluding the Inconsistency Scale; Snyder, 1997, p. 55). These coefficients suggest the MSI-R scales appear relatively stable across time (Juhnke, 2002). Cronbach's alpha coefficients of internal consistency for all MSI-R scales except the Inconsistency Scale ranged between .70 to .93 with a mean coefficient of .82 (Snyder, 1997, p. 55). Such coefficients reflect the instrument's internal consistency. Related to validity, each of the instrument's 13 scales was able to differentiate between clinical and nonclinical couples at the $p < .001$ level. Concomitantly, other research studies comparing "broad-band multidimensional measures of psychopathology and personality functioning in adults and children or adolescents" (p. 68) suggest concurrent validity with appropriate and corresponding scales on the Minnesota Multiphasic Personality Inventory (MMPI) and the Personality Inventory for Children.

Scales

The MSI-R is comprised of 13 scales, including two validity scales and one global affective scale. The first validity scale, Inconsistency (INC), reports random or careless responses, which may also be indications of confusion or deliberate attempts at noncompliance (Snyder, 1997). High scores on the INC may suggest random scoring or a lack of investment in the assessment process. Conversely, low scores may indicate an overall investment in the testing process and potentially a more positive perception of most MSI-R relationship domains (e.g., communications, finances). The second scale, Conventionalization (CNV), reports the clients' "tendencies to distort the appraisal of their relationship in a socially desirable direction." (p. 20). High scores on this scale suggest defensiveness and resistance to discussing conflict within the relationship. Here, for example, when the authors have counseled a couple mandated into family treatment by the courts or child protective services, or when legal counsel of one member of the couple has "highly encouraged" the clients to participate in family counseling before custody cases go to trial, these couples sometimes present with highly inflated CNV scores. Such scores may at first appear incongruent with the couple presenting for relationship counseling. This is because the scores initially may seem to suggest the couple is saying, "The relationship is fine. Nothing is wrong or broken." However, what they may be attempting to suggest is they "don't need help" or they are "perfect" partners or parents and warrant full custody of their children. Low CNV scores, conversely, are frequently associated with moderate overall relationship distress. Here, couples are reporting concerns within their marriages.

The Global Distress (GDS) Scale reports "overall dissatisfaction with the relationship" (p. 21). High GDS scores suggest significant relationship dissatisfaction that likely has existed for a significant time. Such scores are relatively common with the authors' client couples when one partner struggles with addictions and the other does not, or when one partner has actively participated in long-term infidelity and the other has not. Here, the scores may reflect the nonaddicted or noncheating partner viewing the addicted or cheating partner as causing the relationship dissatisfaction. The score further indicates that the nonaddicted or noncheating partner views the other partner as critical and uncaring. Concomitantly, the chaos and dysfunction of living with an addicted or cheating partner is often strikingly apparent when the nonaddicted or noncheating partner compares his or her relationship to other relationships that are perceived as loving, caring, and void of addiction, dysfunction, or infidelity.

Another MSI-R scale is the Affective Communication (AFC) Scale. The AFC Scale is the "best single measure of emotional intimacy experienced" by the couple (Snyder, 1997, p. 21) and reflects dissatisfaction related to perceived partner affection and understanding. High scores denote extensive dissatisfaction related to expressed love and affection within the relationship (Juhnke, 2002). On the other hand, low scores suggest the couple experiences their relationship as happy and fulfilling and their partners as loving and supportive. In couples where addiction is present for both partners, the authors have generally found these scores are more moderate than one might initially anticipate. Here, although the addicted clients' spouses may not be endorsing feelings of great affection and support, they tend to report feeling "understood" and often "accepted" by each other.

The Problem-Solving Communication (PSC) Scale measures the "couple's general ineffectiveness in resolving differences and measures overt discord rather than underlying feelings of estrangement" (Snyder, 1997, p. 22). Couples scoring high on this scale are reporting chronic arguing within the marriage. Many times, these client couples are unable or unwilling to look at voiced partner complaints through their spouse's eyes. These clients often view their partner as intentionally mean and highly rigid. By contrast, couples presenting low PSC scores appear invested in their marital relationship and display behaviors or make statements suggesting they want or expect the relationship to improve. In the authors' experiences, couples endorsing low PSC scores are those either where the marriage is in the early developmental stages or where the identified stressor (e.g., infidelity, addictions) is perceived as being of limited consequences.

The Aggression (AGG) Scale reports intimidation and physical aggression. High scores on this scale denote at least moderate levels of intimidation and physical aggression (e.g., pushing, grabbing, or slapping; Snyder, 1997, p. 23). Here, at least one of the partners is endorsing perceptions of intimidating behaviors or physical aggression by his or her partner. Again, it has been the authors' experience that when sole child custody is being sought or when one or more partners fulfill antisocial personality disorder criteria, AGG Scale scores are typically higher. Conversely, lower scores suggest an absence of physical aggression or intimidation. It should be noted that client couples could have significant relationship struggles and stressors without having inflated AGG Scale scores.

The Time Together (TTO) Scale assesses "the couple's companionship as expressed in terms of the time they spend together in leisure activity" (p. 23). Spending time as a couple is an important part of relationship development and continuance. High TTO scores suggest the couple does not spend adequate time together. Here, the partners may well be spending the majority of their waking time hours away from one another with little emotionally significant quality time together. Low TTO scores suggest time together. It is important to determine if partners scoring low on this scale are actually enjoying time together or if they are "together but separate." Here, for example, the couple might report that they are spending time "together." However, one is playing video games while the other is in the same room but watching soap operas.

The Disagreement about Finances (FIN) Scale reports relationship disharmony resulting from financial management. Most client couples counseled by the authors, even highly affluent couples, endorse at least moderate FIN Scale scores. High scores indicate financial concerns, lack of confidence in the partner's money management, and frequent arguments over money within the relationship. Low scores suggest agreement in the way money is managed. In the authors' experiences, the partner earning the highest salary is often the person reporting the greatest amount of dissatisfaction on this scale.

Another scale within the MSI-R is the Sexual Dissatisfaction (SEX) Scale. According to Snyder (1997) this scale "reflects the respondent's level of discontent with the frequency and quality of intercourse and other sexual activities" (p. 24). High scores suggest "extensive dissatisfaction" (p. 25) related to the sexual relationship and frequency. Low scores suggest a generally positive sexual relationship. These lower scoring SEX folks view their sexual relationship with their partner as being favorable. For most couples counseled by the authors and who report low SEX Scale scores and favorable sexual relations, they claim the presence of open and frequent acts of affection such as holding hands, gentle touching, and nonsexual kissing (e.g., a peck on the cheek). Thus, when both partners perceive affection within the relationship, the authors typically find clients who score low on the MSI-R SEX Scale.

The Role Orientation (ROR) Scale is not necessarily a scale noting marital discord. Rather, it is a scale that reflects incongruence between partners' perceptions of traditional vis-à-vis nontraditional family roles. Here, high scores indicate a belief in more contemporary parenting and marital roles; low scores indicate more traditional parenting and marital roles. Thus, discord can result if spouses have highly differing expectations, assumptions, and beliefs related to how one and one's spouse will participate in such roles (Juhnke, 2002; Snyder, 1997).

The Family History of Distress (FAM) Scale reports "disruption of relationships within the respondent's family of origin" (Snyder, 1997, p. 25). High scores on the FAM Scale suggest significant family of origin conflict and dysfunction. Low scores suggest the endorser experienced a fairly positive family of origin experience.

The remaining two scales measure concerns about children and parenting. The Dissatisfaction with Children (DSC) Scale measures "emotional and behavioral adjustment of their children, quality of the parent-child relationship and negative impact of child rearing demands." (p. 25). High DSC Scores suggest "greater levels of distress in respondents' relationships with their children" (p. 26). Couples endorsing lower scores typically indicate overall satisfaction with their children.

The final scale is the Conflict over Child Rearing (CCR) Scale. Unlike the parent–child relationship addressed in the DSC Scale, the CCR measures the conflict between parents because of child-rearing practices. High CCR scores suggest "extensive conflict in the partners' interactions regarding children" (Snyder, 1997, p. 26). In other words, there likely exists discord between partners related to the way one or both discipline or rear children in the home, as well as discord related to the distribution of child-rearing responsibilities. Low CCR scores suggest the opposite. Low scores suggest satisfaction with one's partner's child-rearing responsibilities and disciplining of the children.

EVA MARIE'S MSI-R

Given Eva Marie is married and Robert is not, we will review Eva Marie's MSI-R responses in this section (see Figure 13.1). In addition, we will provide Ernest's scores. As you will remember, Ernest is Eva Marie's husband. This will allow the authors to discuss Eva Marie and Ernest's perceptions of their marital relationship. Specifically, we will use the MSI-R scales to help identify potential areas of marital dissatisfaction.

Validity Scores

As always, the authors begin their review of client profiles with the client's Validity scores. Specifically, the authors want to determine if the client responded in a manner that suggests she was invested in the assessment process, responded to question stems in a manner that suggested accurate or truthful endorsements, and responded in a manner that was relatively consistent.

Both Eva Marie and Ernest responded to all question stems on their respective MSI-R instruments. Examination of the couple's scores on both the Inconsistency and Conventionalization Scales supports further interpretation of the remaining instrument scales. In other words, both Eva Marie and her husband, Ernest, appear to have endorsed the MSI-R questions stems in a manner that suggests they were at least moderately invested in the assessment process. Specifically, their Inconsistency Scale scores were noted in the low range. This suggests that both partners attended to item content but may have mixed sentiments regarding various aspects of their relationship. Neither spouse

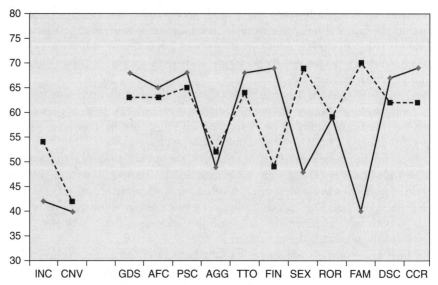

FIGURE 13.1 Eva Marie (solid line) and Ernest's (hashed line) MSI-R.
Abbreviations: INC=Inconsistency; CNV=Conventionalization; GDS=Global Distress;
AFC=Affective Communication; PSC=Problem-Solving Communication; AGG=Aggression;
TTO=Time Together; FIN=Disagreement About Finances; SEX=Sexual Dissatisfaction;
ROR=Role Orientation; FAM=Family History of Distress; DSC=Dissatisfaction with
Children; CCR=Conflict Over Child Rearing

appears to report distorted appraisals of their marriage in an unrealistic, positive manner. Stated differently, both Eva Marie and Ernest admit relationship difficulties and stressors, without blatant attempt to paint their marriage in a glowing or "perfectly heavenly" manner. In addition, Eva Marie and Ernest's low scores on the Conventionalization Scale suggest they are willing to discuss perceived conflicts within their marriage and suggest both partners readily admit relationship distress and concerns.

The couple's Global Distress scores are high. These high scores suggest both Eva Marie and Ernest have a predominate level of overall relationship dissatisfaction. Here, it is important to note that Eva Marie's score is higher than Ernest's score. Thus, it is possible that Eva Marie scores suggest she believes the relationship is in "worse shape" than Ernest believes. Given these scores, Eva Marie and Ernest likely perceive each other as uncaring, critical, and cold, and therefore not meeting each other's perceived needs within the marriage.

Many times, the authors see this type of scoring in relationships where both partners are highly dissatisfied and believe the other partner's behaviors have "caused" the relationship's demise. These scores are further supported by both Eva Marie's and Ernest's Affective Communication Scale scores. Again, their high scores on the Affective Communication Scale suggest that Eva Marie and Ernest perceive a lack of affection and understanding by their partner. Given that both score on this scale at such high levels, it is clear that each has extensive relationship dissatisfaction and likely feels his or her partner lacks warmth, understanding, and support. Simply stated, the couple's scores suggest they have mutually created what each believes is an intolerable living situation.

The couple is likely openly arguing and bickering with one another without gaining mutually satisfactory responses from each other or mutually agreed upon resolutions. Stated differently, their Problem-Solving Communications Scores suggest they are ineffectively arguing with one another and unable to resolve their differences in an effective manner. This arguing appears chronic and pervasive throughout most areas of their lives. Given these scores are so high, both likely perceive their partner as being intentionally critical, harsh, unsympathetic, and likely disparaging. In addition, it is highly unlikely that either Eva Marie or Ernest can allow him- or herself to listen to each other's concerns or even accept his or her partner's voiced concerns.

Although earlier based on the Conventionalization Scale, it was suggested that both partners would likely be willing to discuss their concerns, the authors have found that clients presenting with such high Affective Communication Scale and the Problem-Solving Communications Scale scores typically wish to proclaim the other's faults and have an agenda to blame his or her partner for both real and perceived failures to provide affectionate and nurturing support. Stated differently, if given the chance, Eva Marie and Ernest would likely focus their time discussing his or her partner's perceived failures and lack of support vis-à-vis discussing ways in which the relationship could improve.

Knowing Eva Marie as well as we now do, we would likely anticipate Eva Marie's Aggression Scale score to be exceptionally low. Here, Ernest's Aggression Scale score is in the low range, too. Thus, although the two appear to be actively arguing with one another, neither Eva Marie nor Ernest are reporting significant levels of intimidation or physical aggression, such as pushing, slapping, or hitting within their marriage.

According to Eva Marie's and Ernest's Time Together Scale scores, the couple spends little if any time together. Thus, it is apparent that both Eva Marie and Ernest invest their energies away from one another and likely attempt to remain apart as much as possible. When forced to encounter one another, they likely interact little and their interactions are likely guarded and argumentative.

Based on Eva Marie's and Ernest's Disagreement About Finances Scale scores, it is evident that Eva Marie's significantly higher score suggests she lacks confidence and is suspect of the manner in which Ernest uses the couple's money. Ernest's score is in the low range. This suggests Ernest is generally accepting, if not supportive, of the manner in which Eva Marie manages the family's money. Clearly, however, the person with the greater concern is Eva Marie. Given that Ernest reportedly does not earn enough money to support Eva Marie and Ernest's living independently from Eva Marie's mother, the authors believe it is highly plausible that Eva Marie perceives Ernest as a "free loader" who is simply living at Eva Marie's mother's home and doing little to financially support Eva Marie or her aging mother. In addition, given Eva Marie's significant overall anxiety as reported on earlier testing instruments, it is likely that she is concerned about having enough money to adequately live once her mother passes. Thus, she may well be irritated that Ernest does not do more to contribute to the family's finances and perceives there is little she can do to change his lack of financial contributions.

The couple's Sexual Dissatisfaction Scale is interesting. Given that Eva Marie has scored higher dissatisfaction on all scales than Ernest, one might anticipate that Eva Marie would be more dissatisfied on this scale than Ernest would be. This is not the case. The authors suspect that Eva Marie's significant anxiety level is reflected in her low Sexual Dissatisfaction Scale Score. In other words, given Eva Marie's general anxiousness and the high probability that she feels greater anxiety and discomfort being sexually intimate with a man she believes contributes little to her life and she perceives as caustic, cold, uncaring, argumentative, blaming, and unsympathetic to her emotional needs, she likely finds the infrequent sexual activities quite acceptable. This clearly is not the case with Ernest. He reports clear discontent with the frequency of his sexual activities with Eva Marie, and this scale reflects this dissatisfaction.

Eva Marie's and Ernest's Role Orientation Scale are relatively unremarkable, although Ernest scores at the higher end of the moderate level and Eva Marie scores at the lower end of the moderate level. Thus, their scores indicate that Ernest may believe in a slightly more contemporary family role than Eva Marie may believe in.

Given what we know about both Eva Marie and remembering Eva Marie's earlier statement that Ernest grew up in an "alcoholic" family and did not want children, how can we anticipate Eva Marie and Ernest might score on the Family History of Distress Scale? As you readers have already perceived, Eva Marie seems to romanticize her early life and family of origin experiences. Here, her father is painted as being perfect and although the family struggled with being away from "The Valley" and family and friends, Eva Marie portrays a very loving and caring family of origin experience. Thus, her low scores on the Family History of Distress Scale suggest she likely experienced a very positive family of origin experience. Ernest, on the other hand, reportedly grew up in an alcoholic home. Most families that experience substance abuse or dependence behaviors find their family of origin experiences as chaotic and dysfunctional. This seems to be the case with Ernest. His Family History of Distress Scale suggests he had significant disruption in family relationships as well as conflict and active dysfunction.

Given that Eva Marie and Ernest did not have children, the authors could not administer the Dissatisfaction with Children or Conflict over Child Rearing Scales. However, for teaching purposes only, if Eva Marie and Ernest did have a 16-year-old biological son and a 14-year-old biological daughter, how would we anticipate Eva Marie and Ernest could score on these scales? Given their relationship dissatisfaction, blaming behaviors, perceptions that the other is too harsh, critical, and unsupportive, and their lack of time with one another, we would anticipate elevated scores on both scales by both Eva Marie and Ernest. In other words, Eva Marie and Ernest would likely endorse items on the Dissatisfaction with Children Scale suggesting significant levels of distress in their relationships with their children.

Concomitantly, the authors' would anticipate an elevated score on the Conflict over Child Rearing Scale. Specifically, the authors would anticipate scores suggesting that Eva Marie and Ernest have significant disagreement and discord with one another's disciplining and child-rearing behaviors. In addition, it is plausible that at least Eva Marie will believe Ernest fails to invest adequate childrearing time with the children and fails to support Eva Marie's child-rearing roles. Again, because Eva Marie and Ernest do not have children, the authors could not administer either the Dissatisfaction with Children or Conflict over Child Rearing Scales. However, based on the authors' knowledge of Eva Marie's clinical intake assessment and instrument scores generated thus far, the authors would anticipate the above scoring.

SUBSTANCE ABUSE SUBTLE SCREENING INVENTORY—3

Another testing instrument that the authors have found to have superior clinical utility is the Substance Abuse Subtle Screening Inventory—3 (SASSI-3). Over 20 years ago, the authors were trained how to administer, score, and interpret the original SASSI. Since then, the SASSI has undergone two major revisions and the instrument's utility has greatly increased. This is one of the most widely used substance abuse related assessments in the mental health profession today and was identified as one of the primary specialty assessment instruments that counselors should be trained in (Juhnke, Vacc, Curtis, Coll, & Paredes, 2003).

GENERAL SASSI-3 OVERVIEW

The SASSI-3 was authored by Miller, Roberts, Brooks, and Lazowski in 1997 and is the newest version of the original SASSI that was published in 1988 (Miller et al., 1997). The SASSI was designed to "identify individuals with a high probability of having a substance dependence disorder, even if those individuals do not acknowledge substance misuse or symptoms associated with it" (Miller et al., 1997, p. 2). The SASSI-3 was developed for persons 18 years of age and older (F. Miller, personal communication, July 3, 2001) with a minimum of a 3.2 grade reading level (Substance Abuse Subtle Screening Inventory Institute [SASSI], 2012). The instrument takes approximately 15 minutes to complete (F. Miller, personal communications, July 3, 2001) and is composed of 93 questions. The instrument can be ordered directly from the SASSI Institute at 1 (800) 726-0526.

Side one of the instrument contains 26 face-valid items. These items are highly transparent and directly relate to Alcohol and Other Drug (AOD) use. They provide information regarding the extent to which the addicted family member acknowledges AOD use and define the extent and nature of the AOD problem. The second side of the instrument contains 67 question stems to which the addicted family member endorses either "True" or "False." Unlike side one obvious questions, side two questions are typically nontransparent and subtle. Thus, clients will not likely be able to identify their responses as being directly related to AOD use.

SASSI-3 Reliability and Validity

Test–retest reliability for the Face-Valid Alcohol Scale was 1.0, test–retest for the Face-Valid Other Drug Scale was 1.0, and test–retest for the various subscales ranged between .92 and .97 (F. Miller, personal communication, July 3, 2001). The alpha coefficient for the entire instrument was .93 (F. Miller, personal communication, July 3, 2001).

Miller reports the SASSI-3 has a positive predictive power of 98.4% (personal communication, July 3, 2001). Positive predictive power indicates the ratio of true positives to test positives. In other words, 98.4% of the time the SASSI-3 correctly identified persons who actually had an AOD problem. The instrument also demonstrates exceptionally high concurrent validity. For example, the SASSI-3 matched the addicted client's clinical diagnoses 95% of the time and demonstrated concurrent validity with a number of instruments including the (a) Michigan Alcohol Screening Test (MAST), (b) Minnesota Multiphasic Personality Inventory—2, and (c) MacAndrew Scale—Revised (MAC-R; Lazowski, Miller, Boye, & Miller, 1998).

Scales

The SASSI-3 has ten scales. Two of these scales are face-valid scales that require clients to describe the extent and nature of their AOD use. One of these scales is related to alcohol (Face-Valid Alcohol) and the other is related to all other psychoactive substances (Face-Valid Other Drug). Persons endorsing high Face-Valid Alcohol or high Face-Valid Other Drug scores are likely openly acknowledging AOD misuse, consequences resulting from such use, and loss of control related to their AOD use (Miller et al., 1997). High scores on either or both of these two scales may suggest the need for supervised detoxification (Miller et al., 1997).

The Symptoms Scale asks clients to endorse symptoms or problems resulting from their AOD abuse (Miller et al., 1997). Those with high Symptom Scale scores are likely to be heavy users and be part of a social milieu (e.g., family, peers) where AOD use is prevalent. Thus, it may be difficult for these persons to perceive the negative aspects of remarkable AOD use. In other words, given that their friends and family likely use, they may consider abstinence an abnormality rather than typical.

The Obvious Attribute Scale indicates the degree to which clients acknowledge characteristics typical of AOD using persons (Miller et al., 1997). In other words, persons endorsing a high number of these scale items are indicating a high number of behaviors and characteristics typically indicated by persons who are substance dependent or in recovery from their substance use. High scores suggest clients are receptive to clinical intervention (e.g., group counseling) and able to identify with the experiences of other substance-dependent persons. Conversely, very low Obvious Attribute Scores suggest clients who are reticent to acknowledge characteristics commonly associated with substance-dependent persons and personal flaws.

The Subtle Attributes Scale denotes persons who may either be attempting to present themselves in a most favorable light by denying their substance dependence or who may not recognize their behaviors as problematic or associated with AOD use (Miller et al., 1997). Persons who have endorsed a high number of Subtle Attributes Scale items, especially when the number of these items is higher than their Obvious Attributes Scale items, find it challenging to admit the degree to which AOD is prevalent and problematic within their lives.

Two other scales that directly complement one another and enrich the assessment process are the Defensiveness and Supplemental Addiction Measure Scales. As is the case with all assessment instruments, the scores and clinical profiles are used in conjunction with the counselor's clinical judgment to ensure appropriate assessment and intervention. The SASSI-3 Defensiveness Scale identifies persons who may respond defensively. However, the counselor must use her clinical judgment to determine if the defensiveness revolves around AOD abuse issues or other issues (e.g., addicted family member personality traits, immediate life circumstances). Those endorsing a high number of Defensiveness Scale items are attempting to present themselves in a favorable light and minimizing "evidence of personal problems" (Miller et al., 1997, p. 36). When the Defensiveness Scale is used in conjunction with the Supplemental Addiction Measure Scale, counselors can better assess if the client's defensiveness relates to AOD abuse or other areas. Thus, when both the Defensiveness Scale and the Supplemental Addiction Measure Scale are elevated, there is increased evidence that the client's defensiveness revolves around AOD abuse. However, the counselor must weigh all evidence to make this determination and use her best clinical judgment when making the final clinical diagnosis.

Another important aspect of the Defensiveness Scale is related to low scores at or below the 15th percentile. Such low scores may be indicative of self-abasing or overly self-critical clients. These clients may have problems related to low self-esteem and have "feelings of worthlessness and hopelessness, loss of energy, and suicidal ideation" (Miller et al., 1997). Given the robust correlation between feelings of hopelessness and suicide, it would be important to assess such clients for suicidal ideation and to provide appropriate intervention.

The Family vs. Control Subjects (Family) Scale identifies persons who may not be AOD abusing themselves, but who likely have family members or significant others who are AOD abusing (Miller et al., 1997). The Family Scale should not be used as a codependency scale. Rather, it should be used to assess whether the client is overly focused on others and the others' needs rather than the addicted client's needs. Persons scoring high on this scale may benefit from counseling goals that include establishing appropriate and healthy boundaries.

The Correctional Scale indicates the client's "relative risk for legal problems" (Miller et al., 1997, p. 39). Although the scale was not created to identify specific antisocial psychopathology, it does identify persons who, even if they discontinue their AOD abuse, may potentially require additional counseling services related to areas such as anger and impulse control. Persons scoring high on this scale may also have a checkered history of difficulties with the legal system.

The final scale is the Random Answering Pattern Scale. This scale suggests the client's scores are likely suspect or invalid should the person have a Random Answering Pattern Scale Score of 2 or more. Such scores may also be indicative of persons who are unable to read at the required level or who do not speak English as their primary language.

ROBERT'S SASSI-3

Because Robert was diagnosed during the clinical assessment interview with alcohol dependence and had elevated MAC-R, AAS, and APS scores on his MMPI-2, and Eva Marie does not have a history of alcohol abuse, the authors will review Robert's SASSI-3 clinical scales and profile (Figure 13.2). For the basis of this review, the authors will

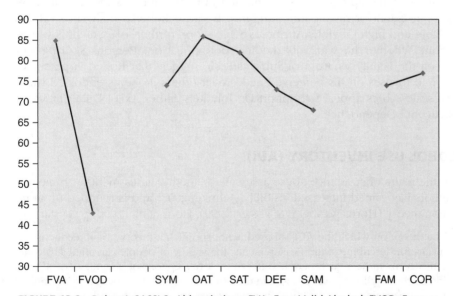

FIGURE 13.2 Robert's SASSI-3. Abbreviations: FVA=Face-Valid Alcohol; FVOD=Face-Valid Other Drugs; SYM=Symptoms; OAT=Obvious Attributes; SAT=Subtle Attributes; DEF=Defensiveness; SAM=Supplemental Addictions Measure; FAM=Family vs. Control Subjects; COR=Correctional

report Robert's test-taking behaviors as "compliant." In other words, he has sufficiently invested himself in taking the instrument and responding in a relatively truthful manner. However, Robert has intentionally and purposefully endorsed his drinking and drugging behaviors and experiences in a manner that fails to describe the full extent of those drinking behaviors and experiences. Stated differently, he has complied with the testing experience but has purposefully attempted to present his endorsements in a more positive manner than actual reality.

Validity Scores

Robert's Random Answering Pattern (RAP) score of 0 suggests he has not answered the SASSI-3 in a haphazard or random fashion. Instead, it suggests that he was invested in the test taking experience. This perception is further supported, because Robert has responded to all question stems.

Clinical Scores

Robert's high Face-Valid Alcohol and Symptoms scales scores suggest that Robert acknowledges extensive alcohol use with accompanying negative consequences, whereas Robert's low Face-Valid Other Drugs scale scores indicate that he denies the abuse of nonalcoholic substances. These responses match Robert's verbal report that occurred during his clinical intake assessment interview. The high Obvious Attributes Scale score combined with his high Subtle Attributes Scale score suggest that Robert may be open to seeing similarities between himself and other substance-dependent people, but that he may be unable to see the full implications of his current problematic alcohol abuse. Robert's moderately high Defensiveness Scale Score suggests that Robert may be attempting to present himself in a favorable manner and may be denying the full extent of his alcohol struggles. Because Robert's high Face-Valid Alcohol Scale score and high Obvious Attributes Scale score, further assessment is warranted to determine whether he warrants medical detoxification. Persons scoring similar to Robert on the Family vs. Control Subjects Scale suggest that Robert is potentially egocentric and focuses on his perceived needs over others. Robert's endorsed validity and clinical scale scores appear to support Dr. Juhnke's earlier Axis I DSM Clinical Diagnosis of Alcohol Dependence.

ALCOHOL USE INVENTORY (AUI)

Within the realm of substance abuse assessment, another assessment instrument used by the authors has gained increased visibility (Juhnke, 2002) and is founded upon multiple-condition theory (Horn, Wanberg, & Foster, 1990). Horn et al. (1990, p. 1) state:

> The theory on which the AUI is based is not so much a theory about alcoholism as it is a means for describing, with measurements, the variety of people classified as alcoholic. It is a theory about how such people differ in their perceptions of benefits derived from drinking, in their styles of drinking, and in their thoughts about how to deal with drinking problems. It is a theory in which each person who is said to be alcoholic is regarded as a distinct gestalt, a pattern of many different factors. It is thought that such different Gestalts derive from different dynamics in etiology and require different treatments if problems are to be mitigated.

The instrument, although having similarities to the MMPI-2's MAC-R Scale and the SASSI-3, provides another type of assessment based on 24 scales that measure "different features of involvement" with alcohol use (Horn et al., 1990, p. 1).

General AUI Overview

Rychtarik, Koutsky, and Miller (1998) state that the AUI "is one of the most comprehensive and systematically developed measures of alcohol problems available" (p. 107). The AUI was authored by Horn et al. in 1986 and was designed "to measure different features of involvement with the use of alcohol" (Horn et al., 1990, p. 2). The instrument has 228 multiple-choice questions and takes approximately 35 to 60 minutes to administer (Pearson, 2012). It is reported as appropriate for clients ages 16 and older who have at least a sixth-grade reading level (S. Nadau, personal communication, June 22, 2001). The AUI is a Pearson test product and can be purchased at Pearson, 1 (800) 627-7271.

AUI Reliability and Validity

Internal consistency reliability was reported between .67 and .93 and test–retest reliability was indicated between .54 and .94 for all scales (Horn et al., 1990, p. 24). It should be noted that only one scale score was identified below .60, and that 17 of the 21 scales in which test–retest was used were noted as being higher than .80 (Horn et al., 1990). The instrument authors report the AUI has content validity as "it was developed out of a process that ensured that the content would be relevant for making decisions in treatment programs" (p. 30) and support the instrument's construct validity via a number of related research studies. Interestingly, however, the authors suggest that an adequate criterion cannot be defined to support the notion of criterion-related validity:

> There is no agreed-upon operations for specifying alcoholism or any particular undesirable condition associated with alcohol abuse, be it called alcohol dependence or something else. Even if there were consensus agreement that the criterion is, say, an alcohol dependence syndrome. . . there is no consensus agreement about how to measure it. . . It would be circular in the extreme. . . to validate the AUI against a criterion defined by a subset of AUI measures. (p. 31)

Validity Scales

Unlike the SASSI-3 and MMPI-2, the AUI does not appear to have specific scales designed to determine the veracity of client-endorsed responses. Instead, the authors report there exists no superior scale to assess veracity:

> The question of the veridicality of an AUI profile, then, is one of figuring out how much of what the person has presented in the profile is genuine disclosure and how much represents attempts to hide....How can one spot this type of person? AUI scores and profile are not the best indicators. A better indicator is an interview pertaining to these scores. There is no good lie detector for any questionnaire (much as it may be claimed that there is), and the AUI is no exception to this rule. But with a client who is not conscientious about dealing with the AUI, a well-directed talk about his or her scores can serve three important purposes. (Horn et al., 1990, pp. 52–53)

The authors then describe in great detail how to conduct an interview with clients to help clients address possible discrepancies between their AUI scores and existing clinical intake information. In addition, the authors provide a thorough explanation of how to help clients clarify what they may have endorsed on the AUI vis-à-vis what their true symptoms are. Finally, the authors describe potential profile configuration discrepancies between the DISRUPT1 and DISRUPT2 scales that may be indicative of persons attempting to respond to the AUI in a more socially acceptable and positive manner. Thus, if the DISRUPT2 scale is higher than the DISRUPT1 scale there exists a high probability that the test taker has attempted to present himself in a guarded and more positive manner.

Clinical Scales

The AUI has 17 primary scales subdivided into four areas: (a) Drinking Benefits (i.e., drinking to: [1] improve sociability and mental functioning [SOCIALIM], [2] enhance mental alertness and creativity [MENTALIM], [3] manage moods [MANAGMOOD], and [4] cope with marital problems [MARICOPE]), (b) Drinking Styles (i.e., GREGARUS [social drinking vis-à-vis those who drink alone], COMPULSV [i.e., constantly thinking about alcohol], and SUSTAIND [drinking with no abstinence periods; "somewhat intoxicated every day" {Horn et al., 1990, p. 7}], (c) Drinking Consequences (i.e., loss of control over behavior when drinking [LCONTORL], social role maladaption [ROLEMALA], delirium [DELIRIUM], hangover [HANOVER], and marital problems resulting from drinking [MARIPROB]), and (d) Concerns and Acknowledgments (i.e., acknowledgment of the quantity of consumed alcohol [QUANTITY], guilt associated with drinking [GUILTWOR], prior attempts to deal with the drinking [HELPBEFR], readiness for help [RECEPTIV], and awareness of drinking problems [AWARENES]). Six second-level scales are also provided (Horn et al., 1990, p. 7). These scales include the following: (a) Enhanced (those who consume alcohol to enhance their functioning [ENHANCED]), (b) Obsessed (persons who hide bottles, sneak drinks and drink prior to bed [OBSESSED]), (c) DISRUPT1 (those who report alcohol consumption as resulting in life disruptions [lost job, severe hangovers]), (d) DISRUPT2 (persons who experienced uncontrolled life disruption as a result of their drinking and report symptomatology typically associated with heavy drinkers: "has used alcohol substitutes such as shaving lotion" {Horn et al., 1990, p. 8}]), (e) ANXCONCN (anxiety, worry, guilt, shame related to drinking), and (f) ALCINVOL (a client noted "broad involvement with alcohol" [Horn et al., 1990, p. 8]).

ROBERT'S AUI

Again, because of Robert's alcohol abuse behaviors that reflect his DSM Axis I Clinical Diagnosis of Alcohol Dependence, the authors will use Robert as the AUI protagonist (Figures 13.3, 13.4, 13.5, and 13.6). Typically, one would anticipate, given Robert's antisocial personality disorder diagnosis and his upcoming court date with the possibility of incarceration for grand theft, that Robert would attempt to present himself in a most favorable and nonsubstance-abusing manner. In other words, one would anticipate that Robert, at best, would present in a guarded manner and not fully disclose his alcohol-abusing behaviors. Thus on the AUI, one would anticipate that Robert's DISRUPT2 Scale score, a less transparent scale that reflects endorsements suggesting life disruptions as a result of heavy drinking, would be significantly higher than his DISRUPT1 Scale Score. However, to help fully demonstrate the AUI scales to readers, the authors will have Robert present himself in a more accurate manner and endorse items more truthfully without the significant guardedness or deceit anticipated of someone with antisocial personality disorder.

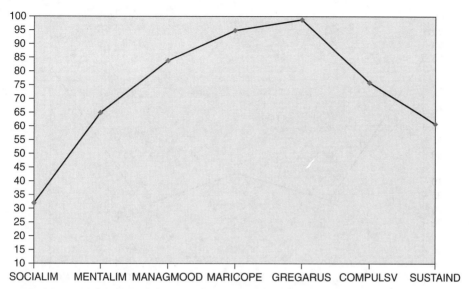

FIGURE 13.3   Robert's Alcohol Use Inventory Benefits and Styles. Abbreviations: SOCIALIM=Improve sociability and mental functioning; MENTALIM=Drink to improve mental functioning; MANAGMOOD=Manage Mood; MARICOPE=Cope with marital problems; GREGARUS=Social Drinking; COMPULSV=Compulsive drinking; SUSTAIND=Sustained versus periodic drinking

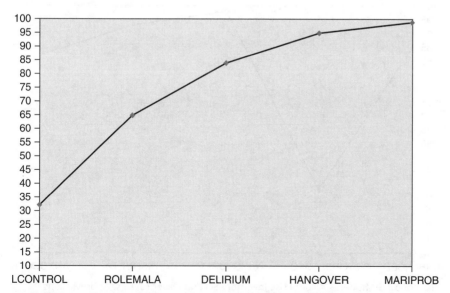

FIGURE 13.4   Robert's Alcohol Use Inventory Consequences. Abbreviations: LCONTROL=Loss of control over behavior when drinking; ROLEMALA=Social role maladaption; DELIRIUM=Delirium; HANGOVER=Hangover; MARIPROB=Marital problems resulting from drinking

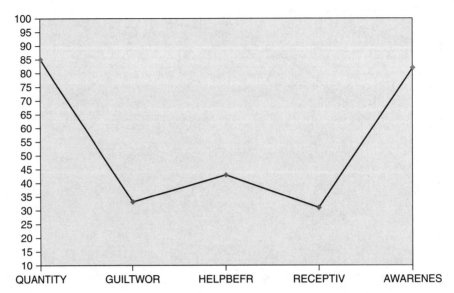

FIGURE 13.5 Robert's Alcohol Use Inventory Concerns and Acknowledgements. Abbreviations: QUANTITY=Quantity of daily use when drinking; GUILTWOR=Guilt and worry associated with drinking; HELPBEFR=Prior attempts to deal with drinking; RECEPTIV=Readiness for help; AWARNES=Awareness of drinking problem

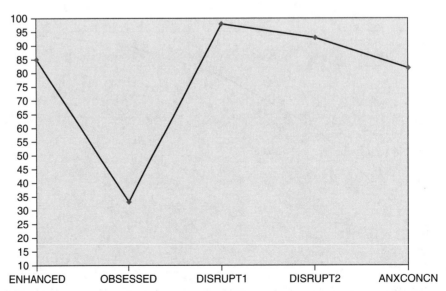

FIGURE 13.6 Robert's Alcohol Use Inventory Second-Order Factors. Abbreviations: ENHANCED= Drinking to enhance functioning; OBSESSED=Obsessive, sustained drinking; DISRUPT1=Uncontrolled life disruption due to drinking directly stated; DISRUPT2=Uncontrolled life disruption due to drinking indirectly stated; ANXCONCN=Anxiety related to drinking

Validity Scores

If, in fact, Robert endorsed the AUI in a relatively honest, open, and nonguarded manner, all AUI question stems would have a corresponding endorsement by Robert. In addition, his DISRUPT1 and DISRUPT2 scales would both be elevated, and Robert's DISRUPT1 Scale score would be higher than his DISRUPT2 Scale score (Figure 13.6). Again, remember the AUI does not have Validity scores, but the DISRUPT1 and DISRUPT2 configurations may well provide insight related to the manner in which the test taker approached and endorsed the AUI.

Clinical Scores

Most of Robert's AUI clinical scores are highly inflated. In particular, three of the four scales related to perceived drinking benefits (Figure 13.3) are inflated. These inflated scale scores suggest Robert believes his alcohol consumption improves his mental alertness, aids him in releasing undesirable "pent up" feelings related to possible worry or anger, and helps him more effectively respond to his girlfriend's perceived nagging and quipping behaviors. The highest of these scores is Robert's MARICOPE Scale score (Figure 13.3). His high score on this scale suggests that his girlfriend's nagging and quipping behaviors provoke his drinking behaviors. Stated differently, Robert likely believes his girlfriend's nagging behaviors "force" him to drink. His lowest score would be his SOCIALIM Scale score. Here, Robert's SOCIALIM score suggests he is self-confident and does not need alcohol to feel that way. It further suggests he has confidence in his interpersonal skills, and he likely enjoys being around others or he has a high need for interpersonal interaction.

This lower SOCIALIM Scale Score matches Robert's high GREGARUS Scale Score (Figure 13.3). Together, these scores suggest Robert is highly sociable and outgoing. Actively drinking with friends, partying at bars and social events, and alcohol consumption during most festive occasions appear to be part of Robert's overall persona. Stated differently, Robert is not a shy, socially inept person who uses alcohol as a means to loosen up to gain social confidence. Instead, Robert is likely a party animal who is outgoing and socially confident with or without alcohol.

Robert's moderately high to high scores on the COMPULSV and SUSTAIND (Figure 13.3) support his DISRUPT1 and DISRUPT2 scales (Figure 13.6), suggesting he is admitting classic symptoms of what is traditionally considered alcoholism. His scores suggest he constantly thinks about alcohol consumption and drinks to a point of intoxication most days—not just weekends. His high scores on LCONTROL, ROLEMALA, and MARIPROB (Figure 13.4) combined with his moderate DELIRUIM and HANGOVER scores suggest Robert's: (a) drinking behaviors typically get out of control, making him aggressive, loud, and possibly belligerent; (b) work, interpersonal, and significant other relationships have likely have suffered as a result of his drinking; (c) marriages (former) and significant other relationships (e.g., current live-in girlfriend relationship) have been compromised because of Robert's drinking behaviors (e.g., lying, violence, infidelity); (d) live-in partner problems are likely perceived at least partly from Robert's drinking behaviors; and (e) drinking behaviors have likely resulted in run-ins with the police or potentially illegal behaviors. Again, these scores confirm the diagnoses rendered by Dr. Juhnke during the clinical face-to-face assessment interview.

If Robert had responded truthfully to the AUI, he would likely have scored moderately high to high on QUANTITY and AWARENES (Figure 13.5). This would suggest Robert is aware of his drinking problem, and he understands the amount of alcohol he consumes within a typical week is significantly higher than most others' alcohol consumption. However, given Robert's antisocial flair he likely would score low to moderately low on GUILT-WOR, HELPBEFR, and RECEPTIV. Thus, he has no or little feelings of guilt associated with his alcohol consumption, he is not ready to begin alcohol treatment or initiate alcohol abstinence, and he likely has attempted to reduce or eliminate his alcohol consumption on his own terms without help in the past. In addition, given these scores, this is not Robert's first "Ah-ha" insight into the existence of his drinking problems.

Finally, Robert's high DISRUPT1, DISRUPT2, and ALCINVOL scale scores in combination with his low ENHANCED, OBSESSED, ANXCONCN, and RECPAWAR scale scores suggest he likely is a person whose drinking problems are highly evident to most others. In addition, his drinking behaviors are likely sustained and he is gregarious and outgoing even when not drinking. Thus, when he drinks he is even more outgoing and gregarious. Concomitantly, Robert has little if any anxious concerns about his drinking behaviors. Furthermore, Robert likely does not feel as though he truly needs alcohol to function well and likely does not hide or sneak his drinking behaviors.

SUICIDE PROBABILITY SCALE (SPS)

The Suicide Probability Scale (SPS) is one of the most frequently used, formal paper-and-pencil suicide assessment instruments on the market today. Given the significant frequency of suicide ideation, suicide behaviors, and suicide deaths, mental health professionals must understand how to assess clients for suicide (Granello & Juhnke, 2009; Juhnke, Granello, & Granello, 2010). The authors believe this instrument can be helpful to entry and moderately experienced counselors when assessing clients for suicide risk and can aid in suicide prevention and intervention planning. The SPS can be purchased directly through Western Psychological Associates at 1 (800) 648-8857.

General SPS Overview

The SPS is a standardized suicide assessment instrument, authored by Cull and Gill (2002). The SPS is a brief, self-report instrument designed to "aid in the assessment of suicide risk in adolescents and adults" (Cull & Gill, p. 1). It was developed for persons 14 years of age and older with a minimum fourth-grade reading level. The scale takes less than 20 minutes to administer, complete, and score.

The scale is composed of 36 self-report question stems. Persons being assessed use a 4-point Likert scale (ranging from *none* to *most/all of the time*) to report the frequency of their subjective experiences (e.g., "I feel so lonely I cannot stand it") and past behaviors ("When I get mad, I throw things"; Cull & Gill, 2002, p. 2). The author's clients typically report the scale to be easily understandable and "simple" to complete (Valadez, Juhnke, Coll, Granello, Peters, & Zambrano, 2009). Although some of the question stems are relatively transparent and directly speak to the topic of suicide (e.g., "In order to punish others, I think of suicide") many are nontransparent and subtle (e.g., "Things seem to go well for me").

SPS Reliability and Validity

Cull and Gill (2002) sought to determine the SPS's reliability and validity in an effort to demonstrate its clinical utility. They attempted this by first conducting two test–retest reliability analyses. Participants in the first test–retest consisted of "80 individuals of various ages, educational levels and ethnic backgrounds" (p. 44). The intent of using this diverse participant pool was to suggest test–retest reliability among a more generalized, heterogeneous population. Three weeks later, the same participants completed the scale a second time. The correlation of the two scale administrations was ".92 ($p < .001$), indicating a high level of test-retest reliability" (p. 44).

A second test–retest was conducted with 478 participants. Time between these two administrations was 10 days. Cull and Gill (2002) reported, "The test–retest reliability for the entire group was .94" (p. 45). Cull and Gill believe these results suggest the SPS has high test–retest reliability. According to Cull and Gill (2002), content relevance and concurrent validity were investigated by "correlating SPS items with an experimental Minnesota Multiphasic Personality Inventory (MMPI) scale specifically designed to measure threatened suicide" (Cull & Gill, 2002, p. 45). Participants in this study included 51 clinical patients comprised mostly of clients who had attempted suicide. The resulting correlations had a median of .27 and ranged between −.19 and .54. Correlations of .30 or greater ($p < .05$) were noted among 15 of these item questions (p. 45). Cull and Gill report, "The size and number of these correlations provide evidence that the SPS is content relevant and substantially related to an externally developed index of suicide risk" (p. 45).

Criterion-related validity was also demonstrated by the Suicide Probability Scale's ability to discriminate between criterion groups of "normals" ($n = 562$), psychiatric inpatients ($n = 260$), and suicide attempters ($n = 336$). This demonstration was evidenced by using "point-biserial correlations between items and criterion classifications, mean differences between groups, and cross-validated classification accuracies" (p. 48). According to Cull and Gill, "The differences between the group means for the various criterion groups were all highly significant ($p = .001$)" (p. 51).

Although there was initial debate between Balkin and Juhnke regarding the instrument's inclusion in this book because of potential concerns regarding validity and the datedness and homogeneity of the sample used (Cull & Gill, 2002), the authors believe inclusion of the SPS is warranted. The SPS is likely one of the only available testing instruments specifically focused on suicide and one of the most widely recognized and used suicide assessment instruments on the market today (Valadez et al., 2009). Concomitantly, the SPS requires counselors to perform both thorough suicide assessment interviews with their clients and investigate multiple areas of suicide risk. Thus, Balkin and Juhnke believe this increases the probability that counselors using the instrument will sufficiently assess client suicide risk and create more thorough, logical suicide prevention and intervention plans.

Validity Scales

Like the AUI authors, the SPS authors did not create specific Validity Scales. However, Cull and Gill (2002) describe ways in which test administrators can use perceived differences and similarities between Suicide Probability scores and clinical perceptions to best ensure the clients' clinical needs are adequately met. This might include seeking appropriate client releases of confidential information to conduct interviews with family members and friends who can provide perceptions and evidence specific to the client's past and current suicide behaviors as well as perceptions regarding the client's immediate danger to self. The instrument does have some serious limitations, including high rates of false positives among low-risk clients and high rates of false negatives with high-risk clients (Golding, 1985). Never should a sole score on an assessment be used to ascertain the disposition of a client, and the SPS is no exception to this ethical responsibility.

Clinical Scales

The SPS is composed of four subscales and three different types of overall suicide assessment risk scores based on a total weighted score, a normalized T score, and a suicide probability score (Cull & Gill, 2002; Valadez et al., 2009).

HOPELESSNESS The Hopelessness subscale notes client self-reported perceptions regarding overall dissatisfaction with life and negative expectations about the future. Specifically, the subscale provides a picture of the clients' global pessimism and despair. According to Cull and Gill (2002), subscale content "reflects loneliness, hopelessness, dysphoric mood, a sense of being overburdened by circumstances, and feelings of futility about life and an inability to effect change" (p. 15). Given the strong correlations between suicidal behavior and hopelessness (Beck, Steer, Kovacs, & Garrison, 1985; Granello & Juhnke, 2009; Juhnke et al., 2010), this is a very important subscale. Persons scoring moderately high or high on this subscale are perceived at great risk for suicidal behaviors and warrant interventions that match their degree of self-harm danger. Thus, should a client's T score on the Hopelessness subscale be at or above 70, the counselor may well wish to assess the client's reported reasons to continue living.

SUICIDAL IDEATION This subscale provides counselors a glimpse into the client's suicidal thoughts and behaviors. Individual items within this subscale can provide information regarding "the frequency of suicide ideation, the reasons for contemplating suicide…or whether a suicide attempt…is likely to be impulsive or carefully planned" (p. 15). Clients scoring high on this subscale are reporting frequent thoughts of suicide and warrant further investigation and intervention to ensure safety. Should a client present with a T score of 70 or above, the authors believe it is imperative to ask how the client intends to commit suicide.

NEGATIVE SELF-EVALUATION The third subscale "reflects an individual's subjective appraisal that things are not going well, that others are distant and uncaring, and that it is difficult to do anything worthwhile" (Cull & Gill, 2002, p. 15). As one can imagine, clients scoring high on this subscale may well be at higher suicide risk and therefore warrant close monitoring. Thus, they warrant immediate intervention and protection from self-harm.

HOSTILITY This subscale "reflects a tendency to break or throw things when angry or upset, and includes a cluster of items reflecting hostility, isolation, and impulsivity" (Cull & Gill, 2002, p. 15). Again, high scores suggest someone who warrants close evaluation and potential intervention. Most persons with very high scores on this subscale frequently have enduring patterns of impulsivity and are oppositional towards others. They often use these behaviors as a means to intimidate and cope with perceived unjust demands being placed upon them.

These subscales and their clinical utility make the SPS a helpful clinical tool for most counselors. In addition, SPS subscales can be combined to create three distinct summary score types. The total weighted score is the sum of the individual items on the combined subscales. This sum can be quickly and easily translated into a normalized T

score that has a mean of 50 points and a standard deviation of 10 points. Thus, according to the SPS, the pronounced risk of suicidal behaviors increases as the client's normalized T score rises above the 50-point mean. Cull and Gill (2002, p. 14) write, "Although any absolute cutoff points are arbitrary, a score of 60T or above indicates the need for careful clinical evaluation of suicide." They further report that scores two or more standard deviations above the mean, that is, 70 points or more, are "strong presumptive evidence for instituting suicide precautions" (p. 14). Stated differently, clients who score 70 points or higher should be perceived at significant suicide risk and warrant interventions that match their presenting needs. Thus, a client presenting with a normalized T score of 70 or above may well warrant hospitalization if a least restrictive environment will not provide adequate safety.

A word of warning is also noted by the test authors related to normalized T scores of 40 or less. According to the test authors, such scores "should alert the user to the possibility that the person has consciously or unconsciously sought to minimize his or her actual suicide potential" (p. 14). Again, one would question why a clinical suicide assessment was being conducted with a client who scored in a manner that suggested no immediate suicide risk. Such low scores likely would suggest that the counselor misunderstood the client and the client's suicide risk, or the counselor lacked sufficient clinical judgment to correctly perceive the client's immediate needs, or most likely, the client consciously or unconsciously attempted to present him- or herself in a favorable, nonsuicidal manner.

The final summary score is the suicide probability score. This score has proved itself exceptionally helpful to the authors when they have assessed clients for suicide risk. In essence, this score suggests the "statistical likelihood that an individual belongs in the population of lethal suicide attempters" (p. 14). In other words, the suicide probability score does not indicate that a client has a certain probability of suicide. Instead, the suicide probability score reports the probability that the client fits a profile of those who have made serious, highly lethal suicide attempts and is therefore at extreme risk. Such extreme risk noted by the SPS can then be explained to the client and used either to encourage participation in a least restrictive treatment setting such as intensive outpatient or partial hospitalization, or in the case of an uncooperative client, support one's clinical judgment for involuntary hospitalization to mental health and insurance gatekeepers.

EVA MARIE'S SPS

Through over 20 years of experience counseling and assessing suicide and homicide risk of youth and adults incarcerated or placed in psychiatric hospital settings, we acknowledge that most persons diagnosed with antisocial personality disorder are a far greater danger to others vis-à-vis themselves. This is not to say that persons diagnosed with antisocial personality disorder will not or cannot kill themselves. Rather, the statement is used to indicate that it is far more likely that Eva Marie would have active suicidal ideation and intent than Robert. This is especially true given that Eva Marie (a) feels unsupported by her husband, (b) lives with her mother and thus has little control over finances or decisions that directly affect Eva Marie's life, (c) feels as an only child she cannot abandon her aging mother, and (d) believes she must fulfill a vow she made to Almighty God that she, for better or worse, will never leave her husband. Thus, for demonstration purposes, we will use Eva Marie as the protagonist for the SPS.

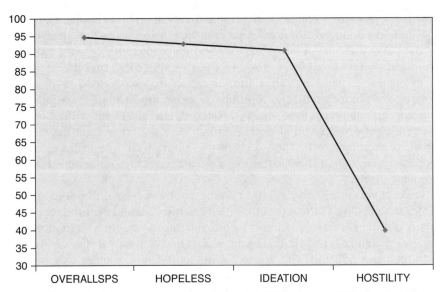

FIGURE 13.7 Eva Marie's Suicide Probability Scale. Abbreviations: OVERALLSPS=Total SPS Score; HOPELESS=Hopeless Scale; IDEATION=Suicide Ideation Scale; HOSTILITY=Hostility Scale

Eva Marie's score on her overall suicide probability score is very high (Figure 13.7) and is more than three standard deviations above the mean. It suggests Eva Marie is at severe suicide risk. Eva Marie's Hopelessness subscale *T* score is very high as well. Likewise, this score is more than three standard deviations above the mean and suggests that Eva Marie has significant life dissatisfaction and negative future expectations.

Her Suicide Ideation subscale is also very high and three standard deviations above the mean. This indicates Eva Marie is actively thinking about suicide. Eva Marie's only two low scores are her Hostility Scale and Negative Self-Evaluation Scale scores. These low scale scores suggest Eva Marie is not impulsive, but rather highly thoughtful and strategic in her behaviors, and she does not see herself in a negative fashion.

As the individual test items endorsed by Eva Marie on these subscales were reviewed with her, Eva Marie reported that she tends to isolate herself from others when she feels angry, depressed, or feels like killing herself. Her statement matches information gathered from Eva Marie's original clinical assessment intake interview and the psychological testing thus far conducted. When asked if Eva Marie was thinking about killing herself, she responded, "I want to. But, I am fearful God will banish me to Hell. I can't win. I am in hell on earth with my mother and useless husband. If I escape by killing myself, I will be sent to Hell by Almighty God."

Based on Eva Marie's statements and her SPS scores, her counselor discussed voluntary inpatient hospitalization with Eva Marie. Her counselor further indicated the hospitalization would provide Eva Marie time away from her mother and husband and allow her to consider what options are available and best for her. Eva Marie expressed relief at her counselor's suggestion and agreed to voluntarily enter St. Michael's Psychiatric Hospital.

THE SUICIDE SCATTT MNEMONIC

General SCATTT Overview

Despite the existence of suicide assessment instruments like the SPS, the SAD PERSONS Scale, the Adapted-SAD PERSONS Suicide Scale, and the IS PATH WARM Scale, the authors have found that less experienced clinical supervisees do not fully comprehend how to immediately intervene once they determine their assessed clients are in fact suicidal and in peril of immediate suicide behaviors. Thus, the looming question for many counselors is, "What do I do now?" Below readers will find a description of the Suicide SCATTT mnemonic (Juhnke, Juhnke, & Hsieh, 2012). The SCATTT provides a basic, step-by-step process that can be used once it is determined that the client is suicidal and warrants a less restrictive environment. The intervention has been used by Juhnke with his clients and reported helpful by his supervisees (Juhnke et al., 2012).

Validity Scales

The SCATTT is a mnemonic. Therefore, it has no validity scales. As is the case with both the AUI and the SPS, counselors are encouraged to use a clinical assessment interview format to provide a context for the assessment.

MNEMONIC PHASES The SCATTT mnemonic is an easily memorized memory aid designed to help supervisees remember the specific steps necessary when intervening for clients assessed as having immediate suicide intent and deemed suicidal by their counselor. Each letter of the mnemonic corresponds to a specific and required suicide intervention phase (i.e., *S*tay, *C*onsult, *A*pprise, *T*erminate, *T*runcate, and *T*ransport; Figure 13.8). SCATTT reminds entry-level counselors of six important suicide intervention plan phases that must occur when it is determined via the previously completed suicide assessments that clients warrant psychiatric hospitalization or another type of least restrictive, monitored, and safe environment (e.g., monitored respite care, partial hospitalization; Juhnke et al., 2012). Supervisees are strongly encouraged to use additional intervention pieces depending on the client's specific needs. The mnemonic and each of the six intervention phases are presented below.

> ***Phase 1: Stay with the Client*** Whenever a client presents suicide intent, the client should never be left alone. Thus, the counselor or another mental health professional

---

Stay with the Client.

Consult with Supervisor(s) and Professional Peers.

Apprise Client of Assessment Findings and Your Professional Judgment.

Terminate Threat (e.g., Remove Any Identified Suicide Instruments [e.g., Guns, Weapons, Knives]).

Truncate Threats That Cannot Be Terminated (e.g., Remove Easy Access to Medications, Ensure Only Supervised Access to Cars).

Transport to Psychiatric Hospital or Least Restrictive Environment Deemed Best by You and Your Supervisors (e.g., Partial Hospitalization, Monitored Foster Care).

FIGURE 13.8 The Suicide SCATTT Mnemonic

must *stay* with the client until hospitalization or an alternative safety monitoring option that corresponds with the client's degree of danger can be arranged.

Phase 2: Consult After stabilizing the immediate situation and ensuring the client's present safety, the counselor should ask another mental health professional or appropriate designee (e.g., police officer, family member) to monitor the client while the counselor *consults* her clinical supervisor. Specifically, the counselor should contact her clinical supervisor and report her suicide assessment findings, the client's immediate degree of suicide risk, and describe how the client is being monitored. Jointly, the counselor and supervisor should develop a hospital intervention or least restrictive monitoring plan that ensures the client's safety and corresponds to the client's noted degree of suicide risk. As the counselor returns to the client, and depending on the jointly agreed-upon suicide intervention plan, the supervisor or supervisor designee should begin contacting area psychiatric hospitals or other clinically appropriate options (e.g., respite care, partial hospitalization programs, psychiatric day center) to determine potential availability. Concomitantly, should it be anticipated that transportation for an involuntary or voluntary hospitalization be required, the supervisor or supervisor designee should begin to secure such transportation.

If the counselor does not have a clinical supervisor, the counselor should implement the "four out of five rule." Here, the counselor consults five professional mental health peers. The professional mental health peers must have equal or greater mental health educational backgrounds (e.g., master's degrees, educational specialist degrees, or doctorates), clinical experience, and treatment licenses (e.g., Licensed Professional Clinical Counselor, Licensed Professional Counselor). Specifically, the counselor will describe the case, the findings from the suicide assessment, and present her proposed clinical recommendations for hospitalization or another least restrictive and safe monitoring option to her professional peers. The counselor will then solicit input from these professional peers in an effort to create the safest clinical intervention and to ensure that the proposed clinical intervention is not overlooking important intervention factors. Should four out of the five professional peers perceive the intervention as clinically appropriate, the counselor should be able to implement the clinical intervention.

Phase 3: Apprise The SCATTT further requires counselors to *apprise* clients of the suicide assessment findings and the counselor's treatment recommendations. A good way to start this phase is by praising clients for recognizing their suicide concerns and for entering counseling. Once counselors praise their clients, counselors then suggest the existence of hope and the possibility for positive change. Next, counselors apprise clients of the suicide assessment findings and treatment recommendations. Finally, if needed, counselors describe differences between voluntary and involuntary psychiatric hospitalizations and potential benefits to voluntary hospitalization.

Should clients indicate they will voluntarily admit themselves into a recommended psychiatric hospital, counselors move to the Transport phase. However, should clients refuse to voluntarily enter a psychiatric hospital, counselors explain potential differences and benefits between voluntary and involuntary hospitalization. Depending upon specific state and relevant laws, clients who voluntarily admit themselves to psychiatric hospitals can often be released if the hospital staff does not perceive them as being imminent dangers to themselves. However, if clients are involuntarily hospitalized, most states require clients to remain for a minimum 72 hours monitoring period. Thus, clients will sometimes prefer to self-admit as a voluntary client with the hope that they will be quickly released vis-à-vis be admitted as an involuntary client and required to stay for a longer time.

If the suicidal client is under the age of majority and depending upon the specific laws of the state where the counselor practices, the counselor will need to apprise the client's parents or legal guardians of the child's suicide risk and hospital recommendation. In general, the authors have found most parents to be supportive of professional recommendations for hospitalization when their children present with significant suicide risk. However, should parents refuse to allow the child to continue treatment or refuse to hospitalize a child who clearly warrants hospitalization, child protective services should be contacted. Because laws vary from state to state, legal counsel should be sought to ensure the counselor practices in a manner congruent to state laws and guidelines.

Phases 4 and 5: Terminate and Truncate the Threat Understanding how the client plans to commit suicide is a critical component of any suicide assessment. Thus, if a client has completed the SPS and indicates she intends to shoot herself with her husband's .45 pistol that is kept in the couple's bedroom lamp stand, the counselor will ask that the gun be removed, locked, and kept in a different home or location until the client is no longer at risk of killing herself. Removing the gun is Phase 4 of the SCATTT. This terminates the suicide threat instrument (i.e., gun) by removing it from the client's availability.

Regretfully, some clients have plans that include suicide instruments where access cannot be terminated. For example, should a client's plan include overdosing on his antidepressant medications, Phase 5 of the SCATTT encourages counselors to *truncate* access to the antidepressants and other drugs. Here, the counselor should secure a release of confidential information, contact the physician prescribing the antidepressant, and inform the physician of the client's suicide plan. The counselor should request that the physician also monitor the client's safety and have the anti-depressant medications dispensed in smaller quantities. Thus, instead of the client having access to a 2-month antidepressant supply, the medication would be dispensed in weekly quantities. Concomitantly, the counselor should require that the client give all current medications to a trusted family member who could then secure and dispense the medications daily. Again, releases of confidential information will need to be signed by the client. The counselor would then meet with the client and the family member dispensing the medications to establish how the medications will be dispensed.

Phase 6: Transport This final phase of the SCATTT is the Transport phase. Here, counselors must ensure that the client has safe and monitored *transport* to the hospital. Depending on the client's emotional presentation, willingness to enter the hospital, and the agency's or school's transportation rules, the authors have found it best to have trusted client family members transport the client to the hospital. However, family transport should be used only when the client is willingly admitting herself into the hospital and poses no foreseeable risk to those transporting her. In addition, for liability reasons and to help ensure everyone's safety, a minimum of two, physically able, adult family members should make the transport. Depending on the situation and immediate needs of the client, the authors have found local police and emergency services workers helpful in transporting clients.

EVA MARIE'S SCATTT

Again, the authors will use Eva Marie as the protagonist for the SCATTT and will continue the vignette where they discontinued the SPS discussion. As you will recall, based on Eva Marie's statements and her SPS scores, her counselor advocated that Eva Marie voluntarily enter St. Michael's Psychiatric Hospital. Thus, for this vignette, her counselor has already apprised Eva Marie of what he thinks is best and Eva Marie has agreed to voluntarily enter St. Michael's Psychiatric Hospital. Thus, the Appraisal phase of the SCATTT is unnecessary. Instead, at this point in the process, her counselor needs someone to stay with Eva Marie to ensure her safety. Therefore, her counselor, Dr. Juhnke, tells Eva Marie he is going to introduce Eva Marie to Dr. Henderson, a female counselor who is present in the office. Eva Marie reports this would be "fine." Dr. Juhnke does not leave the room to find Dr. Henderson. Instead, he text messages Dr. Henderson and asks if she would be willing to monitor a suicidal client in Treatment Room A. Dr. Henderson, knocks on the door. Dr. Juhnke greets Dr. Henderson and introduces Eva Marie to Dr. Henderson.

DR. JUHNKE: Eva Marie, this is Dr. Henderson. She is an exceptional treatment provider and is a partner here at Balkin, Juhnke, and Henderson.

DR. HENDERSON: Hello Eva Marie.

EVA MARIE: Hello. I suppose you're here to guard me.

DR. JUHNKE: Well, Dr. Henderson is an expert in helping people. We want to make certain that you are safe, Eva Marie. Dr. Henderson will stay with you while I check to see about availability at St. Michael's.

EVA MARIE: That will be fine.

DR. HENDERSON: Eva Marie, it sounds as though you are going through a very demanding and difficult time. Your decision to enter St. Michael's is a very logical and important decision. The clients who I have referred there found St. Michael's to be very helpful, friendly, and comfortable.

Let's stop for a moment to review this process. First, and most importantly, Dr. Juhnke never leaves Eva Marie by herself. Instead, he introduces Eva Marie to a colleague. Thus, Eva Marie always has someone with her. In addition, note, Dr. Juhnke does not ask for Eva Marie's permission. He tells Eva Marie that he is introducing her to Dr. Henderson and text messages Dr. Henderson requesting she enter the room. Although some might balk and argue that the counselor should ask permission or seek another release of confidentiality before bringing Dr. Henderson into the room with Eva Marie, Dr. Juhnke believes Eva Marie is a threat to herself and warrants immediate supervision and transport. Thus, Dr. Juhnke informs Eva Marie that she will be introduced to Dr. Henderson. Especially with anxious clients or clients with personality disorders such as borderline personality disorder, telling clients what will happen next reduces anxiety and any potential for "gaminess." Of course, readers should determine what is best for them rather than simply mirror Dr. Juhnke's behaviors. First and foremost, readers should follow ethical principles and laws within their state and profession to ensure that their behaviors are legally and ethically appropriate.

Next, Dr. Juhnke introduces Eva Marie to Dr. Henderson. This is done to promote a sense of comfort and safety for Eva Marie and ensure Eva Marie's safety. Remember, she is an anxious person overwhelmed with feelings. Simply bringing an unannounced stranger into the treatment room would likely fail to engender a sense of comfort for Eva Marie.

Also, note what Dr. Henderson does. She immediately greets Eva Marie in a friendly manner and recounts how Dr. Henderson's clients have found St. Michael's to be a friendly and comfortable place. Think of the power of Dr. Henderson's statement. She embeds the suggestion that Eva Marie will find St. Michael's helpful, too. This should help quell at least some of Eva Marie's concerns and support her perception that she is making the best decision to enter St. Michael's.

If Dr. Juhnke were an entry-level clinician or working with a school district or agency with an immediate supervisor, he would consult with his superiors and provide them with up-to-date information on his intentions to hospitalize this client and the progress therein. If this were the case, he would likely contact his clinical supervisor.

DR. JUHNKE:	Dr. Oldz, this is Jerry.
DR. OLDZ:	Yes, Jerry, how can I help you?
DR. JUHNKE:	We've been consulting about Eva Marie Garza. As you may recall, Eva Marie is a 40-year-old, married, Hispanic-American female, presenting with generalized anxiety disorder. Per your clinical supervision instructions, I administered the Suicide Probability Scale with Eva Marie. She scored quite high on three of the four major scales. When she and I reviewed her high scores, I asked if she was thinking of killing herself. She reported she was planning to kill herself with her husband's .45 caliber handgun after leaving session. The gun is located in the couple's bedroom lamp stand.
DR. OLDZ:	Sounds like you did a good job. Where is Eva Marie right now?
DR. JUHNKE:	She is with Dr. Henderson in Treatment Room A.
DR. OLDZ:	Good Job, Jerry. We want to make certain she remains with someone. What is your plan from here?
DR. JUHNKE:	Eva Marie has agreed to voluntarily enter St. Michael's. I wanted to consult with you and make certain that a referral would be supported by you and by the agency before I make the call to St. Mike's.
DR. OLDZ:	Seems you are making excellent decisions. St. Mike's would be good. How are you planning to transport?
DR. JUHNKE:	As soon as I learn if St. Mike's has availability, I thought I would get a release of confidential information from Eva Marie so that her mother and husband could drive her over to St. Mike's.
DR. OLDZ:	Sounds good. If St. Mike's doesn't have room, you may wish to contact either University Hospital or Grandover Community General Hospital. Keep me posted and let me know how things are going.

As a master's level counselor, the second author often had this type of consultation with his supervisors. At this point, Dr. Juhnke would author a brief note recapping his supervision conversation with Dr. Oldz and include any directives in the client's case notes. Next, Dr. Juhnke would contact the intake coordinator at St. Michael's to determine availability. Typically, a hospital intake coordinator will be familiar with the counselor or counselor's agency and will need to know the type of insurance the client has as well as insurance group numbers and the insurance company's request for preauthorization telephone numbers. Often, they can secure a preauthorization from the client's insurance company for a minimum 72-hour hospital stay.

Because Dr. Juhnke had apprised Eva Marie earlier of both her SPS clinical scores as well as his clinical judgment that she would benefit by voluntarily entering the hospital to ensure her safety, this will not be further discussed. In addition, because Eva Marie has agreed to enter the psychiatric hospital terminating her access to the .45 caliber gun or truncating her access to medications she may have intended to overdose on will not be discussed at this point. (However, before Eva Marie is released from the hospital, both of these issues should be resolved). Therefore, the next pressing issue is transporting Eva Marie to the psychiatric hospital.

In this case, the counselor will not wish to transport. Instead, he will either secure a release of confidential information from Eva Marie, allowing him to seek transportation from Eva Marie's mother and possibly her husband, a friend, a family member, or a priest, or ask that Eva Marie make the telephone calls. Remember, a minimum of two healthy adults should always transport clients.

DR. JUHNKE:	Eva Marie, I just got off the telephone with Shelly. She is the intake coordinator at St. Michael's. Shelly has contacted your insurance carrier and secured a voluntary stay for you. All we need is transportation. Typically, there are two ways we transport our clients. First, we see if the client would prefer to sign a release of confidential information allowing me to contact a family member, friends, or a priest to drive him or her to St. Michaels. We need a minimum of two persons to drive you to St. Michael's. Thus, I will need at least two releases signed and two names with telephone numbers. If you prefer not to sign a release or prefer not to have your family members, friends, or priest drive you, we will contact the San Antonio Police Department and ask for a peace officer to transport you.
EVA MARIE:	I was having a very comfortable conversation with Dr. Henderson. Why don't Dr. Henderson and you drive me to St. Michael's?
DR. JUHNKE:	I am sorry, Eva Marie. I am unwilling to drive. If you wish to sign a release or contact two family members, friends, or others, we would be happy to have them transport you to St. Michael's. If that doesn't work for you, we will contact the San Antonio Police Department and have them transport you.
EVA MARIE:	I certainly don't want the police to transport me; I will call my mother and husband. They will drive me over to St. Michael's.

As this vignette depicts, clients often will rather have friends or family transport them rather than the police. In this case, we do not need a release of confidential information because Eva Marie will contact her family members directly. Incidentally, some may believe it harsh to refuse to transport Eva Marie. Be aware, there are a number of reasons to refuse transporting clients. The authors, as inexperienced, entry-level counselors, have transported clients before. On some of those occasions the clients who originally presented as kind and endearing, became belligerent and argumentative. On another occasion, a client's head lice infested the counselor's car. If these reasons are insufficient to dissuade readers from transporting clients, readers should also know that some auto insurance companies may view transporting clients for business purposes outside the counselor's auto insurance policy. As entry-level counselors, the authors quickly learned that the best transportation options are having others transport.

DISCUSSION

This chapter has provided a general overview of the Marital Satisfaction Inventory—Revised, the Substance Abuse Subtle Screening Inventory—3, the Alcohol Use Inventory, the Suicide Probability Scale, and the Suicide SCATTT mnemonic. Instrument reliability and validity have been reported on all instruments except the SCATTT. As well, descriptions of individual scales have been discussed. Eva Marie and Robert have been used within clinical vignettes depicting how these instruments would be used with each person. Finally, issues regarding transportation of suicidal clients have been addressed.

References

Beck, A. T., Steer, R. A., Kovacs, M., & Garrison, B. (1985). Hopelessness and eventual suicide: A 10-year prospective study of patients hospitalized with suicidal ideation. *American Journal of Psychiatry, 142*(4), 559–563.

Cull, J. G., & Gill, W. S. (2002). *Suicide Probability Scale (SPS) manual.* Los Angeles, CA: Western Psychological Services.

Golding, S. L. (1985). Review of the Suicide Probability Scale. In J. V. Mitchell (Ed.), *The ninth mental measurements yearbook* (pp. 207–210). Lincoln, NE: Buros Institute of Mental Measurements.

Granello, P. F., & Juhnke, G. A. (2009). *Case studies in suicide: Experiences of mental health professionals.* Upper Saddle River, NJ: Merrill-Pearson.

Horn, J. L., Wanberg, K. W., & Foster, F. M. (1990). *Guide to the Alcohol Use Inventory (AUI).* Bloomington, MN: NCS Pearson.

Juhnke, G. A. (2002). *Substance abuse assessment: A handbook for mental health professionals.* New York, NY: Brunner-Routledge.

Juhnke, G. A., Granello, D. H., & Granello, P. F. (2010). *Suicide, self-injury, and violence in the schools: Assessment, prevention, and intervention strategies.* Hoboken, NJ: John Wiley & Sons.

Juhnke, G. A., Juhnke, G. B., & Hsieh, P. (2012). *SCATTT: A suicide intervention plan mnemonic for use when clients present suicide intent.* Retrieved October 30, 2012 from http://www.counseling.org/Resources/Library/VISTAS/vistas12/Article_34.pdf

Juhnke, G. A., Vacc, N. A., Curtis, R. C., Coll, K. M., & Paredes, D. M. (2003). Assessment instruments used by addictions counselors. *Journal of Addictions & Offender Counseling, 23,* 66–72.

Lazowski, L. E., Miller, F. G., Boye, M. W., & Miller, G. A. (1998). Efficacy of the Substance Abuse Subtle Screening Inventory—3 (SASSI-3) in identifying substance dependence disorders in clinical settings. *Journal of Personality Assessment, 71,* 114–128.

Miller, F. G., Roberts, J., Brooks, M. K., & Lazowski, L. E. (1997). *SASSI-3 user's guide: A quick reference for administration and scoring.* Bloomington, IN: Baugh Enterprises.

Pearson. (2012). *Alcohol Use Inventory (AUI).* Retrieved from http://www.pearsonassessments.com/HAI-WEB/Cultures/en-us/Productdetail.htm?Pid=PAaui1000&Mode=summary

Rychtarik, R. G., Koutsky, J. R., & Miller, W. R. (1998). Profiles of the Alcohol Use Inventory: A large sample cluster analysis conducted with split-sample replication rules. *Psychological Assessment, 10*(2), 107–119.

Snyder, D. K. (1997). *Marital Satisfaction Inventory, Revised (MSI-R): Manual* (2nd ed.). Los Angeles, CA: Western Psychological Services.

Substance Abuse Subtle Screening Inventory Institute (SASSII). (2012). *SASSI.* Retrieved from http://www.sassi.com/products/SASSI3/shopS3-pp.shtml

Valadez, A., Juhnke, G. A., Coll, K. M., Granello, P. F., Peters, S., & Zambrano, E. (2009). The Suicide Probability Scale: A means to assess substance abusing clients' suicide risk. *Journal of Professional Counseling: Practice, Theory, & Research,* 37(1), 52–65.

Western Psychological Services (WPS) (2012). *Products: Marital Satisfaction Inventory* Revised (MSI-R) retrieved from http://portal.wpspublish.com/portal/page?_pageid=53,103808&_dad=portal&_schema=PORTAL

CHAPTER 14

Fundamentals of Interpretation in Assessment

OBJECTIVES

After reading this chapter, you will be able to:

1. Understand the structure of an assessment report.
2. Understand the nature of assessment principles in the assessment report.
3. Create and interpret a score report for referrals and clients.
4. Develop a written assessment report.

DEVELOPING A WRITTEN REPORT

An assessment that is comprehensive in nature, uses structured and unstructured measures and interviews, and provides timely information regarding client disposition must be summarized in a manner that is useful to providers, stakeholders, and most importantly, the client. One specific challenge in writing an assessment report is providing appropriate technical information essential to referring bodies and professional stakeholders (e.g., schools, other mental health providers), while simultaneously explaining such information in a manner that is helpful to the client and stakeholders outside the mental health discipline. Therefore, in this chapter we highlight what is included in an assessment report and how such a report must be structured and communicated to the client and relevant stakeholders.

The cases of Robert Jones and Eva Marie Garza presented in Chapter 2 represent comprehensive evaluations of clients in a format consistent with what is seen in many assessment reports. In addition, Chapter 7 on the clinical interview provides in-depth material on information that is relevant to case conceptualization and necessary for the assessment report. Subsequent chapters highlight the use of various types of measures that may be incorporated into an assessment report. With this in mind, we provide an outline and summary of the scope and structure of an assessment report making references, when necessary, to the aforementioned chapters.

In Chapter 7, several important features of the clinical interview were addressed, including the presenting problem, relevant history, mental status exam, medical history, family history/issues, social support, educational/occupational/economic issues, and cultural/spiritual concerns. Many of these elements are addressed in the case studies presented in Chapter 2, along with a formal diagnosis of each of the clients.

In addition, the assessment report includes a list of formal assessments administered, a brief rationale for the administration of the instruments, a statement about the validity of the administration process, a score report on each of the instruments, and an interpretation of scores, as well as how the scores fit the context provided by other information about the client. In other words, the scores of assessment instruments should never stand alone and should be used in conjunction with other information about the client. For clients who obtained scores inconsistent with their case presentation, such discrepancies should be highlighted and addressed in the assessment report.

By providing such structure and information, the diagnosis should be seen as a product, and therefore logical conclusion, from the information presented. In other words, based on the information in an assessment report, the reader, whether a stakeholder, physician, clinician, third-party payor, or so forth, should be able to view the information presented in an assessment report and obtain a strong case conceptualization of the client.

REPORTING SCORES FOR STANDARDIZED INSTRUMENTS

After providing the aforementioned information of the tests administered, rationale, and process of the administration, the counselor provides a score report for each instrument administered. This section of the assessment report requires the counselor to be aware of various aspects of the test and manual, including knowledge of the scale and any pertinent subscales, reliability estimates, and procedures that contribute to a valid administration, scoring, and interpretation of the instrument. Specifically, for each instrument administered counselors should address the following components: (a) scales and subscales, (b) raw scores, (c) standard scores, (d) percentiles, (e) standard error of measurement (*SEM*), and (f) category (if applicable).

The information provided may have appeal to both mental health professionals and laypeople. The information on standard scores and *SEM* provides important guidelines for interpretation that may be of interest to assessment professionals, whereas parents, clients, and consumers may find information related to percentiles and diagnostic indicators as more relevant to their needs. Counselors should keep in mind that the assessment report is a technical report that may be used by a variety of professionals, and therefore needs to include a variety of information that professionals, clients, parents, and stakeholders can utilize. Throughout this chapter, we will use Eva Marie's case in which she is administered the Beck Depression Inventory—II (BDI-II). Examples of how the information is processed will be provided throughout the chapter. Similarly, additional implications for Robert will be addressed through the administration of the Outcome Questionnaire—45.2 (OQ-45.2).

TABLE 14.1	Score Report for Eva Marie on the BDI-II			
Raw Score	Standard Score Clinical (Nonclinical)	Percentile Clinical (Nonclinical)	SEM Clinical (Nonclinical)	Category
28	.36 (1.55)	64th (94th)	3.37 [24.63, 31.37] (2.63[25.37, 30.63])	Moderate to severe

For the case of Eva Marie, a counselor would report the following:

Eva Marie was administered the Beck Depression Inventory—II (BDI-II) to help assess the severity of the depressive symptoms that Eva Marie exhibits. The BDI-II is a 21-item self-report inventory. Clients identify the extent to which they exhibit a variety of diagnostic indicators for depression on a Likert-type scale ranging from 0 (no endorsement) to 3 (increased severity) over the past two weeks. The administration of the BDI-II was under typical conditions. Results from the scores may be deemed as a valid assessment. Table 14.1 represents Eva Marie's scores on the BDI-II.

Eva Marie scored a 28 on the BDI-II, placing her in the 64th percentile among the clinical norm group and the 94th percentile among the nonclinical norm group. Although a score of 28 places Eva Marie in the moderate range of depression, as identified in the manual, when SEM is taken under consideration, Eva Marie could be categorized in the severe range with respect to depressive symptoms.

SCALES AND SUBSCALES After scoring an instrument, counselors should consider the type of scores reported from the instrument. For some instruments, such as the BDI-II, this is rather self-explanatory, as only a total score is derived from the administration of the instrument. Other instruments may provide only scale scores and no total score (e.g., Minnesota Multiphasic Personality Inventory—2—Restructured Form [MMPI-2-RF]). For instruments such as the OQ-45.2, both a total score and subscale scores are derived. The purpose of the administration of the instrument and the use of the test scores are essential in determining whether total scores or subscales should be reported. For example, total scores may be used to get a sense of overall progress or regression for clients, whereas subscale scores may be essential for identifying specific problem areas and creating goals for treatment planning.

RAW SCORES Recall that raw scores alone lack meaning. Only when scores are compared to a norm group do the scores become meaningful. However, not all instruments report scores using a standard score format. For example, instruments such as the MMPI-RF use the *T* scores to report subscale scores, but the instruments such as the BDI-II simply rely on the raw score. The problem with this practice is that raw scores will not convey any information with respect to how a client compares to the general population. Although a client may not initially see this as a problem, what the client really wants to know is whether a score is high or low. Essentially, the clients wants to know what the score means. When the counselor can say, "Compared to others who have taken the same test, your scores is in the upper (or lower) _____ percentile," then the counselor can attribute meaning to the scores. However, this ability is limited simply by reporting raw scores. What raw scores may provide, however, is a sense for how many items were endorsed, particularly on a checklist or self-report inventory, and this may have some meaningful implications to what information is garnered from the assessment and the overall acceptance the clients displays from the interpretation of the assessment.

STANDARD SCORES   Standard scores do provide an ability to make comparisons to the norm group. However, standard scores do not provide information related to the number of items endorsed or answered in a particular manner. So, assessment professionals may place more value on standard scores, whereas laypeople may not have this type of understanding. When deriving standard scores, counselors should pay particular attention to the norm group in which the comparisons are made. Quite often, more than one norm group is used in the development of a test, and the choice of which norm group is used to make comparisons can have important implications with regard to interpretation of the assessment. For example, the BDI-II has two norm groups, a group of 500 outpatient participants from various settings and age groups (13 to 86 years old) and 120 college students. Thus, the BDI-II has two categories: 500 participants representing a clinical subset of the population and 120 college students representing a nonclinical subset of the population. Researchers may argue the appropriateness of suggesting that college students are representative of a nonclinical population that is generalizable to the general population, and such an argument would have merit. Thus, there are pertinent limitations to making comparisons of the BDI-II for individual clients to the norm groups.

However, for the sake of moving this discussion forward to how comparisons are made, suppose Eva Marie was administered the BDI-II and scored a 28, as noted earlier. In order to facilitate interpretation, the counselor converts the raw score to a standard score. The BDI-II provides descriptive statistics for both a clinical group (outpatients) and nonclinical group (college students). In the above example, standard scores were provided for both groups. A counselor may opt to provide scores from a single norm group.

Beck, Steer, and Brown (1996) reported means and standard deviations for outpatients ($M = 22.45$, $SD = 12.75$) and college students ($M = 12.56$, $SD = 9.93$). Applying the concepts of computing standard scores from Chapter 3, the following z scores are noted:

$$\frac{28 - 22.45}{12.75} = .36$$

for outpatients (clinical) and

$$\frac{28 - 12.56}{9.93} = 1.55$$

for college students (nonclinical)

From these computations, counselors can determine that when compared to the clinical group, Eva Marie scored just slightly above the mean, but when compared to the nonclinical group, Eva Marie is over 1.5 standard deviations above the mean. By converting the raw score to standard scores, a counselor is able to explain to Eva Marie that she is within the average range among individuals who seek counseling services for depression and well above the average range among individuals who may not be representative of individuals seeking counseling services.

PERCENTILES   Additional information, particularly for making comparisons, and interpretations, may be ascertained from percentiles. Using the z table from Appendix A the percentiles for the corresponding z scores are available. A z score of .36 corresponds to the 64th percentile; a z score of 1.55 corresponds to the 94th percentile. Hence, Eva Marie is among the top 6% of individuals endorsing depressive symptoms among the nonclinical group but slightly above the middle of the group when compared to a clinical population. Based strictly on the scores from the BDI-II, Eva Marie is like most individuals who are in outpatient counseling and administered the BDI-II, but clearly among the more depressed individuals when compared to people who may not be seeking counseling services.

SEM   A score on a test is time and context bound. Recall from Chapter 4 that *SEM* is used to ascertain a client's true score from the observed score that is the result of an administration of an instrument. To compute the *SEM*, the counselor must be aware of the test–retest reliability estimate of the instrument and the standard deviation of the norm group. Thus,

$$12.75\sqrt{1 - .93} = 3.37$$

for outpatients (clinical) and

$$9.93\sqrt{1 - .93} = 2.63$$

for college students (nonclinical)

By adding and subtracting each of these values from the raw score, the range of possible scores at the 68th percent confidence interval (i.e., 1 standard deviation) are presented in Table 14.1. Counselors interested in reporting the SEM at the 95% confidence interval would simply multiple the *SEM* by 2, yielding the following:

$$2(3.37) = 6.74, [21.26, 34.74]$$

for outpatients (clinical) and

$$2(2.63) = 5.26, [22.74, 33.26]$$

for college students (nonclinical)

CATEGORY   Some manuals for instruments provide indicators for score interpretation. *Cut-scores* refer to scores that are used to determine classifications on a given instrument. For example, Beck et al. (1996) provided cut scores to indicate *mild, moderate,* and *severe* depression. Other instruments may establish cut scores to indicate clinical significance (e.g., MMPI-RF) or diagnostic criteria (e.g., mild mental retardation for IQ scores below 70). Counselors should be cautious about using categories based on scores. A score on a single instrument is not sufficient evidence to provide a label or diagnosis, and to do so based on a single score is unethical. As noted in the above example, the SEM may play a role in categorizing a client. When employing categories consistent with a particular score, counselors should demonstrate evidence based on other assessment tools to substantiate a label, indicator, and/or diagnosis.

For the purposes of evaluating Eva Marie on the BDI-II, a score of 28 is the upper limit for moderate depression; a score of 29 is the lower limit for severe depression (Beck et al., 1996). Therefore, when considering the *SEM*, Eva Marie may be in the moderate to severe level of major depressive disorder. Certainly, evidence from the clinical interview and use of additional assessments may be necessary to substantiate such a diagnosis. Based on the clinical interview, Eva Marie also suffers from anxiety. Often, assessment measures for depression correlate with anxiety measures (Beck et al., 1996). Hence, a counselor working with Eva Marie would need to address whether the client has anxiety, depression, or comorbidity (i.e., the presence of one or more disorders).

WRITING IN PROFESSIONAL LANGUAGE

From the case studies in Chapter 2 and the sample score report on Eva Marie, professionals and laypeople alike easily understand much of the information, particularly the narrative portions in the case studies. However, the score reports are geared toward professionals. Counselors should keep in mind that the assessment report becomes part of the client's record, such as educational records, medical records, employment records, and legal records. Thus, counselors are accountable for how the assessment results are used and interpreted, particularly when such results affect the welfare of the client.

So, who is the client? The request for an assessment of an individual may not come from an individual seeking services but from some other entity (e.g., court, medical professional, organization, school). Hence, the counselor conducting an assessment may be responsible to multiple parties, such as the referring professional or organization, as well as the individual assessed. We will discuss ethical responsibilities to the client and stakeholders later in the chapter; but for now, we will focus on the fact that the assessment report must be written in a manner that pertains to multiple audiences (e.g., client, referring professional or organization).

The assessment report is not only a reflection of the client but also of the counselor conducting the assessment and providing the written report. Professionals look for evidence of a well-written report that reflects a valid administration of the test(s) and knowledgeable interpretation. In addition, multiple forms of evidence should be presented to substantiate any recommendations that are made as a result of the assessment. Writing in a professional language that communicates a logical, coherent case conceptualization is extremely pertinent, as such a report may be used to provide educational placement, medication management, vocational placement, and legal options. For example, juvenile judges often refer adolescents and families to counseling services and expect feedback and recommendations from the counselor to the court regarding the client's disposition. A judge may use such information to render decisions of a case. Hence, based on the counselor's recommendations, a client may be released from the juvenile court, referred for additional treatment, or even detained. In such an instance, what the judge may be looking for is evidence that supports a decision regarding the adolescent's disposition with the juvenile court. Information provided by the counselor may in fact be highly influential in rendering decisions.

Such an assessment is no less important to other professionals, such as a psychiatrist considering medication management issues, schools considering placement, and institutions considering the job placement of an individual. An example may be with the Department of Transportation (DOT), which has specific policies regarding substance abuse for professionals in the transportation industry. Counselors often provide substance abuse assessments for the DOT; the information related in such assessments may have serious ramifications on whether clients are able to continue with their jobs.

Beyond the structure of the assessment report, which has been outlined in this chapter, the manner in which information is conveyed is equally important. Because the assessment report may become part of the client's record in a variety of settings, professionalism is necessary. Counselors should avoid jargon, as professionals outside the mental health industry may need to understand the contents of the report. Although not all professionals may understand the scope of the score report, such information is necessary for those within the mental health field who may know how to interpret such information. The report should be clearly written and grammatically correct. Professionals outside the mental health profession should be able to easily understand the recommendations and the rationale for such recommendations. For example, a school administrator or counselor, judge, or employer examining such a report may communicate a decision and refer to the report as a basis for such a decision.

MAKING RECOMMENDATIONS

Clients, parents/guardians, third-party payors, or other outside entities may request assessment reports. Counselors need to be aware of who the intended audience is for the report and what information should be communicated. Balancing the client's needs and the needs of the referring entity are important considerations. We advocate for a report that is deductive in nature—one that moves from general impressions to specific findings and recommendations. Therefore, recommendations are highlighted near the end of the report and easily distinguished from other aspects of the psychological report. Counselors should deliberate numerous considerations when making recommendations such as the data supporting the recommendations, the client's disposition, the likelihood of following the recommendations, and the scope of the recommendations.

SUPPORTING DATA Recommendations are data driven. The reader of an assessment report should be able to follow a clear logic of how a recommendation was derived. Explicit statements connecting a recommendation to data presented in the assessment report is helpful in providing a strong rationale. For example, a statement reflecting Eva Marie's past history of anxiety and depression may make her a candidate for medication management. Therefore, an assessment report may include a recommendation for a psychiatric consultation. If Eva Marie agrees, providing information from Eva Marie's clinical interview, subsequent sessions, and formal assessments may be helpful to a consulting psychiatrist in rendering a decision related to medication management:

> *Given Eva Marie's disclosure of a long history of anxiety and subsequent score on the BDI-II indicating moderate to severe depression, she may benefit from a psychiatric consultation to evaluate the appropriateness of medication management.*

Thus, the statement provides a cogent recommendation based on data from the clinical interview and administration of the BDI-II.

CLIENT DISPOSITION When making a recommendation, consider the client's amiability toward counseling and prognosis. *Amiability* refers to the client's receptiveness toward counseling. Is the client motivated? Is the client seeking counseling out of personal interest in self-improvement or due to a level of coercion or leverage? An individual who recognizes that he or she has a substance abuse problem may be more amiable toward counseling than an individual court ordered for an assessment. A client's personal motivation to be healthier may certainly facilitate the likelihood of counseling being effective when compared to the individual who attends counseling to escape or reduce logical and natural consequences of behavior.

Based on the data presented and the client's receptiveness and motivation toward counseling and/or assessment, the counselor should consider the client's prognosis. The counselor should avoid using terms that may be implied as overly predictive, such as being too positive or even fatalistic. A statement about prognosis should address the likelihood of success based on the recommendations or the potential for problems to continue. In the case of Eva Marie, the following statement may be appropriate:

> *Eva Marie requested counseling services on her own volition, seeking assistance with her anxiety and evident depression. Based on Eva Marie's apparent amiability toward counseling and verbalized willingness to follow recommendations, Eva Marie may have a good prognosis.*

LIKELIHOOD OF FOLLOWING RECOMMENDATIONS Beyond the client's internal motivation toward counseling, the counselor should consider the feasibility of making recommendations. Not only should the counselor make recommendations that are supported through best practices, but the availability and accessibility to follow through with specific recommendations also is important. According to Eva Marie's assessment report, she works as an assistant to the librarian at a private elementary school. Information as to whether this is a full-time job and provides full health benefits was not addressed. If the counselor recommends a psychiatric consult for Eva Marie, does Eva Marie have the necessary medical benefits to cover the consult and subsequent visits should they be necessary? If she is prescribed psychotropic medication, does Eva Marie possess a prescription drug plan that would cover the cost of ongoing medication?

Hence, the likelihood of a client following recommendations may be less about the client's willingness and more about the client's resources. This is especially true when counseling youth in which transportation, the ability for parents to leave work, school attendance, and financial resources can all be obstacles that interfere with the client's ability to adhere to counselor recommendations. When making a recommendation, consider the resources available and the ability of the client to take advantage of such resources.

SCOPE OF RECOMMENDATIONS The limits of the counselor with respect to an assessment report may be best described as a process in which the counselor has immense responsibility but limited authority. The counselor can make recommendations but has no authority as to whether the client will follow through. In cases where a client is referred by a judge or place of employment, the counselor may have leverage with respect to making recommendations, but follow through on the recommendations is up to the client and the enforcement by the third party.

In addition, when working with referring professionals, agencies, or organizations, counselors should be aware of the information solicited by the referral source and the type of interventions typically used. For example, although a client may be noncompliant with counseling, the counselor does not have the authority to recommend detention or adjudication to a court. These are processes a court may employ depending on the due process of the client. Therefore, the counselor lacks the authority and knowledge to make such recommendations. Rather, the counselor should focus on making recommendations that are more factually based, once again relying on the data from the assessment process to address the client's current disposition and likely challenges and/or strengths.

CONDUCTING AN INTERPRETATION SESSION WITH A CLIENT

The assessment report includes a variety of technical information such as diagnosis(es), score reports, and descriptions employing language specific to mental health professionals. Therefore, a session in which the counselor provides an interpretation of the assessment report for the client is an opportunity to shed light on an otherwise complex report. According to Wall et al. (2003):

> Conveying test results with language that the test taker, parents, teachers, clients, or general public can understand is one of the key elements in helping others understand the meaning of the test results....The test user should indicate how the test results can be and should not be interpreted. (p. 5)

Therefore, considerable preparation and a formal interpretation session for the client is best practice. When a client has no previous contact with a counselor prior to an assessment, the client might not be invested in ongoing sessions with a counselor. Often a client will request that a report is sent to the referral source without ever scheduling an interpretation session. However, counselors should proceed cautiously with such a request. Clients have the right to know assessment results and subsequent interpretations of the information (American Counseling Association [ACA], 2005). Counselors should encourage clients to attend a subsequent session for the purposes of interpreting the assessment report.

Reviewing Informed Consent Procedures

Throughout this chapter, responsibilities to both the client and the referral source were addressed. Nevertheless, the primary responsibility of the counselor is the welfare of the client (ACA, 2005). This does not mean that the recommendations of the counselor always appear beneficial to the client's worldview. On the contrary, what is in the best interest of the client may not be what the client desires. For this reason, the counselor should spend adequate time discussing the nature of informed consent and who may obtain the contents of the assessment report before administration of any counseling assessment. Counselors have the responsibility of assuring the client that the individuals receiving the report have the qualifications to interpret the assessment report properly. Counselors must be aware of Health Insurance Portability and Accountability Act (HIPAA) guidelines when releasing information to another party. Specific forms related to releasing and obtaining information need to be signed, and the party receiving the information must be stipulated.

The counselor should be cautious about releasing information, particularly from the clinical interview. Client disclosures often are made under the pretense of confidentiality. When a counselor obtains consent to release information to a third party, the client must understand the boundaries of what information may be released. In addition, counselors should release information on a need-to-know basis. A common practice is for the counselor to obtain consent to release information from the client and then send the client file. However, this is not best practice, as first and foremost is the client welfare and the third party's need to know. If there is information within the contents of the client's file that the third party does not require in order to render appropriate care or disposition, then such information should not be released.

Reviewing the Instruments Used

During the interpretation session with the client, the counselor will typically address information related to formal and informal assessments. The counselor may highlight information obtained from the clinical interview as well as any standardized measures that were administered. "The specific purposes for the use of such instruments are stated explicitly to the examinee" (ACA, 2005, p. 13). Counselors discuss with the client the nature of each instrument, including the purpose, rationale, and information derived from each instrument.

In the case of Eva Marie, the counselor would review information in the assessment report related to her history, presenting problem, and relevant treatment issues, as well as highlight any formal instruments that were administered. The BDI-II was administered out of concern related to mood disturbance, above what may often be construed from anxiety. Eva Marie's score of 28 places her in the moderate to severe range of major depressive disorder and among the top 6% of individuals who may not be seeking counseling services. Compared to individuals who do seek counseling services, Eva Marie exhibited depressive symptoms that are slightly more severe than average. A counselor making a referral for a psychiatric consultation would identify what may be gained from such a consultation and how the third party may use the information.

Summarizing the Data in Client Language

Counselors should summarize information for clients in a language they can understand. The technical information used in assessment reports is beyond most clients' understanding. Take time to address the nature of a norm group and to whom a client is being compared. In the score report for Eva Marie, comparisons are made to both clinical and nonclinical populations. The nature of different percentiles for the same score may be confusing to a client. Eva Marie's label of moderate to severe depression on the assessment report is easier to explain when comparing Eva Marie to the nonclinical group, as she is in the 94th percentile. Hence, a counselor could explain that 94% of individuals in the nonclinical group scored at or below Eva Marie's score of 28; Eva Marie is in the top 6% when compared to this group.

Explaining Eva Marie's score with respect to the clinical group may be a bit more confusing. How can Eva Marie's placement in the 64th percentile, only slightly above average, be indicative of moderate to severe depression? The client would need to understand that this comparison is based on individuals who are also seeking counseling services. Even though the client may be categorized with moderate to severe depression, the fact that Eva Marie is in the 64th percentile compared to the clinical group may help Eva Marie understand that she is more like other individuals seeking counseling, which can be rather affirming.

As shown in Chapter 2, the assessment reports include a *Diagnostic and Statistical Manual* (DSM) diagnosis, which may also require explanation to the client. A diagnosis may provide information to another mental health care provider in a manner that is easily understood among clinical professionals but may be foreign to a client. Diagnoses may be necessary to obtain reimbursement from third-party payors. However, not all problems and clients require a diagnosis. "Counselors may refrain from making and/or reporting a diagnosis if they believe it would cause harm to the client or others" (ACA, 2005, p. 12). Counselors should provide clients with an explanation of a diagnosis, should one be given, and the implications, as well as treatment strategies, related to the diagnosis.

The assessment process and report may be an intimidating process for clients. Counselors should work hard to normalize the process and place the client's welfare at the forefront while not compromising objectivity. Assessment reports are forthright appraisals of a client's presenting problem(s), relevant history, disposition, and prognosis. Clients may be apprehensive about the assessment process (e.g., court-ordered clients). Counselors make sure that the assessments are administered, scored, and reported with integrity and will be used appropriately. Such ethical intentions should be communicated to the client in order to reduce any anxiety and encourage trust in the assessment process.

TYPES OF INFORMATION DERIVED FROM OUR CASE STUDY

Presentation of Eva Marie's case was emphasized in this chapter. Eva Marie's case included an interpretation of the BDI-II, which is a unidimensional scale. In other words, the interpretation of the instrument is based on a single, total score. To further reiterate the points about instrument interpretation, information related to Robert's case in light of an administration of the OQ-45.2 follows.

The OQ-45.2 is a 45-item scale designed to identify problems and measure progress in three distinct areas: symptom distress, interpersonal relations, and social role. The scale may be administered repeatedly over time to demonstrate progress, stagnation, or regression in the aforementioned areas. Each of the items follows a Likert-type format identifying the frequency a symptom or behavior occurs: *never, rarely, sometimes, frequently,* or *almost always.* A completed instrument produced a Total score and three subscale scores. In addition, there are five critical items that relate to substance abuse, suicidality, and hostility toward others. Given the range of issues with Robert, this instrument was selected to provide insight into problem areas.

Lambert et al. (2004) provided descriptive statistics for several norm groups, consisting of clinical and nonclinical populations. For the purposes of this assessment report, comparisons were made to the community sample (nonclinical). Descriptive statistics for the Total scale scores and subscale scores, as well as the reliability estimates (α), are in Table 14.2.

TABLE 14.2	Descriptive Statistics of the Community Norm Group for the OQ-45.2		
Scale	Mean	SD	α
Total	45.19	18.57	0.84
Symptom Distress	25.43	11.55	0.78
Interpersonal Relations	10.20	5.56	0.80
Social Role	9.56	3.87	0.82

TABLE 14.3	Score Report for Robert Jones on the OQ-45.2			
Scale	**Raw Score**	**Standard Score**	**Percentile**	**SEM (CI 68%)**
Total	32	− 0.71	24 th	7.43 (24.57, 39.43)
Symptom Distress	8	− 1.51	7 th	5.42 (2.58, 13.42)
Interpersonal Relations	10	− 0.04	48 th	2.49 (7.51, 12.49)
Social Role	14	1.15	87 th	1.64 (12.36, 15.15)

Robert is seeking counseling based on the advice of his attorney. Robert has had a history of tumultuous relationships with women resulting in divorce on two occasions, as well as arrests for domestic violence and alcohol consumption. Robert admitted to fighting often and was recently arrested for grand larceny. Robert was administered the OQ-45.2 under typical conditions and results from the scores may be deemed as a valid assessment. Table 14.3 represents Robert's scores on the OQ-45.2.

Notice the OQ-45.2 is a multidimensional scale. The Total Scale score is composed of three subscales. Also notice that if a clinician focuses solely on the Total Scale score, some very important information is missed. In particular, Robert has low scores compared to a nonclinical group in Symptom Distress and Interpersonal Relations. However, Robert's score in Social Role is quite elevated, placing Robert in the 87th percentile. Robert also endorsed three of the five critical items: "After heavy drinking, I need a drink the next morning to get going," "I feel annoyed by people who criticize my drinking (or drug use)," " I feel angry enough at work/school to do something I might regret." An example of how to report Robert's scores on the OQ-45.2 follows.

Robert's Total score on the OQ-45.2, when compared to a nonclinical norm group, place him in the 24th percentile. Robert hardly endorses any symptomatic distress, with placement in the bottom 10% (7th percentile). Robert is in the average range with respect to Interpersonal Relations (48th percentile). However, Robert's score in Social Role was elevated, placing him in the 87th percentile. Elevated scores in Social Role refer to higher levels of "dissatisfaction, conflict, distress, and inadequacy" in areas related to "employment, family roles, and leisure life" (Lambert et al., 2004, p. 2). Robert endorsed items related to stress and dissatisfaction with work, likely emanating from his arrest related to grand larceny, which was pursued by his place of employment. In addition, Robert endorsed three of the five critical items on the OQ-45.2, which were related to substance abuse and Robert's hostility toward others in his work environment. These elevated scores and attributes fit with Robert's clinical profile of alcohol dependence and antisocial personality disorder. Robert may very well be in denial or resistant to addressing his responsibility or role with respect to his treatment of others and the impact of his alcohol abuse.

Robert's attorney referred Robert to counseling. Robert's perception of the problems he is facing appears to be incongruent with the frequency, duration, and severity of the problems presented. Given Robert's resistance toward endorsing such issues, his *prognosis remains guarded at this time. Counseling will focus on confronting Robert with his ongoing alcohol abuse and antisocial problems that affect both his **personal and professional life.***

This score report may accompany the psychological report addressed in Chapter 2, thereby providing a comprehensive review of the client using both qualitative (e.g., session and interview information) and quantitative measures (e.g., standardized assessment instruments). Although the report does not necessarily place the client in a positive light, concerns related to the client's disclosures were supported by data collected in the interview and assessment process. If Robert were to review this assessment report, which he would be entitled to do, he may disagree that the counselor is acting with the client's welfare in mind. However, the counselor may defend such a report by focusing on the data collected and reminding the client that addressing issues of alcohol dependence and threats toward others is pertinent to client welfare. Thus, the counselor must maintain integrity when addressing client strengths, weaknesses, and challenges. The assessment report provided a comprehensive review and summary regarding client issues and disposition, which may affect more than the client but society as well.

References

American Counseling Association. (2005). *ACA code of ethics.* Alexandria, VA: Author.

Beck, A. T., Steer, R. A., & Brown, G. K. (1996). *BDI-II manual.* San Antonio, TX: The Psychological Corporation.

Lambert, M. J., Morton, J. J., Hatfield, D., Harmon, C., Hamilton, S., Reid, R. C., Shimokawa, K., & Burlingame, G. M. (2004). Administration and scoring manual for the OQ 45.2 (Outcome Questionnaire). Salt Lake City, UT: OQ Measures, LLC.

Wall, J., Augustin, J., Eberly, C., Erford, B., Lundberg, D., & Vansickle, T. (2003). *Responsibilities of Users of Standardized Tests (RUST)* (3rd ed.). Alexandria, VA: Association for Assessment in Counseling and Education.

CHAPTER 15

Accountability Issues in Counseling and Assessment

OBJECTIVES

After reading this chapter, you will be able to:

1. Define accountability in relation to the counseling profession.
2. Address challenges to demonstrating accountability in counseling.
3. Evaluate practices of accountability using standardized and nonstandardized measures.
4. Understand effective methods for evaluating assessment outcomes.
5. Apply assessment issues related to accountability to our case studies.
6. Identify assessment processes in program evaluation.

COUNSELING IN AN ERA OF ACCOUNTABILITY

Counselors, regardless of specialization, operate in an era of accountability. *Accountability*, as it relates to counseling, is the use of data to validate the need for services and the outcomes related to those services. Data refer to quantitative or qualitative information used for the justification of services and the results for those services. Naturally, data may be generated from informal assessments, such as information generated through progress notes, or formal assessments, such as information gathered from clinical interviews, mental status examinations, and assessment instruments, rating scales, and surveys.

The demonstration of accountability is broad and ambiguous and can refer to any number of assessments. Satisfaction with services, symptom reduction, improvement in psychosocial functioning, number of clients served, or the frequency of services provided all serve as examples of assessment practices to demonstrate accountability (Balkin & Roland, 2007; Luk et al., 2001). Clearly, the difference between identifying satisfaction with services as an outcome measure versus symptom reduction is notable. An adolescent with disruptive behavior may not like coming to counseling, and perhaps even resents it, yet still makes therapeutic gains. Community mental health agencies often validate their funding by addressing points of service (e.g., number of clients seen) as opposed to providing evidence of effective treatment. Assessing accountability is multifaceted with no recognized measure or operational definition to clarify what should be assessed or measured. For the purposes of this chapter, we recognize that reporting points of service and satisfaction of services can be important components for stakeholders who fund mental health services; however, we will focus more on assessing the effectiveness of counseling services in order to provide counselors with a broad range of tools to demonstrate the relevance and importance of their skills.

Accountability is an ethical mandate of the American Counseling Association (ACA). "Counselors have a responsibility to the public to engage in counseling practices that are based on rigorous research methodologies" (ACA, 2005, p. 9). In addition to the ACA *Code of Ethics* (2005), two prominent areas of legislation affect the counseling profession and the mandate towards accountability: the Health Maintenance Organization Act of 1973 and No Child Left Behind Act of 2001.

The 1973 Health Maintenance Organization (HMO) Act was enacted during the Nixon administration, but the effects on mental health care were not noticeable until the 1980s and beyond because of the substantial growth of managed care companies during this decade (Erickson, 2010). The HMO act introduced managed care to mental health professionals, which influenced mental health professions in several ways. First, managed care companies required preauthorization of care from a primary care physician and quite often a case manager employed by the third-party payor to review requested services. Such a practice created a conflict of interest, as the third-party payor, often an insurance company, could increase profits by limiting and/or denying care. Hence, stated benefit packages touted by employers were often unavailable to individuals requesting access to the benefits. In addition, managed care companies instituted utilization review, in which managed care companies review services, through progress notes, formal letters, phone consultations, and so forth, to identify the necessity and benefit of requested services. For example, a client may have the benefit of mental health services but is unable to utilize those benefits if case reviewers do not believe the services are necessary. Assessment services certainly were affected by these practices. Third-party payors may limit reimbursement for assessment services and specify the monetary amount that will be covered and the number of hours that may be used and reimbursed. Often, the amount allowed was not sufficient to cover cost of materials and the time for the counselor to administer, score, interpret the instruments, and develop a psychological report. Counselors have to justify the need for the assessment services, as well as the cost involved. Such procedures remove decision making from credentialed professionals and onto the third-party payor, which may or may not use informed professionals in the process. Throughout the process, managed care companies could limit providers who could be in-network to service clients under their plan and identify treatment strategies that are needed. Hence, managed care companies may be criticized for enforcing a one-size-fits-all approach to counseling services that disregard the unique needs of each client (Erickson, 2010). Furthermore, managed care companies may be guilty of unfairly restricting access to mental health services. Generally, access to medical services may be attributed to socioeconomic status and obtaining private insurance. However, the opposite may be true for mental health services. Balkin (2006) found that lengths of stay for adolescents in acute care psychiatric hospitalization was shorter when the adolescent had access to private insurance, as opposed to state-funded insurance such as Medicaid. Private insurance companies are much more likely to incorporate utilization review services than state-funded insurance programs. Utilization review is an essential component to cost containment by the insurance companies and seems to affect access to services to a population that previously had more access prior to managed care.

Although managed care companies may scrutinize mental health services unfairly, an unfortunate reality is that mental health services are an easy target for cost containment. Extant research related to the effectiveness of counseling is limited, resulting in a profession that has difficulty providing evidence that counseling is beneficial. Furthermore, some of the blame for the aggressive stance of managed care toward the mental health profession must go to the mental health professionals that abused the system. Prior to managed care companies instituting utilization review, mental health practitioners had free reign with respect to the number of counseling sessions, the utilization of assessment instruments, and the utilization of more intensive types of treatment, such as inpatient hospitalizations with unspecified lengths of stay. The demand for accountability by counseling professionals was both reasonable and necessary.

Accountability practices were affected further by the passage of the No Child Left Behind (NCLB) Act of 2001. NCLB forced school districts to implement high-stakes testing practices to address accountability. School counseling services and mental health services in the schools were tied to educational goals. Hence, if school counseling was to remain a viable component of the educational system, then the benefit of school counseling services should be reflected in educational achievement. The problem is that much of what the school counselor provides is not directly assessed by achievement tests. Rather, the outcomes are more indirect, such as fewer behavior problems in the classrooms, improved crisis management, and higher success in postgraduate placements (e.g., postsecondary education, career-related vocational placements). When students are pulled out of the classroom for responsive services, such as participation in counseling groups, administrators want to be assured that such interventions will be tied to improved academic performance. These types of studies, although needed, are difficult because of the complexity of such studies, which will be discussed later in the chapter.

BARRIERS TO ASSESSING ACCOUNTABILITY IN COUNSELING

Despite the role and function of assessing accountability in counseling, a dearth of outcome studies is apparent in counseling research. Part of the issue stems from training. However, other more practical issues with respect to research design and analysis also limit the prevalence of assessing outcomes and accountability.

The training in research for counselors may be inadequate for assessing accountability in the counseling profession. Often, counselors are master's-level professionals with a single research course that focuses on traditional experimental designs used for large between and within subjects research. In other words, counselors receive training on understanding research methods for comparing large groups, often with an emphasis on being an intelligent consumer of research as opposed to a practitioner of research. As a result, counselors may be less comfortable assessing accountability. Furthermore, inferential statistics require a representative sample, which is not conducive to counseling practice, given that the nature of counseling practice is often centered on individuals, couples, families, and small groups. Outside the school setting, counselors do not have access to large, intact groups with sufficient numbers to make generalizable comparisons. Even in the school setting, where counselors may have access to larger groups, evaluating guidance curriculum may be easier than assessing outcomes from responsive services, which generally occur on an individual or small group basis. Because of this barrier, we recommend counselors become adept with single case study designs—a rather simple process of comparing a single client's progress over time without the reliance on complex statistical analyses.

As mentioned earlier, addressing accountability through measuring outcomes can include a number of possibilities (e.g., satisfaction with services, symptom reduction, improvement in psychosocial functioning, points of service). Throughout the text, assessments were covered that measured operationally defined constructs. However, the notion of outcomes does not follow a singular operational definition, and it is not likely that a single measure can be developed that would adequately address the multiple outcomes necessary for clients served in counseling. For example, consider the outcomes for Eva Marie and how they differ from outcomes for Robert. Identifying a single measure that could adequately address outcomes in counseling for each of these diverse clients would be a challenge. In another example, counseling outcomes across different populations require many different measures. Outcomes for an adolescent diagnosed with anorexia nervosa indicate far different needs than an adult client diagnosed with posttraumatic stress disorder. Outcomes for children and families are much different than outcomes for adults and individuals.

Perhaps an additional challenge is the fact that because outcomes may be so diverse, third-party payors and stakeholders that desire accountability data may be nonspecific as to what exactly constitutes a valid outcome. Counselors and agencies often have some freedom to decide the type of outcomes they wish to measure. For example, a psychiatric hospital may wish to monitor the use of physical restraints, while a counselor in private practice may wish to identify whether individuals participating in a group have improved psychosocial functioning.

Outcome research can be costly. Some popular instruments do have an initial licensing cost or cost per instrument, which may be difficult to justify if the instruments are rather general and a cogent plan is lacking as to how the assessment data will be used to increase accountability and not be cost prohibitive. Outcome instruments require time to administer, score, and interpret. Additional time may be spent inputting data to track general trends for a variety of clients. Counselors, agencies, and organizations that track outcomes may require consultants to help run the data analysis and provide feedback. Although outcome research is important to addressing accountability, careful planning is required to implement accountability research.

Finally, an important acknowledgment about counseling outcomes is that positive outcomes and success are difficult to track and even achieve. For example, in the case study, Robert has a diagnosis of alcohol dependence. If Robert were to become invested in the counseling process and abstain from drugs and alcohol over a 3-month period, would such a commitment be considered a positive outcome or success? What would happen if Robert relapsed after abstaining for 3 months? Does the relapse change the outcome? These are not easy questions. One could argue that for Robert to even commit to counseling, given his long history of alcohol abuse and antisocial tendencies, is a very meaningful success. Certainly 3 months being clean and sober is a major accomplishment. If Robert learns from his relapse experience and continues to focus on his treatment, then perhaps the counseling outcomes are still positive. Of course, if Robert goes back to his antisocial, abusive nature, then he may be deemed a treatment failure.

Although outcome instruments are more readily available for mental health counselors, outcome instruments are lacking for other types of specialization, such as career counseling, rehabilitation counseling, and couple, marriage, and family counseling. Thus, addressing accountability in these environments can be difficult, especially when the presence of formal instruments is rather limited. Often, outcomes are assessed rather subjectively, such as judging if the client has received the services he or she was expecting (e.g., client satisfaction), but such an outcome may not relate to what actually occurred in the counseling process. For example, Robert has a live-in girlfriend, Catherine, who abuses cocaine and alcohol and contacted the police because of Robert's abuse. If Robert and Catherine were to request couples counseling and the relationship continued to deteriorate, resulting in a break-up, how should such an outcome be judged? From a client perspective, such an outcome may not be what Robert wanted but may be what Catherine wanted. Furthermore, given both Catherine and Robert's addiction, being separated may actually be in their best interest from a mental health perspective. Judgments of the outcome of counseling may vary, depending on what occurred and various perspectives of the client(s) and counselor.

Clearly, creating lasting, personal change through the course of counseling is a tall task. Counselors need to be realistic in identifying achievable outcomes with clients. Moreover, finding outcome assessments that are useful may also be a challenge. Sederer, Dickey, and Eisen (1997) provided eight criteria to address in implementing accountability assessment: (a) the assessment should be pertinent to the client in terms of being both useful and expedient; (b) the assessment should be able to measure change over time; (c) the assessment should be generalizable with diverse populations; (d) the assessment should be easy to implement (e.g., administer and score); (e) the assessment should not be cost prohibitive; (f) the assessment should be a collaborative process, involving both the client and the counselor; (g) the assessment should be implemented as a standard of practice; and (h) results of the assessment can be used to address accountability standards for informing practice and presenting data to stakeholders (Lambert & Hawkins, 2004; Sederer et al., 1997). In the following section, we will introduce some nonstandardized and standardized instruments that may be useful in addressing accountability in counseling.

NONSTANDARDIZED AND STANDARDIZED ASSESSMENT OF ACCOUNTABILITY

Given the broad nature of tracking outcomes, counselors should consider carefully the type of accountability assessment that may be most beneficial. Nonstandardized assessments offer the advantage of being able to individualize counseling outcomes that will be assessed. However, counselors may have difficulty communicating meaning of nonstandardized assessment results, as comparisons to others are not likely. Rather, the focus will usually be on the documentation of client progress when compared to the client's *baseline*, the client's symptoms and/or behavior prior to counseling intervention. The use of nonstandardized assessments requires planning, as the counselor will want to document baseline behavior or characteristics prior to beginning a specific intervention or task to address client change.

Standardized assessments, on the other hand, are often normed, which provide the opportunity to make comparisons and determine the extent to which the client's characteristics or behavior is extreme or outside the norm. However, standardized assessments may be rather generic and not address the specific problem(s) of what brought the client to counseling. Often, standardized assessments are used repeatedly to ascertain client change. There are two concerns with this process. First, not all measures were designed to be repeatedly administered. For example, in order to track improvement in Eva Marie's depression that accompanies her anxiety, the Beck Depression Inventory—II (BDI-II) may be administered repeatedly over time. However, the BDI-II was not developed for this purpose. The BDI-II was developed to measure the presence and severity of depression, not track client progress. Counselors should be cautious about the valid nature of the scores when using an instrument in this way. A second consideration is the presence of a *testing effect*. The repeated use of an instrument may result in the client becoming wise to what is being measured, therefore compromising the validity of the scores obtained on an administration. For example, the client may attempt to present him- or herself in the best possible light, in order to demonstrate improvement. A client could also exacerbate symptoms in order to prolong counseling, if that was what the client desired. Standardized outcome assessments are available, and these instruments were developed with the intent of being used for repeated measurement, resulting in a more valid assessment process.

Nonstandardized Assessment—Goal Attainment Scaling

Goal attainment scaling is a nonstandardized assessment in which individualized goals are measured and converted to a *T*-like score (i.e., mean of 50, *SD* of 10). Goals are scored and can be measured against a baseline. Goal attainment scaling was first published by Kiresuk and Sherman (1968), in which they presented how goals could be set, measured, and placed in a quasi-standardized format (i.e., a *T* score) to demonstrate progress in rehabilitation counseling. The reason the format is considered quasi-standardized is because a standard score, the *T*-score, is being used, but a comparison to baseline behavior for the individual is made, as opposed to the traditional comparison to a normative sample.

STEPS TO GOAL ATTAINMENT SCALING Turner-Stokes (2009) outlined a five-step process to using goal attainment scaling in assessing accountability. The first step is to identify the goals. Goals for counseling often are identified from the clinical interview/initial assessment. Goals should be stated in measurable terms. We advocate for goal setting to be a collaborative process between the counselor and client. Turner-Stokes suggested using the "SMART principle" to set goals, indicating that goals should be "specific, measurable, attainable, realistic, and timely" (p. 365). Although there is no limit to the number of goals that can be set, we encourage counselors to limit goals to three or four. Too many goals may become overwhelming to address, treat, and track.

The second step is to weight the goals. Weighting the goals allows for the client and counselor to identify both the importance and difficulty of each goal. Hence, goals that are more important or more difficult to achieve can be given more weight. To weight the goals, both the importance and the difficulty should be considered. The client is asked to identify the importance (I) of the goal and provide the following to each goal: 0 (*not at all important*), 1 (*a little important*), 2 (*moderately important*), or 3 (*very important*). A similar system is used to evaluate the difficulty (D) of each goal: 0 (*not at all difficult*), 1 (*a little difficult*), 2 (*moderately difficult*), or 3 (*very difficult*). Using this rating system, each goal can be weighted by multiplying (I × D). For example, a goal for Robert might be to attend counseling so he can appease the court. Robert may view attending counseling to be very important (3) and only a little difficult (1). Weight = I × D, or 3 × 1. Hence, attending counseling would receive a weight of 3. Note that any goal that receives a 0 on either importance or difficulty will be eliminated from the evaluation. The reason is that if a goal receives a 0 on importance, then the goal should not be a focus of counseling; if the goal receives a 0 in terms of difficulty, then time may be better spent on goals that are more difficult to accomplish and more meaningful. Turner-Stokes (2009) indicated that weighting of goals should be considered an optional process, because the benefits of incorporating weighting into the goal attainment scaling may not be beneficial. When weighting is not used, all goals will be weighted as 1. Perhaps a reason to avoid weighting goals might be from a lack of insight on the client's behalf. A natural goal for Robert is to abstain from alcohol. Because of Robert's antisocial nature and denial, Robert would be likely to view abstaining from alcohol as of little importance (1) and not difficult (0)—both of which are untrue. So, according to the weighting formula, 1 × 0 = 0, abstaining from alcohol would be eliminated, yet is still relevant if Robert is to make any progress in counseling.

The third step in goal attainment scaling is to define the expected outcome for each goal (Turner-Stokes, 2009). Once the expected outcome is defined for each goal, a measure at baseline and subsequent follow-up measures should be assessed using a 5-point scale from −2 to +2. In this scale, a 0 denotes that the *expected outcome was met*. A score of −1 indicates the client was *slightly below the expected outcome*; −2 indicates the client was *much below the expected outcome*; +1 indicates the client was *slightly above expectations*; +2 indicates the client was *far above expectations*.

The fourth step is the establishment of baseline data. As noted in the previous step, both baseline data and subsequent follow-up measures will use the 5-point scale from −2 to +2. For each of the goals, a baseline measure is assessed. Usually, baseline measures will be scored at a −1 or −2, thereby noting that the goal represents an area in which the client needs to improve.

The fifth step is the goal attainment scoring. The client and counselor may wish to identify the frequency in which goals will be evaluated (e.g., every week, once per month). We also recommend a collaborative process when rating the goals. Once goals are rated, either at baseline or subsequent sessions, the *T* score is calculated. For the purposes of goal attainment scaling, the *T* score represents an aggregate score that can be tracked over time. As a general rule, a *T* score of 50 represents that on average, the client is at the expected level of functioning; 60 represents the client is above the expected level of functioning; 70 represents the client is far above the expected level of functioning. Scores below 50 have the opposite effect. A *T* score of 40 represents the client is below the expected level of functioning; 30 represents the client is far below the expected level of functioning. The *T* score is computed with the following formula:

$$T = 50 + \frac{10 \sum (W_i X_i)}{\sqrt{[(1 - p) \sum W_i^2 + p(\sum W_i)^2]}}$$

"where W_i is the weight assigned [to each goal (if equal weights, $W_i = 1$)], X_i is the numerical value achieved (between −2 to +2), and p is the expected correlation of the goal scores" (Turner-Stokes, 2009, p. 364). Turner-Stokes indicated that p might be estimated at .30, which simplifies the equation to the following:

$$T = 50 + \frac{10 \sum (W_i X_i)}{\sqrt{[(.7 \sum W_i^2) + .3(\sum W_i)^2]}}$$

Although the formula may appear a little intimidating or complex, goal attainment scale calculators, which use Excel files, are available on the Internet. A case example using goal attainment scaling follows later in the chapter.

Standardized Assessment

As noted earlier in the chapter, many standardized instruments were not developed specifically for outcome accountability assessment. Counselors should be sure to select instruments that not only measure the construct or goals of interest but also were developed for outcome measurement. Such instruments are more likely to produce reliable and valid scores over repeated measures and be sensitive to change (Lambert & Hawkins, 2004). With this in mind, we will discuss two common outcome measures that meet these criteria, along with being relatively inexpensive and appropriate for master's-level counselors.

OQ AND Y-OQ INSTRUMENTS The OQ and Y-OQ measures are outcome questionnaires, for adults and youth, respectively, developed by OQ Measures. The OQ-45.2 is an adult measure with three subscales—Symptom Distress, Interpersonal Relationships, and Social Role—and a total score. The OQ-45.2 was highlighted in Chapter 14. To review, the scale may be administered repeatedly over time to demonstrate progress, stagnation, or regression in the aforementioned areas. Each of the items follows a Likert-type format identifying the frequency that a symptom or behavior occurs: *never, rarely, sometimes, frequently,* or *almost always.* In addition, there are five critical items that relate to substance abuse, suicidality, and hostility toward others. Internal consistency estimates for scores on the subscales range from .78 to .82; the scores for the Total subscale have an internal consistency estimate of .84. Items on the Symptom Distress subscale tend to emphasize symptoms for anxiety and depression. Items on the Interpersonal Relationships subscale tend to emphasize the client's ability to get along with others, such as friends and family. Items on the Social Role subscale tend to emphasize the ability for the client to be purposeful and productive in essential life tasks, such as school and/or work (Hanson, 2005).

The Y-OQ includes different forms, the most comprehensive being the Y-OQ-2.0, which was developed to be completed by parents, and a self-report version for adolescents to complete, the Y-OQ-2.0 SR. The parent form and self-report form were not designed to be interchangeable or equivalent. However, both instruments have 64 items and use the same subscales. The subscales include Interpersonal Distress, Somatic, Interpersonal Relationships, Critical Items, Social Problems, and Behavior Dysfunction. A Total score is also available. Reliability estimates for scores on the YOQ-2.0 range from .74 to .93 on the subscales and .97 for the Total score (Burlingame et al., 2005); reliability estimates for scores on the YOQ-2.0 SR range from .73 to .91 on the subscales and .96 for the Total score (Wells, Burlingame, & Rose, 2003). Items on the Interpersonal Distress subscale tend to emphasize symptoms for anxiety and depression. Items on the Somatic subscale tend to emphasize somatic complaints, such as headaches, stomachaches, and dizziness. Items on the Interpersonal Relationships subscale tend to emphasize attitude and communication with adults, such as parents and teachers, as well as peers. The Critical Items subscale measures symptoms consistent with psychosis (e.g., delusions, hallucinations), suicide, and disordered eating. Items on the Social Problems subscale tend to emphasize delinquent or aggressive behavior or the tendency to break rules or social norms. Items on the Behavior Dysfunction subscale tend to be consistent with symptoms for ADHD, emphasizing impulsivity, inattention, and low frustration tolerance.

Despite a Total score being available on both instruments, the subscales are probably more helpful. Elevations on the subscales highlight problem areas that may be helpful in addressing issues related to treatment planning, goal setting, and subsequent counseling sessions. The instruments developed by OQ measures tend to have strong psychometric properties and are reasonably priced, which facilitates broad use in a number of settings. Generally, individuals and organizations can purchase a license, which enables repeated use of the instrument without additional costs. More importantly, the instruments were designed for repeated use and address change over time. A practical feature of these instruments is that increases and decreases in Total scores can be tracked, which may indicate meaningful change (improvement or deterioration) that is clinically significant.

OHIO SCALES The Ohio Scales are a set of mental health outcome instruments used by the Ohio Department of Mental Health and licensed users outside of Ohio. The licensing fee for mental health providers outside of Ohio is quite reasonable, and all materials (instruments, manuals, licensing agreements) may be accessed on the Internet from the Ohio Department Of Mental Health. The instruments are divided into two categories: Adult Outcomes Instruments and Youth Outcomes Instruments.

The adult outcomes instruments are referred to as the Ohio Mental Health Consumer Outcomes System and include two forms: a self-report inventory, known as a Consumer Form, and a Provider Form. The purpose of the Adult Consumer Form is for the client to self-report "perceptions of quality of life, effects of health on functioning, medication concerns, symptom distress, and recovery/empowerment" (Ohio Department of Mental Health, 2009, p. 5-1). The Adult Consumer Form is composed of 67 items with the last 6 items reflecting demographic information. Items 1–61 reflect four sections. The first section measures Quality of Life and includes a subscale measure on Financial Status. The second section measures Safety and Health Outcomes. The third section measures Symptom Distress. The fourth section represents Making Decisions Empowerment and includes six subscales: (a) Self-esteem/Self-efficacy, (b) Power/Powerlessness, (c) Community Activism and Autonomy, (d) Optimism and Control Over the Future, (e) Righteous Anger, and (f) Overall Empowerment. The first three sections of the Adult Consumer Form use a Likert-type format with higher scores indicative of more severity or problematic areas. The fourth section, Making Decisions Empowerment, uses a 4-point scale ranging from *agree* to *disagree*. Once again, higher scores represent more severity or problematic areas. Initial studies on internal consistency estimates for scores on the Adult Consumer Form range from .77 to .93, indicating adequate reliability evidence. Further validity evidence is needed.

The Provider Adult Form may be used by counselors to ascertain functioning with regard to interpersonal relationships and social roles, adult living skills, housing status, involvement in the judicial system, risk to self and others, and victimization (Ohio Department of Mental Health, 2009). The Provider Adult Form is not parallel to the Consumer Form. Two domains are measured on the Provider Adult Form. The first domain is Functional Status and includes items that reflect issues such as socialization and social support, housing stability, adult living skills, addictive behaviors, judicial system involvement, and aggressive behaviors. The second domain, Safety and Health, assesses victimization and risk of harm to self or others. The instrument uses 4- and 5-point scales, as well as a check-list format to identify areas of concern. As a general rule, lower scores indicate more areas of concern. Initial reliability estimates are adequate, with internal consistency for scores from the normative sample at .72. No validity evidence was presented in the manual.

Unlike the Adult Outcome Instruments, the Youth Outcome Instruments consist of three somewhat parallel forms to be completed by the counselor, primary caregiver (e.g., parent), and youth. The Parent and Youth forms consist of 48 items that measure four domains: (a) Problem Severity, (b) Functioning, (c) Hopefulness, and (d) Satisfaction with Behavioral Health Services. The clinician form measures Problem Severity and Function-ing and includes an additional scale on Restrictiveness of Living Environment. Each of the sections uses a 4- to 6-point response format. Problem Severity is measured by 20 items, with higher scores indicating more severity; Functioning is measured by 20 items, with higher scores indicating increased functioning, and therefore less severity; Hopefulness is measured by 4 items, with higher scores indicating more severity or decreased hopeful-ness; Satisfaction with Behavioral Services is measured with 4 items, with higher scores indicating decreased satisfaction. Reliability estimates for internal consistency of scores range from .65 to .97. Additional validity evidence was demonstrated through correlations to other outcome instruments, such as the Child and Adolescent Functional Assessment Scale.

The benefits of the Ohio Scales are similar to the instruments published by OQ Measures. The instruments were designed for repeated use and address change over time. A practical feature of these instruments is that increases and decreases in scores can be tracked, which may indicate significant change (improvement or deterioration) that is clinically significant. As with any assessment, counselors should be cautious in interpreting these instruments. Although the breadth of the instruments addresses numerous issues typical in counseling, not much information may be gleaned regarding specific problem areas. For example, a client with a primary diagnosis of a substance abuse disorder or eating disorder may not find the questions on these instruments spe-cific enough to be helpful. An assessment instrument may be valid only when applied appropriately.

EVALUATING CLIENT PROGRESS AND IMPROVEMENT

Both nonstandardized and standardized assessments may be used to identify accountabil-ity issues in counseling. Yet, counselors should be aware that such assessment might identify client improvement or progress, yet not necessarily indicate that a client made sufficient progress or a client is doing well. For example, an adult client may endorse a number of items indicative of symptom distress. Recall that high scores on a 5-point scale indicate increased severity. Thus, a client who endorsed *almost always* (5) at baseline for items measuring symptom distress and then endorses *frequently* (4) one month later cer-tainly showed improvement, but the progress is not sufficient to deem the client well. When using assessment instruments to assess client outcomes, counselors need to be aware of the meaning of client responses and not simply pay attention to whether scores demonstrate improvement or deterioration. A client who indicates thoughts of self-harm *frequently*, as opposed to *almost always*, is still at risk.

To this end, goal attainment scaling may have a distinct advantage over a standardized measurement instrument when assessing client outcomes. The same limitation may apply to goal attainment scaling, in which change from *much below the expected outcome* (−2) to *slightly below the expected outcome* (−1) indicates improvement but not sufficient progress where the client has achieved a therapeutic goal. The difference, however, with goal attainment scaling is that two types of scores are provided—a score on each goal ranging from −2 to +2 to indicate the extent to which a goal has been met or not met and a T-like score, which serves as an aggregate score for all the goals. The *T* score is similar to a more global assessment for the individual, indicating more holistic progress. The disadvantage here is that a client could have made significant gain in a few areas, indicated by +2, but on one goal, the client could have −1, indicating a problem area. Because the *T* score is an aggregate score, high levels of progress in some areas may influence the *T* score, even though the client is still struggling in other areas. Hence, a *T* score of 60 may indicate that the client is above the expected level of therapeutic goal attainment, yet the client could still have some deficits (−1 or −2) in some areas. Looking at both the aggregate *T* score, as well as the scores for each goal, is important to consider the extent to which the client has made progress.

APPLYING GOAL ATTAINMENT SCALING TO EVA MARIE

In Chapter 14, the OQ-45.2 was discussed in relation to Robert. Therefore, Chapter 14 may be useful to review how a standardized outcome assessment may be used and reported. With this in mind, we will focus on using a nonstandardized outcome measure, goal attainment scaling, to address how such a measure can be used to inform practice.

From Eva Marie's case study, we know that Eva Marie's presenting concern is her severe and problematic anxiety. In an effort to evade and perhaps alleviate her anxiety, Eva Marie adopts an extremely unassertive and accommodating persona, which results in many additional life stressors, such as living with her mother, staying with her husband, and maintaining a job that is relatively unsatisfying. These additional stressors not only add to her stress but also contribute to some underlying depression as well.

As part of Eva Marie's treatment plan, Eva Marie and her counselor set some therapeutic goals that may also be used to measure progress. Her counselor informs Eva Marie that with her participation and consent, they can monitor her progress collaboratively and inform Eva Marie's insurance company should additional sessions be necessary beyond what is already certified. Eva Marie agrees to this plan and together they identify the following goals:

1. ***Eva Marie will be able to identify negative thoughts that lead to irrational or unhealthy behaviors or decisions and trigger anxiety symptoms.*** Because cognitive-behavioral therapies represent evidence-based practice to treating anxiety and mood disorders, her counselor begins with a treatment goal to address cognitive distortions and/or irrational beliefs.

2. ***Eva Marie will process and role-play assertiveness strategies to cope with anxiety-producing situations.*** Eva Marie tends to avoid conflict, particularly with her husband and mother. However, the avoidance of conflict and the negative outcomes that continually emanate from such avoidance result in increased anxiety anyway. By addressing ways to be more assertive, Eva Marie may be better able to exert more control in her life and alleviate some of her anxiety.

3. ***Eva Marie will engage in career exploration exercises.*** Eva Marie's job as an assistant to a school librarian contributes to her feelings of depression and adds to her stress. Her counselor knows that 30% or more of an individual's waking hours is spent at work in a given week. Therefore, engaging in career exploration activities may lead to Eva Marie enhancing her own feelings of self-efficacy and developing future goals of finding a more satisfying career.

A number of other goals could be set as well, but goals should be limited in number in order to add focus to future counseling sessions and not overwhelm the client. This does not mean that the client cannot come to counseling and process issues outside the listed goals. Rather, the purpose is to frame the client's goals and expectations for counseling.

Now that treatment goals were identified, Eva Marie and her counselor discuss weighting the goals with respect to importance and difficulty. Eva Marie admits that her negative thoughts tend to happen automatically and contribute to increased feelings of anxiety and sometimes depression. Furthermore, she is not always aware she is engaging in negative thinking. Although she notes that she needs to be more conscientious of her self-fulfilling prophecies, she often feels overwhelmed at home with her husband and mother and does not know how to manage those relationships. She also admits to being so frustrated and bored at her job that she comes home angry and depressed, which often results in negative interactions with her mother and husband. Clearly, the problems identified and the goals to address them have a systemic attribute (i.e., one problem affects another problem). Therefore, Eva Marie and her counselor decide to weight the goals equally.

The counselor collaborates with Eva Marie to establish baseline measures. He explained the rating scale of -2 to $+2$ for each goal and the meaning of the T score. Together, Eva Marie and her counselor identify the scores for each of the goals (see Table 15.1).

To compute the T score using Goal Attainment Scaling, the counselor applies the following computation:

$$T = 50 + \frac{10\sum(W_iX_i)}{\sqrt{[(.7\sum W_i^2) + .3(\sum W_i)^2]}}$$

$$= 50 + \frac{10[(1)(-2) + (1)(-2) + (1)(-1)}{\sqrt{.7(3) + .3(3^2)}}$$

$$= 50 + \frac{-50}{\sqrt{2.1 + 2.7}} = 50 + \frac{-50}{2.19} = 27.2$$

As expected, Eva Marie begins counseling below the expected levels of goal attainment. After 4 weeks of weekly counseling, some improvement was noted. Specifically, Eva

TABLE 15.1 Baseline and 1-Month Data for Eva Marie

Goal	Weight	Score	1 Month
Negative thoughts	1	−2	−1
Assertiveness	1	−1	−1
Career exploration	1	−1	0

Marie was able to notice some of her automatic negative thinking patterns. Although she notices her cognitive distortions and irrational beliefs, she lacks the coping skills to change her thought processes at this time. Hence, the counselor and Eva Marie rate her as somewhat improved but still problematic with a -1. In terms of assertiveness, Eva Marie admits nothing has changed in the way she interacts with her mother and husband. Therefore, her score for assertiveness is unchanged. Eva Marie did complete the O*NET Interest Profiler and Work Importance Profiler. Eva Marie is excited about continuing to explore career options and is even considering going back to school to complete a 4-year degree. Therefore, Eva Marie has met her career exploration goal. Based on her progress after 4 weeks, her counselor computes her T score:

$$T = 50 + \frac{10 \sum (W_i X_i)}{\sqrt{[(.7 \sum W_i^2) + .3(\sum W_i)^2]}}$$

$$= 50 + \frac{10[(1)(-1) + (1)(-1) + (1)(0)}{\sqrt{.7(3) + .3(9)}}$$

$$= 50 + \frac{-20}{2.19} = 40.90$$

The counselor and Eva Marie note the progress made toward her goals, moving from a T score of 27 to 41. However, the counselor reminds Eva Marie that if all goals were attained at an adequate level (e.g., all scores were 0), she would have a T score of 50. This serves as some objective data that encourages Eva Marie to continue in counseling. Furthermore, her counselor has some accountability data to justify further counseling sessions.

GOING BEYOND THE CLIENT: USING ASSESSMENT IN PROGRAM EVALUATION

Assessment is more than a means of helping clients; assessment can be used to improve programs that serve clients. In this respect, counselors not only assume responsibility for client care but may also play a role in oversight for the programs and procedures used by clients. Counselor training in assessment and research provides a strong background for serving organizations and agencies from a more global and holistic context. School counselors often sit on committees to determine services for students in special education programs. School counselors may also provide oversight for school accountability issues, such as educational achievement or grant-funded programs. Counselors who serve in mental health agencies, college counseling centers, rehabilitation counseling centers, and so forth may implement assessment processes to determine if programs and interventions are effective.

Although there are numerous types of program evaluation, the purpose of this section is to highlight how counselors can use assessment to evaluate and improve the programs and services rendered to clients. We selected the Accountability Bridge Counseling Program Evaluation Model by Astramovich and Coker (2007) to highlight the role of assessment in program evaluation. Interested readers are encouraged to read "Program Evaluation: The Accountability Bridge Model for Counselors" for more in-depth information about this program evaluation model. The goal of the Accountability Bridge Counseling

Program Evaluation Model is a system of planning, delivering, implementing, and evaluating counseling programs and services for clients. The Accountability Bridge Counseling Program Evaluation Model involves both the service providers and the stakeholders in two relating cycles. The *counseling program evaluation cycle* is centered on planning, implementation, and evaluation of counseling services. The *counseling context evaluation cycle* includes using evaluation data from the counseling program evaluation cycle and initiating planning, identifying needs, and establishing service objectives.

Assessment plays an important role in each of these cycles. From the counseling program evaluation cycle, counselors may use assessment strategies to monitor and refine programs once they are implemented and evaluate outcomes. In this cycle, the assessments assume both a formative and summative nature. As programs are being implemented, counselors should identify if the programs are having an initial effect through formative assessment strategies. These strategies may include nonstandardized assessment processes. A summative assessment process should follow the formative assessment. The results of the summative assessment are communicated to the stakeholders so they can begin their strategic planning. Stakeholders may desire objective data, so standardized assessment tools may be more appropriate for the summative assessment. Assessment processes continue in the counseling context evaluation cycle, where stakeholders may initiate a needs assessment to determine service objectives in future planning and programs. In conducting a needs assessment, counselors may use their skills interviewing, observing, and researching issues that will require focus from a given agency, program, or organization.

Assessment is an integral component to program evaluation. Counselors may employ assessment strategies to ensure the quality of care on behalf of clients but also to determine client needs and initiate programs and services in the community. For example, college counselors may implement a program to address drinking and drug use on a college campus. School counselors may implement a social skills group for students who struggle in this area. By being aware of the needs of the program environment and community at large, counselors may play an active role in strategic planning, program development, service delivery, and outcome measurement.

At the beginning of this book, we identified that counselors have the opportunity to identify populations of interest and determine the scope of their practice. Assessment skills affect all areas of counseling across all populations. The ability to assess clients and the programs that serve them is essential to counseling practice. Counseling outcomes are not only dependent on the services provided to the client but also the extent to which programs meet the needs of counselors who serve clients. Assessment, therefore, is a systemic dynamic that permeates the programs and services delivered by counselors to the population at large.

References

American Counseling Association. (2005). *ACA code of ethics*. Alexandria, VA: Author.

Astramovich, R. L., & Coker, J. K. (2007). Program evaluation: The Accountability Bridge Model for Counselors. *Journal of Counseling & Development, 85*, 162–172.

Balkin, R. S. (2006). A reexamination of trends in acute care psychiatric hospitalization for adolescents: Ethnicity, payment, and length of stay. *Journal of Professional Counseling: Practice Theory and Research, 34*, 49–59.

Balkin, R. S., & Roland, C. B. (2007). Re-conceptualizing stabilization for counseling adolescents in brief psychiatric hospitalization: A new model. *Journal of Counseling & Development, 85,* 64–72.

Burlingame, G. M., Wells, M. G., Cox, J. C., Lambert, M. J., Latkowski, M., & Justice, D. (2005). *Administration and scoring manual for the Y-OQ (Youth Outcome Measures).* Salt Lake, City, UT: OQ Measures LLC.

Erickson, G. (2010). Managed care and the mental health professions: History and effects on outpatient care. *Graduate Student Journal of Psychology, 12,* 3–7.

Hanson, W. E. (2005). Review of the OQ-45.2. In R. A. Spies & B. S. Plake (Eds.), *The sixteenth mental measurements yearbook.* Lincoln, NE: Buros Institute of Mental Measurements. Retrieved from Mental Measurements Yearbook with Tests in Print database.

Kiresuk, T., & Sherman, R. (1968). Goal attainment scaling: A general method of evaluating comprehensive mental health programmes. *Community Mental Health Journal, 4,* 443–453.

Lambert, M. J., & Hawkins, E. J. (2004). Measuring outcome in professional practice: Considerations in selecting and using brief outcome instruments. *Professional Psychology: Research and Practice, 35,* 492–499. doi: 10.1037/07357028.35.5.492

Lambert, M. J., Morton, J. J., Hatfield, D., Harmon, C., Hamilton, S., Reid, R. C., Shimokawa, K., … , Burlingame, G. M. (2004). Administration and scoring manual for the OQ 45.2 (Outcome Questionnaire). Salt Lake City, UT: OQ Measures, LLC.

Luk, E. S. L., Staiger, P., Mathai, J., Wong, L., Birleson, P., & Adler, R. (2001). Children with persistent conduct problems who dropout of treatment. *European Child and Adolescent Psychiatry, 10,* 28–36.

Ohio Department of Mental Health. (2009). *The Ohio mental health consumer outcomes system procedural manual* (11th ed.). Columbus, OH: Author.

Sederer, L. I., Dickey, B., & Eisen, S. V. (1997). Assessing outcomes in clinical practice. *Psychiatric Quarterly, 68,* 311–325. doi:0033–2720"7/1200-0311$12.50/0

Turner-Stokes, L. (2009). Goal attainment scaling (GAS) in rehabilitation: A practical guide. *Clinical Rehabilitation, 23,* 362–370. doi:10.1177/0269215508101742

Wells, M. G., Burlingame, G. M., & Rose, P. M. (2003). *Administration and scoring manual for the Y-OQ-SR 2.0 (Youth Outcome Questionnaire-Self Report).* Salt Lake, City, UT: OQ Measures LLC.

APPENDIX A

AREA UNDER THE NORMAL CURVE

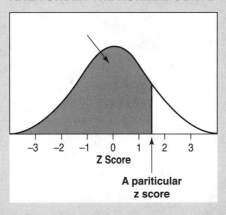

z	.00	.01	.02	.03	.04	.05	.06	.07	.08	.09
−3.0	.0013	.0014	.0014	.0015	.0015	.0016	.0016	.0017	.0018	.0018
−2.9	.0019	.0019	.0020	.0021	.0021	.0022	.0023	.0023	.0024	.0025
−2.8	.0026	.0026	.0027	.0028	.0029	.0030	.0031	.0032	.0033	.0034
−2.7	.0035	.0036	.0037	.0038	.0039	.0040	.0041	.0043	.0044	.0045
−2.6	.0047	.0048	.0049	.0051	.0052	.0054	.0055	.0057	.0059	.0060
−2.5	.0062	.0064	.0066	.0068	.0069	.0071	.0073	.0075	.0078	.0080
−2.4	.0082	.0084	.0087	.0089	.0091	.0094	.0096	.0099	.0102	.0104
−2.3	.0107	.0110	.0113	.0116	.0119	.0122	.0125	.0129	.0132	.0136
−2.2	.0139	.0143	.0146	.0150	.0154	.0158	.0162	.0166	.0170	.0174
−2.1	.0179	.0183	.0188	.0192	.0197	.0202	.0207	.0212	.0217	.0222
−2.0	.0228	.0233	.0239	.0244	.0250	.0256	.0262	.0268	.0274	.0281
−1.9	.0287	.0294	.0301	.0307	.0314	.0322	.0329	.0336	.0344	.0351
−1.8	.0359	.0367	.0375	.0384	.0392	.0401	.0409	.0418	.0427	.0436
−1.7	.0446	.0455	.0465	.0475	.0485	.0495	.0505	.0516	.0526	.0537
−1.6	.0548	.0559	.0571	.0582	.0594	.0606	.0618	.0630	.0643	.0655
−1.5	.0668	.0681	.0694	.0708	.0721	.0735	.0749	.0764	.0778	.0793
−1.4	.0808	.0823	.0838	.0853	.0869	.0885	.0901	.0918	.0934	.0951
−1.3	.0968	.0985	.1003	.1020	.1038	.1056	.1075	.1093	.1112	.1131
−1.2	.1151	.1170	.1190	.1210	.1230	.1251	.1271	.1292	.1314	.1335
−1.1	.1357	.1379	.1401	.1423	.1446	.1469	.1492	.1515	.1539	.1562

z	.00	.01	.02	.03	.04	.05	.06	.07	.08	.09
−1.0	.1587	.1611	.1635	.1660	.1685	.1711	.1736	.1762	.1788	.1814
−.9	.1841	.1867	.1894	.1922	.1949	.1977	.2005	.2033	.2061	.2090
−.8	.2119	.2148	.2177	.2206	.2236	.2266	.2296	.2327	.2358	.2389
−.7	.2420	.2451	.2483	.2514	.2546	.2578	.2611	.2643	.2676	.2709
−.6	.2743	.2776	.2810	.2843	.2877	.2912	.2946	.2981	.3015	.3050
−.5	.3085	.3121	.3156	.3192	.3228	.3264	.3300	.3336	.3372	.3409
−.4	.3446	.3483	.3520	.3557	.3594	.3632	.3669	.3707	.3745	.3783
−.3	.3821	.3859	.3897	.3936	.3974	.4013	.4052	.4090	.4129	.4168
−.2	.4207	.4247	.4286	.4325	.4364	.4404	.4443	.4483	.4522	.4562
−.1	.4602	.4641	.4681	.4721	.4761	.4801	.4840	.4880	.4920	.4960
.0	.5000	.5040	.5080	.5120	.5160	.5199	.5239	.5279	.5319	.5359
.1	.5398	.5438	.5478	.5517	.5557	.5596	.5636	.5675	.5714	.5753
.2	.5793	.5832	.5871	.5910	.5948	.5987	.6026	.6064	.6103	.6141
.3	.6179	.6217	.6255	.6293	.6331	.6368	.6406	.6443	.6480	.6517
.4	.6554	.6591	.6628	.6664	.6700	.6736	.6772	.6808	.6844	.6879
.5	.6915	.6950	.6985	.7019	.7054	.7088	.7123	.7157	.7190	.7224
.6	.7257	.7291	.7324	.7357	.7389	.7422	.7454	.7486	.7517	.7549
.7	.7580	.7611	.7642	.7673	.7704	.7734	.7764	.7794	.7823	.7852
.8	.7881	.7910	.7939	.7967	.7995	.8023	.8051	.8078	.8106	.8133
.9	.8159	.8186	.8212	.8238	.8264	.8289	.8315	.8340	.8365	.8389
1.0	.8413	.8438	.8461	.8485	.8508	.8531	.8554	.8577	.8599	.8621
1.1	.8643	.8665	.8686	.8708	.8729	.8749	.8770	.8790	.8810	.8830
1.2	.8849	.8869	.8888	.8907	.8925	.8944	.8962	.8980	.8997	.9015
1.3	.9032	.9049	.9066	.9082	.9099	.9115	.9131	.9147	.9162	.9177
1.4	.9192	.9207	.9222	.9236	.9251	.9265	.9279	.9292	.9306	.9319
1.5	.9332	.9345	.9357	.9370	.9382	.9394	.9406	.9418	.9429	.9441
1.6	.9452	.9463	.9474	.9484	.9495	.9505	.9515	.9525	.9535	.9545
1.7	.9554	.9564	.9573	.9582	.9591	.9599	.9608	.9616	.9625	.9633
1.8	.9641	.9649	.9656	.9664	.9671	.9678	.9686	.9693	.9699	.9706
1.9	.9713	.9719	.9726	.9732	.9738	.9744	.9750	.9756	.9761	.9767

z	.00	.01	.02	.03	.04	.05	.06	.07	.08	.09
2.0	.9772	.9778	.9783	.9788	.9793	.9798	.9803	.9808	.9812	.9817
2.1	.9821	.9826	.9830	.9834	.9838	.9842	.9846	.9850	.9854	.9857
2.2	.9861	.9864	.9868	.9871	.9875	.9878	.9881	.9884	.9887	.9890
2.3	.9893	.9896	.9898	.9901	.9904	.9906	.9909	.9911	.9913	.9916
2.4	.9918	.9920	.9922	.9925	.9927	.9929	.9931	.9932	.9934	.9936
2.5	.9938	.9940	.9941	.9943	.9945	.9946	.9948	.9949	.9951	.9952
2.6	.9953	.9955	.9956	.9957	.9959	.9960	.9961	.9962	.9963	.9964
2.7	.9965	.9966	.9967	.9968	.9969	.9970	.9971	.9972	.9973	.9974
2.8	.9974	.9975	.9976	.9977	.9977	.9978	.9979	.9979	.9980	.9981
2.9	.9981	.9982	.9982	.9983	.9984	.9984	.9985	.9985	.9986	.9986
3.0	.9987	.9987	.9987	.9988	.9988	.9989	.9989	.9989	.9990	.9990

APPENDIX B

COMPETENCIES IN ASSESSMENT AND EVALUATION FOR SCHOOL COUNSELORS
Approved by the American School Counselor Association
on September 21, 1998,
and by the Association for Assessment in Counseling
on September 10, 1998[1]

The purpose of these competencies is to provide a description of the knowledge and skills that school counselors need in the areas of assessment and evaluation. Because effectiveness in assessment and evaluation is critical to effective counseling, these competencies are important for school counselor education and practice. Although consistent with existing Council for Accreditation of Counseling and Related Educational Programs (CACREP) and National Association of State Directors of Teacher Education and Certification (NASDTEC) standards for preparing counselors, they focus on competencies of individual counselors rather than content of counselor education programs.

The competencies can be used by counselor and assessment educators as a guide in the development and evaluation of school counselor preparation programs, workshops, inservice, and other continuing education opportunities. They may also be used by school counselors to evaluate their own professional development and continuing education needs.

School counselors should meet each of the nine numbered competencies and have the specific skills listed under each competency.

Competency 1.   School counselors are skilled in choosing assessment strategies.
   a. They can describe the nature and use of different types of formal and informal assessments, including questionnaires, checklists, interviews, inventories, tests, observations, surveys, and performance assessments, and work with individuals skilled in clinical assessment.
   b. They can specify the types of information most readily obtained from different assessment approaches.
   c. They are familiar with resources for critically evaluating each type of assessment and can use them in choosing appropriate assessment strategies.
   d. They are able to advise and assist others (e.g., a school district) in choosing appropriate assessment strategies.

Competency 2.   School counselors can identify, access, and evaluate the most commonly used assessment instruments.
   a. They know which assessment instruments are most commonly used in school settings to assess intelligence, aptitude, achievement, personality, work values, and interests, including computer-assisted versions and other alternate formats.
   b. They know the dimensions along which assessment instruments should be evaluated, including purpose, validity, utility, norms, reliability and measurement error, score reporting method, and consequences of use.
   c. They can obtain and evaluate information about the quality of those assessment instruments.

---

[1]A joint committee of the American School Counselor Association (ASCA) and the Association for Assessment in Counseling (AAC) was appointed by the respective presidents in 1993 with the charge to draft a statement about school counselor preparation in assessment and evaluation. Committee members were Ruth Ekstrom (AAC), Patricia Elmore (AAC, Chair, 1997-1999), Daren Hutchinson (ASCA), Marjorie Mastie (AAC), Kathy O'Rourke (ASCA), William Schafer (AAC, Chair, 1993-1997), Thomas Trotter (ASCA), and Barbara Webster (ASCA).

Competency 3.   School counselors are skilled in the techniques of administration and methods of scoring assessment instruments.

a. They can implement appropriate administration procedures, including administration using computers.
b. They can standardize administration of assessments when interpretation is in relation to external norms.
c. They can modify administration of assessments to accommodate individual differences consistent with publisher recommendations and current statements of professional practice.
d. They can provide consultation, information, and training to others who assist with administration and scoring.
e. They know when it is necessary to obtain informed consent from parents or guardians before administering an assessment.

Competency 4.   School counselors are skilled in interpreting and reporting assessment results.

a. They can explain scores that are commonly reported, such as percentile ranks, standard scores, and grade equivalents. They can interpret a confidence interval for an individual score based on a standard error of measurement.
b. They can evaluate the appropriateness of a norm group when interpreting the scores of an individual or a group.
c. They are skilled in communicating assessment information to others, including teachers, administrators, students, parents, and the community. They are aware of the rights students and parents have to know assessment results and decisions made as a consequence of any assessment.
d. They can evaluate their own strengths and limitations in the use of assessment instruments and in assessing students with disabilities or linguistic or cultural differences. They know how to identify professionals with appropriate training and experience for consultation.
e. They know the legal and ethical principles about confidentiality and disclosure of assessment information and recognize the need to abide by district policy on retention and use of assessment information.

Competency 5.   School counselors are skilled in using assessment results in decision-making.

a. They recognize the limitations of using a single score in making an educational decision and know how to obtain multiple sources of information to improve such decisions.
b. They can evaluate their own expertise for making decisions based on assessment results. They also can evaluate the limitations of conclusions provided by others, including the reliability and validity of computer-assisted assessment interpretations.
c. They can evaluate whether the available evidence is adequate to support the intended use of an assessment result for decision-making, particularly when that use has not been recommended by the developer of the assessment instrument.
d. They can evaluate the rationale underlying the use of qualifying scores for placement in educational programs or courses of study.
e. They can evaluate the consequences of assessment-related decisions and avoid actions that would have unintended negative consequences.

Competency 6.   School counselors are skilled in producing, interpreting, and presenting statistical information about assessment results.

a. They can describe data (e.g., test scores, grades, demographic information) by forming frequency distributions, preparing tables, drawing graphs, and calculating descriptive indices of central tendency, variability, and relationship.
b. They can compare a score from an assessment instrument with an existing distribution, describe the placement of a score within a normal distribution, and draw appropriate inferences.
c. They can interpret statistics used to describe characteristics of assessment instruments, including difficulty and discrimination indices, reliability and validity coefficients, and standard errors of measurement.

    d. They can identify and interpret inferential statistics when comparing groups, making predictions, and drawing conclusions needed for educational planning and decisions.

    e. They can use computers for data management, statistical analysis, and production of tables and graphs for reporting and interpreting results.

Competency 7.   **School counselors are skilled in conducting and interpreting evaluations of school counseling programs and counseling-related interventions.**

    a. They understand and appreciate the role that evaluation plays in the program development process throughout the life of a program.

    b. They can describe the purposes of an evaluation and the types of decisions to be based on evaluation information.

    c. They can evaluate the degree to which information can justify conclusions and decisions about a program.

    d. They can evaluate the extent to which student outcome measures match program goals.

    e. They can identify and evaluate possibilities for unintended outcomes and possible impacts of one program on other programs.

    f. They can recognize potential conflicts of interest and other factors that may bias the results of evaluations.

Competency 8.   **School counselors are skilled in adapting and using questionnaires, surveys, and other assessments to meet local needs.**

    a. They can write specifications and questions for local assessments.

    b. They can assemble an assessment into a usable format and provide directions for its use.

    c. They can design and implement scoring processes and procedures for information feedback.

Competency 9.   **School counselors know how to engage in professionally responsible assessment and evaluation practices.**

    a. They understand how to act in accordance with ACA's *Code of Ethics and Standards of Practice* and ASCA's *Ethical Standards for School Counselors.*

    b. They can use professional codes and standards, including the *Code of Fair Testing Practices in Education, Code of Professional Responsibilities in Educational Measurement, Responsibilities of Users of Standardized Tests,* and *Standards for Educational and Psychological Testing,* to evaluate counseling practices using assessments.

    c. They understand test fairness and can avoid the selection of biased assessment instruments and biased uses of assessment instruments. They can evaluate the potential for unfairness when tests are used incorrectly and for possible bias in the interpretation of assessment results.

    d. They understand the legal and ethical principles and practices regarding test security, copying copyrighted materials, and unsupervised use of assessment instruments that are not intended for self-administration.

    e. They can obtain and maintain available credentialing that demonstrates their skills in assessment and evaluation.

    f. They know how to identify and participate in educational and training opportunities to maintain competence and acquire new skills in assessment and evaluation.

Definitions of Terms

Competencies describe skills or understandings that a school counselor should possess to perform assessment and evaluation activities effectively.

Assessment is the gathering of information for decision making about individuals, groups, programs, or processes. Assessment targets include abilities, achievements, personality variables, aptitudes, attitudes, preferences, interests, values, demographics, and other characteristics. Assessment procedures include but are not limited to standardized and unstandardized tests, questionnaires, inventories, checklists, observations, portfolios, performance assessments, rating scales, surveys, interviews, and other clinical measures.

Evaluation is the collection and interpretation of information to make judgments about individuals, programs, or processes that lead to decisions and future actions.

APPENDIX C

STANDARDS FOR ASSESSMENT IN MENTAL HEALTH COUNSELING

The purpose of these training standards is to provide a description of the knowledge and skills that mental health counselors need in the areas of assessment and evaluation. Because effectiveness in assessment and evaluation is critical to effective counseling, these training standards are important for mental health counselor education and practice. Consistent with existing Council for Accreditation of Counseling and Related Educational Programs (CACREP) standards for preparing counselors, they focus on standards for individual counselors and the recommended content of counselor education programs. These standards represent aspirations for competent professional practice and can be used by counselor and assessment educators as a guide in the development, delivery, and evaluation of mental health counselor preparation programs, workshops, in-services, and other continuing education opportunities. They may also be used by mental health counselors to evaluate their own professional development and continuing education needs.

During training, mental health counselors should aspire to meet each of the following assessment standards and have the specific skills listed under each.

Standard I. Mental health counselors use structured and semi-structured clinical interviews, and qualitative assessment procedures (e.g., role playing, life line assessments, direct and indirect observation). Mental health counselors are able to:

1. Define the differences and similarities between structured and semi-structured clinical interviews.
2. Describe the advantages and disadvantages of structured and semi-structured clinical interviews in practice.
3. Use both structured and semi-structured clinical interviews as a means to develop goal setting and treatment intervention plans.
4. Understand the advantages and disadvantages of qualitative assessment procedures.
5. Apply the concepts of continuous assessment and wraparound services.

Standard II. Mental health counselors are skilled in instrument evaluation, selection, and usage. Mental health counselors are able to:

1. Select, administer, score, analyze and interpret commonly used clinical mental health instruments.
2. Identify the strengths and limitations of instruments.

Standard III. Mental health counselors are knowledgeable of diversity issues and the specific uses of mental health instruments. Mental health counselors are able to:

1. Identify the purposes of commonly used clinical mental health instruments.
2. Identify limitations of instruments, including the inaccurate portrayal of persons from diverse backgrounds (e.g., culture, age, sexuality, spirituality), particularly as presenting with atypical thoughts, emotions, behavior, or psychopathology.
3. Identify appropriate and inappropriate uses of commonly used clinical mental health instruments.

Standard IV. Mental health counselors critically evaluate instruments. Mental health counselors are able to:

1. Define and describe the various types of reliability and validity, as well as measures of error.
2. Identify acceptable reliability levels for personality, projective, intelligence, career and specialty instruments.
3. Identify the types and acceptable levels of validity typically associated with personality, projective, intelligence, career and specialty instruments.
4. Evaluate norming methods used to establish testing instruments commonly used within mental health counseling.

5. Identify where and how they may locate and obtain information about testing instruments commonly used within mental health counseling.
6. Identify means to locate and obtain assessment instruments for special populations (e.g., visually impaired persons, non-readers).
7. Use computer administered and scored instruments.

Standard V. Mental health counselors use a broad spectrum of assessment instruments, including general personality, projective, intelligence, career, and specialty instruments which identify specific pathology or mental health in a defined area. Mental health counselors are able to:

1. Use instruments which aid in diagnosing psychopathology (e.g., structured and semi-structured diagnostic interviews, omnibus measures of psychopathology).
2. Assess mood disorders (e.g., depression, mania, cycling mood).
3. Assess anxiety disorders (e.g., phobic and avoidance responses, lingering reactions to stressors).
4. Assess disorders of behavior dysregulation (e.g. chemical addictions, eating disorders, impulse control disorders, sexual disorders, sleep disorders).
5. Assess psychological disorders associated with somatic symptoms (e.g., somatization disorders, life-style induced physical illness).
6. Assess personality traits and disorders of personality.
7. Assess mental capacity and function (e.g., intelligence, aptitude, achievement, academic skills, learning process, and characteristics).

Standard VI. Mental health counselors use assessment to develop effective treatment interventions and goal setting. Mental health counselors are able to:

1. Use assessment findings from personality, projective, intelligence, career, and specialty instruments to provide clinical interventions addressing concerns and problems.
2. Use assessment findings from personality, projective, intelligence, career, and specialty instruments to establish treatment goals.
3. Use multiple assessment sources (e.g., direct observation, assessment instruments, structured clinical interviews) and integrate these results in a manner that benefits clients.

Standard VII. Mental health counselors are skilled in communicating assessment results. Mental health counselors are able to:

1. Describe and obtain informed consent, when appropriate.
2. Indicate what has to occur before information from testing instruments can be provided to persons other than the test taker.
3. Communicate assessment instrument results in a helpful, non-threatening manner that benefits clients.
4. Present assessment results to clients and other nonprofessional audiences using clear, unambiguous, jargon-free language which recognizes both client strengths and client problems in a manner which communicates respect and compassion.

Standard VIII. Mental health counselors can determine the efficacy of treatment programs and clinical interventions by using multiple assessment instruments with program participants. Mental health counselors are able to:

1. Use repeated testing evaluation designs that aid in the determination of program efficacy.
2. Create or select standardized instruments that can measure treatment outcomes.

Standard IX. Mental health counselors continually enhance their professional development within the area of assessment. Mental health counselors:

1. Participate in assessment training and development workshops, conferences, and other educational experiences that promote continual professional development related to assessment.

2. Are aware of advancements within the area of assessment by keeping abreast of current assessment topics written within the profession's journals and other professional sources (e.g., books, test reviews, distance learning).
3. Join professional associations that provide relevant assessment and mental health information.

Standard X. Mental health counselors are aware of the appropriate use of assessment instruments in research and in accordance with the Code of Ethics and Standards of Practice of the American Counseling Association and the American Mental Health Counseling Association. Mental health counselors:

1. Engage in research that uses assessment instruments in a manner that reflects the intended purpose of the instrument.
2. Use assessment instruments within the practice of research in a manner that does not cause harm to program participants.
3. Choose assessment instruments which have potential to increase participant insight and promote greater participant mental health.

Standard XI. Advanced or supervising mental health counselors and counselor educators who train mental health counselors promote assessment skill acquisition. Counselor educators and supervisors:

1. Meet Standard I through Standard X above.
2. Use curriculum instruction methods that promote assessment and evaluation skill acquisition.

Standard XII. Mental health counselors, supervising counselors, and counselor educators comply with the most recent codes of ethics of the American Counseling Association (ACA), American Mental Health Counseling Association (AMHCA), National Board for Certified Counselors (NBCC), and with the laws and regulations of any state licensing board in which the counselor is licensed to practice mental health counseling. Mental health counselors practice in accord with the Code of Fair Testing Practices in Education, Standards for Educational and Psychological Testing, Responsibilities of Users of Standardized Tests, and Rights and Responsibilities of Test Takers: Guidelines and Expectations.

Definitions of Terms

Assessment: active collection of information about individuals, populations, or treatment programs.

General Instruments: well-established, broad-spectrum instruments, which provide multiple indicators regarding the client (e.g., *MMP I-II, MCMI-III, 16PF:5th Ed.*). Typically, general assessment instruments are composed of clinical subscales, which indicate preferred behaviors or recurrent patterns of thinking or behaving.

Guidelines: recommendations in assessment training and professional practice to mental health counselor educators and mental health counselors.

Instruments: standardized or nonstandardized tests, interviews, rating scales, inventories, or checklists used by mental health counselors to better understand the client, the client's past history, the client's current social, employment, physical or interpersonal environment, the client's intellectual functioning, the client's personality, or the client's presenting concerns.

Qualitative: detailed descriptions of situations, events, people, interactions, and observed behaviors.

Specialty instruments: instruments designed primarily to provide specific information regarding a client's functioning. For example, these instruments might be used to provide specific information related to a client's substance abusing behaviors (e.g., *SASSI- III*) or related to a client's presenting degree of depression (e.g., *The Beck Depression Inventory – 2nd ed.*).

Standards: minimal levels of skill, knowledge, or training.

Structured clinical interviews: clinical interviews with individuals, couples families, or groups in which the mental health counselor asks questions precisely as directed by the instrument's author(s). Questions are posed in the order defined by the authors and responses are recorded according to specific directions.

Unstructured clinical interviews: clinical interviews in which the mental health counselor is free to pursue related lines of inquiry to gain needed or pertinent information.

These standards were developed as a joint effort between the Association for Assessment in Counseling and Education (AACE) and the American Mental Health Counseling Association (AMHCA). The joint committee included Dr. Bradley T. Erford (Chair), Dr. Rob Gerst, Dr. Valerie Schweibert, Dr. Debra Wells, and Dr. F. Robert Wilson. Initial drafts of these standards were constructed through substantial input from Dr. Gerald Juhnke, Dr. Dale Pietrzak, Dr. Sondra Smith, Dr. William Kline, and Dr. Richard Balkin.

APPENDIX D

STANDARDS FOR ASSESSMENT IN SUBSTANCE ABUSE COUNSELING

These training standards provide a description of the knowledge and skills needed by substance abuse counselors in the areas of assessment and evaluation. Because effectiveness in assessment and evaluation is critical to effective counseling, these training standards are important for substance abuse counselor education and practice. Consistent with existing Council for Accreditation of Counseling and Related Educational Programs (CACREP) standards for preparing counselors, they focus on standards for individual counselors and the content of counselor education programs. The standards, which represent aspirations for competent professional practice, can be used by counselor and assessment educators as a guide in the development and evaluation of substance abuse counselor preparation programs, workshops, in-services, and other continuing education opportunities. They may also be used by substance abuse counselors to evaluate their own professional development and continuing education needs.

During training, substance abuse counselors should meet each of the following assessment standards and have the specific skills listed under each standard.

Standard I. Substance abuse counselors are able to assess the effects and withdrawal symptoms of commonly abused drugs. Substance abuse counselors can:
1. Assess for and recognize acute intoxication syndromes for commonly abused chemicals (i.e., alcohol, benzodiazepines, marijuana, cocaine).
2. Assess for and recognize withdrawal complications (i.e., seizures, delirium tremens, hallucinations).
3. Assess for and recognize the effects of cross-addiction and dual addiction disorders.
4. Assess for and recognize symptoms of inhalant use (e.g. the smell of fuel on clothes, red eyes, runny nose, cough).

Standard II. Substance abuse counselors can assess the broad spectrum of concomitant disorders. Substance abuse counselors can:
1. Assess for other addictive disorders (i.e., gambling, food, sex).
2. Determine if a psychological disorder (i.e., anxiety, depression, panic, Post Traumatic Stress Disorder) was present prior to, or the result of, clients' substance use.
3. Assess for Attention-Deficit/Hyperactive Disorder (AD/HD).
4. Assess for suicidal or homicidal ideation.
5. Assess for the presence or possibility of domestic violence.
6. Use and interpret the results of adult and adolescent intelligence instruments.

Standard III. Substance abuse counselors are skilled in evaluating the technical quality and appropriateness of testing instruments. Substance abuse counselors can:
1. Identify acceptable reliability levels for instruments.
2. Identify appropriate types of validity for commonly used instruments.
3. Evaluate the procedures used to validate commonly used instruments.
4. Locate testing instruments and information about instruments for special populations (e.g. visually impaired, nonreaders).
5. Use computerized assessment instruments.
6. Articulate the limitations of commonly used instruments within the substance abuse counseling field.

Standard IV. Substance abuse counselors are knowledgeable regarding qualitative assessment procedures including structured and semi-structured clinical interviews. Substance abuse counselors:

1. Are familiar with the advantages and disadvantages of structured and semi-structured clinical interviews.
2. Are familiar with qualitative assessment procedures (e.g. role playing, life line assessments, direct and indirect observations).
3. Understand the advantages and disadvantages of qualitative assessment procedures.
4. Understand the concepts of continuous assessment and wraparound services.

Standard V. Substance abuse counselors employ multiple methods when assessing clients and monitoring the efficacy of treatment. Substance abuse counselors:

1. Use paper and pencil or computerized instruments and structured interviews, as appropriate.
2. Whenever possible, consult with and interview family, friends, and other corroborating sources of information, while always obtain written consent to gather information from sources other than the client.
3. Monitor client progress throughout the counseling process.

Standard VI. Substance abuse counselors are skilled in interpreting assessment results with clients. Substance abuse counselors can:

1. Interpret assessment results in a helpful manner that emphasizes clients' strengths as well as possible problem areas.
2. Explain to clients the steps that are necessary to share testing results with others (e.g. informed consent).

Standard VII. Substance abuse counselors are skilled in using assessment results to develop and evaluate effective treatment interventions. Substance abuse counselors can:

1. Accurately score, analyze, and interpret the results of testing.
2. Create specific treatment plans based upon the results of testing.

Standard VIII. Substance abuse counselors are aware of the need for professional development within the assessment area. Substance abuse counselors:

1. Participate in training needed to keep abreast of new assessment instruments, procedures, and issues.
2. Keep up to date with advancements in the field of assessment by reading the appropriate professional journals, test manuals, and reports.
3. Join professional associations that provide relevant assessment and substance abuse information.

Standard IX. Substance abuse counselors are aware of the appropriate use of assessment instruments in research. Substance abuse counselors use assessment instruments:

1. To determine the efficacy of their interventions.
2. Appropriate for the intended population/clients.
3. In accordance with the *American Counseling Association's Ethical Standards, Code of Fair Testing Practices, Standards for Educational and Psychological Testing, Responsibilities of Users of Standardized Tests,* and *Test Takers, Rights and Responsibilities.*

Standard XI. Counselor educators and supervisors of substance abuse counselors-in-training are able to effectively train counselors in the area of substance abuse assessment. Counselor educators and supervisors:

1. Keep current with scholarship related to how to teach counselors-in-training how to best use assessment instruments in their work with clients.
2. Are knowledgeable in the selection, use, evaluation, and interpretation of assessment instruments.

Definitions of Terms

Assessment: active collection of information about individuals, populations, or treatment programs.

Instruments: standardized or nonstandardized tests, interviews, rating scales, inventories, or checklists used by mental health counselors to better understand the client, the client's past history, the client's current social, employment, physical or interpersonal environment, the client's intellectual functioning, the client's personality, or the client's presenting concerns.

Standards: minimal levels of skill, knowledge, or training.

Structured clinical interviews: clinical interviews to individuals, couples, families, or groups in which the mental health counselor asks questions precisely as directed by the instrument's author(s). Questions are posed in the order defined by the authors and responses are recorded according to specific directions.

Unstructured clinical interviews: clinical interviews in which the mental health counselor is free to pursue related lines of inquiry to gain needed or pertinent information.

These standards were developed as a joint effort between the Association for Assessment in Counseling and Education (AACE) and the International Association of Addictions and Offenders Counselors (IAAOC). The joint committee included Dr. Bradley T. Erford (Chair), Dr. Gerald Juhnke, Dr. Russell Curtis, Mr. Joe Jordan, Dr. Kenneth Coll.

APPENDIX E

MARRIAGE, COUPLE AND FAMILY COUNSELING ASSESSMENT COMPETENCIES

The Marriage, Couple, and Family Counseling Assessment Competencies provide a description of the knowledge and skills counselors aspire to possess in order to be effective in assessment and evaluation. These assessment competencies, which represent aspirations for competent professional practice, can be used as a guide in the development and evaluation of counselor education programs, workshops, in-services, and other continuing education opportunities. The competencies are the result of collaboration between the Association for Assessment in Counseling and Education (AACE) and the International Association of Marriage and Family Counselors (IAMFC) professionals in the field and represent the only existing assessment competencies for marriage, couple and family counselors to date.

Competency 1. *Counselors understand the historical perspectives of systems concepts, theories and assessment methods that are fundamental to marriage, couple and family counseling. Marriage, couple and family counselors can...*

a. Understand and articulate systems concepts, theories and historical perspectives that provide the conceptual foundation for marriage, couple and family assessment.

b. Compare and contrast various models of marriage, couple and family assessments, and explain their unit of measure and the meaning of the results.

c. Assess issues of gender development, human sexuality, intergenerational dynamics, and couple processes.

d. Assess marriages, couples and families across the family life cycle (i.e., premarital, newlyweds, parents with young children, parents with adolescents, parents with adult children and relationships in later life).

e. Assess a broad spectrum of concomitant disorders, such as addictive disorders (e.g. alcohol, drugs, gambling, food), and psychological disorders (e.g., anxiety, depression, panic).

f. Use and interpret the results of child, adolescent and adult intelligence instruments.

g. Evaluate the strengths and limitations of various theoretical models of marriage, couple and family assessment and diagnosis.

Competency 2. *Counselors understand basic concepts of standardized and non-standardized testing and other assessment techniques. Marriage, couple and family counselors can...*

a. Explain the differences between norm-referenced and criterion-referenced assessment.

b. Articulate the need for and use of environmental assessment.

c. Understand and use performance assessments.

d. Understand the use of individual and group test and inventory methods.

e. Effectively make and document behavioral observations during assessment.

f. Understand the limitations of computer-managed and computer-assisted assessment methods.

Competency 3. *Counselors understand quantitative and qualitative concepts of assessment. Marriage, couple and family counselors can...*

a. Carefully evaluate the specific theoretical bases and characteristics, score validity, score reliability and appropriateness of the instrument being used.

b. Understand statistical concepts including scales of measurement, measures of central tendency, indices of variability, shapes and types of distributions, and correlations.

c. Use qualitative assessment procedures including unstructured, semi-structured, and structured clinical interviews.

d. Select, use, evaluate, and interpret assessment instruments.

Competency 4.   *Counselors understand the strengths and limitations of models of assessment and diagnosis, especially as they relate to the assessment and evaluation of individuals, groups, and specific populations. Marriage, couple and family counselors can...*

a. Demonstrate clinical competence when assessing marriages, couples and families of various cultural backgrounds including differences in age, gender, sexual orientation, ethnicity, language, disability, culture, spirituality, and other factors related to the assessment and evaluation of individuals, groups, and specific populations.

b. Evaluate the accuracy and cultural relevance of behavioral health and relational diagnoses.

c. Use various assessment methods that identify clients' strengths, resilience and resources.

d. Ensure that computer-generated test administration and scoring programs function and are interpreted properly so that clients are provided accurate test results.

e. Screen and develop adequate safety plans for substance abuse, child and elder maltreatment, domestic violence, physical violence, suicide potential, and dangerousness to self and others.

f. Provide assessments and deliver developmentally appropriate services to clients, such as children, adolescents, elders, and persons with special needs.

g. Apply individual, marital, couple and family assessments appropriate to specific presenting problems, practice settings, and cultural contexts.

h. Accurately score, analyze, and interpret the results of standardized testing instruments.

i. Conduct structured clinical interviews, obtain an accurate biopsychosocial history and assess intergenerational dynamics and contextual factors related to clients' family of origin (e.g., genograms).

j. Apply qualitative assessment procedures (e.g., role playing, family sculptures, life-line assessments, direct and indirect observations) and understand their advantages and disadvantages.

Competency 5.   *Counselors use various ethical strategies for selecting, administering, and interpreting assessment and evaluation instruments and techniques in marriage, couple and family counseling. Marriage, couple and family counselors can...*

a. Act in accordance with the *ACA Code of Ethics* (American Counseling Association, 2005), *Code of Fair Testing Practices* (Joint Committee on Testing Practices, 2004), *Ethical Code of the International Association for Marriage and Family Counselors* (IAMFC, 2005), *Standards for Educational and Psychological Testing* (American Educational Research Association, American Psychological Association & National Council on Measurement in Education, 1999), *Responsibilities of Users of Standardized Tests* (Association for Assessment in Counseling, 2003), and *Rights and Responsibilities of Test Takers* (Joint Committee of Testing Practices, 2002).

b. Select appropriate standardized measures based on developmental stage and interpersonal processes (e.g., couple, partner, family, system dynamics, or severity of presenting problems).

c. Identify psychometric limitations when selecting and using an instrument.

d. Follow all directions and researched procedures for selection, administration and interpretation of all evaluation instruments and use them only within proper contexts.

e. Maintain test security and avoid prior coaching or dissemination of test materials which can invalidate test results.

References

American Counseling Association. (2005). *ACA code of ethics.* Alexandria, VA: Author.

American Educational Research Association, American Psychological Association, and the National Council on Measurement in Education. (1999). *Standards for educational and psychological testing.* Washington DC: American Psychological Association.

Association for Assessment in Counseling. (2003). *Responsibilities of users of standardized tests* (RUST). Alexandria, VA: Author.

International Association for Marriage and Family Counselors. (2005). *Ethical Code of the International Association of Marriage and Family Counselors.* Retrieved from http://www.iamfc.com/ethical_codes.html

Joint Committee on Testing Practices. (2004). *Code of fair testing practices in education.* Washington, DC: Author

Joint Committee on Testing Practices. (2000). *Rights and responsibilities of test takers: Guidelines and expectations.* Washington, DC: Author.

National Board of Certified Counselors. (2005). NBCC *code of ethics.* Greensboro, NC: Author.

Documents Reviewed for the Development of Assessment Competencies

American Counseling Association. (2005). *ACA code of ethics and standards of practice.* Alexandria, VA: Author.

Association of Marital and Family Therapy. (2004). *Marriage and family therapy core competencies.* Retrieved from http://www.aamft.org

Council for Accreditation of Counseling and Related Educational Programs. (2009). *CACREP Standards.* Retrieved from ttp://www.cacrep.org/template/index.cfm

National Board of Certified Counselors. (2005). *NBCC code of ethics.* Greensboro, NC: Author

These standards were developed as a joint effort between the Association for Assessment in Counseling and Education (AACE) and the International Association of Marriage and Family Counselors (IAMFC). The joint committee included Dr. Jeffrey W. Garrett (Chair), Dr. Richard. S. Balkin, Dr. James M. Devlin, Dr. Bradley T. Erford, Dr. Brandé Flamez, Samantha Mendoza, Dr. Robert Smith, and Dr. Janet Wall.

APPENDIX F

CAREER COUNSELOR ASSESSMENT AND EVALUATION COMPETENCIES
Adopted by the
National Career Development Association
on January 10, 2010
Association for Assessment in Counseling and Education
on March 20, 2010

The purpose of these competencies is to provide a description of the knowledge and skills that career counselors must demonstrate in the areas of assessment and evaluation. Because effectiveness in assessment and evaluation is critical to effective career counseling, these competencies are critical for career counselor practice and service to students, clients, and other customers.

The competencies can be used by counselors as a guide in the development and evaluation of workshops, inservice, and other continuing education opportunities, as well as to evaluate their own professional development, and by counselor educators as a guide in the development and evaluation of career counselor preparation programs.

Competent career counselors strive to meet each of the eight numbered competencies and exhibit the specific knowledge, understandings, and skills listed under each competency.

Career Counselors are skilled in:

Competency 1. *choosing assessment strategies.* **Career counselors ...**
a. can describe the nature and use of different types of formal and informal assessments, including questionnaires, checklists, interviews, inventories, tests, observations, surveys, and performance assessments, and they work with individuals skilled in clinical assessment.
b. can specify the types of information most readily obtained from different assessment approaches.
c. can identity the type of information needed to assist the client and select the assessment strategy accordingly.
d. are familiar with resources for critically evaluating each type of assessment and can use the resources to choose appropriate assessment strategies.
e. are able to advise and assist organizations, such as educational institutions and governmental agencies, in choosing appropriate assessment strategies.
f. use only those assessments for which they are properly and professionally trained.

Competency 2. *identifying, accessing, and evaluating the most commonly used assessment instruments.* **Career counselors ...**
a. know which assessment areas are most commonly assessed in career counseling, such as ability, skills, personality, preference work style, career thoughts and barriers, work values, and interests, including alternate formats.
b. know the factors by which assessment instruments should be evaluated, including developmental procedures, target audience, purpose, validity, utility, norms, reliability and measurement error, score reporting method, cost, and consequences of use.
c. obtain and evaluate information about the quality of career assessment instruments used.
d. use the highest quality instruments available with their students, clients, or customers.

Competency 3. *using the techniques of administration and methods of scoring assessment instruments.* **Career counselors ...**
a. implement appropriate administration procedures, including administration using computers.

b. follow strict standardized administration procedures as dictated by the directions and resulting interpretation.

c. modify administration of assessments to accommodate individual differences consistent with publisher recommendations and current statements of professional practice.

d. provide consultation, information, and training to others who assist with administration and scoring and follow the guidance of others who are more extensively trained.

Competency 4. *interpreting and reporting assessment results.* **Career counselors ...**

a. can explain scores that are commonly reported, interpret a confidence interval for an individual score based on a standard error of measurement, and always consider the impreciseness of assessment results.

b. evaluate the appropriateness of a norm group when interpreting the scores of an individual or a group.

c. are skilled in communicating assessment information to the client and others, including peers, supervisors and the public.

d. evaluate their own strengths and limitations in the use of assessment instruments and in assessing clients with disabilities or linguistic or cultural differences.

e. know how to identify professionals with appropriate training and experience for consultation.

f. follow the legal and ethical principles regarding confidentiality and disclosure of assessment information, and recognize the need to abide by professional credentialing and ethical standards on the protection and use of assessments.

Competency 5. *using assessment results in decision making.* **Career counselors ...**

a. recognize the limitations of using a single score in making an educational or career decision and know how to access multiple sources of information to improve decisions.

b. evaluate their own expertise for making decisions based on assessment results, and also the limitations of conclusions provided by others, including the reliability and validity of computer-assisted assessment interpretations.

c. determine whether the available technical evidence is adequate to support the intended use of an assessment result for decision making, particularly when that use has not been recommended by the developer of the assessment instrument.

d. can evaluate the consequences of assessment-related decisions and avoid actions that would have unintended negative consequences.

Competency 6. *producing, interpreting, and presenting statistical information about assessment results.* **Career counselors ...**

a. can describe data (e.g., test scores, grades, demographic information) by forming frequency distributions, preparing tables, drawing graphs, and calculating descriptive indices of central tendency, variability, and relationship.

b. can compare a score from an assessment instrument with an existing distribution, describe the placement of a score within a normal distribution, and draw appropriate inferences.

c. interpret statistics used to describe characteristics of assessment instruments, especially reliability coefficients, validity studies, and standard errors of measurement.

d. can use computers for data management, statistical analysis, and production of tables and graphs for reporting and interpreting results.

Competency 7. *engaging in professionally responsible assessment and evaluation practices.* **Career counselors ...**

a. act in accordance with ACA's Code of Ethics and Standards of Practice and NCDA's Ethical Guidelines.

b. adhere to professional codes and standards, including the Code of Fair Testing Practices in Education, to evaluate counseling practices involving assessments.

c. understand test fairness and avoid the selection of biased assessment instruments and biased uses of assessment results.

d. do not violate the legal and ethical principles and practices regarding test security, reproducing copyrighted materials, and unsupervised use of assessment instruments that are not intended for self-administration.

e. obtain and maintain available credentialing that demonstrates their skills in assessment and evaluation and update their skills on a regular basis.

Competency 8. *using assessment results and other data to evaluate career programs and interventions.* **Career counselors ...**

a. collect data to determine the impact of the career development activities on clients.

b. use appropriate statistics when comparing groups, making predictions, and drawing conclusions about career programs and strategies.

c. use evaluation results to improve current practices or implement more successful techniques to assist the client.

d. can explain evaluation results to relevant persons, colleagues, agencies, and other stakeholders.

Definition of Terms

Competencies describe knowledge, understanding, and skills that a career counselor must possess to perform assessment and evaluation activities effectively.

Assessment is the systematic gathering of information for decision making about individuals, groups, programs, or processes. Assessment targets include abilities, achievements, personality variables, aptitudes, attitudes, preferences, interests, values, demographics, beliefs, and other characteristics. Assessment procedures include, but are not limited to, standardized and non-standardized tests, questionnaires, inventories, checklists, observations, portfolios, performance assessments, rating scales, surveys, interviews, card sorts, and other measurement techniques.

Evaluation is the collection and interpretation of information to make judgments about individuals, programs, or processes that lead to decisions and future actions.

Committee:

Cheri Butler (NCDA, Chair), Belinda McCharen (NCDA, Chair), Janet Wall (AACE/NCDA, Chair), Rick Balkin (AACE), Lori Ellison (AACE), Chester Robinson (AACE), Brian Taber (NCDA), Pat Nellor Wickwire (AACE).

APPENDIX G

American Educational Research Association, American Psychological Association, & National Council on Measurement in Education. (1999). *Standards for educational and psychological testing.* Washington, DC: American Educational Research Association.

American Speech-Language-Hearing Association. (1994). *Protection of rights of people receiving audiology or speech-language pathology services.* ASHA (36), 60-63.

Joint Committee on Testing Practices. (1988). *Code of fair testing practices in education.* Washington, DC: American Psychological Association.

National Association of School Psychologists. (1992). *Standards for the provision of school psychological services.* Author: Silver Springs, MD.

National Council on Measurement in Education. (1995). *Code of professional responsibilities in educational measurement.* Washington, DC: Author.

THE RIGHTS AND RESPONSIBILITIES OF TEST TAKERS: GUIDELINES AND EXPECTATIONS

Test Taker Rights and Responsibilities Working Group of the Joint Committee on Testing Practices August, 1998

As a test taker, you have the right to:

1. Be informed of your rights and responsibilities as a test taker.
2. Be treated with courtesy, respect, and impartiality, regardless of your age, disability, ethnicity, gender, national origin, religion, sexual orientation or other personal characteristics.
3. Be tested with measures that meet professional standards and that are appropriate, given the manner in which the test results will be used.
4. Receive a brief oral or written explanation prior to testing about the purpose(s) for testing, the kind(s) of tests to be used, if the results will be reported to you or to others, and the planned use(s) of the results. If you have a disability, you have the right to inquire and receive information about testing accommodations. If you have difficulty in comprehending the language of the test, you have a right to know in advance of testing whether any accommodations may be available to you.
5. Know in advance of testing when the test will be administered, if and when test results will be available to you, and if there is a fee for testing services that you are expected to pay.
6. Have your test administered and your test results interpreted by appropriately trained individuals who follow professional codes of ethics.
7. Know if a test is optional and learn of the consequences of taking or not taking the test, fully completing the test, or canceling the scores. You may need to ask questions to learn these consequences.
8. Receive a written or oral explanation of your test results within a reasonable amount of time after testing and in commonly understood terms.
9. Have your test results kept confidential to the extent allowed by law.
10. Present concerns about the testing process or your results and receive information about procedures that will be used to address such concerns.

As a test taker, you have the responsibility to:

1. Read and/or listen to your rights and responsibilities as a test taker.
2. Treat others with courtesy and respect during the testing process.
3. Ask questions prior to testing if you are uncertain about why the test is being given, how it will be given, what you will be asked to do, and what will be done with the results.
4. Read or listen to descriptive information in advance of testing and listen carefully to all test instructions. You should inform an examiner in advance of testing if you wish to receive a testing accommodation or if you have a physical condition or illness that may interfere with your performance on

the test. If you have difficulty comprehending the language of the test, it is your responsibility to inform an examiner.

5. Know when and where the test will be given, pay for the test if required, appear on time with any required materials, and be ready to be tested.

6. Follow the test instructions you are given and represent yourself honestly during the testing.

7. Be familiar with and accept the consequences of not taking the test, should you choose not to take the test.

8. Inform appropriate person(s), as specified to you by the organization responsible for testing, if you believe that testing conditions affected your results.

9. Ask about the confidentiality of your test results, if this aspect concerns you.

10. Present concerns about the testing process or results in a timely, respectful way, if you have any.

The Rights of Test Takers: Guidelines for Testing Professionals

Test takers have the rights described below. It is the responsibility of the professionals involved in the testing process to ensure that test takers receive these rights.

1. Because test takers have the right to be informed of their rights and responsibilities as test takers, it is normally the responsibility of the individual who administers a test (or the organization that prepared the test) to inform test takers of these rights and responsibilities.

2. Because test takers have the right to be treated with courtesy, respect, and impartiality, regardless of their age, disability, ethnicity, gender, national origin, race, religion, sexual orientation, or other personal characteristics, testing professionals should:
   a. Make test takers aware of any materials that are available to assist them in test preparation. These materials should be clearly described in test registration and/or test familiarization materials.
   b. See that test takers are provided with reasonable access to testing services.

3. Because test takers have the right to be tested with measures that meet professional standards that are appropriate for the test use and the test taker, given the manner in which the results will be used, testing professionals should:
   a. Take steps to utilize measures that meet professional standards and are reliable, relevant, useful given the intended purpose and are fair for test takers from varying societal groups.
   b. Advise test takers that they are entitled to request reasonable accommodations in test administration that are likely to increase the validity of their test scores if they have a disability recognized under the Americans with Disabilities Act or other relevant legislation.

4. Because test takers have the right to be informed, prior to testing, about the test's purposes, the nature of the test, whether test results will be reported to the test takers, and the planned use of the results (when not in conflict with the testing purposes), testing professionals should:
   a. Give or provide test takers with access to a brief description about the test purpose (e.g., diagnosis, placement, selection, etc.) and the kind(s) of tests and formats that will be used (e.g., individual/group, multiple-choice/free response/performance, timed/untimed, etc.), unless such information might be detrimental to the objectives of the test.
   b. Tell test takers, prior to testing, about the planned use(s) of the test results. Upon request, the test taker should be given information about how long such test scores are typically kept on file and remain available.
   c. Provide test takers, if requested, with information about any preventative measures that have been instituted to safeguard the accuracy of test scores. Such information would include any quality control procedures that are employed and some of the steps taken to prevent dishonesty in test performance.
   d. Inform test takers, in advance of the testing, about required materials that must be brought to the test site (e.g., pencil, paper) and about any rules that allow or prohibit use of other materials (e.g., calculators).
   e. Provide test takers, upon request, with general information about the appropriateness of the test for its intended purpose, to the extent that such information does not involve the release of proprietary

information. (For example, the test taker might be told, "Scores on this test are useful in predicting how successful people will be in this kind of work" or "Scores on this test, along with other information, help us to determine if students are likely to benefit from this program.")

f. Provide test takers, upon request, with information about re-testing, including if it is possible to re-take the test or another version of it, and if so, how often, how soon, and under what conditions.

g. Provide test takers, upon request, with information about how the test will be scored and in what detail. On multiple-choice tests, this information might include suggestions for test taking and about the use of a correction for guessing. On tests scored using professional judgment (e.g., essay tests or projective techniques), a general description of the scoring procedures might be provided except when such information is proprietary or would tend to influence test performance inappropriately.

h. Inform test takers about the type of feedback and interpretation that is routinely provided, as well as what is available for a fee. Test takers have the right to request and receive information regarding whether or not they can obtain copies of their test answer sheets or their test materials, if they can have their scores verified, and if they may cancel their test results.

i. Provide test takers, prior to testing, either in the written instructions, in other written documents or orally, with answers to questions that test takers may have about basic test administration procedures.

j. Inform test takers, prior to testing, if questions from test takers will not be permitted during the testing process.

k. Provide test takers with information about the use of computers, calculators, or other equipment, if any, used in the testing and give them an opportunity to practice using such equipment, unless its unpracticed use is part of the test purpose, or practice would compromise the validity of the results, and to provide a testing accommodation for the use of such equipment, if needed.

l. Inform test takers that, if they have a disability, they have the right to request and receive accommodations or modifications in accordance with the provisions of the Americans with Disabilities Act and other relevant legislation.

m. Provide test takers with information that will be of use in making decisions if test takers have options regarding which tests, test forms or test formats to take.

5. Because test takers have a right to be informed in advance when the test will be administered, if and when test results will be available, and if there is a fee for testing services that the test takers are expected to pay, test professionals should:

a. Notify test takers of the alteration in a timely manner if a previously announced testing schedule changes, provide a reasonable explanation for the change, and inform test takers of the new schedule. If there is a change, reasonable alternatives to the original schedule should be provided.

b. Inform test takers prior to testing about any anticipated fee for the testing process, as well as the fees associated with each component of the process, if the components can be separated.

6. Because test takers have the right to have their tests administered and interpreted by appropriately trained individuals, testing professionals should:

a. Know how to select the appropriate test for the intended purposes.

b. When testing persons with documented disabilities and other special characteristics that require special testing conditions and/or interpretation of results, have the skills and knowledge for such testing and interpretation.

c. Provide reasonable information regarding their qualifications, upon request.

d. Insure that test conditions, especially if unusual, do not unduly interfere with test performance. Test conditions will normally be similar to those used to standardize the test.

e. Provide candidates with a reasonable amount of time to complete the test, unless a test has a time limit.

f. Take reasonable actions to safeguard against fraudulent actions (e.g., cheating) that could place honest test takers at a disadvantage.

7. Because test takers have the right to be informed about why they are being asked to take particular tests, if a test is optional, and what the consequences are should they choose not to complete the test, testing professionals should:

   a. Normally only engage in testing activities with test takers after the test takers have provided their informed consent to take a test, except when testing without consent has been mandated by law or governmental regulation, or when consent is implied by an action the test takers have already taken (e.g., such as when applying for employment and a personnel examination is mandated).

   b. Explain to test takers why they should consider taking voluntary tests.

   c. Explain, if a test taker refuses to take or complete a voluntary test, either orally or in writing, what the negative consequences may be to them for their decision to do so.

   d. Promptly inform the test taker if a testing professional decides that there is a need to deviate from the testing services to which the test taker initially agreed (e.g., should the testing professional believe it would be wise to administer an additional test or an alternative test), and provide an explanation for the change.

8. Because test takers have a right to receive a written or oral explanation of their test results within a reasonable amount of time after testing and in commonly understood terms, testing professionals should:

   a. Interpret test results in light of one or more additional considerations (e.g., disability, language proficiency), if those considerations are relevant to the purposes of the test and performance on the test, and are in accordance with current laws.

   b. Provide, upon request, information to test takers about the sources used in interpreting their test results, including technical manuals, technical reports, norms, and a description of the comparison group, or additional information about the test taker(s).

   c. Provide, upon request, recommendations to test takers about how they could improve their performance on the test, should they choose or be required to take the test again.

   d. Provide, upon request, information to test takers about their options for obtaining a second interpretation of their results. Test takers may select an appropriately trained professional to provide this second opinion.

   e. Provide test takers with the criteria used to determine a passing score, when individual test scores are reported and related to a pass-fail standard.

   f. Inform test takers, upon request, how much their scores might change, should they elect to take the test again. Such information would include variation in test performance due to measurement error (e.g., the appropriate standard errors of measurement) and changes in performance over time with or without intervention (e.g., additional training or treatment).

   g. Communicate test results to test takers in an appropriate and sensitive manner, without use of negative labels or comments likely to inflame or stigmatize the test taker.

   h. Provide corrected test scores to test takers as rapidly as possible, should an error occur in the processing or reporting of scores. The length of time is often dictated by individuals responsible for processing or reporting the scores, rather than the individuals responsible for testing, should the two parties indeed differ.

   i. Correct any errors as rapidly as possible if there are errors in the process of developing scores.

9. Because test takers have the right to have the results of tests kept confidential to the extent allowed by law, testing professionals should:

   a. Insure that records of test results (in paper or electronic form) are safeguarded and maintained so that only individuals who have a legitimate right to access them will be able to do so.

   b. Should provide test takers, upon request, with information regarding who has a legitimate right to access their test results (when individually identified) and in what form. Testing professionals should respond appropriately to questions regarding the reasons why such individuals may have access to test results and how they may use the results.

   c. Advise test takers that they are entitled to limit access to their results (when individually identified) to those persons or institutions, and for those purposes, revealed to them prior to testing.

Exceptions may occur when test takers, or their guardians, consent to release the test results to others or when testing professionals are authorized by law to release test results.

   d. Keep confidential any requests for testing accommodations and the documentation supporting the request.

10. Because test takers have the right to present concerns about the testing process and to receive information about procedures that will be used to address such concerns, testing professionals should:

   a. Inform test takers how they can question the results of the testing if they do not believe that the test was administered properly or scored correctly, or other such concerns.

   b. Inform test takers of the procedures for appealing decisions that they believe are based in whole or in part on erroneous test results.

   c. Inform test takers, if their test results are under investigation and may be canceled, invalidated, or not released for normal use. In such an event, that investigation should be performed in a timely manner. The investigation should use all available information that addresses the reason(s) for the investigation, and the test taker should also be informed of the information that he/she may need to provide to assist with the investigation.

   d. Inform the test taker, if that test taker's test results are canceled or not released for normal use, why that action was taken. The test taker is entitled to request and receive information on the types of evidence and procedures that have been used to make that determination.

The Responsibilities of Test Takers: Guidelines for Testing Professionals

Testing Professionals should take steps to ensure that test takers know that they have specific responsibilities in addition to their rights described above.

1. Testing professionals need to inform test takers that they should listen to and/or read their rights and responsibilities as a test taker and ask questions about issues they do not understand.

2. Testing professionals should take steps, as appropriate, to ensure that test takers know that they:

   a. Are responsible for their behavior throughout the entire testing process.

   b. Should not interfere with the rights of others involved in the testing process.

   c. Should not compromise the integrity of the test and its interpretation in any manner.

3. Testing professionals should remind test takers that it is their responsibility to ask questions prior to testing if they are uncertain about why the test is being given, how it will be given, what they will be asked to do, and what will be done with the results. Testing professionals should:

   a. Advise test takers that it is their responsibility to review materials supplied by test publishers and others as part of the testing process and to ask questions about areas that they feel they should understand better prior to the start of testing.

   b. Inform test takers that it is their responsibility to request more information if they are not satisfied with what they know about how their test results will be used and what will be done with them.

4. Testing professionals should inform test takers that it is their responsibility to read descriptive material they receive in advance of a test and to listen carefully to test instructions. Testing professionals should inform test takers that it is their responsibility to inform an examiner in advance of testing if they wish to receive a testing accommodation or if they have a physical condition or illness that may interfere with their performance. Testing professionals should inform test takers that it is their responsibility to inform an examiner if they have difficulty comprehending the language in which the test is given. Testing professionals should:

   a. Inform test takers that, if they need special testing arrangements, it is their responsibility to request appropriate accommodations and to provide any requested documentation as far in advance of the testing date as possible. Testing professionals should inform test takers about the documentation needed to receive a requested testing accommodation.

   b. Inform test takers that, if they request but do not receive a testing accommodation, they could request information about why their request was denied.

5. Testing professionals should inform test takers when and where the test will be given, and whether payment for the testing is required. Having been so informed, it is the responsibility of the test taker to appear on time with any required materials, pay for testing services and be ready to be tested. Testing professionals should:
   a. Inform test takers that they are responsible for familiarizing themselves with the appropriate materials needed for testing and for requesting information about these materials, if needed.
   b. Inform the test taker, if the testing situation requires that test takers bring materials (e.g., personal identification, pencils, calculators, etc.) to the testing site, of this responsibility to do so.
6. Testing professionals should advise test takers, prior to testing, that it is their responsibility to:
   a. Listen to and/or read the directions given to them.
   b. Follow instructions given by testing professionals.
   c. Complete the test as directed.
   d. Perform to the best of their ability if they want their score to be a reflection of their best effort.
   e. Behave honestly (e.g., not cheating or assisting others who cheat).
7. Testing professionals should inform test takers about the consequences of not taking a test, should they choose not to take the test. Once so informed, it is the responsibility of the test taker to accept such consequences, and the testing professional should so inform the test takers. If test takers have questions regarding these consequences, it is their responsibility to ask questions of the testing professional, and the testing professional should so inform the test takers.
8. Testing professionals should inform test takers that it is their responsibility to notify appropriate persons, as specified by the testing organization, if they do not understand their results, or if they believe that testing conditions affected the results. Testing professionals should:
   a. Provide information to test takers, upon request, about appropriate procedures for questioning or canceling their test scores or results, if relevant to the purposes of testing.
   b. Provide to test takers, upon request, the procedures for reviewing, re-testing, or canceling their scores or test results, if they believe that testing conditions affected their results and if relevant to the purposes of testing.
   c. Provide documentation to the test taker about known testing conditions that might have affected the results of the testing, if relevant to the purposes of testing.
9. Testing professionals should advise test takers that it is their responsibility to ask questions about the confidentiality of their test results, if this aspect concerns them.
10. Testing professionals should advise test takers that it is their responsibility to present concerns about the testing process in a timely, respectful manner.

Members of the JCTP Working Group on Test Taker Rights and Responsibilities:
- Kurt F. Geisinger, PhD (Co-Chair)
- William Schafer, PhD (Co-Chair)
- Gwyneth Boodoo, PhD
- Ruth Ekstrom, EdD
- Tom Fitzgibbon, PhD
- John Fremer, PhD
- Joanne Lenke, PhD
- Sharon Goldsmith, PhD
- Julie Noble, PhD
- Douglas Smith, PhD
- Nicholas Vacc, EdD
- Janet Wall, EdD

APPENDIX H

Many recent events have influenced the use of tests and assessment in the counseling community. Such events include the use of tests in the educational accountability and reform movement, the publication of the *Standards for Educational and Psychological Testing* (American Educational Research Association [AERA], American Psychological Association [APA], National Council on Measurement in Education [NCME], 1999), the revision of the *Code of Fair Testing Practices in Education* (Joint Committee on Testing Practices [JCTP], 2002), the proliferation of technology-delivered assessment, and the historic passage of the *No Child Left Behind Act* (HR1, 2002) calling for expanded testing in reading/language arts, mathematics, and science that are aligned to state standards.

The purpose of this document is to promote the accurate, fair, and responsible use of standardized tests by the counseling and education communities. RUST is intended to address the needs of the members of the American Counseling Association (ACA) and its Divisions, Branches, and Regions, including counselors, teachers, administrators, and other human service workers. The general public, test developers, and policy makers will find this statement useful as they work with tests and testing issues. The principles in RUST apply to the use of testing instruments regardless of delivery methods (e.g., paper/ pencil or computer administered) or setting (e.g., group or individual).

The intent of RUST is to help counselors and other educators implement responsible testing practices. The RUST does not intend to reach beyond or reinterpret the principles outlined in the *Standards for Educational and Psychological Testing* (AERA et al., 1999), nor was it developed to formulate a basis for legal action. The intent is to provide a concise statement useful in the ethical practice of testing. In addition, RUST is intended to enhance the guidelines found in ACA's *Code of Ethics and Standards of Practice* (ACA, 1997) and the *Code of Fair Testing Practices in Education* (JCTP, 2002).

Organization of Document: This document includes test user responsibilities in the following areas:
- Qualifications of Test Users
- Technical Knowledge
- Test Selection
- Test Administration
- Test Scoring
- Interpreting Test Results
- Communicating Test Results

Qualifications of Test Users

Qualified test users demonstrate appropriate education, training, and experience in using tests for the purposes under consideration. They adhere to the highest degree of ethical codes, laws, and standards governing professional practice. Lack of essential qualifications or ethical and legal compliance can lead to errors and subsequent harm to clients. Each professional is responsible for making judgments in each testing situation and cannot leave that responsibility either to clients or others in authority. The individual test user must obtain appropriate education and training, or arrange for professional supervision and assistance when engaged in testing in order to provide valuable, ethical, and effective assessment services to the public. Qualifications of test users depend on at least four factors:
- **Purposes of Testing:** A clear purpose for testing should be established. Because the purposes of testing direct how the results are used, qualifications beyond general testing competencies may be needed to interpret and apply data.

- **Characteristics of Tests:** Understanding of the strengths and limitations of each instrument used is a requirement.
- **Settings and Conditions of Test Use:** Assessment of the quality and relevance of test user knowledge and skill to the situation is needed before deciding to test or participate in a testing program.
- **Roles of Test Selectors, Administrators, Scorers, and Interpreters:** The education, training, and experience of test users determine which tests they are qualified to administer and interpret.

Each test user must evaluate his or her qualifications and competence for selecting, administering, scoring, interpreting, reporting, or communicating test results. Test users must develop the skills and knowledge for each test he or she intends to use.

Technical Knowledge

Responsible use of tests requires technical knowledge obtained through training, education, and continuing professional development. Test users should be conversant and competent in aspects of testing including:

- **Validity of Test Results:** Validity is the accumulation of evidence to support a specific interpretation of the test results. Since validity is a characteristic of test results, a test may have validities of varying degree, for different purposes. The concept of instructional validity relates to how well the test is aligned to state standards and classroom instructional objectives.
- **Reliability:** Reliability refers to the consistency of test scores. Various methods are used to calculate and estimate reliability depending on the purpose for which the test is used.
- **Errors of Measurement:** Various ways may be used to calculate the error associated with a test score. Knowing this and knowing the estimate of the size of the error allows the test user to provide a more accurate interpretation of the scores and to support better-informed decisions.
- **Scores and Norms:** Basic differences between the purposes of norm-referenced and criterion-referenced scores impact score interpretations.

Test Selection

Responsible use of tests requires that the specific purpose for testing be identified. In addition, the test that is selected should align with that purpose, while considering the characteristics of the test and the test taker. Tests should not be administered without a specific purpose or need for information. Typical purposes for testing include:

- **Description:** Obtaining objective information on the status of certain characteristics such as achievement, ability, personality types, etc. is often an important use of testing.
- **Accountability:** When judging the progress of an individual or the effectiveness of an educational institution, strong alignment between what is taught and what is tested needs to be present.
- **Prediction:** Technical information should be reviewed to determine how accurately the test will predict areas such as appropriate course placement; selection for special programs, interventions, and institutions; and other outcomes of interest.
- **Program Evaluation:** The role that testing plays in program evaluation and how the test information may be used to supplement other information gathered about the program is an important consideration in test use.

Proper test use involves determining if the characteristics of the test are appropriate for the intended audience and are of sufficient technical quality for the purpose at hand. Some areas to consider include:

- **The Test Taker:** Technical information should be reviewed to determine if the test characteristics are appropriate for the test taker (e.g., age, grade level, language, cultural background).
- **Accuracy of Scoring Procedures:** Only tests that use accurate scoring procedures should be used.
- **Norming and Standardization Procedures:** Norming and standardization procedures should be reviewed to determine if the norm group is appropriate for the intended test takers. Specified test administration procedures must be followed.

- **Modifications:** For individuals with disabilities, alternative measures may need to be found and used and/or accommodations in test taking procedures may need to be employed. Interpretations need to be made in light of the modifications in the test or testing procedures.
- **Fairness:** Care should be taken to select tests that are fair to all test takers. When test results are influenced by characteristics or situations unrelated to what is being measured. (e.g., gender, age, ethnic background, existence of cheating, unequal availability of test preparation programs) the use of the resulting information is invalid and potentially harmful. In achievement testing, fairness also relates to whether or not the student has had an opportunity to learn what is tested.

Test Administration

Test administration includes carefully following standard procedures so that the test is used in the manner specified by the test developers. The test administrator should ensure that test takers work within conditions that maximize opportunity for optimum performance. As appropriate, test takers, parents, and organizations should be involved in the various aspects of the testing process.

Before administration it is important that relevant persons
- are informed about the standard testing procedures, including information about the purposes of the test, the kinds of tasks involved, the method of administration, and the scoring and reporting;
- have sufficient practice experiences prior to the test to include practice, as needed, on how to operate equipment for computer-administered tests and practice in responding to tasks;
- have been sufficiently trained in their responsibilities and the administration procedures for the test;
- have a chance to review test materials and administration sites and procedures prior to the time for testing to ensure standardized conditions and appropriate responses to any irregularities that occur;
- arrange for appropriate modifications of testing materials and procedures in order to accommodate test takers with special needs; and
- have a clear understanding of their rights and responsibilities.

During administration it is important that
- the testing environment (e.g., seating, work surfaces, lighting, room temperature, freedom from distractions) and psychological climate are conducive to the best possible performance of the examinees;
- sufficiently trained personnel establish and maintain uniform conditions and observe the conduct of test takers when large groups of individuals are tested;
- test administrators follow the instructions in the test manual; demonstrate verbal clarity; use verbatim directions; adhere to verbatim directions; follow exact sequence and timing; and use materials that are identical to those specified by the test publisher;
- a systematic and objective procedure is in place for observing and recording environmental, health, emotional factors, or other elements that may invalidate test performance and results; deviations from prescribed test administration procedures, including information on test accommodations for individuals with special needs, are recorded; and
- the security of test materials and computer-administered testing software is protected, ensuring that only individuals with a legitimate need for access to the materials/software are able to obtain such access and that steps to eliminate the possibility of breaches in test security and copyright protection are respected.

After administration it is important to
- collect and inventory all secure test materials and immediately report any breaches in test security; and
- include notes on any problems, irregularities, and accommodations in the test records.

These precepts represent the basic process for all standardized tests and assessments. Some situations may add steps or modify some of these to provide the best testing milieu possible.

Test Scoring

Accurate measurement necessitates adequate procedures for scoring the responses of test takers. Scoring procedures should be audited as necessary to ensure consistency and accuracy of application.

- Carefully implement and/or monitor standard scoring procedures.
- When test scoring involves human judgment, use rubrics that clearly specify the criteria for scoring. Scoring consistency should be constantly monitored.
- Provide a method for checking the accuracy of scores when accuracy is challenged by test takers.

Interpreting Test Results

Responsible test interpretation requires knowledge about and experience with the test, the scores, and the decisions to be made. Interpretation of scores on any test should not take place without a thorough knowledge of the technical aspects of the test, the test results, and its limitations. Many factors can impact the valid and useful interpretations of test scores. These can be grouped into several categories including psychometric, test taker, and contextual, as well as others.

- **Psychometric Factors**: Factors such as the reliability, norms, standard error of measurement, and validity of the instrument are important when interpreting test results. Responsible test use considers these basic concepts and how each impacts the scores and hence the interpretation of the test results.
- **Test Taker Factors:** Factors such as the test taker's group membership and how that membership may impact the results of the test is a critical factor in the interpretation of test results. Specifically, the test user should evaluate how the test taker's gender, age, ethnicity, race, socioeconomic status, marital status, and so forth, impact on the individual's results.
- **Contextual Factors:** The relationship of the test to the instructional program, opportunity to learn, quality of the educational program, work and home environment, and other factors that would assist in understanding the test results are useful in interpreting test results. For example, if the test does not align to curriculum standards and how those standards are taught in the classroom, the test results may not provide useful information.

Communicating Test Results

Before communication of test results takes place, a solid foundation and preparation is necessary. That foundation includes knowledge of test interpretation and an understanding of the particular test being used, as provided by the test manual.

Conveying test results with language that the test taker, parents, teachers, clients, or general public can understand is one of the key elements in helping others understand the meaning of the test results. When reporting group results, the information needs to be supplemented with background information that can help explain the results with cautions about misinterpretations. The test user should indicate how the test results can be and should not be interpreted.

Closing

Proper test use resides with the test user—the counselor and educator. Qualified test users understand the measurement characteristics necessary to select good standardized tests, administer the tests according to specified procedures, assure accurate scoring, accurately interpret test scores for individuals and groups, and ensure productive applications of the results. This document provides guidelines for using tests responsibly with students and clients.

References and Resource Documents

American Counseling Association. (1997). *Code of ethics and standards of practice.* Alexandria, VA: Author.

American Counseling Association. (2003). *Standards for qualifications of test users.* Alexandria, VA: Author.

American Educational Research Association, American Psychological Association, National Council on Measurement in Education. (1999). *Standards for educational and psychological testing.* Washington, DC: American Educational Research Association.

American School Counselor Association & Association for Assessment in Counseling. (1998). *Competencies in assessment and evaluation for school counselors.* Alexandria, VA: Author.

Joint Committee on Testing Practices. (2000) *Rights and responsibilities of test takers: Guidelines and expectations.* Washington, DC: Author.

Joint Committee on Testing Practices. (2002). *Code of fair testing practices in education.* Washington, DC: Author.

RUST Committee
Janet Wall, Chair
James Augustin
Charles Eberly Brad
Erford David
Lundberg Timothy
Vansickle

APPENDIX I

STANDARDS FOR MULTICULTURAL ASSESSMENT (2ND ED.)
Preface

The Association for Assessment in Counseling (AAC) is an organization of counselors, counselor educators, and other professionals that advances the counseling profession by providing leadership, training, and research in the creation, development, production, and use of assessment and diagnostic techniques.

The increasing diversity in our society offers a special challenge to the assessment community, striving always to assure fair and equitable treatment of individuals regardless of race, ethnicity, culture, language, age, gender, sexual orientation, religion or physical ability. This is especially important given the increased emphasis placed on assessment spawned by national and state legislation and educational reform initiatives.

This document, *Standards for Multicultural Assessment*, is an attempt to create and maintain an awareness of the various assessment standards that have been produced by various professional organizations. It is a compilation of standards produced by several professional associations.

This publication is based on a study completed by the Committee on Diversity in Assessment under the direction of the AAC Executive Council. The first version of this document was published in 1992, and was also published as an article in *Measurement and Evaluation in Counseling and Development* (Prediger, 1994). The original publication was prompted by a request from Jo-Ida Hansen, Chair of the 1991-1992 Committee on Testing of the American Association for Counseling and Development (now ACA). The original publication was prepared by Dale Prediger under the direction of the AAC Executive Council.

Because of advances in professional standards in the past decade, it was necessary to update and expand upon the first version. This revised document was created by a committee of members from the AAC, chaired by Dr. Wendy Charkow-Bordeau along with committee members, Drs. Debbie Newsome and Marie Shoffner. This publication was commissioned by the Executive Council of the Association for Assessment in Counseling.

AAC also wishes to thank Drs. Pat Nellor Wickwire and Janet Wall for their care and assistance in finalizing this document and coordinating its production.

AAC hopes that all counselors, teachers, and other assessment professionals find this document to be useful in improving their assessment practices.

Table of Contents

STANDARDS FOR MULTICULTURAL ASSESSMENT

Purpose

The Association for Assessment in Counseling (AAC), a division of the American Counseling Association (ACA), presents this revised compilation of professional standards. Although AAC believes that tests, inventories, and other assessment instruments can be beneficial for members of all populations, AAC recognizes that the increasing diversity in client backgrounds presents special challenges for test users. The standards assembled here address many of these challenges that are specifically related to the assessment of multicultural populations.

Although a number of standards in this compilation have relevance for the use of assessment instruments in psychological screening, personnel selection, and placement, they were selected because they have special relevance for counseling and for multicultural and diverse populations. Standards that apply in the same way for all populations (e.g., general standards for norming, scaling, reliability, and validity) are not included. Readers may consult the source documents and other publications for universal testing standards.

AAC urges all counselors to subscribe to these standards and urges counselor educators to include this compilation in programs preparing the "culturally competent counselor" (Sue, Arredondo, & McDavis, 1992, p. 447). Finally, AAC supports other professional organizations in advocating the need for a multicultural approach to assessment, practice, training, and research.

Definition of Multicultural and Diverse Populations

A precise definition of multicultural and diverse populations is evolving. The multicultural competencies outlined by Sue et al. (1992), and then revised by Arredondo and Toporek (1996), define the following five major cultural groups in the United States and its territories: African/Black, Asian, Caucasian/European, Hispanic/Latino, and Native American. Arredondo and Toporek differentiated between these cultural groups, which are based on race and ethnicity, and diversity, which applies to individual differences based on age, gender, sexual orientation, religion, and ability or disability.

In revising the *Standards for Multicultural Assessment*, an inclusive definition of multiculturalism and diversity was used. For the purposes of this document, multicultural and diverse populations include persons who differ by race, ethnicity, culture, language, age, gender, sexual orientation, religion, and ability.

Source Documents

Five documents which include professional standards for assessment in counseling were used as sources for this compilation.

1. *Code of Fair Testing Practices in Education* (2nd ed.) (CODE) (Joint Committee on Testing Practices [JCTP], 2002). Available for download at *http://aac.ncat.edu*.
2. *Responsibilities of Users of Standardized Tests* (3rd ed.) (RUST). (ACA & AAC, 2003). Available for download at *http://aac.ncat.edu*.
3. *Standards for Educational and Psychological Testing* (2nd ed.) (SEPT). (American Educational Research Association, APA, & National Council on Measurement in Education, 1999). Ordering information is available from APA, 750 First Street N.E., Washington, D.C. 20002-4242 or on-line at *http://www.apa.org/science/standards.html*.
4. *Multicultural Counseling Competencies and Standards* (COMPS). (Association for Multicultural Counseling and Development, 1992). These standards can be viewed in the 1996 article by Arredondo and Toporek. Full reference information is listed below in the reference section.
5. *Code of Ethics and Standards of Practice of the American Counseling Association* (ETHICS). (ACA, 1996). Ordering information can be obtained from ACA, 5999 Stevenson Avenue, Alexandria, VA, 22304-3300. The ethical code and standards of practice may also be viewed on-line at *http://www.counseling.org/resources/ethics.htm*.

Classification of Standards

Sixty-eight standards specifically relevant to the assessment of multicultural and diverse populations were identified in a reading of the five source documents. The content and intent of these standards were analyzed and classified. Assessment roles, functions, and tasks cited in these standards were clustered into three major groups.

Selection of Assessment Instruments
  Content and Purpose (n = 13)
  Norming, Reliability, and Validity (n = 18)
  Administration and Scoring of Assessment Instruments (n = 16)
  Interpretation and Application of Assessment Results (n = 21)

The Standards

The 68 standards are listed below by cluster and source.

Selection of Assessment Instruments: Content and Purpose

1. Evaluate procedures and materials used by test developers, as well as the resulting test, to ensure that potentially offensive content or language is avoided. (CODE, Section A-7)
2. Select tests with appropriately modified forms or administration procedures for test takers with disabilities who need special accommodations. (CODE, Section A-8)
3. For individuals with disabilities, alternative measures may need to be found and used.
4. Care should be taken to select tests that are fair to all test takers. (RUST)
5. Test developers should strive to identify and eliminate language, symbols, words, phrases, and content that are generally regarded as offensive by members of racial, ethnic, gender, or other groups, except when judged to be necessary for adequate representation of the domain. (SEPT 7.4)
6. In testing applications where the level of linguistic or reading ability is not part of the construct of interest, the linguistic or reading demands of the test should be kept to the minimum necessary for the valid assessment of the intended construct. (SEPT, Standard 7.7)
7. Linguistic modifications recommended by test publishers, as well as the rationale for modifications, should be described in detail in the test manual. (SEPT, Standard 9.4)
8. In employment and credentialing testing, the proficiency language required in the language of the test should not exceed that appropriate to the relevant occupation or profession. (SEPT, Standard 9.8)
9. Inferences about test takers' general language proficiency should be based on tests that measure a range of language features, and not on a single linguistic skill. (SEPT, Standard 9.10)
10. Tests selected for use in individual testing should be suitable for the characteristics and background of the test taker. (SEPT, Standard 12.3)
11. Culturally competent counselors understand how race, culture, and ethnicity may affect personality formation, vocational choices, manifestation of psychological disorders, help-seeking behavior, and the appropriateness or inappropriateness of counseling approaches. (COMPS, 13)
12. Culturally competent counselors have training and expertise in the use of traditional assessment and testing instruments. They not only understand the technical aspects of the instruments but also are aware of the cultural limitations. This allows them to use test instruments for the welfare of clients from diverse cultural, racial, and ethnic groups. (COMPS, 29)
13. Counselors are cautious when selecting tests for culturally diverse populations to avoid inappropriateness of testing that may be outside of socialized behavioral or cognitive patterns. (ETHICS, Section III.C.5)

Selection of Assessment Instruments: Norming, Reliability, and Validity

1. Evaluate the available evidence on the performance of test takers of diverse subgroups. Determine to the extent feasible which performance differences may have been caused by factors unrelated to skills being assessed. (CODE, Section A-9).
2. Technical information should be reviewed to determine if the test characteristics are appropriate for the test taker (e.g., age, grade level, language, cultural background). (RUST)

3. Where there are generally accepted theoretical or empirical reasons for expecting that reliability coefficients, standard errors of measurement, or test information functions will differ substantially for various subpopulations, publishers should provide reliability data as soon as feasible for each major population for which the test is recommended. (SEPT, Standard 2.11)

4. If a test is proposed for use in several grades or over a range of chronological age groups and if separate norms are provided for each grade or age group, reliability data should be provided for each age or grade population, not solely for all grades or ages combined. (SEPT, Standard 2.12)

5. When significant variations are permitted in test administration procedures, separate reliability analyses should be provided for scores produced under each major variation if adequate sample sizes are available. (SEPT, Standard 2.18)

6. Norms, if used, should refer to clearly described populations. These populations should include individuals or groups to whom test users will ordinarily wish to compare their own examinees. (SEPT, Standard 4.5)

7. When credible research reports that test scores differ in meaning across examinee subgroups for the type of test in question, then to the extent feasible, the same forms of validity evidence collected for the examinee population as a whole should also be collected for each relevant subgroup. Subgroups may be found to differ with respect to appropriateness of test content, internal structure of test responses, the relation of test scores to other variables, or the response processes employed by the individual examinees. Any such findings should receive due consideration in the interpretation and use of scores as well as in subsequent test revisions. (SEPT, Standard 7.1)

8. When credible research reports differences in the effects of construct-irrelevant variance across subgroups of test takers on performance on some part of the test, the test should be used if at all only for the subgroups for which evidence indicates that valid inferences can be drawn from test scores. (SEPT, Standard 7.2)

9. When empirical studies of differential prediction of a criterion for members of different subgroups are conducted, they should include regression equations (or an appropriate equivalent) computed separately for each group or treatment under consideration or an analysis in which group or treatment variables are entered as moderator variable. (SEPT, Standard 7.6)

10. When a construct can be measured in different ways that are approximately equal in their degree of construct representation and freedom from construct-irrelevant variance, evidence of mean score differences across relevant subgroups of examinees should be considered in deciding which test to use. (SEPT, Standard 7.11)

11. When credible research evidence reports that test scores differ in meaning across subgroups of linguistically diverse test takers, then to the extent feasible, test developers should collect for each linguistic group studied the same form of validity evidence collected for the examinee population as a whole. (SEPT, Standard 9.2)

12. When a test is translated from one language to another, the methods used in establishing the adequacy of translation should be described, and empirical and logical evidence should be provided for score reliability and the validity of the translated test's score inferences for the uses intended in the linguistic groups to be tested. (SEPT, Standard 9.7)

13. When multiple language versions of a test are intended to be comparable, test developers should report evidence of test comparability. (SEPT, Standard 9.9)

14. When feasible, tests that have been modified for use with individuals with disabilities should be pilot tested on individuals who have similar disabilities to investigate the appropriateness and feasibility of the modifications. (SEPT, Standard 10.3)

15. When sample sizes permit, the validity of inferences made from test scores and the reliability of scores on tests administered to individuals with various disabilities should be investigated and reported by the agency or publisher that makes the modification. Such investigations should examine the effects of modifications made for people with various disabilities on resulting scores, as well as the effects of administering standard unmodified tests to them. (SEPT, Standard 10.7)

16. When relying on norms as a basis for score interpretation in assisting individuals with disabilities, the norm group used depends upon the purpose of testing. Regular norms are appropriate when the purpose involves the test taker's functioning relative to the general population. If available, normative data from the population of individuals with the same level or degree of disability should be used when the test taker's functioning relative to individuals with similar disabilities is at issue. (SEPT, Standard 10.9)
17. When circumstances require that a test be administered in the same language to all examinees in a linguistically diverse population, the test user should investigate the validity of the score interpretations for test takers believed to have limited proficiency in the language of the test. (SEPT, Standard 11.22)
18. Counselors carefully consider the validity, reliability, psychometric limitations, and appropriateness of instruments when selecting tests for use in a given situation or with a particular client. (ETHICS, Section E.6.a)

Administration and Scoring of Assessment Instruments
1. Provide and document appropriate procedures for test takers with disabilities who need special accommodations or those with diverse linguistic backgrounds. Some accommodation may be required by law or regulation. (CODE, Section B-2)
2. For individuals with disabilities, accommodations in test taking procedures may need to be employed. Appropriate modifications of testing materials and procedures in order to accommodate test takers with special needs are to be arranged. (RUST)
3. Include notes on any problems, irregularities, and accommodations in the test records. (RUST)
4. A systematic and objective procedure is in place for observing and recording environmental, health, emotional factors, or other elements that may invalidate test performance and results; deviations from prescribed test administration procedures, including information on test accommodations for individuals with special needs, are recorded. Carefully observe, record, and attach to the test record any deviation from the prescribed test administration procedures. Include information on test accommodations for individuals with special needs. (RUST)
5. The testing or assessment process should be carried out so that test takers receive comparable and equitable treatment during all phases of the testing or assessment process. (SEPT, Standard 7.12)
6. Testing practice should be designed to reduce threats to the reliability and validity of test score inferences that may arise from language differences. (SEPT, Standard 9.1)
7. When testing an examinee proficient in two or more languages for which the test is available, the examinee's relative language proficiencies should be determined. The test generally should be administered in the test taker's most proficient language, unless proficiency in the less proficient language is part of the assessment. (SEPT, Standard 9.3)
8. When an interpreter is used in testing, the interpreter should be fluent in both the language of the test and the examinee's native language, should have expertise in translating, and should have a basic understanding of the assessment process. (SEPT, Standard 9.11)
9. People who make decisions about accommodations and test modifications for individuals with disabilities should be knowledgeable of existing research on the effects of the disabilities in question on test performance. Those who modify tests should also have access to psychometric expertise for so doing. (SEPT, Standard 10.2)
10. If a test developer recommends specific time limits for people with disabilities, empirical procedures should be used, whenever possible, to establish time limits for modified forms of timed tests rather than simply allowing test takers with disabilities a multiple of the standard time. When possible, fatigue should be investigated as a potentially important factor when time limits are extended. (SEPT, Standard 10.6)
11. Those responsible for decisions about test use with potential test takers who may need or may request specific accommodations should (a) possess the information necessary to make an appropriate selection of measures, (b) have current information regarding the availability of modified

forms of the test in question, (c) inform individuals, when appropriate, about the existence of modified forms, and (d) make these forms available to test takers when appropriate and feasible. (SEPT, Standard 10.8)

12. Any test modifications adopted should be considered appropriate for the individual test taker, while maintaining all feasible standardized features. A test professional needs to consider reasonably available information about each test taker's experiences, characteristics, and capabilities that might impact test performance, and document the grounds for the modification. (SEPT, Standard 10.10)

13. If a test is mandated for persons of a given age or all students in a particular grade, users should identify individuals whose disabilities or linguistic background indicates the need for special accommodations in test administration and ensure that those accommodations are employed. (SEPT, Standard 11.23)

14. Counselors provide for equal access to computer applications in counseling services. (ETHICS, Section A.12.c)

15. When computer applications are used in counseling services, counselors ensure that: (1) the client is intellectually, emotionally, and physically capable of using the computer application; (2) the computer application is appropriate for the needs of the client; (3) the client understands the purpose and operation of the computer applications; and (4) a follow-up of client use of a computer application is provided to correct possible misconceptions, discover inappropriate use, and assess subsequent needs. (ETHICS, Section A.12.a)

16. Prior to assessment, counselors explain the nature and purposes of assessment and the specific use of results in language the client (or other legally authorized person on behalf of the client) can understand, unless an explicit exception to this right has been agreed upon in advance. (ETHICS, Section E.3.a)

Interpretation and Application of Assessment Results

1. Interpret the meaning of the test results, taking into account the nature of the content, norms or comparison groups, other technical evidence, and benefits and limitations of test results. (CODE, Section C-1)

2. Review the procedures for setting performance standards or passing scores. Avoid using stigmatizing labels. (CODE, Section C-4)

3. For individuals with disabilities, interpretations need to be made in light of the modifications in the test or testing procedures. (RUST)

4. When test results are influenced by irrelevant test taker characteristics (e.g., gender, age, ethnic background, cheating, availability of test preparation programs) the use of the resulting information is invalid and potentially harmful. (RUST)

5. Factors such as the test taker's group membership and how that membership may impact the results of the test is a critical factor in the interpretation of test results. Specifically, the test user should evaluate how the test taker's gender, age, ethnicity, race, socioeconomic status, marital status, and so forth, impact on the individual's results. (RUST)

6. If local examinees differ materially from the population to which the norms refer, a user who reports derived scores based on the published norms has the responsibility to describe such differences if they bear upon the interpretation of the reported scores. (SEPT, Standard 4.7)

7. In testing applications involving individualized interpretations of test scores other than selection, a test taker's score should not be accepted as a reflection of standing on a characteristic being assessed without consideration of alternate explanations for the test taker's performance on that test at that time. (SEPT, Standard 7.5)

8. When scores are disaggregated and publicly reported for groups identified by characteristics such as gender, ethnicity, age, language proficiency, or disability, cautionary statements should be included whenever credible research reports that test scores may not have comparable meaning across different groups. (SEPT, Standard 7.8)

9. When tests or assessments are proposed for use as instruments of social, educational, or public policy, the test developers or users proposing the test should fully and accurately inform policy-makers of the characteristics of the tests as well as any relevant and credible information that may be available concerning the likely consequences of test use. (SEPT, Standard 7.9)

10. When the use of a test results in outcomes that affect the life chances or educational opportunities of examinees, evidence of mean test score differences between relevant subgroups of examinees should, where feasible, be examined for subgroups for which credible research reports mean differences for similar tests. Where mean differences are found, an investigation should be undertaken to determine that such differences are not attributable to a source of construct underrepresentation or construct-irrelevant variance. While initially the responsibility of the test developer, the test user bears responsibility for users with groups other than those specified by the developer. (SEPT, Standard 7.10).

11. When score reporting includes assigning individuals to categories, the categories should be chosen carefully and described precisely. The least stigmatizing labels, consistent with accurate representation, should always be assigned. (SEPT, Standard 8.8)

12. When there is credible evidence of score comparability across regular and modified administrations, no flag should be attached to a score. When such evidence is lacking, specific information about the nature of the modification should be provided, if permitted by law, to assist test users properly to interpret and act on test scores. (SEPT, Standard 9.5 and 10.11)

13. In testing persons with disabilities, test developers, test administrators, and test users should take steps to ensure that the test score inferences accurately reflect the intended construct rather than any disabilities and their associated characteristics extraneous to the intent of the measurement. (SEPT, Standard 10.1)

14. In testing individuals with disabilities for diagnostic and intervention purposes, the test should not be used as the sole indicator of the test taker's functioning. Instead, multiple sources of information should be used. (SEPT, Standard 10.12)

15. Agencies using tests to conduct program evaluations or policy studies, or to monitor outcomes, should clearly describe the population the program or policy is intended to serve and should document the extent to which the sample of test takers is representative of that population. (SEPT, Standard 15.5)

16. Reports of group differences in average test scores should be accompanied by relevant contextual information, where possible, to enable meaningful interpretation of these differences. Where appropriate contextual information is not available, users should be cautioned against misinterpretation. (SEPT, Standard 15.12)

17. Culturally competent counselors possess knowledge about their social impact on others. They are knowledgeable about communication style differences, how their style may clash or facilitate the counseling process with minority clients, and how to anticipate the impact it may have on others. (COMPS, 7)

18. Culturally competent counselors have knowledge of the potential bias in assessment instruments and use procedures and interpret findings keeping in mind the cultural and linguistic characteristics of the clients. (COMPS, 22)

19. Counselors recognize that culture affects the manner in which clients' problems are defined. Clients' socioeconomic and cultural experience is considered when diagnosing mental disorders. (ETHICS, Section E.5.b)

20. Counselors are cautious in using assessment techniques, making evaluations, and interpreting the performance of populations not represented in the norm group on which an instrument was standardized. They recognize the effects of age, color, culture, disability, ethnic group, gender, race, religion, sexual orientation, and socioeconomic status on test administration and interpretation and place test results in proper perspective with other relevant factors. (ETHICS, Section E.8) 21. In reporting assessment results, counselors indicate any reservations that exist regarding validity or reliability because of the circumstances of the assessment or the inappropriateness of the norms for the person tested. (ETHICS, Section E.9.a)

References

American Counseling Association. (1996) *Code of ethics and standards of practice.* Alexandria, VA: Author.

American Counseling Association and Association for Assessment in Counseling. (2003). *Responsibilities of users of standardized tests.* Alexandria, VA: Author.

American Educational Research Association, American Psychological Association, and National Council on Measurement in Education. (1999). *Standards for educational and psychological testing* (2nd ed.). Washington, DC: American Educational Research Association.

Arredondo, P., & Toporek, R. (1996). Operationalization of the multicultural counseling competencies [Electronic version]. *Journal of Multicultural Counseling and Development, 24,* 42-79.

Association for Multicultural Counseling and Development. (1992) *Multicultural counseling competencies and standards.* Alexandria, VA: American Counseling Association.

Joint Committee on Testing Practices. (2002). *Code of fair testing practices in education.* Washington, DC: Author.

Prediger, D. J., (1992) *Standards for multicultural assessment.* Alexandria, VA: Association for Assessment in Counseling.

Prediger, D. J. (1994). Multicultural assessment standards: A compilation for counselors. *Measurement and Evaluation in Counseling and Development, 27,* 68-73.

Sue, D. W., Arredondo, P., & McDavis, R. (1992). Multicultural counseling competencies and standards: A call to the profession. *Journal of Counseling and Development, 70,* 477-486.

INDEX